Sex, Love, and Families

Catholic Perspectives

Edited by

Jason King and Julie Hanlon Rubio

LITURGICAL PRESS
ACADEMIC

Collegeville, Minnesota
www.litpress.org

Cover design by Ann Blattner. *Improvisation 27 (Garden of Love II)* by Vasily Kandinsky, oil on canvas. Courtesy of Wikimedia Commons.

The editors are grateful to Porsia Tunzi, doctoral student in historical and cultural studies of religion, Graduate Theological Union, Berkeley, California, for her work on the index.

3   4   5   6   7   8   9

Library of Congress Cataloging-in-Publication Data

Names: Rubio, Julie Hanlon, editor. | King, Jason E. (Jason Edward), 1971– editor.
Title: Sex, love, and families : Catholic perspectives / [edited by] Julie Hanlon Rubio and Jason King.
Description: Collegeville, Minnesota : Liturgical Press, 2020. | Includes bibliographical references. | Summary: "A collection of essays which engage with and respond to realities shaping contemporary family life, like religious pluralism, technology, migration, racism, sex and gender, incarceration, consumerism, and the call to holiness"— Provided by publisher.
Identifiers: LCCN 2019041364 (print) | LCCN 2019041365 (ebook) | ISBN 9780814687949 (paperback) | ISBN 9780814687956 (epub) | ISBN 9780814687956 (mobi) | ISBN 9780814687956 (pdf)
Subjects: LCSH: Families—Religious life. | Families—Religious aspects—Catholic Church. | Sex—Religious aspects—Catholic Church. | Marriage—Religious aspects—Catholic Church. | Catholic Church—Doctrines.
Classification: LCC BX2351 .S46 2020 (print) | LCC BX2351 (ebook) | DDC 261.8/358—dc23
LC record available at https://lccn.loc.gov/2019041364
LC ebook record available at https://lccn.loc.gov/2019041365

"I cannot think of any duo more competent or attractive for hosting a Catholic discourse on *Sex, Love, and Family* than Jason King and Julie Hanlon Rubio. Today, in the United States, millions agree to disagree about what constitutes good sex, good love, and good family, but that agreement is usually followed by a silence because few are willing to hear the differences. Well, those days are over because our editors did not shy away from truly challenging contributors. Pick up this book and discover that you are probably not as conservative (or as progressive) as you thought. These are powerful, thoughtful, and honest pieces and their claims ought to finally end the timid silence that has been way too seductive and self-serving."

> —James F. Keenan, SJ
> Canisius Professor of Theology
> Boston College

"Sex, marriage, and family mores are changing radically. Whether you are celebrating or alarmed, you can learn from the realistic, hopeful, and impactful voices gathered here. They seek the light of faith in LGBTQI identity, campus hook-ups, heartbreaking pregnancy loss, identity-challenging infertility, undocumented siblings, incarcerated parents, interchurch families, 'secular Catholic' families, twenty-first century parenting, marital love as abiding friendship, discipleship through divorce, and more. *Sex, Love, and Families* would make an excellent course text; no student would skip the readings and the discussions would run themselves."

> —Lisa Sowle Cahill
> Monan Professor of Theology
> Boston College

Contents

Sex, Love, and Families

Lived Christianity in Context

Jason King and Julie Hanlon Rubio

For Christians, Jesus reorients all things—including sex, love, and families. In the earliest days of the church, while some believers chose celibacy over marriage, others organized their families and homes to foster compassion, forgiveness, and service. Some early marriage rites included prayers for the couple to become expressions of God's peace on earth. The goal was a "renewed and restructured family and community life in which discipleship had priority for all."[1] The work of trying to understand sex, love, and families in light of Christ has been an ongoing task of Christianity. In every era, thinking and practice develop in response to the challenges of the day. Each era calls for new developments.

Today, people are asking questions about sex that the Catholic theology of the past could not have envisioned. Contemporary Catholics are diverse in race, class, ethnicity, sexual orientation, gender identity, marital status, and family form. Waiting to have sex until marriage is normative only in very traditional subcultures. The vast majority of adults have sex before they marry.[2] A majority of births to women under thirty occur outside of marriage.[3] Relationships are increasingly shaped by Tinder, Grindr, and Bumble. With tens of millions of users, these apps and others like them have reshaped dating so thoroughly that it is nearly impossible to date without using them. Pornography has become mainstream—and now

1. Julie Hanlon Rubio, *A Christian Theology of Marriage and Family* (Mahwah, NJ: Paulist Press, 2003), 50.

2. Lawrence Finer, "Trends in Premarital Sex in the United States, 1954–2003," *Public Health Reports* 122, no. 1 (2007): 73–78.

3. Jason DeParle and Sabrina Tavernise, "Unwed Mothers Now a Majority Before Age of 30," *New York Times*, February 18, 2012, A1.

often mediates expectations of sexual encounters.[4] Tolerance of sexual violence is declining in the wake of the #MeToo movement. Consciousness of gender equity and diversity is growing. A majority of Catholics support artificial contraception, cohabitation, and same-sex marriage.[5] Sexual desire is viewed more positively, and sexual intimacy and fulfillment are highly valued.

Given all of these changes, it is understandable that conversations now center on how to negotiate gender and sex in and outside of marriage. Consent is becoming more central to discussions about sex, especially in response to hookup culture and in the context of growing awareness of sexual harassment and sexual violence.[6] There is less focus on purity and more on love, freedom, self-care, and justice. In evaluating relationships, people ask: Is there a balance of power in the relationship? How are gender norms operating? Does the relationship preserve and promote the dignity of those involved? Does it encourage openness and generosity? Catholic sexual ethics has just begun to address questions like these.

Conversations on love have also shifted in response to cultural changes, and now include reflections on structural forces that make love difficult to sustain and on goods that couples attempt to embody. Only half of first marriages make it to their twentieth anniversary.[7] While children, sexual fidelity, and lifelong marriage are still desired by most, people are marrying later and marriage rates have declined due to economic forces and growing trepidation. Cultural forces of individualism and materialism engender worries about if, when, and whom to marry. Marriage is becoming more and more an upper-class phenomenon.[8] Increasing numbers of widows, divorced people, and single parents raise questions about love in diverse, and often challenging, situations. Poverty, incarceration,

4. Pamela Paul, *Pornified: How Pornography Is Damaging Our Lives, Our Relationships, and Our Families* (New York: Holt Paperbacks, 2005).

5. See, for example, Pew Research Center, "Attitudes on Same Sex Marriage," https://www.pewforum.org/fact-sheet/changing-attitudes-on-gay-marriage/; and Pew Research Center, "Catholics-Contraceptives," https://www.pewresearch.org/catholics-contraceptives/.

6. The CDC indicates 30 percent of women and 10 percent of men have experienced rape, physical violence, and/or stalking by a partner. Intimate partner violence resulted in 2,340 deaths in 2007—accounting for 14 percent of all homicides. National Center for Injury Prevention and Control, "Preventing Intimate Partner Violence," https://www.cdc.gov/violenceprevention/pdf/ipv-factsheet.pdf.

7. Casey E. Copen, Kimberly Daniels, Jonathan Vespa, and William D. Mosher, "First Marriages in the United States: Data From the 2006–2010 National Survey of Family Growth," *National Health Statistics Report* 49 (2012): 1–22.

8. Pew Research, "The Decline of Marriage and Rise of New Families," November 18, 2010, https://www.pewsocialtrends.org/2010/11/18/the-decline-of-marriage-and-rise-of-new-families/.

work stresses, and chronic illnesses force couples to reflect on the nature of their love and commitment. Single and married laypeople are interested in how to grow in love amid the struggles of ordinary life.

Contemporary families also face new challenges that give rise to new questions. Social media sites such as Facebook, Instagram, and Snapchat vie for our time and attention.[9] Adults are conflicted about how to balance work and life and how to raise children in an increasingly complex world without being "helicopter" or "snowplow" parents. They struggle to resist consumerism and the domination of technology in the home, attempt to keep teens safe from violence and bullying, and strive to cultivate good values. Poverty, declining job security and low wages, racism, and migration make family life more difficult.[10] Those with more money have access to housing, education, and networks that make family life easier and more stable. In contrast, the poor and middle class marry less often, have fewer resources to support them in parenting, and face increased social and economic risks.[11] Households are much more diverse in members, marital status, religious affiliation, and practices. In light of these changes, family ethics involves questions of how to engage structural injustice and how to cultivate intentional practices within households that contribute to family flourishing.

Why This Book?

The Catholic tradition has to face these new challenges. The church can neither abandon its past nor retreat into it. How does it grow, develop, and respond faithfully to Christ? The two editors of this book have been teaching sex, marriage, and family at Catholic universities for more than twenty years, and these questions have been on our mind for some time. We saw the shifts we described above in the new kinds of students that were coming to Catholic colleges and universities, many without a Catholic background and some uninterested in it. Their assumptions about family, sex, and love were new, radically so at times. They raised questions and reflected on experiences that a typical course on "Christian marriage" did not address. In our extended families, professional circles, and among our friends, we also noticed different lived realities of marriage and family life, the declining

9. Sherry Turkle, *Alone Together: Why Expect More from Technology and Less from Each Other*, rev. ed. (New York: Basic Books, 2017).

10. Annette Lareau, *Unequal Childhoods: Class, Race, and Family Life*, 2nd ed. (Berkeley: University of California Press, 2011).

11. Robert D. Putnam, *Our Kids: The American Dream in Crisis* (New York: Simon & Schuster, 2015).

influence of Catholic teaching, and a lack of awareness of the new situation in most Catholic parishes. When we met over lunch at a professional conference a few years ago, we decided to put together a collection of essays in response to these new challenges.

We knew we needed to gather scholars, not just the best in the field, but those not trapped in debates of previous decades. Too often, the field of moral theology breaks down around issues related to two major papal documents of the twentieth century: *Humanae Vitae* (1968) and *Veritatis Splendor* (1993). In *Humanae Vitae*, Pope Paul VI reaffirmed Catholic teaching against artificial contraception, and, in *Veritatis Splendor*, Pope John Paul II defended absolute moral norms. Debates among theologians often focus on the possibility of dissent or disagreement in the context of an overarching fidelity versus the necessity of fidelity to the magisterium and the absolute moral norms it defends. Theologians gather at different academic conferences, write for different publications, and participate in different online forums. As a result, scholars in the field can remain locked in distinct circles, only rarely coming together to talk about sex and gender or address the new realities shaping family life.

We wanted something different for our book. We invited scholars not to voice different sides of old arguments but to begin new conversations about what was facing the church and the world. We looked for people whose work was complex and added something new to the dialogue. We included scholars with a spectrum of views, including some who could not easily be categorized as belonging to one camp or another. We wanted people who spoke not to the context of the mid-twentieth century but to the diverse experiences of today. We were interested in finding writers who drew on the tradition and applied it in new ways, complicating existing narratives and breaking new ground.

Many of the moral theologians we sought out bracket controversial issues around love, sex, and marriage in order to engage in constructive ethical conversation. Some write about virtue and character, about how to live faithfully in a pluralistic and complex world. They ask new questions: What does it mean to love a spouse, a child, or a parent? How can people grow in their ability to love? What is good sex? What is good parenting? How can a home be more open—to the church and to the world? Another group focuses attention on pressing social issues of poverty, labor, racism, sexism, migration, and human rights. Many now identify their field as "social ethics" rather than moral theology. They care deeply about social issues and yet analyze their impact on love, sex, and family, bringing social ethics and personal ethics together. We asked these scholars to apply the wealth and insights of the Catholic tradition in the new terrain of sex, love, and family. We hoped that in applying the wisdom of the tradition to a changing world, they would deepen and enrich our understanding of what it means to live a good life.

We embarked on this project because we wanted to envision new possibilities for authentic ways of living in the face of new realities. Many Catholic colleges and universities no longer have a Catholic majority. Professors welcome "Nones," Protestants, Muslims, Hindus, and Jews, along with agnostics and atheists to their classrooms. Even among Catholic students, many are loosely affiliated, and few come from homes in which Catholicism is central. Some are more closely affiliated through Catholic parishes and high schools, and a minority are very devout, with strong ties to Catholic youth groups, homeschooling networks, and traditionalist parishes. These undergraduates come to Catholic campuses that embody their Catholic identity in diverse ways.[12] Graduate students too are looking for newer perspectives. At most universities and schools of theology and ministry, Catholic laymen and laywomen study alongside religious sisters, brothers, and men preparing for priesthood. Diverse in age, background, and religious traditions, they come from all over the world and bring very different experiences of love, sex, and families. The presence of diverse views, racial and ethnic backgrounds, nationalities, sexual orientations, and gender identities on university and seminary campuses is raising new questions. There is a pressing need to rethink how Christian teachings on sex, love, and families are being taught and discussed.

Outside higher education, in living rooms, church basements, online forums, and other spaces, adult Catholics with increasingly fragile ties to institutional Catholicism are also looking for new perspectives. Reflecting on their own experiences, they raise new questions about sex, love, and families. Or, becoming frustrated with the way these issues are discussed in ecclesial spaces, they are becoming disengaged with religion. A small percentage enthusiastically seeks a countercultural Catholic family life while a somewhat larger group is interested but pulled in many directions. We wanted to offer essays that could be helpful for people trying to navigate the often fraught relationship between faith and sexuality, no matter where they are coming from.

In academic circles, the ethics of sex, love, and family can be dismissed as "pelvic issues" by some, while for others social ethics is viewed as insufficiently theological and only loosely connected to traditional conceptions of a virtuous life. The essays gathered in this volume, however, show, love, sex, and family intersect with every social issue one can think of—technology, incarceration, race, migration, health care, income inequality, sexism, LGBTQ justice, citizenship, labor, environmental

---

12. Jason King, *Faith with Benefits: Hookup Culture on Catholic Campuses* (New York: Oxford University Press, 2017), chapter 2.

justice, and sexual violence. The essays in this book also show the impact of structural injustice on people's personal lives—on sexual practice, identity, dating, cohabiting, marriage, friendship, infertility, miscarriage, pregnancy, child and elder care, homemaking, religious practice, and time. We hope that readers of this book will see how theologically rich, socially engaged, intellectually sophisticated, and deeply practical the field of Christian family ethics can be.

Conclusion

This volume includes essays from some of the most creative and insightful scholars addressing questions of sex, love, and family in order to bring the Catholic tradition to bear on new contexts. We hope their insights will be helpful to people with varied relationships to Catholicism in their own discernment about the moral life. We imagine this volume contributing to Pope Francis's project of recentering the church as "field hospital" on discipleship in everyday life. In this discussion, traditional and progressive Catholics; single, partnered, married, and divorced people; strong and struggling families, all have a place at the table and an opportunity to share their wisdom. We hope this book will contribute to spirited conversations about relationality and social justice, care for those we love and care for the vulnerable, familial flourishing, and healing the world.

PART I

SEX

Only in the modern era did Catholics come to a more positive understanding of the equal dignity of men and women and of sex as contributing to the "intimate partnership of life and love" of a married couple (*Gaudium et Spes* 48).[1] Theologians have since mined the tradition, recovering the love poetry of the Song of Songs, the spiritual writings of saints and mystics who spoke of love for God using imagery drawn from courtship and marriage, and biblical stories previously sidelined due to a focus on elevating celibate life. Still, Catholic sexual ethics has struggled to articulate a sexual ethic for new generations less wedded to core teachings on sex outside of marriage, contraception, homosexuality, and gender identity, yet struggling with pressures of hookup culture and the normativity of casual sex, as well as the prevalence of sexual violence, sexism, and heterosexism.

The contemporary Catholic Church rearticulated its teaching on sex in *Humanae Vitae* (1968). In the encyclical, Pope St. Paul VI used a natural law methodology to argue that, because the sexual act is essentially unitive and procreative, these two essential characteristics or ends of sex ought not be separated. A few decades later, Pope St. John Paul II added a personalist perspective to this teaching in his theology of the body.[2] The pope argued that the meaning of the body is nuptial; men and women are made for self-giving to each other. Both John Paul II and Paul VI emphasized long-standing church teaching against contraception and for

---

1. On this development, see Michael G. Lawler, *Marriage and Sacrament: A Theology of Christian Marriage* (Collegeville, MN: Liturgical Press, 1993), 52–72.

2. Michael Waldenstein, *Man and Woman He Created Them: A Theology of the Body* (New York: Pauline Books and Media, 2006). Best estimates indicate that approximately 3 percent of Catholic couples use NFP.

limiting sex to heterosexual marriage. They modernized those teachings by arguing that traditional rules were compatible with respect for persons and their desires for intimacy and unity, though critics point to gender essentialism and physicalism in their thought as well as a failure to see the goodness of same-sex relationships.

In this section, we bracket ongoing debates about norms in sexual ethics in order to offer essays that speak to current concerns. Jennifer Beste highlights research showing the dissatisfaction most college students report with hookup culture, while Megan McCabe shows that dating relationships too are often marred by sexism and violence. Elizabeth Antus uses research on women's pain in sexual intercourse to illustrate how gendered norms shape sexual practice in harmful ways. All three argue for recovering values and virtues from the tradition (e.g., freedom, desire, vulnerability, interdependence, mutuality, love, justice, fidelity, and self-care) that can better enable human flourishing. Kathryn Lilla Cox's essay challenges traditional ideas about marriage and parenting by engaging literature on infertility. Kent Lasnoski's upholds a more traditional model of gender relations and argues for a vision of marriage as a "vocation to virtue" located in a household wedded to standards of poverty, chastity, and obedience. In contrast, essays by Hoon Choi and Cristina Traina consider the influence of gender norms on marriage and parenting and suggest ways to begin moving beyond them, and Craig Ford creatively employs natural law reasoning in conjunction with contemporary gender studies to reconsider Catholic thinking on trans/gender identity. Together, these essays engage a full range of questions in sexual ethics and provide resources for engaging conversation about sex and gender.

Chapter 1

Hookups, Happiness, and Human Flourishing

Jennifer Beste

When I first added college hookup culture as a topic in my sexual ethics course, I was surprised by the skepticism that many students brought to the research findings I presented. The material was interesting, they said, but how could adult researchers really understand the dynamics of hookup culture if they weren't college students exposed to the same media and peer culture, living in residence halls, and going to college parties? As a sophomore, Zach,[1] put it, "They just don't live our reality day in and day out. I doubt their analyses are accurate."

Together, we soon became excited about a new approach that students said they could trust: they would become "ethnographers" who would attend and observe their own parties *sober*, then analyze their own social reality.[2] After several years of reading approximately seventy-five ethnography papers each semester, it dawned on me that a wider audience could benefit from students' eye-opening analyses and insights. With their consent, I began to collect papers and engage in a qualitative analysis of the data.[3] My students turned out to be far more adventurous than I

---

1. Names have been changed for the sake of privacy.

2. This ethnographic assignment, requiring eight to twelve hours of observations in total, consisted of the following main tasks and questions: (1) Describe how your peers are acting at parties. Examine the interactions and dynamics of peers according to gender, race and ethnicity, and sexual orientation. (2) Why do you think your peers are acting the way they are? (3) Analyze power dynamics at college parties according to gender, race and ethnicity, and sexual orientation. (4) Do the peers you are observing seem happy and fulfilled? What dynamics, if any, would you change to be personally happier at parties?

3. Though it is impossible for a qualitative researcher to interpret data with pure objectivity, it is possible to be self-reflexive, aware of how subjectivity and biases can influence the process of

anticipated, observing parties not just at our own Catholic university but at private and public universities in seven different states. At a second Catholic institution, I later completed qualitative analysis of students' theological and ethical reflections on party and hookup culture. An extensive analysis of these student-centered research projects can be found in my book *College Hookup Culture and Christian Ethics: The Lives and Longings of Emerging Adults.*[4] In this essay, I share what I have learned from my students about prospects for happiness and fulfillment in contemporary party and hookup culture.

Ethnographers' Reflections on Happiness at College Parties

Individual ethnographies on college parties were predictably diverse, but all 126 students in my study observed the following sequence of events at parties. First, there were pregaming rituals involving consumption of alcohol in preparation for the actual party. Second, upon arrival at parties, drinking resumed and peers proceeded to grind on the dance floor. Third, as the evening progressed, ethnographers observed peers hooking up, finding a private place at the party to hook up, or leaving in pairs for "the guy's place."[5]

When asked if they thought their peers were happy and fulfilled at parties, 10 percent of ethnographers offered an uncomplicated yes, typically citing that peers had been smiling and laughing as they drank and socialized. The rest, perceiving that some, most, or all of their peers were dissatisfied, gave reasons falling into these

---

interpretation. Throughout the coding process, I intentionally utilized multiple procedures to check that my interpretations of repeated themes and theoretical constructs were grounded in the data itself and not simply an imposition of my own biases and perspectives. To ensure that my qualitative analysis represented as accurately as possible the ethnographers' collective account of their social reality, I asked for feedback from students in my sexual ethics courses from 2010 to 2012. During every semester that I read ethnography assignments, I took notes on reoccurring ideas, themes, and particular quotations, later checking with students on which ideas were representative of their college party culture and which appeared as exaggerations. When classes came to a consensus that a particular description of a party behavior or sexual act was extreme and not representative of typical college parties, I deleted it. Finally, besides my own qualitative coding, I hired two students—one white female undergraduate and one white male undergraduate from a different university (neither of whom took my sexual ethics course)—to code portions of the relevant text and identify repeating ideas and themes.

4. Jennifer Beste, *College Hookup Culture and Christian Ethics: The Lives and Longings of Emerging Adults* (New York: Oxford University Press, 2017).

5. According to my students' analyses, hookups can be defined as casual sexual activity (ranging from kissing to intercourse), usually fueled by alcohol, between strangers, acquaintances, or casual friends. While hookups appear spontaneous, there are implicit rules to hookup culture, including the expectation of interactions being solely physical, not emotional or otherwise "relational."

categories: (1) some peers were happy with drinking and hooking up, while others appeared unhappy or distressed; (2) partiers were momentarily happy, until the next morning when they woke up sober and had to deal with negative emotions and other consequences of their drunken behavior; and (3) their peers were definitely unhappy and unfulfilled with parties and/or hookups within the culture. Of course, even the most careful observations and interviews can never guarantee clear access to others' states of being. When explaining why they thought peers were unhappy, my students drew on their own and their friends' experiences of parties and hookups. Their reasons for dissatisfaction were based on one or more of the following four explanations. First, students expressed a sense of emptiness, loneliness, and depression post-hookup. This was especially prominent among females in my study, but broader social-scientific literature finds that both college men and women who experienced negative emotions post-hookup have a higher risk of depressive symptoms.[6] Second, because the ideal of an emotionless, unattached hookup rarely translates into reality, both men and women expressed a sense of disillusionment or hurt post-hookup and a longing for more. Third, many women expressed experiencing serious loss of self-esteem as a result of how they were treated by their hookup partner and fellow peers. Nora echoed many of her peers' comments in the following reflection:

> I know several people, myself included, who have woken up the next morning either to a reaction of "Oh, my gosh, I can't remember if we had sex" or to just an overwhelming depression. Finally, last year I was so depressed by drunken, meaningless hookups that I swore I would not touch anyone until it actually meant something. It made me much happier. Having such a nonchalant attitude about sexuality leads to a lack of self-esteem, which only perpetuates the cycle because you try to earn respect through sexual encounters.[7]

Fourth, many female ethnographers reported that they and their friends are unhappy due to negative sexual experiences that ranged from "bad sex" to sexual assault and rape. Both men and women observed how sexually aggressive and predatory many men were as they sought hookups:

> Male students will unfairly target the females who appear to be the most drunk since they are the easiest target to have a random hookup. (Jake)

6. Jesse Owen, Frank Fincham, and Jon Moore, "Short-Term Prospective Study of Hooking Up Among College Students," *Archives of Sexual Behavior* 40, no. 2 (2011): 331–41.

7. In order to protect confidentiality and anonymity, I used pseudonyms. As necessary, I made slight edits in students' quotations to avoid awkwardness that occurred occasionally in students' writing.

A couple of the men were trying to get this very drunk girl to come home with them. She turned down a few, but eventually accepted one offer around 1:30 a.m. She then left with the man basically carrying her because she could not walk. Many women and men at the party repeated this behavior throughout the evening. (Kelly)

My students' accounts of how normalized this kind of sexual behavior is at parties reflects the broader epidemic of sexual assault on college campuses. In the latest comprehensive study of 150,072 college students at twenty-seven universities, 26.1 percent of senior women, 29.5 percent of TGQN (transgender, genderqueer, or nonconforming, questioning) seniors, and 6.3 percent of senior males reported being victims of sexual assault involving completed penetration or unwanted sexual touching as a result of physical force or incapacitation.[8]

Social Dynamics That Students Would Change

When students were asked if they would change any dynamics at parties to make themselves personally happier, only one out of 126 ethnographers reported he would make no changes. The rest mentioned they would change one or more of the following dynamics:

1. Reduce or eliminate pressure on women to look a certain way and compete with one another for male approval.

2. Change men's culture of entitlement, objectification, and violence; men need to treat women with respect.

3. Stop judging; develop a culture that allows students and their peers to be accepted for who they truly are.

4. Eliminate the expectation of excessive drinking; replace binge and black-out drinking with social drinking.

5. Redefine a "successful party night" such that it does not require a hookup; parties would be more fun without this social expectation.

To be clear, student reflections did not reveal a puritanical fantasy of abolishing excessive drinking or hookups. Students simply thought they would enjoy

---

8. David Cantor, Bonnie Fisher, Susan Chibnall, Reanne Townsend, Hyunshik Lee, Carol Bruce, and Gail Thomas, *Report on the AAU Campus Climate Survey on Sexual Assault and Sexual Misconduct* (Rockville: Westat, 2015).

themselves much more if they didn't feel pressure to do these things in order to be viewed as fun and fit in with their peers. Michelle echoed many of her peers when she wrote:

> Even though people typically appear to have a good time at these parties, I think it is hard to actually do so. There are so many expectations of college students in the party scene. They have to look the right way, act the right way, drink the right way, and even hook up the right way. If someone does not conform to these societal norms and peer pressures, then they are in jeopardy of social rejection. It gets to be a little overwhelming. Parties would be more fun if people could just relax and forget about living up to some standard society has set.

My own college students' experience with party and hookup norms is corroborated, it turns out, by a vast amount of research that many of my students did not immediately trust. At best, only a small minority of students are truly positive about hookups. Sociologist Lisa Wade, author of *American Hookup*, finds that 15 percent of college students are true hookup enthusiasts, 33 percent of college students opt out of hookups and would prefer no sexual activity in college if their only option is casual sex, and the rest are ambivalent.[9] If the majority are privately dissatisfied, how is it possible that hookup culture remains normative and entrenched on college campuses? Sociologists repeatedly find that the phenomenon of pluralistic ignorance drives hookup culture. This occurs when people wrongly believe that their feelings and beliefs are different from those of others. By misperceiving others' preferences, many choose to follow norms that few privately support. In the context of hookup culture, undergraduates think they aren't as comfortable with hookups as their peers, so they don't reveal their discomfort or dissatisfaction. Because they don't want to appear abnormal, they conform to the hookup norm.

As a professor, I have been struck by the discrepancy between (1) students' public persona and comments in class discussions and (2) views expressed in private journal reflections and one-on-one conversations. Each semester, some of the men and women who endorse a positive stance toward hookup culture publicly reveal negative experiences privately:

> Many times we wake up to regret [hookups] the next morning. Even when we do regret our actions, it is easy to put on an air of happiness in order to simply fit in. (Tammy)

9. Lisa Wade, *American Hookup: The New Culture of Sex on Campus* (New York: W. W. Norton & Co., 2017).

From my own hookup experiences, I would say that I have zero fulfillment the next day, but while it is happening, I feel happy and successful. For people who do not know me though, they cannot see the disappointment because to outsiders it is masked. I am always upset after the hook up, because while it's happening I have the feeling that it will lead to something more, like a relationship. This is never really the case though; once you are sober and wake up the next day, you just have the feeling of being used for physical pleasure, which never creates a happy satisfied attitude. (Olivia)

Fueling all of this, of course, is our dominant popular cultural narrative about sex and gender. According to my students, most youth have been consuming images and videos from pop culture (movies, television shows, and social media) since middle school that depict college as the time to be wild, drink excessively, and hook up with as many people as possible. They arrive at college eager to hit the party scene and experience the most fun-filled years of their lives. And yet, their positive expectations about hookups in particular fail to meet the reality of their actual experiences of hookups. Why is this, and can Catholic theology offer any insights?

Becoming Fully Human Through Poverty of Spirit

As a Catholic theologian, I wondered if my students could benefit from insights in the Catholic tradition that might shed light on their dissatisfaction within hookup culture and also assist them with choices concerning sexuality and relationships that would make them (and their peers) happier. To this end, I began assigning a short spiritual classic called *Poverty of Spirit* by Johann Baptist Metz after students had discussed party and hookup culture.[10] While the title can be off-putting, students realize soon enough that poverty of spirit does not mean Jesus was (and we ought to become) miserable—end of story. Focusing on the desert temptations, Metz helps his readers understand that Jesus was fully vulnerable, just as we are, and he insists that Christ's humanity saves us and "gives us the courage to be true to ourselves."[11] Out of love for humanity, God willingly experienced powerlessness in order to overcome the separation between divine and human and make possible the experience of intimate union with us:

What the devil really fears is the powerlessness of God in the humanity Christ has assumed. Satan fears the Trojan horse of an open human heart that will re-

10. Johann Baptist Metz, *Poverty of Spirit* (New York: Paulist Press, 1998).
11. Ibid., 14.

main true to its native poverty, suffer the misery and the abandonment that is humanity's, and thus save humankind. Satan's temptation is an assault on God's self-renunciation, an enticement to strength, security and spiritual abundance; for these things will obstruct God's saving approach to humanity in the dark robes of frailty and weakness.[12]

As students grasp that Jesus actually embraces the opposite of the hypermasculine traits many expect the Son of God to claim in moments like these, I give them the following assignment:[13]

> (1) Imagine that Metz's Jesus has returned to earth as a sophomore transfer student at your university. You have a conversation with Jesus and ask, "What does embracing poverty of spirit mean to you?" and "What does the embrace of poverty of spirit look like specifically for a college student?" What does he say?
> (2) He then asks you, "What do you think are the main challenges to embodying poverty of spirit in college?" What do you say?
> (3) Describe how Jesus acts throughout the evening at a party you're both attending. How does he relate to his peers, and how do his peers respond to him?

As several undergraduates and I coded 150 student interpretations of poverty of spirit, three dominant themes arose. The most important aspect of poverty of spirit for them was interdependence. My students imagined Metz's college-aged Jesus as a person who takes great joy interacting with his peers. He is also comfortable acknowledging his need for support from God and others in order to grow and flourish. Being made in God's image and loved into existence as a unique person is more than enough for Jesus. Many of my students, by contrast, struggle to experience a stable sense of self-worth based simply on their *being*. Socialized to be self-sufficient individuals in a cutthroat society of clear winners and losers, they internalize that identity and self-worth are based not on *being* but on *doing* (individual achievements) and *having* (social status and materialism):

> Parents, professors, grad schools, and future employers all pressure me to succeed. I feel as though the content on my resume, the likes I get on Facebook, and the recognition of my achievements all equate my value as a human being. I am bombarded from every angle with messages saying that I'm not good enough and that I have to be better if I want to be successful. (Bella)

---

12. Ibid., 11.
13. This is an abridged version of the assignment due to space constraints.

This constant drive for vigilant self-improvement to be the best and outdo their competitors deeply affects students' attitudes toward sexuality and intimate relationships. Hookups appear as the most "reasonable" choice in college because they are the most time-efficient way to meet desires for sex, approval, and social validation:

> Hookups give stressed-out college students a chance to finally let their hair down and have sex with a random stranger that they won't have to deal with back in their daily lives. They do not want another person to cause them stress during the school week, so they need to find someone that they can hook up with and forget about. (Ella)

Furthermore, students note that our culture associates strength and success with self-sufficiency, which creates discomfort and shame about their need for relationships and support. Students emphasize that, if they express desire for a relationship after hooking up, they fear they will be labeled needy, clingy, and pathetic. Twenty years earlier, it was considered normal on my college campus to openly seek exciting experiences of falling in love, intense connection, and being in a committed relationship. Today, social influences make youth and young adults ashamed of their most basic needs for genuine affirmation, emotional intimacy, and support.

Second, in addition to interdependence, students identified self-love as a key aspect of embracing poverty of spirit and becoming fully human. Interestingly, many students were simultaneously attracted to and afraid of Metz's call to accept all aspects of ourselves—our gifts as well as limitations and vulnerabilities:

> Another obstacle we face is in accepting our weaknesses and limitations. So many college students try to run from imperfection and manipulate ourselves to perfection. We are so uncomfortable with struggle, limitations, pain, and failure and we see them as diseases that can be fixed by working harder or masking them with distractions. Instead of embracing these parts of our humanity, we run from them. (Natalie)

Students were similarly intrigued by Metz's account of self-love involving a courageous rejection of the status quo in favor of accepting our unique calling. In *Poverty of Spirit*, Metz highlights how we all experience (as Jesus did) a fundamental temptation to sacrifice our uniqueness in order to secure social validation. Students identify with this temptation to conform because their self-esteem is deeply affected by peer acceptance:

> Friends and popularity still make up such a significant part of how college students view their own self-worth, and therefore many don't feel ready to venture away from the crowd, and stand alone on the path to which they are called. (Grace)

The third major aspect of embracing poverty of spirit and becoming fully human, according to my students, is learning to love our neighbor. Indeed, for Metz, true neighbor love requires that we are willing to be affected, challenged, and transformed by our encounter with others:

> Every genuine human encounter must be inspired by poverty of spirit. . . . We must be able to open up to the other person, to let that person's distinctive personality unfold—even though it often frightens us or repels us. We often keep the other person down, and only see what we want to see; thus we never really encounter the mysterious secret of their being, only ourselves.[14]

In his imagined encounter with Jesus, one student described Jesus explaining neighbor love in the following way:

> You can see God through your friend, classmate, coworker, the stranger you just met at a bar, etc. Life is not just about you; it is bigger than that. Life is more fulfilling when you put your egoistic self-interest aside and consider others' interests as well. If you are serving only your sense of self, you are missing out on the major piece of a satisfying life. When people forsake the people around them or love what they can get from others, they slowly become like the things they love—small, insignificant, and petty. (Matthew)

Asked to identify challenges to loving their neighbor as themselves, students named two. First, egoism is positively encouraged by the messages from US culture (even parents) that college is the time in life to focus on oneself:

> College years are often looked at as a time to be wild and self-indulgent. Society often encourages students to experiment and do what makes them happy. The idea of making ourselves happy makes us selfish and gives us a sense of control that makes it difficult to become fully human. (Aubrey)

Second, students express that fear of vulnerability prevents them from sharing their authentic selves with others and actually feeling and expressing a full range of emotions. Expressing vulnerable emotions is culturally associated with weakness, which creates shame, embarrassment, and loss of status.

> When surrounded by a status-minded social environment where weakness is discouraged, it is extremely hard to accept that it is okay to be vulnerable with others when it comes to feelings and relationships. Revealing these things will negatively impact our social standing. (Evan)

14. Ibid., 44.

> Becoming authentic and vulnerable is also risky because we may get rejected and hurt: Falling in true love is exciting, and something college kids want to do but are afraid of. Overcoming the obstacle of completely taking down your brick wall piece by piece and letting another being in is one of the greatest feats. (Aliyah)

Of course, fears of being vulnerable, relational, and authentic are not novel. Generations of college students have experienced fear of rejection, heartbreak, and betrayals. Aliyah's imagery of a brick wall to protect herself from others, however, resonates with my assessment that the risk students take when they disclose their authentic selves has never been so high. In part, this has to do with technology. Students articulate how social media ratchets up their fears of vulnerability, failure, and shame since their personal lives are made public in unprecedented ways. Within seconds, everyone can witness the embarrassing details of a drunken night out, failures, breakups, and rejections. It is no wonder that, within college culture, so many seek to escape these anxieties by chasing instant highs from alcohol, drugs, and casual hookups, only to feel the return of emptiness and loneliness the next day. It is these cultural crises in authenticity, vulnerability, and relationality that are at the root of the rise and perpetuation of hookup culture as the social norm on college campuses.

Christ Versus Culture

During the first semester I read students' imagined conversations with Jesus as a college sophomore, I was struck by how sharply *all* of them juxtaposed Jesus' way of being and the typical college partier's way of being at parties. While Jesus is similar to his peers in the sense that he loves socializing, having fun, and partying late into the night, the college-aged Jesus stands out from his peers in profound ways: since Jesus is comfortable with who he is, his sense of self-worth is not dependent on conforming to social norms. Students repeatedly imagine Jesus enjoying beers throughout the night, but he does not feel the need to get drunk to fit in. Many imagine that Jesus intentionally does not get drunk because he knows he could do something stupid and hurt someone. Students also imagine Jesus turning down offers from women to hook up because he knows he would simply be using them as a means for self-gratification.

Another main occurrence in student reflections is Jesus reaching out to peers who appear marginalized, vulnerable, or struggling emotionally. Many students visualize Jesus "interacting with women and treating them as equals" (Lindsey). For instance, David writes that Jesus would never be standing around with his friends "rating girls on a 10-point scale in terms of their appearance" and "taking dibs on which one he would try to hook up with." When Jesus encounters passed-out women on couches, he makes sure to find the woman's friends so she gets home safely. Jesus is not afraid of conflict if respecting someone's dignity is at stake: students readily imagine him intervening in situations where men are trying to leave parties with drunk women. Epitomizing the very antithesis to the hypermasculinity that pervades the party scene, Jesus would "cause many people to be uncomfortable," as Caleb wrote. "To be completely vulnerable as a man would greatly challenge what many men think it means to be a man." Similarly, Jordan acknowledged that Jesus would probably take heat for his countercultural respect for women: "People may put him down for this behavior, but he can handle it."

One day in class, I presented the table below and asked my students if I was interpreting them accurately.

College Partier's Way of Being versus Jesus' Way of Being	
College Partier/Hookup Player	*Jesus*
Stoic (unattached, unemotional)	Expressive, empathetic
Self-sufficient and individualistic	Interdependent
Follows crowd	Follows heart, unique calling
Invulnerable, in control	Vulnerable
Ego-driven	Loves neighbor as self
Free to maximize self-interest and pleasure	Free to love God, others, and self

They said yes, and many students went further. As Rob commented, "It isn't just the typical hookup partier or college partier who is opposite to Jesus—it's typical college students. This is how we have to be in our day lives—to be academically successful, get into grad school, and get jobs." Jon chimed in, "Actually—it's even broader than college students—change 'college partier' to 'US citizen.'" Several students nodded their heads. Through their reflections and class discussions, my students helped me realize that their party lives are not so different from their academic lives: both are ruled by the values and priorities presumably needed to succeed in US culture. Their reflections alerted me to how deeply the implicit values and norms of neoliberal capitalism influence all aspects of our lives.

Reflection and dialogue about alternative ways of being in the world offers students opportunities to determine which values and priorities they actually practice in their day and night lives and to discern which way of being they want to embody in the future. Does such reflection enable many young adults to make and "own" decisions that are most likely to lead to greater happiness in all aspects of their lives—including their sexual and relational lives? Anonymous end-of-the-semester evaluations indicate yes. Self-reported examples of students making positive changes in their relationships and lives include stories of going out of their comfort zones to actually ask someone out on a date, relating to their partner more justly by considering their full humanity, and ending relationships that are unjust, abusive, or otherwise unfulfilling.

Conclusion

A key insight I have gained as a result of listening carefully to my students over the past decade is that the dynamics of party and hookup culture have become more and more dehumanizing. Making matters worse, many have become desensitized to their own and others' dehumanization. Students submit to or even embrace the norms of pursuing unattached hookups that lack emotion for multiple reasons that have nothing to do with promoting joy and well-being in their lives. Social acceptance, lack of other perceived social options, and the need to remain in control and invulnerable all play a role. In my student-centered research projects at two universities (focusing on party ethnographies and students' theological reflections), undergraduates have overwhelmingly expressed a deep longing for more than their current social reality offers. Their desires can be summed up simply in three wishes:

1. to be free from narrow social and sexual norms and free to act in ways that truly make them feel affirmed and happy;

2. to be free to express and be accepted for who they truly are;

3. to have supportive relationships marked by authenticity and vulnerability.

The degree of dissatisfaction and suffering within contemporary college party and hookup culture opens students to the possibility that Christ's way of being authentic and intimately connected to others is a more promising path than simply following our dominant culture's path of egoistic self-gratification. Students' longings for genuine love and connection affirm core convictions present in the Catholic tradition that we are created as deeply relational beings and that our joy and fulfillment lie in discerning our own unique calling and experiencing genuine intimacy and communion with others.

Of course, it is possible to repress and deaden our deepest desires to be known and loved for who we are and to know and love others. Industries that produce pornography or even encourage sex with dolls or robots as a replacement for true intimacy testify to this reality. To be able to *feel* such desires for authenticity and intimate connection, one must first be able to experience a sense of safety and basic trust. Tragically, toxic cultural norms and harsh economic conditions that incite fear about one's individual survival can override such higher-order desires.

Given this cultural context, it becomes more crucial than ever to provide young adults with tools and opportunities to seek and find life-giving insights in our theological tradition that are relevant to their struggles. By imaginatively encountering Jesus within their own college culture and comparing Christ's way of being human with dominant US culture's ways of being, my students have been able to reflect critically on their socialization and discern paths more likely to foster happiness and fulfillment. If my students' hunch is correct that neoliberal values have become normative nearly everywhere, it's an exercise we all might want to try.[15]

15. For more research on how neoliberal ideology negatively impacts college students' well-being, see Salman Turken, Hilde Eileen Nafstad, Rolv Mikkel Blakar, and Katrina Roen, "Making Sense of Neoliberal Subjectivity: A Discourse Analysis of Media Language on Self-Development," *Globalization* 13, no. 1 (2016): 32–46; Karin Schwiter, "Neoliberal Subjectivity—Difference, Free Choice and Individualised Responsibility in the Life Plans of Young Adults in Switzerland," *Geographica Helvetica* 68, no. 3 (2013): 153–59.

Chapter 2

Relationships Instead of Hooking Up?

Justice in Dating

Megan K. McCabe

The last decade has seen increased attention on the "hookup culture," including questions from Christian ethicists about its effects on emerging adults.[1] One concern is hookup culture's demand for conformity: social life and romantic expression available to students seems to require participation in party and hookup culture on the majority of college campuses. Some scholars worry about the disconnect between physical activity and intimacy; others about students' reports of unhappiness. And still others are concerned this disconnect will leave students without the skills to foster the emotional intimacy needed to sustain relationships. And patterns of gendered inequality have been identified in both party culture and expectations regarding hookups themselves. The dominant conversation about hookup culture locates problems of sexual violence on campuses within hookup culture. As Jason King argues, "Sexual assault is an extension of stereotypical hookup culture, which exerts a subtle social coercion on everyone."[2] For many, hookup culture is the problem that gives rise to unhappiness and violence on college campuses.

1. Jennifer Beste, *College Hookup Culture and Christian Ethics: The Lives and Longings of Emerging Adults* (New York: Oxford University Press, 2018); Kari-Shane Davis Zimmerman, "In Control? The Hookup Culture and the Practice of Relationships," in *Leaving and Coming Home* (Eugene, OR: Cascade, 2010), 47–61; Kari-Shane Davis Zimmerman, "Hooking Up: Sex, Theology, and Today's 'Unhooked' Dating Practices," *Horizons* 37, no. 1 (2010): 72–91; Conor Kelly, "Sexism in Practice: Feminist Ethics Evaluating the Hookup Culture," *Journal of Feminist Studies in Religion* 28, no. 2 (2012): 27–48; Jason King, *Faith with Benefits* (New York: Oxford University Press, 2017).

2. King, *Faith with Benefits*, 12.

Consequently, Christian ethicists argue in favor of a recovery of dating or committed relationships on campus. If hookup culture fosters unhappiness, inequality, and is marked by gendered and sexual violence, then relationships allow for vulnerability, happiness, and greater equality between women and men.

Evidence suggests, however, that these problems are not so easily rectified by promoting dating and committed relationships. These contexts, especially for emerging adults, are also sites of risk, abuse, and sexual violence. The problems that many identify within hookup and party culture are also problems in dating and relationships. In light of this reality, this essay investigates the presence of violence in dating and relationships before offering a response of a relational virtue ethics.

Danger and Violence in Romantic Relationships

Dating and relationships are contexts with potential for flourishing and joy. They are sites of intimacy and meaningful relationship. And they serve as the context for persons to grow and learn who they will be in relation to others and exactly *how* to relate to others in intimate relationship, which is critical for potential future long-term committed relationships or marriages. Yet, relationships and dating are also marked by intimate partner violence (IPV), sexual coercion, stalking, and patterns of social injustice. These realities are of particular concern precisely because of the formative role that dating plays. That is, there is a danger that learned patterns of abuse will remain part of how young adults relate to others, including to future significant others or spouses. More immediate, such abuse negatively affects the lives of those who are victimized, inhibiting their flourishing and violating their dignity as persons.

Sexual violence, including rape and sexual coercion, occurs in troubling ways within dating contexts.[3] While the majority of rapes on campuses are perpetrated by classmates, boyfriends have been identified as perpetrators of completed rapes for almost a quarter of all rapes on campus but as perpetrators of attempted rapes only approximately 15 percent of the time. These numbers suggest that relationships not only are not immune from acts of sexual violence but also have the potential to be exploited by perpetrators perhaps because of trust that has been built over time or because boyfriends do not seem to fit the stereotypical image of a rapist.

Sexual coercion "occurs when one individual (the *perpetrator*) performs an act of physical force or psychological manipulation to gain greater sexual access to

---

3. Doug P. Vanderlaan and Paul L. Vasey, "Patterns of Sexual Coercion in Heterosexual and Non-Heterosexual Men and Women," *Archives of Sexual Behavior; New York* 38, no. 6 (2009): 987–99; Bonnie S. Fisher, Leah E. Daigle, and Francis T. Cullen, *Unsafe in the Ivory Tower: The Sexual Victimization of College Women* (Thousand Oaks, CA: SAGE Publications, Inc., 2009).

another individual (the *victim*)."[4] Physical coercion may involve physical attempts to have sexual activity with another person, using physical force such as twisting an arm or trying to hold somebody down in order to kiss them, or attempting to use physical force to have intercourse. But coercion may also include forms of psychological manipulation: threatening to end the relationship in order to extract sex, using continual arguments, or threatening to use physical force. Heterosexual men are the most likely to engage in both forms of coercion. This does not mean, however, that men are not victimized. In fact, researchers have found that those who are vulnerable to sexual coercion, both women and men, are likely to believe stereotypes that men constantly desire sexual activity. Women may be vulnerable to coercion because they believe that they must be available to satisfy what they perceive to be a man's needs. And men appear to be vulnerable as they try to live up to the demands of stereotyped masculinity. Such social stereotypes exert pressure and constrain the options of both men and women in coercive contexts. Other women who experience coercion have noted that they went along with sex because they did not think they could stop it from happening. It can take the shape of normalized and eroticized violence. Psychologist Lynn Phillips quotes one young woman:

> My boyfriend would like to hit me and call me a slut and other mean names during sex. He would pretend he was raping me and that I was loving it and just couldn't get enough of him. He wanted to tie me up and stuff, and he liked to dominate me during sex. I didn't know how to handle it, so I thought I should just pretend I enjoyed it too, you know, so we wouldn't get into a hassle. I guess it was partly because I was afraid of him turning on me, but it was also because he was my boyfriend and I thought I should just try to grin and bear it.[5]

Another woman reported going along with unwanted sex because she thought it was owed in a relationship:

> We would be having sex, again, and I wouldn't want it, but he was my boyfriend, you know, so I never really felt like I could let him down by saying no. But a lot of the times it hurt me. . . . I didn't feel like I could exactly say no, but I hoped that he would see me crying and just stop, I don't know, out of guilt or concern or something, even pity. Of course he never did. He'd just keep going, and then afterward, he'd say, "Didn't you like it?"[6]

4. Vanderlaan and Vasey, "Patterns of Sexual Coercion," 992.

5. Lynn M. Phillips, *Flirting with Danger: Young Women's Reflections on Sexuality and Domination* (New York: New York University Press, 2000), 138.

6. Ibid., 145.

The fact that these women were in relationships is what made them vulnerable to coercion and violent behaviors in the context of sex.

Another area of risk in relation to dating for college students is stalking.[7] In fact, stalking is likely more common on college campuses than among the general population. College is a particularly risky time due to the close proximity of students living in and around campus, shared spaces such as dining halls and dorms, and easy access to one's regular schedule. Estimates for the prevalence of stalking among college students ranges from 6 to 27 percent, with women, who may be two to four times more likely to be stalked than men, disproportionately victimized.

Stalking is closely associated with dating relationships on college campuses. It may include attempting to monitor one's partner or their behavior via social media, calling them when they do not want to be called, or attempting to obtain information about them without their knowledge. Over 30 percent of students, including both men and women have been found to engage in these forms of pursuit, which all suggest attempts to control one's significant other.

In some cases, pursuit behaviors occur in the context of wanting a relationship to develop. Beliefs that women should be in relationships are intensified by the stereotype that women are looking for commitment, leaving them vulnerable to attempts to coerce them into dating. Some women have expressed that the only way to successfully reject somebody is the excuse that they already have a boyfriend, not their own wants or choices. They "often told stories of men who acted entitled to relationships, expecting their relational overtures to be accepted, and became angry when rebuffed—sometimes stalking the rejecting woman."[8] Stalking may also mix with coercion. One woman experienced a man insisting that he would not take no for an answer, causing her to give in to finally get him to stop, all while trying to get him to break up with her.

Stalking is a particular risk when relationships have ended.[9] One study found that among female students interviewed, about two-thirds experienced ongoing pursuit after the breakup. And women who experienced intimate partner violence within a dating relationship were at greater risk of stalking post-breakup. These

---

7. Ryan Shorey, Tara Cornelius, and Catherine Strauss, "Stalking in College Student Dating Relationships: A Descriptive Investigation," *Journal of Family Violence* 30, no. 7 (2015): 935–42; Eric G. Lambert et al., "Do Men and Women Differ in Their Perceptions of Stalking: An Exploratory Study Among College Students," *Violence and Victims* 28, no. 2 (2013): 195–209.

8. Elizabeth A. Armstrong and Laura Hamilton, "Gendered Sexuality in Young Adulthood: Double Binds and Flawed Options," *Gender & Society* 23, no. 5 (2009): 600.

9. Jennifer Katz and Hillary Rich, "Partner Covictimization and Post-Breakup Stalking, Pursuit, and Violence: A Retrospective Study of College Women," *Journal of Family Violence* 30 (2015): 189–99.

women are especially likely to be stalked in ways that involve surveillance or intimidation and threats to do harm to oneself, the victim, or the victim's family. Such stalking is additionally worrisome in that it is predictive of post-breakup violence.

Men may use stalking behaviors in an attempt to control or reunite with women who have attempted to end relationships. One study reported, "Men often drew on romantic repertoires to coerce interaction after relationships had ended. One woman told us that her ex-boyfriend had stalked her for months—even showing up at her workplace, showering her with flowers and gifts, and blocking her entry into work until the police had arrived."[10] In such cases, these men may not recognize "that their actions are not courtship-pursuing behaviors but actually forms of stalking."[11] Given social narratives of what "aggressive courtship" looks like, these forms of stalking may receive broader social support from friends, family, or through the influence of popular culture. In fact, while women are more likely than men to perceive stalking as harmful, both men and women have been found to perceive a blurry line between aggressive courtship and stalking.

College students are also at risk of experiencing abuse within their relationships.[12] Up to a third of students have experienced violence within the context of a dating relationship. "Intimate partner violence is a pattern of coercive behaviors that can result in physical injury, psychological abuse, sexual assault, and social isolation."[13] It may take the form of psychological, physical, or sexual violence. Evidence suggests that psychological partner violence, in which a perpetrator is degrading to his or her partner, is the most common form of IPV experienced by college students, with somewhere between 34 to 52 percent of students psychologically victimized by a significant other. Psychological abuse has the potential to escalate to include physical and sexual abuse, which is experienced by 16 to 34 percent of students. Physical violence may range from light pushes or slaps to more serious forms of violence such as punching or even lethal violence. While violence is not directly caused by use of alcohol, alcohol may pose a risk for IPV because

10. Armstrong and Hamilton, "Gendered Sexuality in Young Adulthood," 601.

11. Lambert et al., "Do Men and Women Differ in Their Perceptions of Stalking," 196.

12. Katie M. Edwards and Kateryna M. Sylaska, "The Perpetration of Intimate Partner Violence among LGBTQ College Youth: The Role of Minority Stress," *Journal of Youth and Adolescence* 42, no. 11 (2013): 1721–31; Leah E. Daigle et al., "Intimate Partner Violence Among College Students: Measurement, Risk Factors, Consequences, and Responses," in *The Wiley Handbook on the Psychology of Violence*, Carlos A. Cuevas and Callie Marie Rennison, eds. (Malden, MA: John Wiley & Sons, Ltd., 2016); Heidi Scherer, Jamie A. Snyder, and Bonnie S. Fisher, "Intimate Partner Victimization Among College Students with and without Disabilities: Prevalence of and Relationship to Emotional Well-Being," *Journal of Interpersonal Violence* 31, no. 1 (2016): 49–80.

13. Daigle et al., "Intimate Partner Violence Among College Students," 374.

it does facilitate aggression. Given the alcohol usage that accompanies campus party culture, there is a risk that college relationships or dating will involve IPV.

Abuse in dating contexts is a potential risk for both women and men. The phrase "domestic violence" brings to mind what scholars call "patriarchal terrorism" in which a male partner terrorizes a female partner by isolating her and verbally and physically assaulting her, with a great risk of escalating into lethal violence. While patriarchal terrorism on college campuses does occur,[14] less severe forms of abuse are much more common among college students, often taking the form of partner covictimization. Both women and men report similar levels of victimization, especially when it comes to psychological violence and emotionally abusive relationships. Such abuse "most likely consists of common couple or situational violence, which is a type of partner violence in which both partners engage in typically low-levels of violence that is borne out of disagreements that escalate, not a desire to dominate or control the other partner."[15] This kind of covictimization is worrying precisely because of the formative nature of relationships among emerging adults. When violent patterns of relationship are learned, it takes time and effort to unlearn these ways of relating to others.

Research has found, however, that the IPV among college students does have gendered dimensions. Women typically resort to acts physical force when they are looking for some kind of control or retaliation for emotional hurt, while men are more likely to use physical force when they have been hurt first or as an expression of jealousy. The use of violence in response to jealousy is particularly troubling given that such violence functions not only as an expression of anger but also as a tool for control and power over another. And men who resort to physical violence have been found to have greater problems controlling their anger than women who engage in violence. Given the threat of severity of injury that may result from male violence, and even from social narratives about battered women, male violence may be particularly threatening or fear inducing for women. And one significant study found that although men and women were equally likely to perpetrate some kind of physical violence, "[m]ale college students hit their partner more than twice as often as female college students."[16]

Social narratives about commitment and romantic relationships may encourage women to stay in risky contexts. Phillips argues that a social narrative that

14. Jeremy Bauer-Wolf, "Multiple Warning, No Action" *Inside Higher Ed*, January 22, 2019, https://www.insidehighered.com/news/2019/01/22/slain-university-utah-student-asked-campus -police-help-multiple-times-no-results.

15. Daigle et al., "Intimate Partner Violence Among College Students," 379.

16. Ibid., 382.

sharply distinguishes between "good guys" and "bad guys" makes it easy to see strangers as perpetrators of violence but more difficult to recognize violence in the context of some kind of intimate relationship. One young woman interviewed said of her boyfriend,

> He's basically a really good person, and we share a lot together. It's just that he has a really bad temper, and when he gets upset, he sometimes hits me. God, that sounds so bad. But most times he's really decent, so I don't think of the times he hits me as so severe. . . . It's really very seldom, actually. Well, there was this one time that he had me up against a wall and he was holding my hair and punching me in the stomach. But he really apologized after, and I don't think that will ever happen again. I know this might sound like, whatever, but he's not an abuser.[17]

Phillips also found that assumptions that women's fulfillment is in relationship makes them vulnerable to accepting abuse as normal, especially when it is combined with experiences and social narratives that male violence is acceptable. Women may learn that "love hurts" through a form of cultural osmosis or by watching the kinds of relationships that the women in their lives growing up have.

Some studies indicate that women are more likely than men to slap, push, shove, or throw something at a romantic partner, and others have found that women are more likely to indicate being in a physically abusive relationship. But as one study found, "women who had violent tendencies but were with non-violent partners did not act on these tendencies. This suggests that young women's general aggression is conditioned on being with a violent partner."[18] Thus, it may be true that women are generally more likely to be victimized in an abusive relationship through patterns of control and severe violence and that they participate in abusive acts in bidirectional and dysfunctional relationships.

The perception that perpetrators are always men and victims are always women also obscures the reality of IPV among same-sex couples. One study noted that approximately 43 percent of LGBTQ+ students reported perpetrating some kind of dating violence within the past year. Such abuse may go unrecognized by both victims and potential support networks because of assumptions about abuse and gender.

17. Phillips, *Flirting with Danger*, 169–70.
18. Catherine Kaukinen, Angela Gover, and Jennifer Hartman, "College Women's Experiences of Dating Violence in Casual and Exclusive Relationships," *American Journal of Criminal Justice* 37, no. 2 (2012): 157.

Abuse among LGBTQ+ persons is shaped by negative attitudes about homo-sexuality. For those who experience rejection from friends and family because of their sexual or gender identities, the threat of isolation caused by abuse may be particularly acute. Abused persons may run the risk of being unwillingly outed by an abusive partner, or abusive partners may try to limit access to the queer com-munity. Victims of IPV in same-sex relationships may fear reaching out for help out of concern for being discriminated against. Perpetrators of same-sex IPV are likely to also have experienced internalized homonegativity and/or concealing their sexual identity. And those who experience sexual-orientation-related vic-timization have been found to be a risk for perpetration of psychological abuse. This reality suggests that negative attitudes about homosexuality may participate in the causes of IPV among same-sex couples.

The rates of intimate partner victimization among college students with dis-abilities is worryingly high as well. Students with disabilities are twice as likely as those without to experience IPV. The consequences are also higher. Victims with disabilities were found to be three times more likely to report depressive symp-toms. And persons with multiple disabilities are more likely to report self-harm behavior or stress than students with no or only one disability.[19]

Relationships and dating are contexts of risk and danger, including sexual vio-lence, stalking, and intimate partner violence. These realities suggest that an ethic for romantic relationship must be foundational and able to respond to the abuses of both the hookup culture and those of relationships and dating. Such an ethic must apply to the ways that persons engage one another and to the responsibility for social narratives or assumptions about gender, sexuality, and abuse that give rise to or obscure realities of violence.

Relationality and Its Virtues

Human existence is fundamentally relational. The ability of individuals to flourish and survive requires being in relation to others. And, as Margaret Farley observes, "We are who we are not only because we can to some degree determine ourselves by our freedom but because we are transcendent of ourselves through our capacities to know and to love."[20] Human relationships, including but not limited to romantic relationships, have great potential for human flourishing. Indeed, the Catholic tradition has maintained that they have potential to be

19. Scherer, Snyder, and Fisher, "Intimate Partner Victimization Among College Students."
20. Margaret A. Farley, *Just Love: A Framework for Christian Sexual Ethics* (New York: Con-tinuum, 2008), 213.

graced and sacramental, mediating God's very presence. Yet, romantic and sexual contexts are also sites of risk and danger, including sexual violence, stalking, and intimate partner violence. These realities demand a foundational ethic to guide and shape our capacity for relationship. James Keenan has argued that the human person is "a relational rational being whose modes of relationality need to be rightly realized."[21] We do not merely exist in relationship, but such relationship makes demands on us. We must ask, who are we to be and become in relation to one another and ourselves?

As Keenan argues, this question is ultimately a question of virtue ethics, which recognizes that what we *do* shapes who we *are*. If what we do is coerce, control, and abuse, then those are the ways in which we will be formed to relate to others, potentially even beyond the context of romantic relationship and into ways of relating with friends, family, or even future children. To this end, Keenan offers four cardinal virtues: "Our identity is relational in three ways: generally, specifically, and uniquely. Each of these relational ways of being demands a cardinal virtue: as a relational being in general, we are called to justice; as a relational being specifically, we are called to fidelity; and, as a relational being uniquely, we are called to self-care."[22] The fourth virtue "is prudence which determines what constitutes the just, faithful and self-caring way of life for an individual."[23]

Justice requires that we treat all people equally in ways that recognize and uphold their dignity, including in the contexts of relationships, dating, and sexual encounters. Farley argues that justice means treating persons as ends in themselves and respecting both their capacity for relationship and their capacity for self-determination. "In sexual relations, justice always prompts us to see the other as a subject and not as an object; justice leads us to recognize the importance of never taking advantage of another for the sake of fulfilling our own desires or needs."[24] Justice prohibits sexual coercion, rape, stalking, IPV, and all forms of control-seeking action, which prioritize one's own desires ahead of the dignity of others.

But justice must also be social, attentive to our neighbor, and, according to the standard of the preferential option for the poor, responsive to those who are most vulnerable. Social justice in the context of sexuality and relationship asks not only what is due to another in the context of interpersonal relationship between two people but also what it means to treat others as ends in themselves in the context of community. It requires that persons be responsible bystanders who work to

21. James F. Keenan, "Virtue Ethics and Sexual Ethics," *Louvain Studies* 30, no. 3 (2005): 189.
22. Ibid., 190.
23. Ibid.
24. Ibid., 193.

prevent sexual violence and IPV. It points us in the direction of those who are *made vulnerable* by social narratives and unjust stereotypes. As such, it ought to push for an examination of the social narratives regarding dating and romantic relationships, rape, abuse, sexual orientation, ability, gender, and race that foster not only dating violence but the social conditions that make it difficult to recognize abuse for what it is. Specifically, the racism that prevents black women and the social stigma that prevents LGBTQ+ persons from naming their abuse for fear of bringing negative perceptions to their communities; the social stigma against LGBTQ+ persons that may be internalized, increasing the chances for IPV; or the cultural assumptions about gender that increase the chances of sexual coercion of both women and men must be worked against to foster the social conditions that promote human flourishing in relationships.

Fidelity demands a commitment to particular relationships. It "calls us never to abandon our lover, to recognize rather that our sexual love must deepen, embrace, and extend through intimacy."[25] It prohibits treating one another as disposable. In the context of patterns of abuse and coercion, however, the virtue of fidelity itself has the potential to function in dangerous ways. Those who are abused may come to think that fidelity's demands to not abandon a partner require that they accept abuse or coercion for the sake of a greater moral good.

For this reason, Keenan also offers the virtue of self-care. This virtue asks that one be responsible to oneself and look toward one's own good. "Prudential self-care informed by mercy leads some people to delay as precipitous sexual intimacy, but for others it gently prods them to seek sexual love that has, for long, been an object of fear and dread."[26] In light of various forms of sexual and relational abuse, self-care may also encourage one to prioritize one's own flourishing in contexts of harm or in light of social narratives that encourage acceptance of abuse. Persons do not merely owe justice to others but are owed it *by* others. Through self-care they may come to demand right relationship of their partners.

Virtues are classically defined as a mean between two extremes, one of excess and the other of lack. For example, one obvious vice in relation to fidelity would be moving quickly from partner to partner. But the other vicious extreme might be requiring persons to stay in relation to another regardless of circumstances, which could include abuse and coercion. Individual persons may trend toward one extreme and others toward the other. Consequently, what actions are necessary to foster the virtues may differ from person to person. Virtues are, thus, able to be contextualized according to the specific contours of an individual's life. And it is

25. Ibid., 195.
26. Ibid., 196.

the virtue of prudence that "has the task of integrating the three virtues into our relationships . . . [and] is always vigilant looking to the future, trying not only to realize the claims of justice, fidelity, and self-care in the here and now, but also calling us to anticipate occasions when each of these virtues can be more fully acquired."[27] Prudence helps persons embody the virtues in the concrete realities of their lives.

These virtues ought to help persons grow into the kind of persons who exist in right and just relationship with others and themselves. They provide the guide for the direction in which persons should grow, but "their final expression remains outstanding,"[28] meaning that one's moral growth into ethical relationality is never complete. Through practicing virtuous actions, the person becomes virtuous; the virtues become a kind of "second nature." By acting just one becomes just. If acting in abusive and coercive ways, that is, according to vice not virtue, is formative, then by acting according to virtuous relationality, individuals can grow and be formed into those who relate in ways that promote the flourishing of others and themselves.

College sexual, dating, and relationship contexts are marked by the risks of sexual violence, intimate partner violence, and stalking. While these realities are present beyond campus life, they exist in distinctive ways in college culture and have the dangerous potential to negatively inform the ways in which young adults participate in relationships with family, friends, and romantic or sexual partners. An ethical response that shapes who persons are in relation to one another is necessary to promote the conditions of justice and flourishing. The virtues of justice, fidelity, and self-care, informed by and made concrete by prudence, have the ability to provide the foundational ethic that is necessary to form persons to relate to one another in just and good ways as well as to work to transform the cultural conditions that give rise to violence.

27. Ibid., 191.
28. Ibid., 186.

Chapter 3

"A Woman's Pain Is Not a Gift"

Toward Sexual Flourishing for All

Elizabeth L. Antus

Many practicing Catholics eagerly proclaim today that the Catholic Church wants marriage to include mutual sexual pleasure between spouses. This message is part of a larger development of Catholic doctrine about sexuality and marriage over the past hundred years: while sex should happen only in marriage, it is good not only for the sake of procreation but also for the sake of spousal intimacy and pleasure. But in concert with Catholic theologians who have already critiqued official Catholic teaching on sexuality by supporting the prudential use of birth control and by recognizing the goodness of LGBTQ+ relationships, I also suggest that the Catholic Church needs to take even more seriously the importance of sexual pleasure as a Catholic theological resource—one that does not gain its ethical legitimacy merely through its connection to the possibility of procreation. Though procreation is an important dimension for specific time periods in many romantic partnerships and marriages, sex is not by definition only about openness to children.

I take a distinctively Catholic feminist theological approach so as to analyze the Catholic Church's ongoing androcentrism and lack of sufficient care for women's bodies. I do so through a largely unexplored topic: women's sexual pain disorders, an issue that has received increasing attention in the scientific community since the late twentieth century. Even beyond diagnosable disorders, multiple studies suggest that up to 75 percent of adult women have had painful vaginal sex at some point.[1] Sexual pain is crucial to explore because it constitutes a reality that

---

1. Jen Gunter, "Sex Hurts. Help!" *New York Times*, January 31, 2018, https://www.nytimes.com/2018/01/31/style/sex-pain-causes-solutions.html.

many women in partnerships face, and it has been almost entirely neglected in Catholic theology. This research from doctors, psychologists, and sexologists provides important information that can help guide Catholic discussions of sex. Key aspects of women's healing from sexual pain can illuminate new ways forward for articulating a richer Catholic account of sexual flourishing, for women, men, and people of all genders.

First, I argue that Catholic theology is currently ill-equipped to help name and address women's sexual pain disorders. Sexual pain constitutes a particular type of physical and emotional suffering in which vaginal intercourse causes pain to women in heterosexual partnerships, many of whom are experiencing some misery from it but who may continue to attempt intercourse because they feel pressured by a host of interpersonal, social, and religious expectations to be the "good woman," the female partner who is sexually available to her male partner and whose default is to put him first, before herself. There are no official Catholic documents that acknowledge women's sexual pain, and the Catholic emphasis on good sex primarily as that which channels sexual pleasure toward the non-selfish possibility of procreation does not give Catholic women the proper ethical and theological scripts to see their suffering for what it is. If the Catholic Church cares about human flourishing, it has the responsibility to take seriously women's sexual pain, which means caring in a much fuller way about women's bodies and desires.

Second, various healing options for women addressing their sexual pain suggest ways forward for a better theological approach to sex. This healing often includes a hiatus from intercourse that is simultaneous with practicing other forms of sex that are more focused on the clitoris than the vagina. This practice is indispensable for helping women reconnect with sex as something enjoyable rather than obligatory. This practice also helps them learn what a real no to sex feels like, and learning this no helps them learn the possibility of a yes to sex, an enthusiastic openness that proceeds more from a genuine desire to have satisfying sex rather than an external sense of obligation to submit one's body to another. Authentic sexual freedom shared between partners often results in shared emotional and physical pleasure (often including but not limited to orgasm) and is a key ingredient in what Catholics should consider to be good sex in an ethically robust sense.

Characteristics of Women's Sexual Pain

Even in the scientific community, much is still unknown about women's sexual pain. Current expertise on the matter promotes a flexible biopsychosocial approach in which sexual pain can be understood as having psychological and physical dimensions that are always shaped and given meaning in particular social and religious contexts. Though perhaps some sexual pain is more on the "physical" or "medical" end in terms of causes, while other sexual pain is more on the "psychological" end, a multidimensional approach is always important. Even when sexual pain can be attributed to a medical problem such as endometriosis, it can also create a significant psychological experience for the woman. Furthermore, a simplistically medicalizing approach has often meant, historically, that many doctors have viewed women with sexual pain simply as needing to be "fixed" (i.e., so that they can abide by the heteronormative standard of having intercourse with a male partner) without any attention to the broader social scripts about sex and womanhood that may be informing the pain experience from their perspective, especially constrictive heteronormative scripts that heighten their embodied panic. Conversely, pain that is caused primarily by psychological anxiety is truly physically felt within women's bodies, a crucial point given that women with sexual pain in the eighteenth and nineteenth centuries were told by doctors that it was "all in their head." In other words, a multidimensional approach helps debunk reductive views of sexual pain that insist the problem is merely a woman's "broken body" or "feminine hysteria." This approach also demands critical attention to the broader social and religious scripts shaping the perception and experience of sexual pain.[2]

The Diagnostic and Statistical Manual of Mental Disorders from 2013 categorizes women's sexual pain disorders such as dyspareunia (vulvar pain specifically during vaginal intercourse, affecting 10 to 20 percent of women),[3] vulvodynia (vulvar pain felt at various times, affecting at least 15 percent of women),[4] and vaginismus (an involuntary pelvic floor muscle spasm caused by the attempt to insert anything, affecting 5 to 17 percent of women)[5] under the label of "genito-pelvic pain/penetration disorders," or GPPPD. Regarding vulvodynia specifically, it can occur during intercourse, gynecological exams, tampon insertion, and even wearing certain clothes. There are various causes, and the pain can be localized or generalized and provoked or unprovoked. The most common type of localized

2. For a comprehensive overview of various facets of women's sexual pain disorders, see Andrew T. Goldstein, Caroline Pukall, and Irwin Goldstein, eds., *Female Sexual Pain Disorders* (Oxford: Blackwell, 2009).

3. James Sorensen et al., "Evaluation and Treatment of Female Sexual Pain: A Clinical Review," *Cureus*, March 27, 2018, doi: 10.7759/cureus.2379.

4. Amanda Chan, "Vulvodynia, Vaginal Pain, Is Common but Underdiagnosed: Study," *Huffington Post*, September 26, 2011, https://www.huffingtonpost.ca/2011/09/26/vulvodynia-vaginal-pain-women_n_978484.html.

5. Emily Blatchford, "Vaginismus: The Sexual Disorder You've Never Heard Of," *Huffington Post*, October 6, 2016, https://www.huffingtonpost.com.au/2016/06/09/vaginismus-the-sexual-disorder-youve-never-heard-of_a_21391997/.

vulvodynia is provoked vestibulodynia (PVD), which is internal pain near the vaginal opening. Dyspareunia and associated emotional suffering are some common symptoms of PVD. The potentially multiple medical causes of PVD are not currently well understood, and the particular experiences of it vary considerably between women. Though the studies of PVD broken down by racial demographic are still in their infancy, there is some evidence to suggest that the daily vulvar pain of PVD is particularly pronounced for black women.[6]

Relatedly, vaginismus may also be localized or generalized, and it can develop in addition to other sexual pain disorders or occur alone. Women with severe vaginismus often say that when they try to insert a tampon or have intercourse, the experience is like trying to break through a wall. The physical pain is real, and the trigger seems to be uncontrollable anxiety about the insertion of anything into the vagina. Many women with vaginismus develop it after, for example, a traumatic first gynecological exam or an uncomfortable first attempt at intercourse. A statistically high number of women with vaginismus have been sexually abused. Further, given that women of color, particularly Native American women, are at an especially high risk for being sexually abused, it is probable that women of color deal with vaginismus at statistically higher rates than white women do.[7] Much more work needs to be done on the racialized dimensions of sexual pain, an undertaking that would further highlight the structural racism embedded in the health-care system of the United States.[8] Moving forward, though there are more nuances to women's sexual pain disorders, this overview of dyspareunia, vulvodynia, and vaginismus provides a solid basis for altering the shape of Catholic sexual ethics.

Social Scripts and Catholic Views of Sex Facilitate Women's Sexual Pain

Heteronormative social scripts about womanhood and manhood exacerbate the suffering involved in women's sexual pain. I will explore two such scripts and demonstrate how Catholic approaches to sexuality compound their harm.

---

6. Candace Brown et al., "Pain Rating in Women with Provoked Vestibulodynia: Evaluating Influence of Race," *Journal of Women's Health* 25, no. 1 (2016): 57–62, doi: 10.1089/jwh.2015.5223.

7. RAINN, "Victims of Sexual Violence: Statistics," 2019, https://www.rainn.org/statistics /victims-sexual-violence; End Rape on Campus, "Prevalence Rates," N.D., https://endrapeoncampus .org/new-page-3.

8. National Women's Law Center, "Racism in Healthcare—For Black Women Who Become Pregnant, It's a Matter of Life and Death," April 13, 2018, https://nwlc.org/blog/racism-in-health -care-for-black-women-who-become-pregnant-its-a-matter-of-life-and-death/.

First, many straight women who experience sexual pain initially have difficulty recognizing it for what it is because they have been socialized to view sex first and foremost as something they owe to male partners rather than as something they can enjoy in themselves. Some women with sexual pain will continue to have intercourse for years through the pain because they believe that it is an obligation they can still fulfill, and they do not want to feel guilty about leaving their partners "unsatisfied."[9] There is a social script that conditions women to believe that male sexual desire is the fulcrum around which sexual relationships must pivot. Further, even when male partners do not want sex to cause their female partners pain, many have also still been socialized to view sex primarily as something for them. This default social conditioning largely removes women's sexual desire from the equation, for both women and men, respectively. This myopia then conceals women's sexual pain.

Once a woman experiences sexual pain, she cannot "power through" and end it simply with more intercourse. Instead, what typically happens with repeated attempts after the onset of sexual pain is a disastrous cycle in which a woman experiences pain with intercourse and then feels anxiety that exacerbates the pain of subsequent attempts. Many women will endure this cycle for a long time out of the belief that they are fulfilling their obligation, an obligation that defines what sex is: something separate from a woman's capacity for enjoyment and pleasure. Even when consent is technically given in these cases, these encounters do not signal true sexual freedom.

Catholic teaching also does not robustly discuss how sexual pleasure, particularly women's sexual pleasure, is an important good to be cultivated. Many years ago when I was in graduate school for my doctorate in theology, a friend at another Catholic graduate school told me about a disturbing comment made by a male student during a seminar on Christian mysticism. In a discussion about Teresa of Ávila's blending of erotic pleasure and pain in her description of her journey to a spiritual marriage with God, this student said approvingly, "This makes sense, though, because on the wedding night, the wife's pain is a gift she gives her husband." Nobody in the class addressed the comment.

Why is the sentiment of this student intelligible within a Catholic context? We can find part of an answer in official Catholic teachings after Vatican II. Paul VI's 1968 encyclical *Humanae Vitae* condemns the use of birth control by arguing that intercourse must not be done in a manner that is closed to the possibility of procreation and that sexual pleasure must not be separated from this openness

9. Elizabeth G. Stewart and Paula Spencer, *The V Book* (New York: Bantam, 2002), 335.

(HV 12). A couple of decades later, John Paul II's "theology of the body" argues that because sex in marriage is fundamentally self-gift, the spouses must be especially vigilant about not becoming sinfully attached to sexual pleasure.[10] He adds that this self-gift is revealed in a particularly striking way in women, whom he considers to be "receptive" physically, emotionally, and spiritually, a characteristic that constitutes for him the feminine "genius."[11] More recently, Monsignor Cormac Burke writes in this same vein, "Contraceptive intercourse is an exercise in meaninglessness."[12] Noteworthy here is the unquestioned assumption of the constancy of sexual pleasure, along with the concern that this pleasure not take place in disconnection from the possibility of procreation. Otherwise, for Burke, contraceptive sex has no value or purpose.

These mainstream Catholic approaches to sex overlook the fact that many women have sex for all sorts of reasons that have nothing to do with any sexual desire, let alone the insatiable kind. Painful and even simply boring experiences of sex are all too common for women. Furthermore, these approaches imply that the main ingredient of good sex is a view of selfhood that is primarily other-directed toward the partner and toward the possibility of conceiving children. Even though this teaching is androcentrically framed around a certain view of male sexual desire as an erotic yearning that is always present and simply needs to be ethically directed, it is then awkwardly applied to women in a way that underscores Catholic stereotypes of "feminine" relationality. The message to women here is that their sexual desire need not be cultivated but rather should be channeled toward the lofty goal of giving to the other and living into their most meaningful identity: mother.[13] For women struggling with sexual pain, there is virtually nothing in these Catholic views of sexuality that would help them understand their sexual pain

---

10. Even with John Paul's caution, theologians such as David Cloutier and William Mattison argue from a less sex-positive perspective that John Paul makes all too much of sexual pleasure as the romanticized apex of marriage. Though I do not disagree with this concern, these authors also ignore the difficulty that many women have in experiencing any sexual pleasure, so these critiques have little to offer in response to the problem of women's sexual pain. For their arguments, as well as others regarding Catholic theology and marriage, see Lisa Sowle Cahill, John Garvey, and T. Frank Kennedy, eds., *Sexuality and the U.S. Catholic Church* (New York: Crossroad, 2006).

11. John Paul II, *Mulieris dignitatem* (Ottawa: Polyglot, 1988); John Paul II, *Theology of the Body* (Boston: Pauline Books and Media, 1997).

12. Cormac Burke, *The Theology of Marriage* (Washington, DC: The Catholic University of America Press, 2015), 169.

13. John Paul II argues that both men and women are called in marriage to nuptial self-gift culminating in parenthood, but he also says that motherhood *particularly* reveals a special sensitivity to others that women ostensibly already, by definition, have.

as a serious problem and their pleasure as something distinctively good. It would be all too tempting to view their pain as a gift they should give their husbands.

The second commonplace social script that causes suffering for women around their sexual pain claims that vaginal intercourse is the only "real" sex. Women with sexual pain who have a fraught relationship with intercourse thus believe that they are not "real" sexual partners. For women struggling in the midst of this socialization (and not uncommonly against male partners who mirror this message), it does not matter that there are other nonintercourse forms of sex that could be physically and emotionally satisfying. These forms of sex do not "count" because sex is understood to be primarily about satisfying men's desire for intercourse.[14] One can thus see how androcentric, heteronormative scripts about sex worsen women's experiences of their own sexual pain. When women with sexual pain feel that their viability as sexual partners depends on having intercourse, they are pressured to keep trying a type of sex that not only lacks pleasure but actually causes pain.

The official Catholic emphasis on at least potential openness to procreation in all sexual encounters in marriage also reinforces the idea that intercourse is the compulsory sexual norm, a point that ultimately supports an unjust, androcentric framing of sex. Within this frame, all other forms of sex must be understood at best as nonorgasmic elements of foreplay that are always merely preparing for intercourse.[15] When other forms of sex are practiced for their own sake, Catholic teaching views them as exercises in selfishness, regardless of the instances when couples view them as expressions of love. Yet, as many feminist sexological researchers and progressive Catholic theologians have noted, women statistically find other forms of sex more easily pleasurable, especially nonpenetrative activities such as cunnilingus, which focus more on the clitoris than the vagina.

Returning again to Monsignor Burke, his theology of marriage functions as an *apologia* for official Catholic approaches to sex, and he gamely illustrates its

14. Janine Farrell and Thea Cacchioni, "The Medicalization of Women's Sexual Pain," *Journal of Sex Research* 49, no. 4 (2012): 328–36.

15. Some popularizers of John Paul's theology of the body such as Gregory Popcak argue that as long as no contraception is used and sex ends with a man ejaculating inside a woman's vagina, "everything" is allowed. But, as other popularizers of this teaching such as Christopher West point out, if one takes the time to consider the Catholic tradition in light of the range of sexual possibilities beyond oral stimulation, the question of what the Catholic Church would currently accept as foreplay probably still depends to some extent on the sex act, and it is more difficult (though perhaps not impossible) to make the case for the legitimacy of anal penetration as foreplay. See Gregory K. Popcak, *Holy Sex!* (New York: Crossroad, 2008). See also Christopher West, *Good News about Sex and Marriage* (Cincinnati: Servant, 2004). In any case, the theology of foreplay is currently under-thought in the Catholic academic realm.

androcentrism. In discussing the necessity of sex without contraception, he writes, "The greatest expression of a person's desire to give himself is to give the seed of himself. Giving one's seed is much more significant, and in particular much more real, than giving one's heart."[16] Perhaps aware of how gender-exclusive this description is (given the way that Catholic teaching has historically applied the category of "seed" to male reproductive material), Burke adds in a footnote, " 'Seed' is intended here to refer equally to the male or the female generative element."[17] Yet he claims one paragraph later that the key sign of spousal bonding is "the husband's seed in the wife's body."[18] The wife's "seed" has disappeared. Ultimately, here, sex is something that men do inside women. Men are the real agents of sex—the seeds—and women are the backdrop—the dirt.

If, in the official Catholic view of sex, intercourse is the "real" sex, and if women often find other forms of sex more pleasurable, then women's sexual pleasure is not really considered a theological resource by Catholic leadership at this time. Because of the systemic androcentrism here, sexual pleasure is assumed as a reality that simply needs to be channeled properly toward the possibility of procreation through noncontraceptive intercourse. There is no consideration of the reality that many women often participate in intercourse without really enjoying it, a fact that requires a radically different approach to sexuality. Ultimately, then, because official Catholic teaching ignores the needs and desires of women as sexual agents, it also fails to promote a truly unitive vision of sex.

The Healing of Women's Sexual Pain and Its Lessons for Catholic Approaches to Sex

There are many courses of action for healing along biopsychosocial lines that can be salutary both for women who wish to engage in intercourse eventually and for women who do not. Treatment options vary, but many women with sexual pain engage in pelvic floor therapy, a type of physical therapy in which a pelvic floor therapist teaches them exercises to strengthen their pelvic floor and helps stretch their vaginal muscles in healthy ways. This type of physical therapy can also include both vaginal dilators that help desensitize overactive vaginal nerves and biofeedback machinery to help gauge the level of tension within the pelvic floor. The point here is for women to become more in touch with their vaginas, not only to heal from pain, but also to learn how to relax them, which is integral

16. Burke, *The Theology of Marriage*, 168.
17. Ibid.
18. Ibid., 169.

to experiencing sexual pleasure and to feeling a general sense of well-being within their bodies. Some form of psychotherapy is often recommended for the same time period.

The recovery process typically includes the deconstruction of the aforementioned androcentric social scripts and the construction of healthier ones. First, a guiding idea for healing is that women are sexual agents who, when they engage in sexual activity, are entitled to enjoy it. Sex should not be categorized principally as an obligation to sate another. Relatedly, being sexual is not merely about being sexually desirable but also about experiencing oneself as sexually desiring. Though the idea that women are entitled to enjoy sex is more common now than it often has been historically, it is still not "second nature" as far as today's commonplace socialization about sex and gender goes. Furthermore, dyspareunia, vulvodynia, and vaginismus need to be understood as signs that something is wrong rather than par for the course. One married woman in her twenties told her gynecologist when she was diagnosed with vulvodynia, "I had absolutely no idea that it wasn't supposed to hurt there."[19] Though sad, this admission is predictable given our regnant social scripts about sex. But resocializing women and all people about the importance of women's sexual desire is truly possible, and it will help women discern an enthusiastic yes to sex when they are genuinely interested rather than begrudgingly acquiescent.

Catholic views of sex do not have to keep supporting the idea that a wife's pain is a gift she gives her husband. Over the course of the twentieth century and into the twenty-first, the Catholic Church came to appreciate the emotional and physical bonding that occurs in good sex. Today, the Catholic Church should emphasize even more explicitly the importance of sexual desire and pleasure, especially for women. Concomitantly, the Catholic Church should more pointedly denounce not only sexual coercion but any view of sex that paints it as categorically pleasureless for anybody, notably for women. Such a development would help women identify their sexual pain and encourage them to seek healing from a space of love for their bodies. This shift would also require a sea change for men's socialization around sex, for, as a fundamental matter of emotional maturation, they would have to refine the skills of listening, mutuality, and vulnerability— skills that are not only valuable but erotic.

Second, regardless of whether a woman wishes to have intercourse again or not, it is crucial to unlearn the script that makes intercourse the compulsory norm and apex for sexual activity. During recovery, women are advised to take a hiatus

19. Stewart and Spencer, *The V Book*, 299.

from intercourse not only to stop the pain but to relearn how to connect sexually with their bodies in other ways, especially in ways that focus on the clitoris. This relearning is necessary not only so that women may experience sexual pleasure, but also because this sexual pleasure reintroduces them to the experience of sexual desire, of the feeling of engaging in sexual activity because they "feel like it" and not because they "should." In reconnecting to sex from a place of desire, women can cultivate a creativity and openness about what is possible sexually, a transformation that can also be instructive for men who commonly need to unlearn the script of male sexual entitlement and become acquainted with themselves as individuals with particular desires and needs that nobody else is "required" to fulfill. This resocialization helps the embodied memory of painful sex fade for women.

A logical outcome of the Catholic Church taking mutual pleasure more seriously, then, is that it would encourage nonintercourse forms of sex as integral to the physical, emotional, and spiritual health of sexual partnerships, especially marriages. Though the temporary, biologically procreative potential of many partnerships is important, I agree with many Catholic theologians who have already suggested that procreation should not function as the absolutely necessary criterion for determining the goodness of partnerships.[20] As the Catholic Church's recognition of the marriages of infertile couples already suggests, a lack of biological procreation does not necessarily harm a relationship. Though every couple is different, a lack of mutual bonding caused by consistently bad sex is, however, a serious problem that—at least potentially—gravely harms the physical, emotional, and spiritual integrity of the relationship. Barbara Andolsen's recommendation here is apposite: "Catholic ethicists need to name violent or coercive sexual activity, not nonprocreative sexual activity, as the fundamental sexual evil."[21] This is something that most progressive theologians are doing (and Francis at least explicitly condemns sexual violence in *Amoris Laetitia* 54), while most conservative theologians have not yet sufficiently grappled with the horror of sexual violence. I would include here the reality of women's sexual pain disorders, aided by androcentric social scripts, as part of the "fundamental sexual evil" that needs to be named and resisted in the Catholic Church. This naming and

---

20. Cristina Traina, "Under Pressure: Sexual Discipleship in the Real World," in *Sexuality and the U.S. Catholic Church*, 68–93; Lisa Sowle Cahill, *Sex, Gender, and Christian Ethics* (New York: Cambridge University Press, 1996), 108–20; Todd A. Salzman and Michael G. Lawler, *Sexual Ethics* (Washington, DC: Georgetown University Press, 2012), 47–121.

21. Barbara Hilkert Andolsen, "Whose Sexuality? Whose Tradition? Women, Experience, and Roman Catholic Sexual Ethics," in *Feminist Ethics and the Catholic Moral Tradition*, ed. Charles E. Curran, Margaret Farley, and Richard McCormick (New York: Paulist Press, 1996), 207–39, at 225.

resisting would help the Catholic Church develop a better approach to desire in its theology of sexuality and marriage, not just for women with sexual pain disorders, but for all adults in sexual relationships who still look to the guidance of the Catholic Church.

Conclusion

The Catholic Church has already softened its erotophobia in its cautious celebration of sexual pleasure for the unitive bonding in marriage. To develop this doctrine even further, however, the church must do something new: take seriously the embodied realities of women's lives, in all their pains, pleasures, needs, and desires. I have demonstrated via women's sexual pain disorders how this kind of development would tectonically shift Catholic views of sex and marriage. It remains to be seen whether the Catholic Church can shake free of the view that suggests a wife's pain is a gift she gives her husband. The real gift, I would suggest, is that sex can sometimes bespeak divine joy at all in this broken world. I give thanks for the Catholic feminist theology that helps us see how this is so.

Chapter 4

Infertility

A Lens for Discerning Parenthood in Marriage

Kathryn Lilla Cox

"How many children do you have?" "When are you planning on having (more) children?" "Do you want (more) children?" These and similar questions can help us forge connections, get to know someone, and find common ground with family members, friends, coworkers, and even strangers. We frequently cannot perceive, however, that answering the first question with none or zero might mean infertility, since we quickly follow an answer of none or zero with the second or third question. The questioner does not intend to cause pain or suffering. Yet, for married people wrestling with infertility, these and other questions frequently cause pain and suffering. Furthermore, the questions' seeming naturalness as conversation starters (rather than "tell me about your family" or "tell me a story about you") unearth ecclesial and cultural presumptions that heterosexual marriage equals biological children.

The assumption that heterosexual marriage equals biological children disintegrates when infertility forces couples into a discernment process to determine *if* and *how* they will bring children into their marriage.[1] This discernment process is, however, overshadowed and rendered invisible for various reasons within the broader community. Moral theologians, ethicists, and ecclesial teaching prioritize

---

1. This essay focuses on infertility as defined and experienced by heterosexual (opposite sexed) married couples. With this fact and working within the boundaries of how marriage is defined by the Roman Catholic Church magisterium, this essay primarily uses the binary language of male/female, men/women. I recognize, however, that discerning *if* and *how* to bring children into a marriage are also questions for fertile opposite-sexed, same-sexed, and transgendered couples.

discussions regarding the morality of various types of infertility treatments rather than discussions about discernment tools and processes. People struggling with infertility often keep silent about their struggles. The silence ensues because of feelings of shame, inadequacy, failure; their communities provide programming and support for families with children, while having no spaces, resources, or programming to support couples with infertility. The long tradition emphasizing procreation with children as the symbol of embodied love between spouses makes it hard to admit that the symbol of that love, a child, is not coming. Thus, couples are frequently left unaccompanied and unsupported by their faith communities in their discernment of *if* and *how* to have children.

Acknowledging that biological parenthood does not always follow marriage due to infertility and that because of infertility couples must discern *if* and *how* to become parents raises several questions about the vocation of parenthood assumed to be part of the marriage vocation. How are the two vocations, marriage and parenthood, related but distinctive? Are all couples called to parenthood? Is parenthood only a call for some? What does infertility mean when a call to parenthood is assumed or has been discerned? Ultimately, accounting for the experiences of couples grappling with infertility requires systematic theological discussions that address the interconnected but distinctive vocations of marriage and parenthood.[2]

Furthermore, talking openly and honestly about infertility means rethinking theologies of marriage, sexuality, families, and theological anthropology. Women acutely feel the tensions inherent in the theology around marriage, sexuality, family, and anthropology. Tensions appear when women's identity is primarily construed as either virgin or mother. As a married woman with no children, she is neither. When men are no longer virgin or father, they are typically seen as having a vocation outside the home in addition to the potential vocation of fatherhood.

With these questions and realities about infertility, marriage, and parenthood in mind, this essay proceeds by first looking at Roman Catholic teaching on marriage. It then examines some experiences of infertility with implications for our understanding and embodying of the procreative meaning of marriage. After describing the Roman Catholic teaching about infertility treatments, the essay compares responses to infertility in Sacred Scripture. Finally, the essay identifies some criteria for discerning the call to adoptive, biological, and/or foster parenthood for all couples.

---

2. There is precedent for considering parenthood a vocation, in writings that consider the dual vocations of Christian parents. See, for example, Julie Hanlon Rubio, "The Dual Vocation of Christian Parents," *Theological Studies* 63 (2002): 786–812.

Ecclesial Views of Marriage[3]

Current Roman Catholic teaching about marriage relies on a theological anthropology of biological, sexual, and gender complementarity. The church teaches that the purposes of marriage are the bringing forth and education of children, sexual fidelity, mutual support of the spouses, spiritual growth, and outward-looking social concerns. The shorthand for these various purposes of marriage are the procreative and unitive goods of marriage.[4]

During the wedding ceremony, the various goods of marriage are found in the vows and prayers of blessing. The question "Are you open to children?" and the prayers for children within the wedding rite speak to the good of children in marriage. Despite teaching on the plural purposes of marriage, along with expansive theological reflection and analysis, a truncated view of the procreative and unitive goods of marriage as bringing biological children into the world dominates the church's imagination. Subsequently, when people experience infertility, they often wonder what is wrong with them, feel the pain of dashed hopes and desires, and question if they are failing at their marriage duties or if their marriages are invalid. This is the case even as the magisterium teaches that sterility (infertility) is not an impediment to marriage or to its validity or fruitfulness.[5]

Infertility in the Twenty-First Century

The Centers for Disease Control defines infertility "as not being able to get pregnant (conceive) after one year or longer of unprotected sex," or six months of unprotected sex for women thirty-five years and older. Primary infertility

3. The Supreme Court ruling in Obergefell v. Hodges legalized same-sex marriages in all fifty states on June 26, 2015. As a result of this ruling, some Christian churches began performing and permitting both opposite- and same-sex marriages. Some denominations have no official policy with various branches or individual churches having different practices. Other denominations, including the Roman Catholic Church, continue teaching that marriage is between a woman and a man, forbidding same-sex wedding ceremonies or the blessing of same-sex civil marriages. For one discussion of the implications of civil approaches to marriage and the reality of infertility for Christian approaches to marriage, see Cristina S. Richie, "Disrupting the Meaning of Marriage? Childfree, Infertile and Gay Unions in Evangelical and Catholic Theologies of Marriage," *Theology & Sexuality* 19 (2013): 123–42.

4. Language used by the magisterium and theologians to discuss the goods of marriage has varied, changed, or emphasized different things in different eras. For an analysis of how parenthood has been described in modern times, see Jacob Kohlhass, "Constructing Parenthood: Catholic Teaching 1880 to the Present," *Theological Studies* 79 (2018): 610–33.

5. *Code of Canon Law*, 1084.3.

describes a couple with no children trying to conceive. Secondary infertility means a couple has one or more biological children with difficulty conceiving again for the requisite time. Finally, impaired fecundity, related to infertility, is the inability to carry a pregnancy to term.

Infertility as a type of reproductive loss has economic, emotional, medical, spiritual, and social facets. People need to reckon with the economics of the technology; questions around belonging, finitude, and freedom; the loss of a vision of their potential child; and how to handle other people's misperceptions about them as childless couples. The manifestation or experience of these various dimensions exist in both society and the church with cultural and familial differences. In other words, infertility is a medical condition as well as a personal and spiritual crisis that raises questions about one's identity, purpose, and meaning of life.

This reality, the "fact that one will never conceive or bear children," has been described as "not just an experience of profound disappointment. Rather, those who have gone through it describe it as a kind of 'dying,' a loss of both an envisioned future and a possible self, a potential role and a longed-for relationship."[6] This type of loss moves beyond disappointment to a space where identities must be reconfigured, reimagined, and lived into.

Theologian Gina Messina describes her journey through the existential reality of infertility in this way: "Growing up, I believed that motherhood was my destiny, an idea that was constantly reinforced by my family, church, teachers, and surrounding culture. I understood that women were supposed to become mothers, and as a female I aspired to such." As a married Catholic, she eventually found that the very teachings she committed to following "played a critical role in my feelings of inadequacy and shame throughout my quest to become a mother."[7] Intellectually she knew her "life served many purposes in this world," yet she "perceived [her] value as diminished if I could not become a mother." She developed a "ritualistic cycle of grief"; at times she "cursed God for abandoning me, leaving me barren, and refusing me the one role that society and church demanded of me—a role I believed was my call."[8]

6. Maura A. Ryan, "Faith and Infertility," in *Cloning*, ed. Robert B. Kruschwitz (Waco, TX: The Center for Christian Ethics at Baylor University, 2005): 65–74, 66. Men experience sorrow and pain with infertility as well. See Christopher Pramuk, "A Hidden Sorrow," *America*, April 11, 2011, 19–20.

7. Gina Messina, "Cursing God (*infertility*)," in *Encountering the Sacred: Feminist Reflections on Women's Lives*, ed. Rebecca Todd Peters and Grace Y. Kao (New York: T & T Clark, 2019), 119–31, 119.

8. Ibid., 121–22.

The grief accompanying fertility loss means dealing with the "societal expectations of women's roles as mothers, personal feelings of failure, and lamenting the loss of a child that existed in [her] imagination."[9] Letting go of one identity (biological motherhood) and incorporating another identity (adoptive or foster motherhood or not being a mother) is part of many women's stories. Integrating a new identity means acknowledging the pain of being around pregnant women, which includes grappling with feelings of jealousy, anger, sorrow, and abandonment by God when trying to be happy for those who have conceived. It requires dealing with unhelpful comments by those trying to be supportive. It can even include struggling against problematic theological interpretations about women, such as these: infertility is the woman's fault, you are an embarrassment to your husband, or children from artificial insemination or in vitro fertilization (IVF) are not conceived in love.[10]

Infertility in the Magisterial Tradition

The magisterium affirms involuntarily childless marriages resulting from infertility or sterility. Yet, involuntarily childless marriages are rarely discussed in magisterial documents on their own merits. Instead, they are placed within the conversation about marriage's unitive and procreative ends, which ideally results in biological children.[11] As a result, involuntarily childless or biologically infertile marriages are the exceptions that are accepted because the couple wants biological children but cannot have them.

The magisterium recognizes that couples will seek medical remedies for infertility. Therefore, the Congregation for the Doctrine of the Faith (CDF) has issued two documents, *Donum Vitae* and *Dignitatis Personae*, offering guidance regarding the validity of various assistive reproductive technologies for having a child. Both documents affirm procedures aimed at correcting or fixing underlying physiological issues affecting fertility. For example, unblocking fallopian tubes or treating thyroid disease are acceptable. Additionally, the CDF encourages ongoing research into methods for addressing the root cause of infertility.[12]

---

9. Ibid., 121–22, 128.

10. Ibid., 121–25.

11. Joseph A. Selling, "The Childless Marriage: A Moral Observation," *Bijdragen* 42 (1981): 158–73, 158–60.

12. For examples of this type of research, see the related Natural Procreative Technology at https://www.naprotechnology.com/ and the Saint Paul VI Institute for the Study of Human Reproduction at http://www.popepaulvi.com/.

In both documents, however, the CDF prioritizes explaining the reasons for deeming homologous and heterologous artificial insemination, IVF, surrogacy, cloning, and heterologous embryo transfer (also called embryo donation or embryo adoption) as unethical. Meanwhile, the CDF provides very little guidance for couples finding themselves infertile and adhering to church teaching, for those who do make use of technologies deemed unethical, or for the church community who wants to support them.[13]

The CDF briefly touches on parenthood within the context of deeming these various potential medical avenues for childbearing unethical because children deserve to be conceived as a result of the conjugal act. This argument subtly privileges biological parenthood, even as the CDF supports and praises adoptive and foster parenting. Couples pursing adoption experience this bias and preference toward parenting biological children. Sometimes, the questions come from others who ask, "Why not spend money on IVF and have a child of [your] own?" Other times, couples question themselves, "What if we ended up with a kid that was a 'lemon'?" "What if the child was not white—could we really handle raising a child of a different race than us?" "Would we be able to love a child that was not *really* ours'?"[14]

Compounding the privileging of biological procreation for women is the church's emphasis on women's main role as mother. Married women without children find themselves navigating a liminal identity space between "no longer virgin" and "not yet mother." Spiritual motherhood as a response to infertility offers solace to some yet little or no comfort to others. Spiritual motherhood keeps motherhood as the primary category for considering women's contributions to the community, but the spiritual motherhood trope ignores other ways women are in life-giving relationships. Women are friends, companions, partners, daughters, nieces, sisters, sisters-in-law, coworkers, mentors, and leaders. These identities and ways of relating differ from motherhood and offer the community alternative ways of seeing women's multifaceted identities, whether fertile or infertile.[15]

Marriage, Children, and Infertility: Insights from Scripture

Biblical barrenness narratives with their "miracle births" have spoken and still speak to women's hope that God will remove the "curse" of barrenness and "gift" them with child, thus fulfilling their hoped-for identity as mother. But the

---

13. Catholics in various fields have stepped up to fill this gap. See Angelique Ruhi-Lopez and Carmen Santamaria, *The Infertility Companion for Catholics* (Notre Dame, IN: Ave Maria Press, 2012).

14. Messina, "Cursing God (*infertility*)," 126.

15. This would hold true for men and the idea of spiritual fatherhood.

stories are also about the women's relationships as spouses, sisters, employers, and community members. Therefore, exploring the stories of Sarah, Rebekah, Rachel, Manoah's wife, Hannah, and the great Woman of Shunem together provides a complex, rich, and insightful tapestry of wisdom and responses to barrenness that can be helpful for women and couples today.[16]

Their barrenness causes the biblical women to interact with their spouses, God, or community in different ways. Sarah blames God. Rebekah does not. Rachel blames Jacob. Rachel also feels God remembers her and opens her womb, giving her Joseph and Benjamin. We do not know Manoah's wife's response because the story begins with an angelic visitation announcing her upcoming pregnancy. Hannah grieves deeply, pleads with God for a child, and shuts out her husband. Scripture notes that the great Woman of Shunem has no children because her husband is old. It is unclear if she wants children.

The women seek various solutions for their barrenness. Sarah and Abraham try adopting Lot and Eliezer. Surrogates are used by Sarah (Hagar) and Rachel (Bilhah).[17] Rachel tries natural remedies (mandrakes) that fail. Hannah pleads and bargains with God. We do not learn if or how Rebekah, Manoah's wife, and the great Woman of Shunem try to resolve their barrenness. They appear to have tried nothing, going on with other aspects of their lives. Rebekah appears to have wanted children, however, because once pregnant she prays for her pregnancy's safe completion. The great Woman of Shunem, known for her hospitality, does not ask Elisha for a child when he wants to repay her hospitality. Instead, when Elisha determines and promises that she will have a child, she tells him no. She asks Elisha not to deceive her. Furthermore, when her son falls ill, she reminds Elisha that she did not ask for a child, raising questions about her desire for motherhood. Meanwhile, Scripture provides no indication that Manoah's wife wanted motherhood.

The biblical texts also provide glimpses into the men's responses to infertility. Isaac and Manoah do not resort to polygyny. Isaac does pray that God removes Rebekah's childlessness, whereas Manoah seems as confused as his wife about her upcoming pregnancy, indicating possible acceptance of her barrenness. In a culture where the primary purpose of marriage was extending the familial line, Isaac and Manoah's responses, where they do not pursue either polygyny or surrogacy, are remarkable, even more so when read with the other barrenness narratives. Abraham asks God for a biological heir. Abraham and Jacob agree to surrogacy. Polygyny provides children for Jacob with Leah and Elkanah with Peninnah, the

---

16. In what follows, I rely on Janice Pearl Ewurama DeWhyte, *Wom(b)an: A Cultural-Narrative Reading of the Hebrew Bible Barrenness Narratives* (Boston: Brill, 2018), especially chapters 4 and 5.

17. For a biblical analysis from Hagar's perspective see Delores S. Williams, *Sisters in the Wilderness: The Challenge of Womanist God-Talk* (Maryknoll, NY: Orbis Books, 1993).

husbands of Rachel and Hannah, before Rachel and Hannah eventually conceive biological children. Jacob also has children with Leah's maid, Zilpah. Jacob blames God for Rachel's barrenness, while Elkanah wonders why his love for Hannah is not enough for her, why she must be completed by a child. Scripture does not record a response by the Shunammite's husband; it is Elisha and her servant who are concerned.

Scripture reveals that our ancestors, like us today, used various methods for responding to infertility. Scripture also illuminates that solutions or remedies may or may not work, and they do not always solve existential questions of identity. Adoptions fall through. Natural remedies fail. Some couples seemingly seek no recourse. Some pray, while others use every means available to have children.

Surrogacy raises ethical questions about women's capacity to oppress each other, as well as the need to navigate the complex relationship of birth and social motherhood. Adopting, surrogacy, or directing one's energy outward toward communal concerns does not remove everyone's desire to carry and birth a child. Anguish about, blame for, and anger about infertility are all directed at God. The stories of Rachel, Rebekah, and Hannah hint at infertility's toll on marriages. And sometimes after decades of infertility, a biological child arrives. No matter the course of action, decisions had to be made, both by our ancestors in the faith and by us today. Thus, the stories not only provide a framework for considering today's questions and responses to infertility but also point to the need for discerning which approach to take.

Discerning Parenthood When Facing Infertility

An infertility diagnosis pushes a couple into discernment mode where they must first decide to continue trying to have children. If they decide yes, what happens next? If Catholic, they must decide whether to seek treatment by doctors using an approved method like NaPro or interventions (artificial insemination, IVF, HET, or surrogates) deemed unethical by the CDF, along with the various ethical questions for each intervention. When Catholic couples do discern pursuing unapproved methods for bringing biological children into a marriage, this is often a quite lonely process. Many keep their decisions a closely guarded secret, lest they be judged less than Catholic for how they cocreate with God or their children are punished for the parents' decisions.[18] Additionally, economics mat-

---

18. For an analysis looking at the ethics of using various ART's and the need for better pastoral responses to church members who decide to use ART's, see Julie Hanlon Rubio, "Family Ties: A Catholic Response to Donor-Conceived Families," *Christian Bioethics* 21 (2015): 181–98.

ter for couples since insurance may or may not cover various medical treatments. What can they afford? How far down the "infertility treadmill" are they willing to go? For some couples, the economics of reproductive technologies or even adoption remove these options from consideration.

If couples say no to biological children through medical means, then they must discern whether to adopt, foster, or stay childless. If parenting is the desire and call, adopting or fostering includes discerning which stage to enter parenthood—newborn, toddler, child, or teen. Fostering children requires the couple asking if they are equipped financially and emotionally to nurture and care for children who may or may not stay with them. Can they let them go back to families of origin when it is time? Adoption requires considering local or international adoption with their own unique set of ethical questions and considerations. And an involuntary childless couple might discern to stay that way.

Theological analysis regarding discernment for voluntarily childless marriages might be helpful for all couples. Discussing her own discernment, Kendra G. Hotz starts by recognizing that our lives and the tasks to which we are called are multifaceted, collectively forming our identity. Thus, "a woman cannot be reduced to 'mother.' That role may form one note in the song of a woman's life, but it must be in harmony with other notes if it is part of her vocation. Many women like myself find harmony without that note at all." Placing this idea in the context of the broader Christian community and communion of saints with our particular role to play, she further argues, "Our question then is not simply whether having or not having children will be gratifying for us personally, but also whether that choice is a faithful expression of what God is doing—through our lives—in the world. The choice for parenthood is bigger than what pleases me; it is also about God's reconciliation of all things."[19] In other words, considering parenthood as a vocation means placing the decision to have or limit the number of children within the matrix of one's relationships to God, family, and community along with their obligations and responsibilities. A vocation requires that we say no to a good because we are being asked or called to say yes to another good. Hotz observes that her other vocations as theologian and teacher are rarely questioned, yet her discernment about motherhood "has regularly been questioned."[20] This observation highlights the reality that we perceive the vocation of marriage as automatically involving the vocation of parenthood rather than the two vocations as related but distinctive.

19. Kendra G. Hotz, "Happily Ever After (Voluntary Childlessness)," in Todd and Kao, *Encountering the Sacred*, 149–61, at 152–53.
20. Ibid., 155.

If parenthood is a vocation distinct from marriage, then answering certain questions can help with the discernment. Is there a "strong or persistent urge to rear children"? Does the married life being built make sense with future children or does it feel "disharmonious when they picture themselves as parents"? Does the couple find their sense of direction, purpose, commitment to the common good and other relationships fulfilling and meaningful without children?[21] Discernment regarding children must be ongoing because the call could emerge at a later time. Biological procreation as a good of marriage must be upheld. Finally, the couple must maintain an openness to children that might arrive despite a decision not to try to have children.[22]

If involuntarily childless couples can still maintain support for the value of children in marriage, so too can voluntarily childless couples. For both groups, this support and upholding of the biological procreative good within the institution of marriage takes various forms. A couple could be willing to be listed as potential guardians for nieces, nephews, or even friends' children, thus demonstrating not only an openness to children but possible future parenthood. Aunts and uncles are open to children by being active in the lives of nieces and nephews, including their spiritual lives. Couples can advocate "for policies and practices that enhance recreational, healthcare, and cultural opportunities for children." They will work to "ensure there are plenty of resources for the next generation" and that their educational needs are met.[23] Despite both involuntarily and voluntarily childless marriages supporting children in these myriad ways, considering parenthood as a vocation still requires taking seriously the reality that many who feel called are unable to answer. This inability must be addressed spiritually, pastorally, and theologically by the faith community.

Conclusion

Infertility points to the need to consider parenthood within marriage as a discernible vocation. This requires examining the strange liminal space involuntarily childless couples occupy—between those considered sacrificial and holy because they have biological children and those considered selfish and sinful because they are voluntarily childless. The involuntarily childless couples look like voluntarily childless couples because they have no biological children. The involuntarily childless couples, however, share the intentions of those with biological parenthood.

---

21. Ibid., 154.
22. Selling, "The Childless Marriage," 167–71.
23. Hotz, "Happily Ever After (Voluntary Childlessness)," 158–59.

Considering parenthood as a discernable vocation would help eliminate this strange liminal space for involuntarily childless couples. As a vocation, the *if* and *how* (adoptive, biological, or foster children) of parenthood would need discernment for *all* married couples, not just for couples struggling with infertility. Furthermore, discerning how to be parents could help dismantle the bias that biological parenthood is somehow superior to adoptive or foster parenting. Conversations about discernment could begin in pre-Cana classes and could continue in parishes that pair newly married couples with mentor couples married longer. While not alone in discerning the *if* and *how* of parenthood, infertile couples would still have to deal with the tragedy and struggle of a vocational call to biological parenthood that remains unfulfilled. Thus, the ecclesial community has several additional remaining tasks.

Theologically, the work already begun reimagining procreativity as generativity whereby biological procreativity is one way of cocreating with God needs to continue.[24] This also requires retrieving and again highlighting the mutual self-giving of partners in the daily tasks and interactions of marriage. We need to remember that our call as disciples to minister and serve remains broader than what we do within our familial units that have children. Remembering this makes more visible the ministerial work single people and childless couples undertake.

Additionally, since couples wrestling with infertility often feel marginalized, alienated, and unsupported in their church communities, attention needs to be placed here. Sacred space within our churches for both men and women grieving infertility as a reproductive loss needs to be provided. Prayers for children need to include those already born, waiting to be born, grieved due to reproductive loss, or desired and hoped for. Likewise, Mother's and Father's Day blessings should incorporate couples who have had reproductive loss, who are trying to have children, or who are waiting for word regarding fostering or adopting. Spiritual resources need to be available to help those with infertility find a place for this experience in their faith lives. Pain and suffering from infertility cannot be eliminated, but we can remove the silence surrounding infertility as we more mindfully incorporate the reality of infertility into our theology, pastoral practices, and memories as the Body of Christ.

24. See Kathryn Lilla Cox, "Toward a Theology of Infertility and the Role of *Donum Vitae*," *Horizons* 40 (2013): 28–52, 44 and 50; Joseph Loic Mben, "Beyond Procreation: Rereading Aquinas in the Context of Involuntary Childlessness in West and Central Africa," *Horizons* 45 (2018): 19–45, 30; Pope Francis, *Amoris Laetitia* 181.

Chapter 5

Marriage and Householding in Christ

Kent Lasnoski

Catholics, and to some extent other Christians, will likely encounter the narrative of "marriage as a vocation." Popular in marriage prep programs, on marriage blogs, and on websites (e.g., the USCCB's *For Your Marriage* website), the term "vocation" appears without definition, as a thin way of valorizing the state of life. The term ends up as a rhetorical tool rather than a meaningful category for understanding the nature and purpose of marriage. Colloquially, "vocation" connotes a job I have chosen, a practical skill I have learned, hence "vocational school." In popular parlance people also deploy "vocation" to emphasize their own sense of fit to the job or life situation they occupy. By connecting the job with identity, with "who I am," the term "vocation" adds value and meaning to what might otherwise be simply a job. In the context of marriage, books and videos tend to employ "vocation" synonymously with "a calling" and leave it at that. Rich definitions rarely appear, and the serious consequences of calling marriage a vocation are not meaningfully set out. In this content vacuum, people hearing the marriage-as-vocation narrative understandably take away the feeling that they were "meant to" marry this person, that God has stamped his approval on whatever it is they think they're doing by getting married.

The *Code of Canon Law* never uses the word "vocation," suggesting the word is unimportant for a juridical description of matrimony. Furthermore, in its large section on marriage, the *Catechism of the Catholic Church* uses "vocation" two times to refer directly to marriage; on neither occasion does the *Catechism* define the term or spell out meaningful consequences of matrimony's vocational status, leaving the word orphaned to the simple definition of "calling." For example: "The vocation to marriage is written in the very nature of man and woman as they came from the hand of the Creator" (*Catechism of the Catholic Church*, 1603). This use of vocation leaves unchallenged the reader's notion of what she thinks marriage is about while validating her preexisting thoughts or feelings on marriage. Marriage is, after all, written into her very nature. What nonintuitive truth is left to learn? The 2009 pastoral letter by the United States Conference of Catholic Bishops, *Love and Life in the Divine Plan*, improves slightly on the situation, offering a section on "Marriage as a Vocation" that suggests the need for discernment before enjoining the indissoluble bond. The bishops fall short, however, failing to define vocation and highlight its nonvoluntary characteristics and consequences. The vocation narrative is not beyond rehabilitation, though. In this essay, I sketch what marriage as a vocation might entail.

Consent to Marriage

If marriage and home life are a vocation, a calling, it must come *from someone* (origin) and beckon us *to something* (mission). The dignity of a person's entering marriage comes in great part from its origin. The value of marrying comes less from my own independent decision than from the act of the one who has called me to it. Currently, couples slide into marriage without discernment, without listening for or to God's call. Folks often marry unconsciously, either because Grandma keeps pressuring or because "it's just the next step." The Creator, Redeemer, and Sanctifier of the universe calls spouses by name, to follow in obedience the path of matrimony and householding he sets before them. As an act of obedience to *God*, a union of the spouses' wills to God's, the decision to marry takes on inestimable value. If we remain at this level of response, however, without defining what spouses are called *to*, we are left with the same self-validation story.

God calls spouses *to* a clearly defined state in life, a certain kind of relationship that generates a practice of householding. God fashioned the nature of matrimony as the permanent, exclusive, faithful, two-in-one-flesh union of man and woman entered for the purpose of procreation and education of children, mutual aid against the tendency to sin, and signifying and making present the indissoluble love of the Son for his bride the church, which is none other than the selfsame love of the Trinity. When spouses marry, they enter a state in life they did not create or define and apprentice themselves under a long-standing practice of holding house together measured by standards they did not write and have no power to change.

The details of canon law and the matrimonial rite bear out the point. Juridically speaking, that is, according to the church's canon law, the verb that makes spouses married is *consent*, not *choose*.[1] Christian marriage is a sacrament, and God is the agent of sacramental grace. Working through their words of consent—the spouses are the ministers of the sacrament, after all—God unites the man and woman irrevocably, indissolubly to each other. Until death, they exist, as it were, *for each other*. They have been turned immovably *toward* each other, given over *to* the other. Come what may, even divorce or hatred, this state of being *for* and *toward* the other does not change. People, it seems, aren't good at making unbreakable promises. God has to step in and make the person into the promise, just as he made himself into a promise through the incarnation. Just as he made himself an enfleshed, living promise to us—his unworthy bride—when he was born, ministered, suffered, died on the cross, and rose from the dead. This is, perhaps, among the most daring and inspiring pieces of the marriage sacrament, that God wants to do something with me, for me, through me, and to me, that I could never accomplish—let alone imagine—on my own. The Father wants to give me irrevocably in love to and for the salvation of another just as he gave the Son irrevocably to and for the salvation of another—his bride the church.

Yet, the consent of the marriage rite is not entirely passive. In fact, the spouses make an act of the will, a choice to express their consent in two moments: at the questions of consent and in the making of the vows themselves. While we are all likely familiar with the vows, the questions of consent may surprise: (1) "N. and N., have you come here to enter into Marriage without coercion, freely and wholeheartedly?" (2) "Are you prepared, as you follow the path of Marriage, to love and honor each other for as long as you both shall live?" (3) "Are you prepared to accept children lovingly from God and to bring them up according to the law of Christ and his Church?"[2] In answering these questions, the spouses affirm the nature and ends of marriage are not in their hands; they consent to be bound by God's generous grace into a freely entered, irrevocable union for the procreation and education of children and the mutual aid of each other. The spouses then express this consent actively through spoken vows that also advert to the fact that much of what they are entering is supra-voluntary, that is, beyond their choosing: "I, N., take you, N., for my lawful wife, to have and to hold, from this day forward,

---

1. See *Code of Canon Law*, 1057.1, "The consent of the parties, legitimately manifested between persons qualified by law, makes marriage"; and 1057.2, "Matrimonial consent is an act of the will by which a man and a woman mutually give and accept each other through an irrevocable covenant in order to establish marriage."

2. *The Order of Celebrating Matrimony: Second Edition* (Collegeville, MN: Liturgical Press, 2016), 60.

for better, for worse, for richer, for poorer, in sickness and in health, to love and to cherish until death do us part."[3]

Householding

Christian marriage is a specification of what the church (at the Second Vatican Council) called the "universal vocation to holiness" given to all Christians, "having the same filial grace and the same *vocation to perfection*" (LG 32). "Perfection" here means "the fullness of Christian life" and "the perfection of charity," to attain which, Christians "must conform themselves to His image seeking the will of the Father in all things" (LG 39–40). Marriage is a species of the generic vocation to imitate Christ and Christ's virtues. Charity, the form of all virtues, sits at the center of Christ's life, but more precisely Christian tradition has identified the "state of perfection" with donning the habit of Christ's evangelical virtues of poverty, chastity, and obedience. While Christians entering religious life explicitly vow "poverty, chastity, and obedience," in marriage couples implicitly enter a life of these evangelical virtues. The Second Vatican Council reminds spouses that "they should imbue their offspring, lovingly welcomed as God's gift, with Christian doctrine and the *evangelical virtues*" (LG 41, 42). Furthermore, "all the faithful of Christ [including spouses] are invited *and held to pursuing* the holiness and perfection of their own proper state. Indeed, they have an obligation to so strive" (LG 41, 42).[4] Holy matrimony, then, is not a terrifying calling to a series of unfortunate events endured with a stiff upper lip. No, marriage is a vocation to virtue, a vocation to become the image of Christ the poor, chaste, and obedient bridegroom of the church.

According to St. Thomas Aquinas, a virtue is a habit that "disposes an agent to perform its proper operation or movement" (ST IaIIae, 49.1). As a habit, virtue is a second nature, a disposition. While virtues, or the habits of living well, dwell within an individual, communities originate and mediate their enactment in the form of practices. Virtues require communities because novices learn *from masters* the standards of excellence that determine the virtue's enactment. Virtues, as existing in practices, are therefore traditioned, handed down like the skill of carpentry—from father to son, master to apprentice. But what, specifically, is a practice, and how is marriage a practice? Alasdair MacIntyre defines "practice" as "any coherent and complex form of socially established cooperative human activity through which goods internal to that form of activity are realized in the course of trying to achieve those standards of excellence which are appropriate to, and

---

3. Ibid., 62.

4. The English translation on the Vatican website omits "et tenentur," which I have replaced, as it is present in the official Latin.

partially definitive of, that form of activity, with the result that human powers to achieve excellence, and human conceptions of the ends and goods involved, are systematically extended."[5] In other words, a practice is a coherent, purposeful set of activities. Those activities are subject to standards of excellence. Those activities naturally accomplish a set of goods when performed in accord with the standards. Those goods essentially make the people who achieve them better at achieving them in the future. For example, casting, setting the hook, reeling, netting, etc., are all activities, but fishing is a practice that integrates them all into a coherent whole. Likewise, promise keeping, sexual intercourse, changing diapers, cooking meals, and arguing are activities integrated into the practice of marriage. What integrates them is the ends (internal goods) of the practice and the communally held standards to which they are accountable.

When it comes to the "internal goods" of marriage, that is, those goods only intelligible in terms of the practice, the church has enumerated three:[6] (1) *consortium vitae*, interpersonal communion or the sharing of the whole of life, which tends toward mutual aid against sin; (2) the procreation and education of the child; and (3) the sacramental sign of marriage (signifies and makes present the love of Christ for his own bride, the church). In one sense, we may call these three goods *ontological*. Like the wings of a bird, they are, in part what make a bird precisely a bird. Without them, we don't have a marriage. In another sense we may call them *aspirational*. Like this or that particular flight of a bird, they are aimed at but not always achieved to their perfection.

Standards of excellence protect these goods ontologically and aid couples in their achievement aspirationally. As has been said, entering a practice means accepting the community's preexisting, socially established standards of excellence and "the inadequacy of my own performance as judged by them."[7] Because practices have histories, entering a practice means becoming a sharer in that history. It becomes plain at this point that, as a vocation to a particular kind of householding, Christian marriage is *already* a project much larger than my own "nuclear family," extending intergenerationally into the depths of an unsounded, authoritative past that communicates standards of excellence to us. In the case of marriage, these standards emerge from the church as authoritative community,[8] and they relate

5. Alasdair MacIntyre, *After Virtue: A Study in Moral Theology*, 3rd ed. (Notre Dame, IN: University of Notre Dame, 2007), 189–91.

6. For the traditional three constitutive goods of marriage, see Pope Pius XI, *Casti Connubii* 17–33.

7. MacIntyre, *After Virtue*, 190.

8. See Kent Lasnoski, *Vocation to Virtue: Christian Marriage as a Consecrated Life* (Washington, DC: Catholic University of America Press, 2014), chapter 5.

to each of the internal goods above. The closer the practitioner adheres to the standards, the more easily and extensively will the internal goods develop. Looking again to the marriage rite, we see the standards of *freedom, totality, fidelity, irrevocability,* and *receptivity.* Furthermore, since *Christian* spouses are called to a following of Christ and his own evangelical virtues in their marriage, *poverty, chastity,* and *obedience* emerge as standards further extending the spouses' abilities to achieve the goods internal to marriage.

The three questions of consent and the vows themselves contain the first set of standards. Full freedom protects and extends the couples' *sharing* of the whole of life in their project of householding for the kingdom. Freedom here means two things: lacking coercion and having gratuitousness, that is, being a gift rather than a commoditized exchange. Vows made under coercion are invalid, and "love" given conditionally, only in exchange for certain benefits, is not spousal love. Spouses don't love each other because they are soul mates but because they are Christians who, like Christ, have freely given themselves over for the sake of another without demand of repayment. *Sharing* assumes free gift and reciprocity, not price and payment. Totality and receptivity, for their part, protect and extend procreation/ education because the couple open to fecundity gives the whole of the self to the spouse. Furthermore, the posture of receptivity invites the totality of the other person in the sharing of the whole life and invites the gift of children from God in the great act of Christian hospitality. In welcoming the stranger, either a newborn or the next-door neighbor, we always seem to receive more than we give. Irrevocability and fidelity protect and extend all three goods of marriage. Psychological awareness that God has joined them in an unbreakable bond strengthens the spouses to view and solve their problems with the confidence that God has ordered them to and for the mutual aid of each other. Fidelity, moreover, strengthens the good of procreation, giving children a witness to the reality of a love that is loyal in the particular and ever-true to its word. Furthermore, fidelity amplifies the mutual aid against sin inasmuch as each spouse gains confidence and grace to grow closer to Christ precisely from the trust and good opinion each places in the other. Like a positive feedback loop, fidelity promotes increased trust that engenders fidelity, that again boosts trust, and so on.

Poverty, Chastity, Obedience

Focusing on the wider ecclesial context of marriage as a vocation to a particular kind of householding specifies the universal, baptismal consecration of *all* Christians to the *one* holiness of the church, that is, Christ's own holiness, exemplified by the evangelical counsels or virtues of poverty, chastity, and obedience. These counsels, considered in turn, move ever closer to the interior of the person and thus ever closer to the heart of marriage and its three goods.

Working from the outside in, we begin with poverty. Simply speaking, poverty as a standard for the practice of Christian marriage means detachment from property, that is, things external to myself yet appropriated to me. St. John Chrysostom tells couples the word "mine" should be banished from the household.[9] Beyond sharing bank accounts, computers, cars, etc., conjugal poverty proceeds from the deep realization that, just as I am utterly destitute before God, so too am I destitute in the face of my spouse. I have nothing but the gift of myself to give, and even that I have on loan from the Father of Lights. If even my own life is not my possession, how much less is my spouse or anything we share in the household strictly "mine"? Taken one step further, the marriage itself is not mine but ours. Spouses must together write the story of their householding for the kingdom, generously giving over control of that narrative to each other and the Lord.

Developing this virtue in marriage can take many forms, but I believe it is best effected when couples put themselves in situations of *real* interdependence and voluntary poverty. Be in a position to need the people around you and be in a position to help others in their authentic needs, and the glory and gratuity of God's love become ever more resplendent. Inasmuch as through its lens all things are seen as gift received and shared, poverty protects all three goods of marriage. Children, ever at risk of becoming commodities in a consumer society, are seen as the priceless gift of God's love given in response to the spouses' gift of love to each other. Mutual aid against concupiscence, ever at risk of being reduced to a logic of justice, deal-making, and negotiation, is experienced as the relief of a true need that inspires reciprocal love in both spouses. Finally, poverty teaches spouses to rely on God's grace for the gift of indissolubility in marriage rather than their own sense of emotive satisfaction.

In the context of religious life, chastity involves the renunciation of one's biological, procreative faculties, but in marriage chastity is simply the virtue of temperance applied to sexuality. Chastity amounts to sexual self-possession and the spouses' reverence for each other as body-soul unities and sexed persons, which protects all three goods of marriage. As Pope St. John Paul II puts it in his *Theology of the Body*, the conjugal union restates the marital vows. So, chastity is an *exclusive* self-*gift* of spouses to each other, a reflection of the free consent and lifelong commitment in the vows. In addition, chastity is an openness to the gift of the spouse that entails an openness to children in every conjugal act, echoing

9. John Chrysostom, "Homily 20 on Eph 5," in St. John Chrysostom, *On Marriage and Family Life*, ed. and trans. David Anderson and C. Roth (Yonkers: St. Vladimir's Seminary Press, 1986).

the promise to "accept children lovingly from God." When brought to perfection, then, temperate spouses so reverence each other as recipients of the gift of self that their sexual activity embodies the goods of marriage and supports their marital vocation.

Finally, and perhaps most challenging, is the standard of obedience. In their project of householding for God, spouses must give over not only their goods and their bodies but also their very wills, the center of their being. To whom, though, must they give their wills? To each other? To God? The answer is to both. First, as a couple, the spouses must see their decision to enter marriage as an act of obedience to Christ and his call to holiness, his invitation to an unexpected adventure. Furthermore, couples should consider major, and even minor, decisions in terms of obedience to the will of God as discerned through mutual prayer and prudence.

But how do couples mediate God's will for their lives? One approach is through a *regula vitae*, a rule of life much like that of religious communities. In mutually creating the rule and mutually submitting to it, the spouses consecrate each moment of the day to the particular task (even if it is leisure) by which they have discerned God calling them to live. Such an approach strengthens the couple's sense of being on a mission, and raises the dignity of their householding together. Such a vision insulates couples from the corrosive effects of consumeristic, self-serving visions of the household as a place principally of consumption and self-satisfaction, offering instead a vision of marriage as something great in the making, as an adventurous risk worth taking.

In sum, the practice of obedience in marriage is principally the disposition of a couple to submit their shared will or vision about what their marriage holds to the greater will of God for their marriage and to submit their own individual wills to the reality that they are to be loved and served by each other. Adventurous couples can embody these dispositions in the habit of prayerful discernment of God's will in all decisions, by living according to a rule of life, and by undertaking the challenge of allowing oneself to be sacrificially loved by another.

Conclusion

I began with the claim that the marital crisis is a linguistic one, namely, that Christians lack a coherent, substantive narrative that describes what marriage is, why they ought to marry, and what they should be doing in marriage and householding. In response, I argue that Christian couples should search in two places: (1) the rite of marriage itself and (2) the church and its history of radical Christian discipleship. The rite of marriage tells us the story of what marriage is (a sharing of the whole of life initiated by freely consenting to being bound indissolubly by God to another person) and gives us standards by which to live that way of life (freely, faithfully, totally, fruitfully). The wider milieu of Christianity (discipleship, the imitation of Christ) specifies further standards by which to live marriage *precisely as a Christian vocation*: namely, by imitating the virtues of Christ the poor, chaste, and obedient bridegroom. Spouses, like the rich young man, should hear the call of Christ's challenge, "There is still one thing lacking. Sell all that you own and distribute the money to the poor; . . . then come, follow me" (Luke 18:22; cf. Matt 19:21).

Chapter 6

Beyond "Helping Out"

Fathers as Caregivers

Hoon Choi

When fathers in heterosexual marriages are challenged about their lack of involvement in parenting ("housework" and child caring), the most common response is that they "help out." They often follow these comments with some remarks about their "other" (public) obligations, other housework done in lieu of parenting (mowing the grass, handiwork, "heavy lifting," etc.), or worse yet their innate abilities or lack thereof. These comments imply that parenting and domestic spheres belong mostly, or even essentially, to mothers. Progressive fathers might be less inclined to believe in any innate nature that excludes them from fully participating as a parent. Nonetheless, they often either end up not doing much of the housework or child caring or get praised for "helping out" by making their child(ren)'s lunches or "babysitting."

Studies support my general experiences. Men with gender-egalitarian ideals tend to fall back to more "traditional" roles *at home* and choose career aspirations over familial-domestic obligation. Given the same constraints, however, women are more willing to cut back on career aspirations. "[H]ousework and child care . . . have proven to be much more rigid over time, with persistently large gender gaps in time spent on child care and household labor."[1] On the other hand,

---

1. Jennifer Glass, Robin W. Simon, and Matthew A. Andersson, "Parenthood and Happiness: Effects of Work-Family Reconciliation Policies in 22 OECD Countries," *American Journal of Sociology* 122, no. 3 (2016): 886–929; David S. Pedulla and Sarah Thébaud, "Can We Finish the Revolution? Gender, Work-Family Ideals, and Institutional Constraint," *American Sociological Review* 80, no. 1 (2015): 116–39; William J. Scarborough, Ray Sin, and Barbara Risman, "Attitudes and the Stalled Gender Revolution: Egalitarianism, Traditionalism, and Ambivalence from 1977 through 2016,"

some studies show that men are doing a bit more domestic work—but even then, only four hours a week (up from two hours a week in 1965, roughly the same as 1995)—and spending a bit more time with their children.[2] While there are small changes and complex sets of determinants, the domestic *work* of parenthood remains with mothers. "Good fathers" simply "help out."[3]

To move beyond such a deeply ingrained metaphor toward mutuality in parenting, I aim to do the following: (1) suggest a practical need for a new model, (2) highlight the ways in which societal constructions and Catholic theology on parenting are limiting, and (3) look to Jesus as a helpful model that can move fathers beyond these limitations.

Caregiver as a New Model for Fatherhood

From my vantage point as a heterosexual Catholic father, I want to make a case for using a different metaphor. Rather than thinking of fathers as helpers, which relegates parenthood to the periphery of men's lives, one can think of fatherhood using a new metaphor: caregiver.[4] To be sure, the caregiver as a metaphor does not

---

Gender & Society 33, no. 2 (2019): 173–200. To be sure, there may be many factors operating here. The economic recession, for example, has a tendency to build public anxiety in anticipation of the rise in unemployment, which can stimulate the feeling that jobs should be reserved for men in times of scarcity. See Scarborough et al., "Attitudes and the Stalled Gender Revolution," 194.

2. S. M. Bianchi, L. C. Sayer, M. A. Milkie, and J. P. Robinson, "Housework: Who Did, Does or Will Do It, and How Much Does It Matter?," *Social Forces* 91, no. 1 (2012): 55–63; "Fifty Years of Change Updated: Cross-National Gender Convergence in Housework," *Demographic Research* 35, no. 16 (2016): 464 and 466; Kim Parker and Wendy Wang, "Modern Parenthood: Roles of Moms and Dads Converge as They Balance Work and Family," *Pew Research Social and Demographic Trends*, March 14, 2013.

3. I am aware that not all families are born into an equal setting and families may have different economic realities. Nevertheless, the "work" of parenthood, regardless of the economic realities, remains uneven along gender lines. From the American Time Use Survey (ATUS), on an average day, 19 percent of men reported doing housework like laundry, cleaning, and other tasks, compared to 49 percent of women. When the female spouse is the breadwinner, men do less housework, regardless of the recession as variant. Men might experience "gender role threat" and perhaps attempt to compensate in this way (except in cooking). See US Bureau of Labor Statistics, "American Time Use Survey: 2017 Results," June 28, 2018; Yasemin Besen-Cassino and Dan Cassino, "Division of House Chores and the Curious Case of Cooking: The Effects of Earning Inequality on House Chores among Dual-Earner Couples," *About Gender—Rivista internazionale di studi di genere* 3, no. 6 (2014): 25–53.

4. "Care-provider" might also serve a similar function. My intention, however, is to move away from the societal norms that identify fathers too restrictively as "provider." My hesitancy of using a "caretaker" metaphor is that it has both too strong a connection to taking care of *things* and properties and too much of a self-serving connotation.

solely belong to fathers nor is it the only metaphor that captures fatherhood, and some fathers already function as caregivers in their families. Still, my intention is to add to current metaphors for fatherhood so as to free the existing descriptors from being boxed-in. In this way, some positive characteristics of fatherhood received from the past (e.g., leader, counselor, protector, role model, provider, etc.) can remain viable without being essentialized in relation to fatherhood. Moreover, the metaphor contributes to equity, not just in philosophy, beliefs, and expressions, but also in the actions and lived experiences of parents. While imperfect, a caregiver metaphor would fill the gap created by some of the received descriptors of fatherhood.

Impetus for the Caregiver Metaphor for Fatherhood

My desire for the metaphor of caregiver for fatherhood only came to me after actually becoming a father and a married partner. Prior to my marriage, I did what I could to prepare myself for it: got a job with a stable income, talked to and learned from people who were already married, learned about mutual sacrifice and respect necessary for a successful marriage, went through a preparatory training (pre-Cana), and learned to put the spouse first before anything else but not to romanticize it so that I am prepared to do the hard work necessary for a successful marriage and parenting. In a relatively short period of being married—just over five years—there was one aspect that I did not know that would become a substantial part of marriage: being a caregiver.

When my partner and I were married, we immediately planned to have children. I was in my mid-thirties, and, by my Korean cultural standards, I was already starting out a bit late. Luckily, my partner was able to conceive right away. The good news was short-lived, however, as we found out that we had an early pregnancy loss. It was devastating, especially because we were so excited about the prospect of having our first child. The space here does not permit me to explain the complexity of an early pregnancy loss. The emotions, guilt, confusion, as well as cramping, bleeding, nausea, fever, chills, expelled tissues, the recovery process, all while trying to work, live, and do the everyday necessities of a pre-tenured family life do not even start to capture this complexity.

I did my best, but I was ill-prepared to give care while going through complex emotional struggles myself. Because the female body reacts to early pregnancy loss like a child delivery, I needed to care for my partner's mind and body as a postpartum, postnatal mind and body. I was not prepared. Even when we had a remarkable number of people empathizing, supporting, and, in fact, sharing so many stories of their early pregnancy losses (and wondered why hardly anyone was talking about something so prevalent), I was not ready. I was certainly unprepared to face another early pregnancy loss afterward. Even when she had a successful gestation of our first child on our third try, my partner needed to deliver the baby through a Caesarean section. I was unprepared to take on caregiving duties to my newborn child and my patient-partner. As if that were not enough, we had another early pregnancy loss after that. That third, and the last early pregnancy loss, was especially difficult because this time we had to surgically remove the embryo. No one can really be prepared for that. While not all experiences of marriage are identical, all marriages require mutual caregiving for all members, albeit to a differing degree and through a variety of conditions and stages. There are factors, however, that marred what was often already a very difficult situation.

Caregiving and the Social Fear of Emasculation

Despite my honest and best effort, the gender norms of our society contributed to this ill preparedness. Caregiving is rarely associated with maleness in the Western societies. Studies have shown that men often take on jobs that are associated with caregiving or female-dominated only by default when so-called traditionally male occupations are unavailable.[5] This reluctance may be due in part to the "wage penalty" on men in caregiving professions (such as nursing) versus the wage dividend awarded to men in more technical-allied occupations.[6] The hesitancy is not, however, due only to lower wages. It is also associated with fear of emasculation: being feminized or stigmatized as "effeminate and/or homosexual through an association with women, or by doing a woman's job."[7] To compensate for such a "threat," men sometimes adopt strategies to reestablish masculinity by "re-labeling, status enhancement, [and] distancing from the feminine."[8] A male librarian may relabel himself as an "information scientist," a male cabin crew

5. For example, in their study of "seeker, finders, and settlers," Susan Williams and Wayne Villemez found that more than 80 percent of men in "traditional female jobs" are "finders" who did not actively search for these jobs but "fell into" them. Susan L. Williams and Wayne L. Villemez, "Seekers and Finders: Male Entry and Exit in Female-Dominated Jobs," in *Doing Women's Work: Men in Non-traditional Occupations*, ed. Christine L. Williams (Newbury Park: Sage, 1993), 75; Ruth Simpson, "Masculinity at Work: The Experiences of Men in Female Dominated Occupations," *Work, Employment and Society* 18, no. 2 (2004): 349–68.

6. Janette S. Dill, Kim Price-Glynn, and Carter Rakovski, "Does the 'Glass Escalator' Compensate for the Devaluation of Care Work Occupations? The Careers of Men in Low- and Middle-Skill Health Care Jobs," *Gender and Society* 30, no. 2 (2016): 334–60.

7. Ben Lupton, "Maintaining Masculinity, Men Who Do 'Women's Work,'" *British Journal of Management* Special Issue 11, no. 3 (2000): S38.

8. Simpson, "Masculinity at Work," 359–62.

member may downplay service functions of their job and enhance their status by highlighting "safety and security" demands, a male teacher might take on football coaching, and a male nurse might distance himself from other female nurses by describing himself as having a "cool head," enjoying pressure and challenge, or associating and building relationships with the doctors.[9] All of this is to say that to encourage caregiving roles for men in any capacity—professional, ecclesial, personal/familial—is no easy task.

Catholic Theology on Parenting: A Limited Resource

Roman Catholic teaching on parenting is only somewhat helpful. The official teachings have certainly developed. The absence of fathers is discouraged, and fathers are encouraged to be involved in the family by sharing in the education of children, taking a job that promotes the unity and stability of the family, and living a Christian life (e.g., *Familiaris Consortio* 25).[10] While such teachings open up possibilities for fathers in the domestic sphere and enhance possibilities for women whose "equal dignity . . . fully justifies [their] access to public functions," they also limit women "as mothers" to "an irreplaceable role" and thus cannot entail renouncing their femininity or escaping the maternal obligations to the family as their priority (*Laborem Exercens* 19, 23). There is no similar emphasis on paternal obligation to the family.

The result of such teachings is that the masculine symbol of "bridegroom" for God connects only to male-human aspects of love that highlight love of bridegroom and father (love of "Israel" as a child) in abstract terms. The female symbol for God, on the other hand, represents female-human aspects that highlight particular characteristics of mothers' love—"*Can a woman forget* her sucking child," "As one whom his *mother* comforts, so will I comfort you," "Like a child quieted at its mother's breast"—many of which convey carrying (the pain), nourishing, and comforting qualities.[11] Such a teaching also claims that the absence of such essential and complementary roles and priorities "creates obstacles in the normal

---

9. Ibid., 359–61. Even same-sex couples think "the 'more masculine' partner and the 'more feminine' partner should generally be responsible for stereotypically male and female chores." Natasha Quadlin and Long Doan, "Sex and Gender More Important Than Income in Determining Views on Division of Chores," *American Sociological Association* (2016), http://www.asanet.org/press-center/press-releases/americans-think-sex-should-determine-chores-straight-couples-masculinity-and-femininity-same-sex.

10. I choose to highlight Pope John Paul II because he has written most directly, prolifically, and influentially on this topic in the recent past. See similarities in Pope Francis's *Amoris Laetitia* 176.

11. *Mulieris dignitatem* 8. See Susan A. Ross, "Can God Be a Bride?," *America* 191, no. 13 (November 1, 2004): 12–15; Ross, *Extravagant Affections* (New York: Continuum, 1998), 97–115.

development of children who would be placed in the care of such persons."[12] Followers of this teaching would be left with little room for imagination outside of strict gender complementarity or for a vision toward caregiving as an essential role for fathers. The most current teachings about gender qualities—highlighting the "feminine genius" and stressing the importance of the "well-defined" presence of male and female figures—do not usher in this caregiving vision either, though it *does* help to have some hints of development in the teaching acknowledging a "certain flexibility of roles and responsibilities" (*Amoris Laetitia* 173–74). The language that encourages fathers to be "close to his wife, share everything, joy and sorrow, hope and hardship. And to be close to his children as they grow" is also helpful (AL 177). These nascent thoughts suggest a way forward: to overcome the *limitations* of these metaphors for fatherhood by discovering the *fullness* of fatherhood.

Alternative Theological Resources: Fullness of Being and Jesus as Model

If fullness of fatherhood is the issue, can Christian traditions retrieve a model that might help fathers discover their full potential? In the Protestant tradition that "does not await invention but discovery" and in the Catholic sacramental tradition that "encounters" the invisible God that already exists in the visible material realities, one can certainly discover *within the tradition* that which might help fathers move beyond the constraints that hinder their fullness of being.[13] One important resource, then, is the theological understanding of the fullness of being in terms of the Trinity.

Trinitarian existence that does not compromise any one of the identities over and against another is an appropriate metaphor for fatherhood (and indeed personhood). It is especially appropriate in a society where a hegemonic identity often outweighs or overwhelms other possible identities for fathers. To downplay one persona of the Trinity would be at least incomplete and at most blasphemous. Correspondingly, since we are made in the image and likeness not only of God but also of a trinitarian God (*imago trinitatis*), to describe only partially what it means

---

12. Congregation for the Doctrine of the Faith, *Considerations Regarding Proposals to Give Legal Recognition to Unions between Homosexual Persons* 7; cf. The Congregation for Catholic Education's Instruction, *"Male and Female He Created Them": Toward a Path of Dialogue on the Question of Gender Theory in Education.*

13. Martin Marty, *The Public Church* (New York: Crossroad Publishing, 1981), 1; Richard P. McBrien, *Catholicism* (New York: Harper Collins Publishers, 1994), 9–10.

to be human would be incomplete and would place unjust restrictions on God's will.[14] While one will never achieve the fullness of what it means to be a human being in this life, it is a Christian obligation to live *more fully* as God intended us to do so. Thus, if a certain form of fatherhood (e.g., that of a leader, councilor, protector, role model, provider, etc.) has been hyper-emphasized, Christians have an obligation to interrupt those tendencies and to bring about a more authentic fullness by highlighting those aspects that have been traditionally neglected.

Jesus did this kind of interruption in his life, ministry, death, and resurrection, so one can see in Jesus a method for moving beyond limiting understandings of manhood and open oneself to engaging in fatherly caregiving. Biblical scholar Brittany E. Wilson considers four ways Jesus disrupted many norms associated with manliness.[15] While Jesus' body was biologically male, his body is both culturally construed in a way that does not evidence Jesus' manliness according to cultural norms in his time *and* understood as divine. His body is not "fixedly male." At that time, "real men" had to be socially elite, be able to maintain bodily boundaries (as "impenetrable penetrators"), project proper bodily demeanor (be free of deformities, disabilities, or defects), and have power and self-mastery over the body and emotions.[16] His unconventional conception without a male progenitor at birth, his performance of "superstitious" miracles, his display of emotions, his call to abandon family, and the deformity of his pierced/invaded body through emasculating crucifixion at his death and even after resurrection are all ways he disrupted gender norms. Like the eunuchs and non-elite-circumcised Jews, Jesus was not "manly" in his cultural milieu.[17] Jesus' way is "to fight Satan: by undergoing bodily invasions or an 'unmanning' process, by carrying the wound from it, and by depending on God's power whereby powerlessness and loss become victorious."[18] That is why he asks his followers to remember him in the breaking of the bread. Just as Jesus was a social outcast, surpassed bodily boundaries, carried a pierced body, and displayed emotions, his followers are charged to "break" their bodies, disrupt what is considered emasculating, and fight against evil.

14. See my treatment of *imago trinitatis* in "Imagine! An Examination of Race and Gender in Korean American Catholicism," in *Embracing Our Inheritance: Jubilee Reflection on Korean American Catholics (1966–2016)*, ed. Simon Kim and Daeshin Kim (Eugene, OR: Pickwick Publications, 2016), esp. 105.

15. Brittany E. Wilson, *Unmanly Men: Refiguration of Masculinity in Luke–Acts* (New York: Oxford University Press, 2015) and "Gender Disrupted: Jesus as a 'Man' in the Fourfold Gospel," *Word & World* 36, no. 1 (2016): 24–35.

16. Wilson, *Unmanly Men*, 39–75.

17. Wilson, "Gender Disrupted," 25–35.

18. Wilson, *Unmanly Men*, 241–63.

It behooves his followers, especially fathers, to act more like "non-men" and to "break" their bodies up against the cultural male expectations.[19] By acting and living in ways that parallel Jesus' way of being, a father can become *more fully human* through "letting go of one's false ego-driven self" that machismo culture has created, risking and embracing his vulnerability and loneliness in the process of accepting his finitude and his calling as a father, and pursuing justice in solidarity with others who welcome caregiving as a metaphor for fathers against Satan's whisper to "be like the rest of humanity."[20] Rather than simplistically embracing cultural norms, then, fathers would accept the ways in which they love as a caregiver, not as a "secondary" duty, but as an integral part of parenting and fathering and following Jesus.

Conclusion: Jesus the Suffering Caregiver

As I look back at my confused, anxious, and unprepared state during the early part of my marriage, I wonder about what might have helped. I think at least some level of understanding of fatherhood that included (socially hidden) expectations for grief, loss, lament, and mutual caregiving may have helped me cope better and give better care for my partner and my child. After all, Jesus handled his agonizing realities by moving beyond his set of social norms not by conquering emotions but by being in touch with them. By not being completely in control of his emotions, by becoming anxious, distressed, and agitated to the point of being sorrowful or "deeply grieved even to death" (Matt 26:38; Mark 14:34) and to the point of asking God to remove "this cup" (Matt 26:39, 42; Mark 14:36; Luke 22:42), Jesus broke from the tradition of manliness of his time.[21]

When I wondered why God had forsaken my family, when I just wanted the suffering to end, I would not have felt so confused and inadequate. I would have realized that Jesus suffered, felt, and wanted the way I did. I would have been better positioned to move forward with grief and give better care for my partner and me, just the way Jesus moved forward carrying his grief and nevertheless taking moments to care for his disciples "whom he loved," to commit his mother to their care (John 19:26-27), and even to ask for forgiveness for those who put him to death (Luke 23:34). The gendered understanding of fatherhood had prevented

---

19. Ibid., 263; Wilson, "Gender Disrupted," 34–35.

20. See Jennifer Beste's treatment of the theological vision of Johann Metz's *Poverty of Spirit* in her "Poverty of Spirit within Party and Hookup Culture: Undergraduates' Engagement with Johann Metz," *Horizons* 44, no. 1 (2017): 108–36.

21. Wilson, "Gender Disrupted," 32.

me from accepting and experiencing life's inconsistencies as meaningful and from living out many sides of being more fully a father and a human. As Christians need multiple descriptors for God—and since we are made in the image and likeness of that God—we need multiple symbols to describe ourselves. Perhaps understanding fatherhood using different metaphors, including "caregiver," will bring about the fullness of humanity in all fathers.

To be sure, more work is required. This metaphor needs to be scrutinized and developed. It does, however, fill some gaps created from the "helper" metaphor, which preserves the notion that fathers are there to "help," while mothers are the main players in parenting. For too long, mothers have been parenting without proper recognition, and their work of parenting is often ignored as their *indispensable* duty as mothers. Indeed, many women with professional careers are accused of neglecting parental duties by "wanting to have it all." Meanwhile, fathers are allowed to have careers and are often *admired* for doing some amount of parenting; they often want it all *and* have it all. This clear double standard is upheld at least partly through metaphors like fathers as helpers, which can contribute either to direct essentializing of gender or indirect complacency, that is, while supporting equality verbally or in their workplaces but not in the domestic sphere.

The metaphor of father as caregiver disrupts this trend. It encourages an approach where one of the *essential* duties of a father is to be mutually participatory in giving care to one's spouse, child(ren), and other duties around the house. By doing so, perhaps *only* by doing so, fathers can truly recognize the privilege from which they have benefited and start to work to undo years of societal constructions that allowed such an imbalance in married relationships. It also might prepare fathers better to receive and give care when care is needed in the inevitable times of struggle in marriage.

Some might see, however, the irony of attempting to argue for the caregiver metaphor within a Catholic Christian framework. I am painfully aware that such a scaffolding contributes to the problem of essentialization, or the idea that women and men as mothers and fathers are equal but fundamentally different. The undoing of such a framework is necessary to move beyond a model that categorizes parents as playing essentially different and complementary roles *strictly* based on gender. My aim in suggesting caregiver as a metaphor for fatherhood is to continue Jesus' dismantling work as he charged his disciples to do in his "remembrance" and to contribute more particularly to an expansive understanding of fatherhood in a Catholic Christian context. Since both goals require some kind of systematic and structural change, my intention here was a modest one: to initiate the process by accurately describing the unjust status quo and by adding a new descriptor in an effort to contribute positively toward the yet realized goals of feminist movements.

The Catholic understanding of "fullness of humanity" that gestures toward the trinitarian God guides a follower through this process.

In the end, I am not able to work out the metaphor comprehensively. I only argue that the current gendered understanding of fatherhood cannot bring about the authentic and integral Christian family. Caregiver is but *a* metaphor with an initial step toward a more authentic understanding. It is only one of many that must be added to understand the complexity of fatherhood, which must necessarily go against the toxic and limited grains of the societal understanding of it today. Ultimately, however, one can only realize an adequate form of Christian fatherhood if it reflects the divinity and fullness of humanity in Jesus—but all human realities fall short of that in the context of sin. Still, it behooves Christian families to do the will of God in that context of sin despite these inadequacies. We may discover that with the grace of God we are indeed more capable of bringing about a greater level of the fullness of our being within our families and in the wider society than we think.

To actualize this capability, more voices from different localities must be in concert to get a better grasp of fatherhood, most urgently from economically and racially disadvantaged and nonbinary and/or same-sex vantage points. My hope is that thinking about this metaphor will start this process that may propel our understanding of fatherhood to more adequate, comprehensive, and just forms that reflect how we are created, in the image and likeness of God with many faces.

Chapter 7

How Gendered Is Marriage?

Cristina L. H. Traina

Legally, marriage is a contract that unites any two people and their property until further notice. It has a few other practical implications, like the ability to file taxes jointly, draw on each other's Social Security, and avoid testifying against each other in certain civil cases. In the past, marriage secured property, family alliances, and sometimes political power. It still does, but that's not what inspires the wedding industry. The toasts you heard at the last wedding you attended probably did not include taxes. They most likely conjured marriage as a lifelong partnership of romantic love that founds a household. Despite the apparent neutrality of "two persons," partnership, romance, and household open the door to all the gendered messages we've absorbed from our wider culture about how to work together, how to communicate love, and what needs to be done by whom—even when the partners are of the same gender.

This should not surprise or distress us. As the philosopher Judith Butler argued long ago, gender is everywhere: all cultures assign meanings to our sexed bodies.[1] Our culture's ideas of masculinity and femininity are the building blocks out of which, and often against which, we construct our social identities, and they come along with us into marriage—in our conscious and unconscious expectations, in our habits of being, and in others' unspoken expectations of us, particularly around parenting.[2] To this culture of gender, Roman Catholicism adds an explicitly gendered sacrament: an outward sign of grace given to sustain a heterosexual couple's joint

---

1. Judith Butler, *Gender Trouble: Feminism and the Subversion of Identity* (New York: Routledge, 1990).

2. Darcy Lockman, *All the Rage: Mothers, Fathers, and the Myth of Equal Partnership* (New York: HarperCollins, 2019).

journey through the world. In what follows, I look at how Roman Catholic teaching on gender and marriage reflects the norms of masculinity and femininity that still permeate our culture, how more inclusive and dynamic views of gender as a product of culture are beginning to affect official Roman Catholic positions, and how these developments may shape future theologies of marriage and gender.

Men Are from Mars, Women Are from Venus[3]

Women's receptive nature is paramount in understanding women's genius. Men's nature is generative: Men are called to give their lives—even unto death—for the defense and protection of women.[4]

We've all heard it: men and women are just different—not just slightly dissimilar, but so far apart that we fill disparate social roles and have to communicate across culture gaps of interplanetary proportions. United States culture has tended to visualize women as chatty, catty, nurturing, self-sacrificing, emotionally wise, receptive or submissive, and "natural" with children; we paint men as silent, steady, competitive, self-focused, rational, assertive or dominating, and clueless with kids, unless they are coaching a child's sports team.[5] If you've ever heard a boy called a crybaby in a situation in which a girl would have been comforted or a woman called a b**ch in a situation in which a man would have been praised for standing his ground, you've witnessed these gender norms in action. Television talk show hosts and stand-up comics make a living from these characterizations. Revlon and Harley Davidson depend on them. The pink of Mother's Day and the green and brown of Father's Day confirm them. (When was the last time you saw a Mother's Day card with a golf theme, or a Father's Day card covered in roses?) The corollary is that the attraction between these polar opposites leads to marriage, which leads to children, which makes the world go round.

Most of us live according to a version of this vision. Over 97 percent of Americans are cisgender—identify with their birth sex—*and* are attracted to the opposite sex.[6] Even though marriage comes later and marriage rates have dropped, about

---

3. John Gray, *Men Are from Mars, Women Are from Venus* (New York: HarperCollins, 1992).

4. Mary Jo Anderson, "Feminine Genius," https://www.catholicculture.org/culture/library/view.cfm?recnum=6709.

5. Adding to the list takes us into territory in which race, ethnicity, and class fracture the agreement. For instance, US white culture has traditionally viewed both Black and white men, and Black women, as sex-obsessed and white women as disinterested in sex.

6. Anna Brown, "5 Key Findings about LGBT Americans," Pew Research Center, https://www.pewresearch.org/fact-tank/2017/06/13/5-key-findings-about-lgbt-americans/. I have included people who identify as bisexual in this number.

80 percent of Americans marry a person of the opposite sex at some point.[7] According to one estimate, about 90 percent of people become parents worldwide.[8]

The data Darcy Lockman gathers in her recent work *All the Rage* illustrate just how thoroughly our cultural visions of gender permeate marriage, especially with regard to care of home and children.[9] As Lockman shows, in heterosexual marriages, wives do a disproportionate amount of the household work, the child-rearing, and the mental labor of keeping track of what must be accomplished in both categories, no matter what their employment situation. Even women tend to chalk this phenomenon up to "natural maternal instincts"[10]—an idea Charles Darwin promoted[11]—and women's purported natural superiority at multitasking.[12] (However, neuroscience shows that no one can multitask.[13])

Belief in women's natural proclivity for maternity shows up in other ways. Both men and women view women's paid work as more "flexible," justifying social expectations of women's greater responsiveness to child and household needs.[14] In my own experience, for instance, schools call moms first when a child becomes ill; most school volunteer chains target moms; and "room parents" are usually female. Lockman sees these patterns as reflecting the belief—held by both men and women—"that women are better able to rear children."[15] She cites Pew data indicating that 58 percent of men who believe men and women parent differently credit that difference to nature,[16] and 53 percent of adults think that "a mother is better equipped than a father to care for children" beyond breastfeeding.[17] These beliefs may explain why both men and women feel child and household labor are appropriately divided if men are doing about half as much as women.[18]

7. Wendy Wang and Kim Parker, "Record Share of Americans Have Never Married," Pew Research Center, September 24, 2018, https://www.pewsocialtrends.org/2014/09/24/record-share-of-americans-have-never-married/.

8. Anshul Ranjan, "What Percentage of People Become Parents?," Quora, November 17, 2015, https://www.quora.com/Children-What-percentage-of-people-become-parents. The percentage includes both biological and adoptive parents.

9. Darcy Lockman, *All the Rage: Mothers, Fathers, and the Myth of Equal Partnership* (New York: HarperCollins, 2019).

10. Ibid., 70.

11. Ibid., 75.

12. Ibid., 89.

13. Susan Weinschenk, "The True Cost of Multi-Tasking," *Psychology Today*, September 18, 2012, https://www.psychologytoday.com/us/blog/brain-wise/201209/the-true-cost-multi-tasking.

14. Lockman, *All the Rage*, 198.

15. Ibid., 199.

16. Ibid., 57.

17. Ibid., 71.

18. Ibid., 49–50.

The 58 and 53 percent cited above interpret masculinity and femininity as inevitably different ways of being in the world, rooted in a biological distinction that is in turn rooted in the forces that form the universe. For them, the differences that underlie attraction and reproduction are natural, already-given elements of human identity with nearly endless implications for personality, gifts and talents, and weaknesses.

Similarly, as the quote that opens the section illustrates, in recent decades Roman Catholic teaching has embraced a vision of sexual complementarity: the idea that both men and women are created in the image of God and are equally dignified, and yet, because of their different, gender-linked strengths and weaknesses, that they are more whole together than separately. Pope John Paul II in particular thought of human existence as fundamentally about seeking a partner (*Mulieris Dignitatem* 7) who is not just biologically but also spiritually and psychologically complementary (18). He saw sex and gender as the main axis of complementarity. In his view, God designed men and women to search for emotional, vocational, and physical completion through giving themselves to an opposite-sex partner: for priests, brothers, and single men, the church (gendered feminine); and for sisters and single women, Christ (gendered masculine); for most laypeople, a husband or wife. For married people, John Paul II believed this gendered self-gift involved sex that was open to new life. In essence, all people were to enter into a relationship with their gender complement to complete each other and to generate something: faithful Christians, human flourishing through good works, or children.

The gender differences John Paul II saw as innate—like women's sensitivity, intuition, fidelity, and generosity (*Letter to Women* 2)—were not merely about personal relationships but had larger-scale social and political dimensions. For instance, he believed that women's natural disposition to motherhood (MD 18) with its outpouring of love was politically indispensable in an era of social and economic injustice (MD 30). He implied that men, less able to "see persons with their hearts" (LW 12), were blind to the fact that their (masculine) technological advances excluded some people from flourishing; only women's love and sensitivity could reveal this injustice. For Pope Francis too, "the grandeur of women includes . . . their specifically feminine abilities [which] entail a specific mission . . . that society needs to protect and preserve for the good of all" (*Amoris Laetitia* 173).

Pope John Paul II's writings on women and sexuality, the theology of the body that his writings generated, and Pope Francis's exhortation on marriage are all theologies of gender: reflections on mainstream social and biological phenomena of gender in a given time and place from within Roman Catholic sacramental traditions and texts. But does this theological explanation of gender, marriage, and their connection truly express universal, eternal experiences of marriage and gender?

Gender's Elasticity

There has been a great diversity of opinion on this subject, but the generally accepted rule is pink for the boy and blue for the girl. The reason is that pink being a more decided and stronger color, is more suitable for the boy; while blue, which is more delicate and dainty is prettier for the girl.[19]

In matrilineal societies, where women can accumulate wealth and where their competitiveness is rewarded, women are more likely to engage in competition than men, suggesting there are cultural pressures defining women and men's willingness to compete.[20]

As these examples indicate, gender and its markers change with culture over geography and time. Today, in the United States, pink signifies female, and blue, male; men are seen as naturally competitive, and women who "lean in" are thought of as unusually aggressive.[21] We even attribute these differences to creation: for instance, we attribute men's customarily greater competitiveness to their higher testosterone levels.

Context and culture shape visions of "natural" gendered marriage roles, even for popes. John Paul II and Francis have been products of their times and places. Born in Poland in 1920, John Paul II lost his mother when he was eight years old and all his siblings and his father by the age of twenty-two, when he entered seminary. His visions of gender and marriage were shaped by prewar Poland, his early childhood, and possibly his longing for his own absent mother. Francis, born to an expatriate antifascist Italian family in Buenos Aires, began studying for the priesthood at the age of nineteen. Although Francis's family remained

---

19. "Pink or Blue?," *Earnshaw's Infants Department*, June 1918, cited in Jo B. Paoletti, *Pink and Blue: Telling the Boys from the Girls in America* (Bloomington: Indiana University Press, 2012), 85. Paoletti adds that by 1927, *Time* ("Fashions: Baby's Clothes," November 14, 1927) reported that six of ten major American regional department stores still promoted pink rather than blue for boys; Halle's in Cleveland promoted pink for both boys and girls (Paoletti, *Pink and Blue*, 91).

20. Uri Gneezy, Kenneth L Leonard, and John A. List, "Gender Differences in Competition: Evidence from a Matrilineal and a Patriarchal Society," *Econometrica* 77, no. 5 (2009): 1637–44, http://gap.hks.harvard.edu/gender-differences-competition-evidence-matrilineal-and-patriarchal-society.

21. Sheryl Sandberg popularized the term through her *Lean In: Women, Work, and the Will to Lead* (New York: Knopf, 2013).

intact for longer, his vision of gender and marriage too was shaped by the early to mid-twentieth century, Victorian-inspired professional model in which educated husbands conducted careers and wives ran households. That is, the experiences that grounded their theological reflection on "natural" gender were quite particular historically.

Other labor statistics suggest that their own families' visions of gender may have been atypical, even in their own time. For instance, in a study of major northern US cities in 1870, when the Victorian theme of mothers as pure "angels in the house" was becoming popular in US white parenting literature, black married women were almost eight times as likely to work for pay as white married women.[22] They are unlikely to have described gender in this white Victorian mode. (Sojourner Truth's well-known 1851 "Ain't I a Woman?" speech is the classic rejoinder to the Victorian vision of delicate female domesticity.[23]) Likewise, cultures of gender were likely more diverse in Krakow and Buenos Aires than the popes' memories imply.

Biology itself is contextual, not determinative. As Lockman's literature survey indicates, there is truth to the claim that primary caretaking mothers tend to be more attuned and responsive than secondary caretaking fathers and even to the claim that these mothers' brains work differently: caretaking activities showed up in the women's amygdalae, where emotions are processed, rather than in the sociocognitive centers of their brains, where their male partners processed the same activities. But research suggests that this difference is a matter not of genetics but of brain plasticity, of the brain wiring itself for the work it is asked to do. First, both primary and secondary caretaking integrate the emotional and sociocognitive functions of the brain—a win-win for all parents. Second, amygdala activity in fathers who were primary caretakers matched that of primary caretaking mothers. Third, *women's* pregnancies prime their *male partners'* bodies for attachment and caretaking: heterosexual expectant fathers' levels of testosterone drop and prolactin, cortisol, and estrogen rise. In other words, Lockman argues, primary caretakers (usually women) *de facto* parent more "naturally" than their partners (usually men), but sex-linked tendencies are not the cause; this occurs only because their brains have wired themselves to be good at the tasks they face often, and their partners' brains have failed to develop in the same way because they have

---

22. Claudia Goldin, "Female Labor Force Participation: The Origin of Black and White Differences, 1870 and 1880," *Journal of Economic History* 37, no. 1 (1977): 87–108, at 95.

23. Sojourner Truth, "Ain't I a Woman?," Women's Convention (Akron, OH), December 1851, https://sourcebooks.fordham.edu/mod/sojtruth-woman.asp.

not engaged children as much.[24] Attuned parenting is natural to human beings generally, but there is no sex-linked proclivity. Primary-care dads, whether gay or straight, and primary-care moms, whether lesbian or straight, all acquire the brains that help them attune to their children in the same way: through practice.

The key news is that caretaking is a human, not a gendered, trait; nearly any human being can acquire it. The bad news is that we write social scripts of gender into children so unconsciously and early that they are hard to arrest, so that people arrive at adulthood with brains and habits already primed for cultural masculinity or feminine caretaking. Adults inadvertently respond differently to the same behavior in infant and toddler girls and boys, shaping their habits by reinforcing more aggressive behavior in boys and more social behavior in girls or engaging in more physical play with boys and more physical grooming with girls. Soon children themselves begin to police these standards among themselves, and peer pressure does the rest.[25] By the time we reach adulthood, aggressive masculinity and nurturing femininity have become second-nature behavior to most of us, so natural in fact that—as Lockman hypothesizes—few heterosexual, married men or women seem to want to do the work needed to attune men to their children. In addition, as my husband discovered when I was working full-time and he was mostly at home raising our children, it takes a lot of energy to move against the gendered flow of social expectations day in and day out.

The resulting Mars-and-Venus culture is bad for children because it narrows the parenting resources they receive, bad for women because it saddles them with a second shift that men do not perform, and bad for men because it distances them from their partners and children. Redescribing child-rearing traits as parental rather than feminine would help to relieve these unhealthy patterns.

If gendered parenting behavior is actually flexible, are the popes wrong about gender complementarity? It turns out that John Paul II's and Francis's devotion to social justice qualifies their teachings on gender complementarity considerably. John Paul II saw gender inequality as the result of human sinfulness. He assigned "objective blame" to "not just a few members of the Church" for women's historical oppression, adding that historical gender conditioning "has been an obstacle to the progress of women" (LW 3). He called for "*real equality* in every area": "equal pay for equal work, protection for working mothers, fairness in career advancements, equality of spouses with regard to family rights and the recognition of everything that is part of the rights and duties of citizens in a democratic State" (LW 4, italics in original). Equality on this scale erodes some potential claims about gendered

24. Lockman, *All the Rage*, 87–93.
25. Ibid., 96–101.

difference: clearly women are logical, disciplined, outward-focused, and capable of leadership, for instance. Both he and Francis have demanded an end to domestic abuse and to sexual violence (LW 5; AL 54). In addition, Francis calls for "a certain flexibility of roles and responsibilities, depending on the concrete circumstances of each particular family" (AL 175). He adds that gender roles are the products of many factors; we should not see them has having been delivered by God's hand:

> Masculinity and femininity are not rigid categories. Taking on domestic chores or some aspects of raising children does not make [the husband] any less masculine or imply failure, irresponsibility or cause for shame. . . . Overaccentuation of the masculine or feminine . . . does not help children and young people to appreci-ate the genuine reciprocity incarnate in the real conditions of matrimony. Such rigidity, in turn, can hinder the development of an individual's abilities, to the point of leading him or her to think, for example, that it is not really masculine to cultivate art or dance, or not very feminine to exercise leadership. (AL 286)

Francis like John Paul II also argues that the "well-defined presence of both figures, female and male," is the best environment for children (AL 175). Still, despite their insistence that men and women are essentially different and complementary, Francis's document on marriage and John Paul II's writings on women endorse no permanent, definite, meaningful gender differences. For both, in the end, flex-ibility, generosity, reciprocity, and equality, not maintenance of inherited gender roles, are the measures of strong marriages and good parenting.

Implications

In the recent document *"Male and Female He Created Them": Towards a Path of Dialogue on the Question of Gender Theory in Education*, the Congregation for Catholic Education wrote that we are created in a "pre-ordained duality," either male or female (34, 24);[26] essentially different and complementary, in nearly every respect, we should occupy disparate roles in church and family if not in culture. The document leans hard toward essential difference, even affirming the idea that our bodily sex is a product of our essential masculinity or femininity, not the other way around (4).

The popes, however, can be read as offering a "both/and" approach to gender, neither rigid nor completely open ended. This fits experience. To begin with, it

---

26. The document allows for sexual ambiguity but says that cases of unclear sex are to be decided by physicians and receive intervention (24).

acknowledges and celebrates an important difference. By and large, only a fertile woman and a fertile man can produce a child, and only women can become pregnant and give birth. In this way, most men and women are not exactly alike, a real difference that is both blessing and vulnerability. This difference has an enormous impact on how men and women organize their lives in every culture. First, as both popes acknowledge, men have used it to oppress women politically, socially, and economically. Just institutions must account for this difference in ways that do not penalize women and children. In addition, culture will always generate gender characteristics around this inevitable difference. We must learn to see these culturally generated gender characteristics as historical, not innate, and to refrain from using them to justify unjust policies and practices or even to ground a universal theology of marriage.

Second, although we cannot escape cultural gender scripts, we can use them creatively once we are aware of them. For instance, understanding how gay and lesbian couples creatively exploit their gender scripts while parenting might help straight couples break out of their gender molds. Gay men in one study drew on traditional masculine tropes of challenge and adventure in deciding to become parents, so that they could frame necessary decisions to sacrifice recreational time or self-consciously develop their capacities to nurture as part of the larger project of inherited gender ideals of masculine self-making. In other words, they "fothered"—described their nurturing according to a masculine identity script— providing intimate care that both resisted and accepted US paradigms of mascu- linity.[27] Lesbian couples, drawing on their own cultural conditioning to be attuned to others' needs, seem to have an easier time dividing child-rearing and home tasks without conflict than either gay or straight couples.[28] A flexible view of gender also suggests that when gay and lesbian parents exercise the whole culturally gendered spectrum of personality, they do so more critically and self-consciously than many straight parents, because they are intentionally adopting stereotypi- cally opposite-gender traits, modeling role flexibility to their children. What if we raised both boys and girls to see child-rearing as a conscious, adventuresome, shared vocational choice and also to keep their antennae up in anticipation of their partners' desires and needs?

27. Mark Giesler, "Gay Fathers' Negotiation of Gender Role Strain: A Qualitative Inquiry," *Fathering* 10, no. 2 (2012): 119–39.

28. Lockman, *All the Rage*, 106. See, for instance, Timothy J. Biblarz and Judith Stacey's compre- hensive analysis of the literature in "How Does the Gender of Parents Matter?," *Journal of Marriage and Family* 72, no.1 (2010): 3–22.

Third, for well over a millennium, Catholics have seen marriage as both a social, political, and economic institution and a sacramental, vocational union in which sex was excused by procreation. In the modern era, friendship and mutual self-gift moved closer to the fore in theology of marriage and sexuality (the "unitive" dimension), joined eventually by John Paul II's gender theory of head-to-toe complementarity. But, if (as John Paul II and Francis agree at least in part) gender is culture's way of riffing on reproductive biological difference, then the official theology of marriage is due for an overhaul. A theory of fixed gender complementarity is not an adequate foundation for a partnership in which complementarity has more to do in practice with a couple's decision to harmonize a diversity of gifts, preferences, and personalities that have little to do with gender. In my household, for instance, I'm the cook but also the tax-and-finance person; my husband is the mechanic and carpenter but also the decorator. I'm the go-to person for testing term-paper arguments, and my husband is the baby-whisperer. If the real glues of marriage are grace and committed collaboration, and complementary characteristics are not necessarily gender linked, is gender difference necessary to marriage? Come to think of it, is gendered marriage the best or only paradigm for vocation? How does our theology of vocations change if we no longer think of the church as the subordinate Bride of a dominant Christ, no longer see vowed men as "married" to the church, and stop envisioning vowed women as "wives" of Jesus?

Finally, the question of whether gender is purely innate, as John Paul II often implied; is solely a product of culture, as the Congregation for Catholic Education worries; or is a cultural innovation on biology, that uncomfortable middle spot, makes a great difference to our understanding of gender injustice. Gender injustice is a sin, surely, but its origins matter, and here we need to update John Paul II's individualistic theology of gender and sin with a more social and cultural view of both. John Paul II tended to see sin primarily in interpersonal terms; as mentioned above, he blamed even historical Catholic oppression of women on particular members of the church, not its theology, policies, and institutions (LW 3). He argued that gender difference became gender inequality as a consequence of God's post-Fall declaration in Genesis 3:16: "your desire shall be for your husband, and he shall rule over you." In his view, the Fall installed domination in individual men and submissive, manipulative desire in individual women as essential, gendered vices *on top of* their good, preexisting, innate, complementary gender characteristics. Sexism's massive scale was a consequence of all men and women being infected in identical, gendered ways and enacting these warped behaviors in their intimate relationships. This argument implied that gender injustice arose from the collective sins of individual men and women, although, he admitted, women suffered more under it (MD 8, 10, 12). Solving it meant individual repentance and conversion, one by one by one, and a graced return to the complementary, equally dignified roles of masculine and feminine.

If we envision gender ideals as socially generated, the blame for gender injustice shifts toward structures and groups without entirely exonerating individuals. Certainly social, political, and economic systems perpetuate sexual gender privilege. Gender ideals based in "natural" wifely maternity and homemaking function on both the macro scale (think of gendered pay inequity and internalized sexism in hiring) and the micro scale (husbands' focus on work and their resulting economic power, if husbands are socially privileged, or their resentment and alienation, if meaningful well-paid work is not available to them). Lockman is adamant that the stereotype of feminine nurture has stuck because it works to men's advantage (it's convenient to husbands if their wives are willing to handle most of the housework and child coordination, and the men can spend their time off relaxing and "helping" when they feel like it).[29] Still, she points out, women tend to cling to this stereotype resentfully at home, even when they've fully embraced a "liberated" life in other departments. This resistance makes it harder for men who desire truly reciprocal, egalitarian marriages to accomplish them, just as men who state their desires for shared parenting and then wait for their wives to ask for help make it hard for wives to insist on a truly egalitarian parenting paradigms (if wives don't pack the lunches and sign the permission slips, will the children suffer before it occurs to their husbands that these tasks must be done?).

By and large, Lockman paints a picture in which heterosexual married women and men resist problematic cultural gender messaging enough to feel constantly frustrated by their roles but not enough to exert the time and energy needed to change the script. She divides the fault for gender injustice more realistically between culture (quite a lot) and individuals (a bit, given the unrelenting effort required to swim against the stream of cultural expectations). Still, gay and lesbian couples' success at adopting countercultural gender roles should encourage heterosexual couples not only to seek gender justice on a large scale but also to reshape the dominant paradigm by rewriting the scripts of partnership and parenting from within their gendered identities, modeling a more flexible approach to the next generation.[30]

Gender comes with us everywhere we go, including into marriage. The more aware of gender we are, the more we can deploy it justly and creatively within

---

29. Lockman, *All the Rage*, 90.

30. A Dutch study found that de facto egalitarian partnerships often coexisted with strong belief in gender difference—and that men's, rather than women's, strong beliefs in gender equality and role flexibility correlated with equal sharing of home tasks. See Fons J. R. van de Vivjer, "Cultural and Gender Differences in Gender-Role Beliefs, Sharing Household Task and Child-Care Responsibilities, and Well-Being Among Immigrants and Majority Members in The Netherlands," *Sex Roles* 57 (2007): 813–24.

marriage, and the more we can use the vocation of marriage as a platform for transforming policies and theologies that rigidify gender expectations into unjust limitations. A theology of marriage built on a specific vision of gender is viable only as long as that vision of gender remains current both for the partners and for society.[31] As we've seen, even Roman Catholic papal teaching on gender recognizes that gender is culturally and historically malleable. A just and lasting theology of marriage will need to bypass gender altogether, embracing a vision of complementarity that emerges from the gifts and choices particular partners bring to their shared, faithful vocation.

---

31. See David Matzko McCarthy, *Sex and Love in the Home*, new ed. (London: SCM Press, 2004), chapter 9, 175–96.

Chapter 8

Born That Way?

The Challenge of Trans/Gender Identity
for Catholic Theology

Craig A. Ford Jr.

*I who have dwelt in a form unmatched with my desire, I whose flesh has become
an assemblage of incongruous anatomical parts, I who achieve the similitude of
a natural body only through an unnatural process, I offer you this warning: the
Nature you bedevil me with is a lie. Do not trust it to protect you from what I represent, for it is a fabrication that cloaks the groundlessness of the privilege you seek
to maintain for yourself at my expense. You are as constructed as me.*

—Susan Stryker[1]

No lesser light than the pop icon Lady Gaga famously proclaimed through
the testimony of lip-syncing fans across the English-speaking world that, indeed,
"I'm beautiful in my way / 'Cause God makes no mistakes / I'm on the right
track, baby, I was born this way."[2] The song, as many know, is a celebration of
queer identity, a repudiation of the discourse that pathologizes LGBTQ+ persons. Whether through her admonition, "Don't hide yourself in regret / Just love
yourself and you're set" or through her confident advice, "Don't be a drag, just be
a queen," Lady Gaga's work sounds a note that resonates with many progressive
theologians—especially with many progressive *Catholic* theologians—working to

---

1. Susan Stryker, "My Words to Victor Frankenstein above the Village of Chamounix: Performing Transgender Rage," *GLQ: Journal of Lesbian and Gay Studies* 1, no. 3 (1993): 237–54, 240–41.
2. Lady Gaga and Jeppe Laursen, "Born This Way," *Born This Way* (Interscope Records, 2011).
Permission requested.

move the tradition away from condemnation of the lives and the loves of queer persons. This essay seeks to bear its part of the load toward such a realization for the Catholic tradition by pointing up a caution and offering a proposal.

First, the caution. Progressive theologians, following wider conversations in the progressive world, have adopted a view of sex and gender identity that conceives of sexuality and gender as based in a virtually immutable part of the person that is then subsequently "expressed." This has become especially prominent in the progressive conversation about homosexuality. Through some combination of nature and nurture, the account goes, persons just *are* homosexual. They are—to say it differently—"born that way." This sort of paradigm for thinking about sexuality has been remarkably effective, especially since the rationale for discriminating against an individual on the basis of something that they cannot control is rightly unconscionable. What makes such discrimination unjust is that the discrimination occurs on the basis of something that is fundamentally *unchosen*. The problem with this view, as I argue below, is that such a paradigm of thinking does not bode well for transgender or genderqueer persons—and this, because the identities of transgender and genderqueer persons come into focus *precisely* through the enacting of certain choices. In other words, where the legitimacy of identity is based on unchosenness, gays, lesbians, and bisexuals win; transgender and genderqueer persons lose.

Now, the proposal. Following the trajectories both of queer theory and of the Catholic natural law tradition, I would like to suggest below a framework for conceiving of gender identity that avoids placing sexual and gender legitimacy within the phenomenal space of the unchosen. Instead, I want to propose one that conceives of gender identity as fundamentally *curated*—that is, as both meaningfully given and chosen. In order to do this, I draw from the virtue theory that undergirds the Catholic natural law tradition. The argument is that trans/gender[3] identity can rightly be analogized as the acquisition of a virtue—in this case, the virtue of alignment—and that such acquisition can be seen as part of the overall journey toward human flourishing. To get there, I proceed in three stages. In the first, I summarize the current state of the question with respect to transgender identity in Catholic circles. Then, I draw out in greater detail the problems with the "born-this-way" discourse in theologies that seek no longer to exclude transgender and genderqueer persons. Last, I propose the account of gender as alignment as a queer natural law approach to the question of gender identity.

---

3. I use the term "trans/gender" identity in order to highlight that the account I give, while based in the experiences of transgender and genderqueer persons, has a universal significance for persons of all gender identities.

Transgender Identity and Catholic Theology

The last several years have served as the occasion for a burgeoning conversation concerning transgender identity both within and beyond the academy. Most helpful and of primary importance has been the increase in the number of published perspectives from transgender persons themselves—people who share not only their gender journeys but their faith journeys as well.[4] In addition, the theological conversation has itself become larger and more complex over the last twenty-five years, with transgender theologians writing what Joy Ladin identifies as "trans-theology" or theology that "uses transgender perspectives to develop a new understanding of God."[5] Trans-theology, in this sense, critically intervenes in past theologies that would pathologize gender transition by challenging theologies that imply gender essentialism, or the view that every human being is born either male or female and cannot, without sinning, deviate from a cisgender identity.[6] Cisgender theologians, as allies, have also labored to produce trans-theology under the auspices of queer theology, a fairly recently emerged field of study at the intersection of Christian liberation theology and queer theory.[7]

The distinctly *Catholic* theological conversation concerning transgender identity, however, is still in its nascent stages. For example, in June 2019, the Congregation for Catholic Education released *"Male and Female He Created Them,"* a document that constitutes the Vatican's first official pronouncement related to transgender identity.[8] This document solidifies positions taken in the recent past by both Pope Francis and various bishops.[9] These writings, on the whole, regard

---

4. For example, see Christina Beardsley and Michelle O'Brien, eds., *This Is My Body: Hearing the Theology of Transgender Christians* (London: Darton, Longman and Todd, 2016).

5. Joy Ladin, "In the Image of God, God Created Them: Toward Trans Theology," *Journal of Feminist Studies in Religion* 34 (2018): 53–58.

6. One of the most often-cited texts to read in this regard is Justin Tanis's *Transgendered: Theology, Ministry and Communities of Faith* (Cleveland: Pilgrim Press, 2003).

7. See, for example, the various essays in Marcella Althaus-Reid and Lisa Isherwood, eds., *Trans/Formations* (London: SCM Press, 2009).

8. Congregation for Catholic Education, *"Male and Female He Created Them": Towards a Path of Dialogue on the Question of Gender Theory in Education*, February 2, 2019, http://www.educatio .va/content/dam/cec/Documenti/19_0997_INGLESE.pdf.

9. See Francis, *Amoris Laetitia* 56, and the United States Conference of Catholic Bishops, " 'Gender Theory'/'Gender Ideology'—Select Teaching Resources," http://www.usccb.org/issues -and-action/marriage-and-family/marriage/promotion-and-defense-of-marriage/upload/Gender -Ideology-Select-Teaching-Resources.pdf, and "Created Male and Female," http://www.usccb.org /issues-and-action/marriage-and-family/marriage/promotion-and-defense-of-marriage/created -male-and-female.cfm.

transgender identity and the process of transitioning negatively, arguing—to use the words of Pope Francis in *Amoris Laetitia*—that the interventions made by queer theologians and queer thinkers more broadly constitute a "gender ideology" that "denies the difference and reciprocity in nature of a man and a woman and envisages a society without sexual differences, thereby eliminating the anthropological basis of the family" (AL 56).

This view has not gone uncontested. Among those contesting voices, I have argued that this current position taken by Francis and by the bishops is unsustainable for two reasons. First, one can criticize the bishops' deployment of natural law *methodology*. In their refusal to engage the actual perspectives of transgender persons in addition to their dismissal of the critical discussion of gender among scientists and philosophers, the bishops decline to investigate as widely as would be necessary in order to make a normative assessment of human nature vis-à-vis gender identity. Second, one can in fact make a natural law argument in favor of the exploration of gender identity and for the affirmation of all gender identities adopted by a person, when, as a result of adopting a particular gender identity, that person exhibits well-being (*bene esse*)—a sign (though certainly not an infallible one) of human flourishing.[10]

A factor simultaneously contextualizing and limiting the Catholic conversation on transgender identity has been the anthropology that stands at its root. In the twentieth century, the primary architect of this anthropology was John Paul II, especially as exemplified in his theology of the body. As his teachings therein unfold, he articulates two fundamental categories for understanding gender identity: gender essentialism and gender complementarity.[11] As seen above, gender essentialism maintains that each person at an ontological level can be fundamentally distinguished as *either* a male or a female who is furthermore destined for a gender expression *either* as man or as woman, respectively. Gender complementarity, for its part, specifies further that, together, men and women exhibit an ontological polarity that is then realized through their asserted physical, psychological, and emotional compatibilities. Gender essentialism and gender complementarity, in turn, generate a "spousal meaning" to the body that is then fulfilled in marriage as the partners express "the love in which the human person becomes a gift and—through this gift—fulfills the very meaning of being and existence."[12] The official anthropology that undergirds current Catholic

---

10. Craig A. Ford Jr., "Transgender Bodies, Catholic Schools, and a Queer Natural Law Theology of Exploration," *Journal of Moral Theology* 7, no. 1 (2018): 70–98.

11. John Paul II, *Man and Woman He Created Them: A Theology of the Body*, trans. Michael Waldstein (Boston: Pauline Books and Media, 2006).

12. John Paul II, *Man and Woman He Created Them*, 186.

teaching, then, is fundamentally heterosexual, and—when the possibility of the legitimate expression of sexual desire is raised—that same sexuality is ultimately *conjugal*. As a consequence, all questions of sexual ethics ultimately reduce to engagements with one or more of these anthropological themes. All sexual acts outside of marriage are prohibited because they are not conjugal, regardless of the genders of the partners; same-sex desire is wrong because it contravenes the principle of gender complementarity; and transgender identity poses problems because it can be taken to deny gender essentialism.

Progressive Catholic theologians have worked hard to reshape the contours of this official Catholic anthropology. Until now, progressive theological engagements with respect to sexuality and gender have largely been restricted to engagements with gender complementarity, with the result that gender essentialism is either assumed or passed over as an object for analysis. Take progressive interventions into magisterial teaching concerning homosexuality. As is widely known, official church teaching with respect to homosexuality draws a distinction between homosexual inclinations, on the one hand, and homosexual acts, on the other. While the inclination is classified as an objective disorder, it is not *per se* sinful; by contrast, every "homosexual act" constitutes serious sin.[13] Contesting this view, progressive theologians have maintained that homosexual acts are only sinful under circumstances where heterosexual acts would be sinful (e.g., exploitation).[14]

What is more interesting for our analysis, however, is what is left *uncontested* by progressive theologians and the bishops. Both parties concede the existence of the identity of the *homosexual*—that is, both parties accept that a person can experience sexual desire in such a way that sexual desire could be characterized more or less as a veritable *orientation* toward a given type of sexual activity. In other words, just as both parties admit that there exists the heterosexual for whom sexual activity is inclined toward heterosexual acts, so there exists for both parties the homosexual whose sexual activity is inclined toward homosexual acts. For progressive theologians, this point maintains signal importance because, by positing sexuality specifically as an *identity*, progressive theologians have been able to argue that same-sex sexual desire exists outside of the volition of the individual. Same-sex sexual desire (and, on this view, opposite-sex sexual desire, as well) is, therefore, constitutive of the very being of the person in the sense that—through

13. Congregation for the Doctrine of the Faith, *On the Pastoral Care of Homosexual Persons* 3, http://www.vatican.va/roman_curia/congregations/cfaith/documents/rc_con_cfaith_doc_1986 1001_homosexual-persons_en.html.

14. See, for example, Margaret A. Farley, *Just Love: A Framework for Christian Sexual Ethics* (New York: Continuum, 2006), 271–96.

some combination of nature and nurture—homosexuals (as well as heterosexuals) are simply "born that way." This very *unchosenness* of sexual orientation reflects, in a theological key, a certain *givenness* of sexual orientation by God to the person, which then grounds an argument for maintaining that homosexuality as sexual orientation is an aspect of God's creation and is therefore, good and morally unproblematic. "Our sexual anthropology recognizes sexual orientation as an intrinsic dimension of human 'nature,'" write Todd Salzman and Michael Lawler. They continue:

> As such, what is "natural" in sexual activity, which is an expression of the sexual person, will vary depending on whether or not the person's sexual orientation is homosexual or heterosexual. Homosexual acts are "natural" for people with a homosexual orientation, just as heterosexual acts are "natural" to people with a heterosexual orientation.[15]

Born-This-Way Discourse as a Problem

It is impossible to deny that arguments like these have had welcome effects for some members of the queer community, especially for those who might identify in other sectors as gays, as lesbians, and—perhaps more tenuously—as bisexuals. The reason why the born-this-way paradigm works is because it tells a particular story about the relationship between identity and bodily expression, namely, that one expresses with the body who one is "on the inside," where "who one is on the inside" is spatially transformed into the location where one's "truth" is located. To live one's existence as a gay, lesbian, or bisexual person, then, is to "live one's truth" as one's "authentic self." Such born-this-way arguments have been appropriated for use by transgender persons as well—and, no doubt, with the same liberating goal of political and social equality in mind. Such arguments famously incorporate elements that suggest an analogous unchosenness that other queer persons have successfully mobilized—elements as witnessed in the example of a transgender man who maintains of himself that he was "always meant to be a man" or, conversely, of a transgender woman who maintains that she has felt like "a woman trapped inside of a man's body."

But even as it is the case that arguments about human nature bolstered in their contemporary form by the born-this-way paradigm provide the link among various political, legal, ethical, and philosophical discourses, and even as the gains

---

15. Todd Salzman and Michael Lawler, *The Sexual Person: Toward a Renewed Catholic Anthropology* (Washington DC: Georgetown University Press, 2008), 227.

from such a coalescence of discourses have been positive for lesbian, gay, and bisexual persons, it is nevertheless not unambiguously clear how these sorts of arguments depathologize the existences of transgender, genderqueer, and gender nonconforming persons more broadly. Consider, for example, the perspective of transgender woman Siân Taylder, who describes her transition in the following way: "I say 'wanted to be a woman' because that's how it was, plain and simple." She continues,

> I didn't consider myself to have been born in the wrong body, I didn't accuse any divine being of making an almighty mess of things, and, although I have more than a cursory knowledge of psychology, I'm not going to look for excuses there, either, and I'm certainly not going to claim that God intended me to be a woman. I hated being a man, as simple as that; I found it increasingly hard to relate to being a man and so, at the relatively tender age of 27, I decided to "become" a woman— inasmuch as one can "become" a woman. I did it because I was actually quite good at it, I did it because it made me feel a lot more comfortable with myself and I did it, believe it or not, for the reasons outlined above, as an act of rebellion.[16]

The born-this-way framework has even been unsatisfactory among transgender theologians. Jakob Hero, for example, evaluates this sort of discourse not as a liberating one but rather as one based in self-loathing. Calling it the "ideology of the innocent sufferer," Hero writes that such ideology

> leads many of us towards extreme hatred of our pre-transition selves. Even those who may not be inclined to hate every aspect of their pre-transition bodies or identities find themselves pushed into the narrative of the suffering transsexual— the iconic "man trapped in a woman's body" or vice-versa—because this wins our issues the status of birth defect.[17]

But most important for our purposes here, such a "born-this-way" discourse— even one transmuted into its transgender equivalent of body mismatching—ignores a very basic observation: for transgender and genderqueer persons, the "born-this-way" discourse fails *precisely* because the way that they were born *is,*

16. Siân Taylder, "Shot from Both Sides: Theology and the Woman Who Isn't Quite What She Seems," in *Trans/formations*, ed. Marcella Althaus-Reid and Lisa Isherwood (London: SCM Press, 2009), 70–91, 83–84.

17. Jakob Hero, "Toward a Queer Theology of Flourishing: Transsexual Embodiment, Subjectivity, and Moral Agency," in *Queer Religion*, Vol. 2: *LGBT Movements and Queering Religion*, ed. Daniel Boisvert and Jay Emerson Johnson (Santa Barbara: Praeger, 2012), 143–65, 146.

in fact, unsatisfactory. It ignores the reality that, constitutive of each transgender and genderqueer person's gender journey (up to and including the election of gender confirmation surgeries) is the element of *chosenness*—an observation that we honor, today, by calling transgender and genderqueer persons by the names and pronouns associated with their *chosen* gender. Of equally decisive importance for our consideration here is that the born-this-way discourse leaves the gender binary untouched, with the result that the gender essentialism at its root goes uninterrogated. In other words, to say that one is a "man" in a "woman's body" (or vice versa) implies that these two genders are the only ones that truly exist. Yet to believe this—as queer thinkers have insisted—is to validate the ideology that denies that gender exists on a spectrum. Such a denial in turn denies legitimacy to the lives of genderqueer persons and, indeed, to all transgender persons who do not assume a binary notion of gender.

Gender as Alignment: A Queer Natural Law Proposal

What would be a way to conceive of trans/gender identity beyond gender essentialism, beyond the gender binary? Here I propose, perhaps very counter-intuitively for some readers, that we return for insight to the ethical framework of the natural law and, more specifically, to the virtue theory that undergirds it, empowered with some of the insights that have emerged from thinkers working in the area of queer theory.

The natural law tradition that I draw on is rooted in Thomas Aquinas's own development of the same tradition in his *Summa Theologiae*. There, Thomas understands the natural law to be fundamentally our capacity to discern right from wrong, and that, furthermore, this capacity reflects our ability to track God's own plan for human flourishing (ST I–II, q. 91, a. 2). The virtues, as habits that shape us toward the performance of right acts (ST I–II, q. 55, a. 1), incline us to act in accord with God's plan for our flourishing (ST I–II, q. 94, a. 3). Following Aristotle, Thomas understands that the successful acquisition of any virtue for an individual depends on their own internal proclivities (ST I–II, q. 64, a. 2). So if a given person is a particularly fearful person, for example, successful acquisition of the virtue of courage will require that that person exhibit more fortitude in situations where perseverance is called for; by contrast, if a person is particularly rash, successful acquisition of courage will require a more cautious approach toward confrontation. The crucial point to recognize here, though, is that, even though the journey toward a given virtue will necessarily be individualized according to our given constitution, the acquisition of that virtue can be recognized generally across individuals as the recognition that the person has achieved the "mean" between two vicious extremes corresponding to the virtue (ST I–II, q. 64, a. 1). In other words, this account trades on the idea that, even though each person has different work to do in order to become, for example, courageous, there appears to be something uniform about all persons who have successfully completed that work: they can all be recognized as courageous.

What I want to propose here is that gender identity, like courage, is something that we acquire, and furthermore, I want to propose that the journey toward a gender identity is like the journey toward courage, or toward any other acquired virtue on a Thomistic account of it. The virtue corresponding to gender identity would be the virtue of *alignment*, such that when this virtue is rightly realized one avoids, on the one hand, the excess of "naturalization" (in which one unreflectively inhabits one of the binarized gender identities) and, on the other, one avoids the excess of dysphoria (in which one's own gender identity is at variance with one's experience of one's body).

An appreciation for advances in queer scholarship illuminates why naturalization and dysphoria are problems. To call "naturalization" a problem for gender identity is to observe that an internalization of the ideology of gender complementarity and gender essentialism constrains gender expression along binary axes that deny the existence of gender fluidity or the existence of gender as a spectrum. When this occurs—when the gender binary is seen simply as a part of "nature" and therefore prior to social construction—the gender binary becomes naturalized. Someone whose gender expression is "naturalized," then, exhibits a gender performance that reflects a mentality associated with a limited (and therefore false) consciousness of gender. On the other hand, someone whose gender expression is "dysphoric" exhibits a gender performance that reflects a mentality of discomfort with one's own bodily expression of one's own gender. This sort of person may express dissatisfaction with an aspect of their body or gender expression that they see as critical to their self-concept. Last, the "mean" of alignment, as with the other two "extremes," reflects a certain gender performance, but—in this case— the mentality is one that understands gender expression as simultaneously both unconstrained by gender essentialism *and* characterized by an enduring comfort with one's own bodily expression of one's gender. To the extent that one realizes alignment with respect to one's gender, it is to that extent that one is closer to realizing the overall goal of human flourishing, which possesses positive normative value within a natural law framework.

It is important to make a particular point about the relationship between alignment and gender performance. The virtue of alignment (as well as its excesses) are mentalities that one bears with respect to one's gender performance. As such, these mentalities cannot be inspected visually. Someone whose gender performance takes on an especially butch or femme expression does not, for that very reason, reflect the presence of a naturalized gender expression. Likewise, someone who enacts a nonconforming gender expression does not necessarily bear, for that reason, an aligned sense of gender expression. Instead, the virtue of alignment is realized in situations where one's gender is integrated within one's overall being considered as a physical, emotional, and spiritual creature. As with the realization of the other virtues, one is limited in one's ability to describe in advance all the conditions by which it is realized. Instead, one must turn to examples of integrated persons who exhibit the virtue of alignment in order to understand what it looks like to possess the virtue.

There are three principal reasons why such a framework would be helpful for conceiving of gender identity. In the first place, such a view provides a way of making sense of the accounts of gender journey and transition given by transgender theologians themselves. Justin Tanis, for example, conceives of gender fundamentally as a calling. "Like a calling," he writes, "our sense of our own gender arises from within us and, at the same time, seems to come from a source that is beyond our control or volition."[18] Second, and relatedly, such a framework allows us to conceive of gender identity as a *project*. Like the journey toward courage, temperance, or any of the other virtues, the journey toward alignment would be one that involves processes of habituation and the opportunity to practice alignment. It is at this stage where one can justify, ethically, the provision of activities and scenarios that allow for gender identity exploration. But, in the third place, such a framework would be helpful precisely because it allows us to conceive of gender identity as an *individualized project*, insofar as one's journey toward alignment will look different for each person. Using terms internal to the virtue tradition, this means that each person's journey toward gender alignment will consist of their finding the "mean" relative to their own embodiment. So, even though the mean of alignment can potentially be equally realized within each person, the matter of one's own starting location toward that virtue as either more dysphoric or more naturalized depends on one's own proclivities as established through processes of nature and nurture. Moreover, it is such a starting location—unique for each one of us—that can account for the feeling of the "givenness" of gender that we feel we subsequently express without thereby needing to locate that "givenness" within the constraints of a born-this-way discourse. A helpful outcome of such a conception of gender is that it asks each of us to evaluate our gender performance critically: if one feels too dysphoric, what are practices that can bring one into greater alignment? Conversely,

18. Tanis, *Transgendered*, 149.

if one has imbibed gender norms without any critical interrogation (e.g., if one has naturalized a binary notion of gender), what are practices that can bring one into greater alignment through a more reflective understanding of gender?

Most important, however, such a framework helps to accomplish the goal of depathologizing transgender and genderqueer persons, but it does so through the specific recognition that the journey to gender alignment not only is incumbent on transgender and genderqueer persons but is also a requirement for all persons of all genders. We all, in other words, are born into a world in which our gender oscillates between dysphoria and naturalization. To engage this oscillation is to subject our gender identity to the process of *curation*. The task is to bring our gender into alignment and to adopt the practices that allow us to do so responsibly and as informed decision makers in the process—whether those practices be spiritual, mental, hormonal, or surgical.

It is not just transgender persons who make choices to rightly realize their genders. All of us, in fact, do, and all of us are thrown between the twin phenomena of the givenness and chosenness of our gender identities. The adoption of the queer natural law perspective offered here can permit us to lower the stakes for policing how these phenomena are negotiated, insofar as, on this view, even the many bodily interventions taken by cisgender persons can be conceived as "transgendering" practices. After all, when looked at from the point of view of realizing alignment, what substantively separates the cisgender man who makes a steady transition to the physique of a bodybuilder with the help of supplements from the transgender man who trains in the gym while taking hormones in order to realize the same goal? Similarly, what substantively separates the cisgender woman who undergoes cosmetic surgery from the transgender woman who undergoes the same thing, especially when both attempt to do so in order to "bring out their real self"?

In all, what this framework hopes to offer is a way to make sense of gender identity by allowing the journey that transgender persons make to shine light on the gender journeys that *all* of us make, regardless of gender identity. In so doing, the gender binary is loosened, and gender essentialism recedes into the background. Moreover, by placing this work specifically in the idiom of the natural law, this argument maintains further that each person's journey toward gender alignment is a part of the person's overall journey toward human flourishing. For a theological framework like that of the natural law, such a contextualization is important. In such a framework, the natural law provides a way toward knowing how God would have us flourish. This makes all aligned gender identities a part of the story God gives us to tell about what it means for the human being to be fully alive, about part of what it means to live into the reality of grace always already bestowed on us.

PART II

LOVE

Modern Christian theology of marriage developed along with Western culture, moving slowly from an ideal of contractual marriage controlled by families toward companionate marriage rooted in the freedom to choose the one you love.[1] Catholic theology of marriage has flourished in the last several decades, as married theologians link theological reflection on experience, social science, and the best of the tradition to construct a positive vision of married partnership. Ongoing debates include same-sex marriage, divorce, and remarriage, but we bracket those here in order to focus on social structures that impede love and to lift up models and practices that contribute to love's flourishing.

Attentive to Pope Francis's call to welcome, the essays in this section are not limited to marriage but rather consider the diversity of households in which Christians live out the call to love. Bridget Burke Ravizza and Julie Donovan Massey share their research on how couples understand holiness in their married life. Emily Reimer-Barry's ethnographic work with poor women living with HIV-AIDS in Chicago allows her to offer parallel reflections on holiness from populations disadvantaged by poverty, illness, and racism. Both challenge the tradition to listen to the experience of families. In contrast, Richard Gaillardetz and Timothy O'Malley focus on drawing from the tradition (e.g., theologies of friendship, the marriage liturgy, sacramental theology) to challenge some conventional notions of love. Essays by Sandra Sullivan-Dunbar and Kathryn Getek Soltis illustrate how structures of labor and incarceration impede people's ability to live out their duty and desire to love in their families, while also showing how

1. Stephanie Coontz, *Marriage, a History: How Love Conquered Marriage* (New York: Penguin, 2005).

families challenged by unjust structures can yet witness to the deepest values of the tradition. Finally, Kari-Shane Davis Zimmerman and Jana Bennett consider how the church might better serve and learn from singles (unmarried, cohabiting, divorced, or widowed) who love in households and family forms that are rarely considered in Christian theology. Together, these essays offer a window into the diversity of loving relationships embraced by contemporary Christians.

Chapter 9

Love as Holiness in the Daily Lives of Married Couples

Bridget Burke Ravizza and Julie Donovan Massey

When we set out to write *Project Holiness*, a book about marriage in the Catholic tradition, we knew we wanted to deeply root the text in the lives of married persons. Convinced there were abundant examples of holy men and women, ordinary saints, if you will, active in church communities across the country, we first surveyed over two hundred couples in twenty parishes. The respondents not only provided helpful insight into a number of topics but also identified "everyday married saints"[1] from their parishes. From those nominees, and with the help of wonderful pastoral leaders, we were able to connect with and interview fifty couples. The interviews were a mix of focus groups involving several couples and dialogue with single couples; all took place in person. We went into these interviews with the hope that we would gain wisdom from those with whom we spoke. We were not disappointed. In this chapter, you can hear what they can teach us about the powerful call to live holy lives in the context of marriage and family.

The Gift and Power of Married Friendship

"Find a friend." Jerry Simms calls it the "greatest piece of wisdom" he can offer on marriage. When we spoke to Jerry and his best friend and spouse, Lisa, fourteen years into their marriage, they agreed that their close friendship is at the heart of

---

1. The survey item asking respondents to identify couples read: "The researchers are interested in interviewing couples whose marriages are identified by others as being especially vibrant and who serve as models of what holiness can look like in everyday life. Please name one or more couples in your parish community who you would describe in this way."

their marriage and essential to its success. Lisa looked at Jerry and said, "When something really good happens or something really bad happens, you're the first person I want to tell about it." In turn, Jerry described the comfort and security that comes with a mutual knowing, accepting, and appreciating "all of the little things" about each other. Facing Lisa, he said, "I know what you like. I know what you don't like. I know your fears and am able to anticipate them and maybe help deal with [them]." Friendship—marked by deep intimacy, attentiveness, and delight in each other—is clearly the bedrock of Jerry and Lisa's marriage and the foundation on which they raised their three sons.

Theologian Paul Wadell notes that, while we surely enjoy and celebrate our friendships, we often overlook their *moral importance*.[2] We do not fully appreciate the connection between having authentic friends and being good persons. But philosophers such as Aristotle thought extensively about this connection, arguing that we *need* good friendships in order to be virtuous.[3] Christian thinkers like Thomas Aquinas agreed: we need friendships in order to be good. Yet, Aquinas "radically reenvisioned" Aristotle's account of the centrality of friendship in the moral life "by suggesting that human beings are made not only for friendship with one another, but also for friendship with God—what he called charity or *caritas*. Our most exquisite happiness, Aquinas insisted, comes from all of us together seeking and enjoying a life of intimate friendship with God."[4] Not only, then, do our friends help us become better persons, but simultaneously they bring us closer to God. Simply put, they make us holy. Indeed, the couples in our study showed us that married friendship leads to holiness in myriad ways.

Becoming Responsible to Others and Growing in Virtue

Day after day, friendship in marriage requires us to overcome self-centeredness and move toward other-centeredness. High school sweethearts Jim Donlon and his wife, Anne Marie, have been married twenty-nine years. Jim emphasized the self-transcendence prompted by his marriage:

> We're not meant to live by ourselves. I don't think it's an accident that it's in the Book of Genesis that we weren't alone for very long. And that makes you a better person because when you are completely alone, everything you do is completely centered on you. And so when I got married to Anne Marie, it wasn't me anymore.

---

2. Paul Wadell, *Happiness and the Christian Moral Life* (Lanham, MD: Rowman & Littlefield, 2008), 25.

3. Ibid.

4. Ibid.

And boy, when we had kids, I looked through the nursery window and there was that little fat pink thing lying there and oh my God! Now it's not even just the two of us. . . . I really don't think you can live up to the potential of how really good you can be by yourself. I just really don't think you can. It's taking care of somebody, loving somebody, raising somebody, burying somebody; I mean every step along the way.

Jim recognizes the connection between becoming responsible to others—meeting the daily needs of his wife and children over the long haul—and growth in goodness. If one is a faithful friend "every step of the way," one is inevitably invited to grow ever more patient, more loyal, more kind, more generous. Jim also highlights here a core Christian anthropological claim, reflected in the two creation stories in the book of Genesis, that human beings are not meant to live alone.

In one of those stories, God creates the first human being (*adam*) but sees that the creature is lonely and in need of a partner. God declares, "It is not good for you to be alone" (see Gen 2:18), puts the creature to sleep, and—from *adam*—creates two equal companions who unite to become one flesh (Gen 2:24). Moreover, in both creation stories, human beings are made *in God's image* and therefore are made for communion. Wadell explains, "We are living, breathing images of a Trinitarian God whose very life is the fullness and perfection of intimacy. Born from this love, we are called to mirror in our lives the intimacy, friendship, and community we see perfectly displayed in God. *God is intimacy.*"[5] And so the logic goes: if we are made in God's image, and God is intimacy and perfect communion, then we will only flourish in communion with others. The Christian tradition argues that only in loving others do we become our best selves, the selves we were created to be.

Although we are beautifully made in God's image, we nevertheless are imperfect creatures, so maintaining friendship over a lifetime is demanding and requires real work from both partners. Interviewees described the challenge of giving way to the other, of trying to see situations from their spouse's point of view, of compromising, and of "letting go of the need to be right all the time." Jane and Phil Rullo helpfully discuss the power of self-sacrifice and humility in their fifty-two-year marriage. Phil suggests that "you have to leave your ego at the doorstep when you get married, really. You have to have a friendship, [that requires] losing your egocentricity and losing your selfishness and gaining a kind of selflessness. If there is anything important in marriage, it is putting selfishness aside, becoming selfless, and being willing to sacrifice for someone else." Phil points to the very definition

5. Ibid., 77.

of authentic friendship. Friendship is a relationship marked by beneficence and benevolence—that is, *wanting* what is best for the other and *doing* what is best for the other. His wife Jane said:

> I think that's what marriage has done. It has made me want another human being to become the very best they can become and I worked very hard on that. And I think I learned that things don't always go your way. And I always used to think I was right all the time. And I learned I was not right all the time and that you had to give a little and, in turn, that other person gave a little. It was both people working together to make each other better.

Humility and self-sacrifice are just two of the many virtues that spouses in our study both "worked very hard on" and modeled for one another, thus "mak[ing] each other better." For example, Phil praises the virtues of his wife: "I like very much her patience and her capacity for forgiveness. . . . She has always been very respectful of who I am and what I do. I appreciate her great capacity to love. She's a very giving person, and I try to reciprocate that love because she's so generous with it." Jane models particular virtues—patience, respect, love, generosity—that, in turn, shape Phil and call him to be more virtuous.

Mutual Emotional Support and Challenge

In addition to modeling and reciprocating virtue, spouses "take responsibility" for the betterment of their partner by providing ongoing support and encouragement. When balancing responsibilities in the home, workplace, and wider community—and managing accompanying pressures—it is easy to feel "not good enough," even overwhelmed. In the midst of such pressures, these couples rely on one another for emotional replenishment and reinforcement. Al and Christine Kozak, married twenty-five years and raising five children, spoke compellingly about concrete and regular efforts they make to build one another up and boost each other's self-esteem—through spoken words, gestures, and texts—helping them "become successful as a married couple." Al calls his wife *every day* at noon to check in, but he noted that encouragement is particularly important in challenging times, when one's partner is "knocked down" by something, such as not getting a promotion, or a sale, or an article published. In that vein, Donna Erikson expressed gratitude for the support that she received from her husband of thirty-two years, Tim, when her business venture failed, which was a devastating loss: "I said [to Tim], 'You can't fix this. I've got to work on it. Just love me through it, that's all I ask. Just be there and love me through it.' And he did."

It is clear that supporting and encouraging one another—building each other up—is one important way that spouses push each other toward their potential.

Yet spouses do not *only* serve as encouragers and cheerleaders, rightfully reminding their partners of their many gifts and talents. Sometimes spouses need to do the hard work of intimacy by revealing to one's spouse ways that he or she needs to grow. Jeff and Laura Rader, married thirty-four years, with three grown children and "lots of granddaughters," discussed the sometimes tough work of friendship in their marriage. Jeff said, "She challenges me to grow and can be blunt with me sometimes—which is good." Laura responded: "I prefer to call it *caringly direct*." They laughed. "Jeff . . . points out things to me as well. Not as bluntly, but . . . [more laughter] he challenges me to grow in the virtues. I can only change myself, so he can highlight those [areas of growth] for me. But I know that at the end of the day, or the end of the conversation, or the end of him pointing out my faults or an area I need to grow in, he is going to love me through it, so I have a comfort foundation that even when I'm not perfect he loves me and that's good. That's a blessing."

Despite her imperfections and need for growth, the comfort in knowing that Jeff will *love her through it* is a blessing. It is the exact language that Donna Erikson used above—in the midst of loss and worry, she asked her husband not to fix it but to be there and *love her through it*. And he did. This language points to an essential characteristic of married friendship: fidelity.

Covenantal Fidelity

"Fidelity requires us not only not to end or walk out of loving relationships but more importantly to defend and sustain them."[6] This assertion, made by Catholic ethicist James Keenan, captures the essence of fidelity, or faithfulness. The virtue demands that particular, interpersonal relationships—such as relationships with friends, family members, and married partners—be *defended* and *sustained*. Moreover, from a Catholic perspective, Keenan argues that fidelity ought to be informed by mercy, which he specifically defines as "the willingness to enter into the chaos of another to respond to their need."[7]

When a couple participates in the sacrament of matrimony, they promise a lifetime of fidelity to one another, consenting to "be faithful" to one another "in good times and in bad, in sickness and in health." They pledge to "love" and "honor" each other "all the days" of their lives. They make promises to God and each other, which is symbolized by the exchange of rings. Theologian Margaret Farley explains that, once vows and rings are exchanged, spouses are bound to one

6. James Keenan, "Virtue Ethics and Sexual Ethics," *Louvain Studies* 30, no. 3 (2005): 195.
7. Ibid., 192.

another and have a claim over each other; future choices are henceforth choices of either *fidelity* or *betrayal*.[8]

Couples we interviewed spoke pointedly about the meaning of their vows, which grounded their fidelity and framed their daily choices. When describing a challenging period of his marriage, Jim Donlan said: "When did it become an option that you could just leave? Never. I mean, we all stood up on an altar in front of our friends and God and everybody. Those vows are not multiple choice. It isn't 'for better or worse, for richer or poorer: yes, no, yes, no.' It is 'yes' to all of it. So, it isn't an option." Some couples used the language of *covenant* when discussing their vows and responsibilities to be faithful to one another and to God. Angie Smith said, "We took a vow. It was the two of us and God in this covenant relationship. It's not just us. This is our covenant with God," and thus unbreakable. The Catholic tradition has drawn extensively on covenant imagery to argue that marriage is *indissoluble*. Once the spouses become "one body" in marriage, they cannot be broken apart; they have entered an everlasting covenant.

Covenant imagery for marriage appears in both testaments of the Bible. God's covenant with the people, whether expressed as God's relationship to Israel or Christ's relationship to the church, is one of *steadfast fidelity*. We see that God is faithful to the people, even when they let God down, shirking their covenantal responsibilities—by worshiping other gods, breaking the commandments, or forgetting the poor. As Farley notes, "The story of the Covenant is ultimately a story of a God who does not withdraw divine promises or presence, no matter the provocation."[9] God refuses to give up on the beloved people and thus repeatedly forgives and renews the covenant. Such fidelity serves as a model for married couples to imitate.

In fact, we did see couples imitating God's faithfulness and heard them speak beautifully about it. Frank Brown told us, "It's like each day when you wake up . . . you get married again . . . you roll over and say, 'I choose you.' I mean again. No matter what." His wife Kelly agreed, saying, "I would name that value faithfulness, a Christian value. Faithfulness means, 'I say yes to this. I choose this, I believe this no matter what comes.'" *No matter what. No matter what comes.* Couples spoke of *loving each other through* financial difficulties, job loss, literal storms and floods that destroyed homes, and the deaths of family members, including children. One man described as "living fidelity" his accompaniment of his wife as she battled advanced cancer—giving emotional and spiritual support, traveling together for

---

8. Margaret Farley, *Personal Commitments: Beginning, Keeping, Changing*, 2nd ed. (Maryknoll, NY: Orbis Books, 2013), 23.

9. Ibid., 152.

her treatments, and nursing her during her illness. Choosing to defend and sustain one another—and the relationship—in the midst of chaos and hardship. This is living out a pledged fidelity.[10]

Expanding Sacrament

What becomes clear in the discussion of friendship and fidelity above is that, while the sacrament of matrimony is celebrated on the wedding day, the sacramental nature of marriage is ongoing and daily. Thinking expansively about the sacrament of marriage highlights three overlapping "layers" of sacrament: married partners are sacrament to one another; sacraments abound in the home; and spouses and families become sacrament to others.

Spouses as Sacraments to Each Other

Sacraments are the moments large and small in which we glimpse the depth of God's love. Theologian Michael Himes writes, "By 'sacrament' I mean any person, place, thing or event, any sight, sound, taste, touch, or smell that causes us to notice the love which supports all that exists, that undergirds your being and mine and the being of everything about us. . . . For all of you who are married, I hope that one of the deepest, richest, most profound experiences of the fundamental love which undergirds your being is your spouse."[11]

The hope Himes expresses was validated by many couples. Kevin Landwehr, married to Lisa for over forty years and the father of five, reflected on the abiding presence of his wife as a place of encounter with God, "When you love somebody as much as I love Lisa, God just comes along." Phil Rullo, speaking from the wisdom of more than five decades of marriage, reflected on the way in which marriage has brought him closer to God: "And I think if you have love, if you have patience, if you show understanding and gentleness—and there is plenty of that in our relationship—all of those things are Christ-like and God-like. I think all of those things bring us closer to God." Indeed, we are invited daily to open

10. In *Project Holiness*, we discuss concrete ways that couples practice fidelity, particularly in times of conflict or difficulty (106–24). By upholding fidelity as ideal, we do not wish to imply that spouses should remain in a married relationship that is abusive or dehumanizing. For a marriage to live up to its potential, both partners must be faithfully committed to the covenant relationship that includes actively seeking the good of his or her spouse.

11. Michael J. Himes, "Finding God in All Things: A Sacramental Worldview and Its Effects," in *Becoming Beholders: Cultivating Sacramental Imagination and Actions in College Classrooms*, ed. Karen E. Eifler and Thomas M. Landy (Collegeville, MN: Liturgical Press, 2014), 13.

our eyes to the presence of God, not despite the complex and often busy lives we have as couples and families, but *through* the relationships and commitments that mark our days.

Sacraments Abound in the Home

Rituals have an important role to play in marriage and family life, and they help us open our eyes to God's presence in the ordinary. One father reflected on an annual family ritual, "Our daughter, when she was in preschool, made an angel out of paper plates and at Christmastime, we put it on top of the tree. . . . [Years later] it isn't Christmas until she gets home, and I put out the stepladder, and she gets up there and has to put her angel on the tree." Theologian Maureen Gallagher helps us understand why such rituals can be so deeply revered. "[J]ust as the church celebrates sacraments in the community, so does the family ritualize its gifts, its ups and downs, its brokenness, its giftedness. . . . It experiences life every day; at certain times such as birthdays, parties, Sunday dinners or brunches, it takes life in slow motion so its members can come to new realizations, new awareness of what they mean to each other. At such times families take their raw experiences, make them significant, and celebrate them. This is the heart of sacramentality."[12] And so a simple angel made from paper plates comes to have real meaning, slowing down time and reminding the family of their deep connectedness.

Some rituals are daily, such as a mother who lays down with her daughter each night at bedtime and shares a story of her childhood. Now nearing twelve years old, this daughter still wants to hear these nightly renditions of Mom's "when I was a little girl" stories. Other rituals are annual demarcations built around a wider circle of family. One woman spoke of a yearly back-home campout where her siblings and their families camp in their parents' yard. Aptly nicknamed "Moochfest," this is one time each year when the adult children (and their children) mooch off the hospitality of Mom and Dad! These traditions move with a rhythm the members understand and value. Like the seasons of the church year, such rituals mark important times in the life of the family.

Some of the rituals in which couples engaged had more clearly religious connections. One family created a candle with their children, painting on it various images and symbols. When someone in the family became aware of a person needing prayer, they would light the candle and pray together for that intention. Another couple blesses their children each morning as they leave the house. In

---

12. Maureen Gallagher, "Family as Sacrament," in *The Changing Family: Views from Theology and the Social Sciences in Light of the Apostolic Exhortation* Familiaris Consortio, ed. Stanley L. Saxton, Patricia Voydanoff, and Angela Ann Zukowski (Chicago: Loyola University Press, 1984), 10.

an era when school shootings appear in the news on an all-too-regular basis, it is easy to understand the comfort, for parents and kids alike, of a daily blessing.

Pete and Sally Mahon decided early on that the Prayer of St. Francis held deep meaning for them. So they committed to praying it together each night of their marriage. Sally describes their practice, "There are very few nights we don't say it. . . . And it's hard to say when you're mad at each other! But sometimes, one of us would go, 'We should say our prayer,' and you can't not say it then!" The Mahons and many others also spoke of attendance at weekly Mass as a cherished ritual, valuing the eucharistic celebration as an important "check in" with God, a needed "course correction," an opportunity to "recharge," and "a reset button."

Many couples told us, too, about the rich meaning of regularly gathering around the family table. Powerful and important connections can be made between the formal ritual of the Eucharist in church and the familiar experience of family meals at home. Al Kozak points to those connections when saying: "Our kitchen table is a big place for our family. It's where we come back and we have . . . a meal together. You know our Catholic faith and Jesus says, come back to the table. A lot of good discussions have happened at our kitchen table." Jim and Anne Marie Donlon recall their then-teenage sons complaining, "Nobody else's parents make their kids come home for dinner!" Many years later, their commitment to daily family meals was affirmed by their adult son who noted, "We used to give you such a hard time about the dinners. . . . I wouldn't change that. I didn't realize how many people didn't have that growing up and how important it would be in my life."

To call our homes places we encounter the sacraments is to know God is experienced not only in moments and places set apart but in the very everydayness of life. One man we interviewed described it well: "This is real life. This is the nitty-gritty feeding the kids, going to work every day; that's a sacrament too. And I think it's really important for the church to recognize that too and not just have us lowly peons looking up at the great sacraments up there. I think we need to realize what we are doing is really important for the world, really important for God and each other." As sacrament, marriage and family life demonstrate God's grace in the world, most closely to those in the family, but as signs for the wider community as well.

Sacrament to the Wider World

Frank and Kelly Brown understand that the love they share must draw them out into the world where their gifts are needed. As Kelly describes, "It is about us, but has been about more than us. . . . The ultimate end [of the marriage] . . . is to bring more God into the world." Margaret Murphy, married to Matthew for twenty-six years, articulates an outward-looking perspective, one she and Matthew consciously shared with their children:

> And we've always kind of tried to instill that with our kids even when they went from grade school to high school and out: that somehow that love, that compassion, it would be selfish for us just to keep it in our family and say, "Okay, we're all happy. Everybody's good." We always, we talk about this. That's our challenge. *Are we doing enough? Are we giving enough?* You know what I mean? It shouldn't be this big heavy guilt thing but it should be a bit of a challenge and nudge that, *yeah, we're blessed, so what are we doing to extend that?* Our marriage should be a mirror of love to other people.

Notice how the love and compassion experienced *within* Margaret and Matthew's marriage and family moves them to show love and compassion *outside* it. Margaret believes that the resources she and Matthew have are not for their good alone or even the good of their family; rather, their marriage is to mirror God's love ever-outward by sharing what they have with others. For her, a personal relationship with Jesus, while foundational, must be reflected in care for others beyond their family. Margaret sees Jesus as the model for being and acting: "I always tell the kids that Jesus showed us how to live. It was his loving and being true to what he knew he had to do to bring justice, to bring peace, to bring love to the world. That's what got him in trouble. But we're called to do the same. The whole message of social justice: how do we bring that love and healing?"

In our interviews, stories of love and healing abounded, and the ways couples and families became sacrament to others both humbled and inspired us. Our interviewees serve their neighbors by ministering in hospitals and nursing homes, working at shelters, raising money for cancer research and other charities, participating in service trips, bringing the Eucharist to homebound persons, volunteering in parishes and schools, and organizing and distributing food at pantries. Moreover, while not necessarily described as "service," we heard story upon story about reaching out to neighbors who are sick or elderly—whether it be shoveling snow, checking in to ensure safety and well-being, or delivering groceries. John and Nancy Brady, for example, do weekly grocery shopping for a 102-year-old woman, Rita, who has no family in town. John explains how shopping and dropping off groceries feeds Rita's body and spirit: "I mean, I never just go, 'Oh, hi, I'm here. Do you have your list? Okay, thanks.' We visit. So whenever I go to pick up the list . . . I tell Nancy that I am stopping by Rita's. We know it's going to be a while. I sit down, chit chat. I think it's more, it's a lot more than we just do the grocery shopping, for her, and for me, too. . . . It's a social thing. We're doing her a service, so to speak, but more than just the physical groceries." The spiritual nourishment is reciprocal ("for her, and for me, too"), but such long-term, loving care takes discipline; it's not always easy or convenient. Nancy is honest about the difficulty:

> For me, sometimes, quite frankly, it's kind of a pain to do it. Because it's been years now and I have to worry about her grocery shopping on top of ours. And sometimes, I'm like, *Really? Can't we just go to the grocery store and get what I need because I'm in a hurry and I've had a busy week*, or whatever. And it keeps me grounded in [the call that] we're supposed to be taking care of other people. This is what our lives are about. God puts us here to take care of others and not just be in our own little bubble.

These examples of care for neighbor make it clear that there are different kinds of poverty and that being merciful need not mean participating in an organized service effort. In his excellent reflection on mercy, Cardinal Walter Kasper describes a "lack of relationships" as a form of poverty. "As a social creature, the human person can experience various forms of poverty: loneliness and isolation, the loss of a partner, the loss of family members or friends, communication difficulties, exclusion from social intercourse—whether self-caused or forced upon a person—discrimination and marginalization, including the extreme cases of isolation or exile."[13] Consequently, if we return to Margaret's question above: How do we bring love and healing? The answer depends on which neighbor one serves and whether the person's poverty is bodily or spiritual.

One profound way that couples met both the bodily and spiritual needs of neighbors is by extending hospitality—that is, offering welcome to the stranger. Couples took into their home a pregnant niece, a brother with special needs, a young sibling whose parents died, family friends, children from the foster care system, and refugees. One couple with a gay son makes sure their home is a safe place where people can come: "There are still people—friends of ours and community people—who just don't feel like they are welcome in places. At least people feel welcome in our home. We try to make sure of that . . . [though] it's not always clean. Just the fact that— 'Yes, when you want to come over, come. Sit down and we'll talk.'" The condition of the *house* is less important than the welcome provided in this *home*, where guests are lovingly embraced in their authenticity.

---

13. Cardinal Walter Kasper, *Mercy: The Essence of the Gospel and the Key to Christian Life*, trans. William Madges (Mahwah, NJ: Paulist Press, 2013), 143–44.

A Communal Project

For these couples, marriage is fundamentally a holiness project, one deeply rooted in the wider church community. They do not do it alone. They are actively engaged in their parish communities. Regular participation in sacramental life trained their eyes to see holiness in the daily and elemental—bread and wine found on the eucharistic table acting as a call to gather at table in the home, to tell the story and share the gifts just as we do in liturgy. They recognized the ways their communities affirmed and carried them, both in the ongoing joy of witnessing the committed marriages of others and in the many compassionate ways community members stood with and for one another in times of hardship or suffering. These couples were not immune to the difficulties in life; they came to understand that marriage is too difficult to navigate alone, and they relied on the support of others, particularly their faith community.

Chapter 10

An Intersectional View of Love in Marriage

Emily Reimer-Barry

My task in this essay is to explain how some Christian families practice the presence of God in their relationships, especially marriage. To do this well, we must listen to the practical realities and lived experiences of Christians, with special attention to communities marginalized in theological discourse. Communities disproportionately impacted by poverty and racism should have a privileged seat at the table. Women who have experienced intimate partner violence should have a privileged seat at the table. Learning from their stories can shape us and help us reimagine an intersectional spirituality of marriage that would be life-affirming for all.

Defining Spirituality

It can be difficult to define "spirituality" because the term is used in so many different contexts. Philip Sheldrake, a scholar whose expertise lies in Christian spiritual traditions, explains that the origins of the word "spirituality" can be found in the Latin noun *spiritualitas* and the Greek noun *pneuma* (spirit).[1] In its New Testament usage, to be a spiritual person meant to be someone who lived under the influence of the Spirit of God.[2]

While this meaning still holds for many, a wider understanding of spirituality attends to three additional facets. First, spirituality is holistic. Sheldrake explains

---

1. Philip Sheldrake, *Spirituality: A Brief History* (Malden, MA: Wiley-Blackwell, 2013), 2.
2. Ibid.

that spirituality is not one element among many in a person's life but rather should be seen as the integrating factor in life, "attending to life-as-a-whole."[3] Second, spirituality is a quest for the sacred (in Christian terms, a quest for deepened relationship with God). Finally, spirituality in contemporary usage involves a quest for meaning and a sense of purpose in one's life. To be a spiritual person in this sense means that one cares about "ultimate values," values that go far beyond material satisfaction of needs but extend to a deeper sense of human fulfillment. The practice of spirituality thus requires careful attention, awareness of one's emotional life, and constant self-reflection.[4] "Spirituality" is an open-ended invitation to examine one's life and become attuned to the presence of God within everyday life.[5]

Marital Spirituality

Applying Sheldrake's understanding of spirituality to marriage, we can say that marital spirituality is a married couple's holistic, self-reflective quest for the Sacred. A Christian marriage relationship should promote the integral flourishing of both spouses and draw them ever closer to the Sacred through their everyday lives. This is what the grace of the sacraments means in Catholic liturgical theology: through the sacraments we experience the love of God through an outpouring of grace. For a married couple, this is supposed to happen precisely through the couple's relationship. In my marriage relationship, I am supposed to encounter the living God. In our marriage relationship, my partner and I should grow in holiness. Sheldrake explains, "At its most fundamental, spirituality . . . is a complete way of life. In other words, to be a Christian is to live in the world in a certain way."[6] Married life is similarly all-encompassing. I bring my whole self into marriage and live, day to day, in the reality of married life.

But we must avoid sanitized, whitewashed versions of marital spirituality. Christian marriage is not an easy vocation, and marriage is not a perfect institution. Catholic accounts of the purposes of marriage are not static and unchangeable but have in fact developed significantly, even in the last century.[7] The Catholic Church has moved away from a patriarchal understanding of marriage and toward

---

3. Ibid., 3.
4. Ibid., 4.
5. Ibid., 7.
6. Ibid., 25.
7. I elaborate on this point in my book, *Catholic Theology of Marriage in the Era of HIV and AIDS: Marriage for Life* (Lanham, MD: Lexington Books, 2015), 128–31.

a vision of an equal partnership of life and love. The emphases on procreative sex and marital indissolubility, however, continue to obscure other church teachings that value the quality of the couple's intimate relationship.[8] Thus, we need to give attention to real people's lives, as Jesus modeled in his ministry. We can illustrate the challenge of such an approach by empathetic listening to Jimena's and Diva's stories of family life.

Jimena's Story[9]

Born in San Fernando, Mexico, Jimena is thirty-four years old and living at a migrant safe house in Tijuana. Jimena's father was an abusive alcoholic. Her mother left her father when Jimena was nine years old, and then her mother had a string of abusive boyfriends. When her mother remarried, Jimena did not get along with her stepfather, who was verbally abusive. For a while, she lived with extended family members to get away from her stepfather. When her older sister, who was nineteen, found out that she was moving from place to place, she told Jimena, "Let's move to Tijuana." Jimena, now twelve, dropped out of school and moved to Tijuana with her sister and her sister's boyfriend. Things got worse instead of better. After their arrival in Tijuana, her sister's boyfriend attempted to rape her. Jimena says, "I told my sister and my sister did not believe me. Then my sister kicked me out of the house." She lived on the streets until being trafficked to the United States. She says: "The man who helped me cross the border, he was thirty-three years old, and I was fifteen. He made me have sex with him so that he would help me. I lived with him in the US, and he made me have sex with him." Jimena gave birth to a daughter in the United States, and for two years lived with her daughter and the father of her daughter—this abusive man who treated her like a sexual slave. Child Protective Services took her daughter away from her when Jimena was placed in a group home for girls previously trafficked. She never saw her daughter again. When Jimena turned eighteen, she could no longer live at the group home for girls. Without a place to go, she decided to return to Mexico. She struggled with substance abuse and had difficulty finding a job. She did become a parent again but could never offer a safe and stable home to her children, who were cared for within the foster system in Mexico. She continues:

8. Ibid., 127.

9. Jimena [pseud.], interview with the author. Tijuana, Mexico. July 21, 2011. Consecutive interpretation (Spanish–English) provided by Javier Maldonado.

When I think back on my life, it was like one action led to another and led to another, and I went down such a dark path. First there was the bad relationship between my parents, and I had a bad relationship with my mother. I was young when I left home, and never really knew what it meant to have a stable home, to have a loving family. I left home when I was so young, and I lived with my sister, but that was dangerous too. Sometimes her boyfriends wanted to have sex with me. I never had loving supportive parents and brothers and sisters. So I did my best, but my life was chaotic, and disorderly, and difficult. I was always in search of that family experience, that family I never had. But I made bad choices. The wrong choices led me to drugs, so then I was living the life of a user. And I couldn't get my life together.

Jimena is grateful for the stability of her current safe house, where she attends Narcotics Anonymous meetings every morning and meets with a sponsor regularly. She is responsible for cooking and cleaning and has a leadership role among the women, advocating for the women's needs with the director and subdirector. While none of her own children live in the house, she cares for some of the children there. She hopes to recover from addiction and move into a house of her own. "I'm not good to anyone when I'm high. But I can change," she says. "I'm trying very hard." Jimena's resilience and determination are evident, and her hope in a better future is profound.

Diva's Story[10]

Diva Jackson is fifty-two years old and proudly showed me pictures of her six grown children and five grandchildren. On the day we met, she was feeling strong, healthy, and ready to share her story. Diva's experience as a black, HIV-positive, Catholic woman in Chicago influenced her description of married life. Diva explained that her marriage to Lamar is built on trust and companionship. They took care of each other and expected that, since they were both living with HIV, they would have to take care of each other a lot in the future. Diva was confident that, when the time came to care for Lamar, she would be able to do it. "Some days he goes through things where, you know, he can't get out of bed. I have to bring him something to eat and stuff. I've got to take care of him. He's my spouse." Diva felt equipped to care for Lamar because she worked as a nurse's aide. "I have worked in nursing homes. I have dealt with elderly people. I have dealt with the

---

10. Diva Jackson [pseud.], interviewed by the author. March 16, 2006, and July 9, 2014, Chicago, Illinois. Further analysis of Diva's story and its implications for people of faith can be seen in my *Catholic Theology of Marriage in the Era of HIV and AIDS.*

dying. I've dealt with hospice. You know? Nothing really turns my stomach or makes me queasy. I guess that's just one way that God prepared me, you know?" While she believed she could handle the demands of caregiving for her husband, Diva hoped that Lamar would remain healthy for a long time.

> Lamar's very nice. He's very compassionate. He does anything he can for me, and I do anything I can for him. He's very loving. He goes everywhere I go. Sometime we go places and he'll be the only man. We are in each other's corner. When I ache, he aches. When I'm down, he's down. He cooks, he cleans, he washes, he can do whatever a woman can do. He is a companion, and I guess I was looking for that in my early years, my other marriages. I needed love. I need to be loved.

For Diva, marriage to Lamar provided her love and companionship. They engaged in simple acts of companionship as touchstones of what the marital relationship is all about: accompanying one another to doctor appointments, going to church together, reminding each other to take medicines, caring for the home together. Lamar was concerned for Diva's health and encouraged her to take care of herself. "For example, he doesn't want me to do any heavy lifting, because he's concerned for my heart and my lungs. But we have a good understanding. He's a very good companion to me. And sometimes I'm mad at him. Sometimes he doesn't move fast enough for me, but that's my stuff, my problems coming out." Diva's description of her marriage as companionship even in the midst of struggle is captured in a similar story from Cheryl, another study participant.

> It's the little bitty things that you really need to appreciate. If I don't feel like cooking, he'll go out and get some fried chicken, and we'll eat it right from the bucket in the middle of our bed watching a movie. We're casual like that. But every day is a challenge, you know. We aren't perfect, nobody is perfect. You have your good days and your bad days, but we are in this thing together, me and him. And we support each other. This is a big process, a big struggle, HIV. So I think being married helps you deal with it.[11]

Hearing the Challenge

Jimena and Diva tell very different stories of family life. In *Amoris Laetitia*, Pope Francis has encouraged Catholics to "stop looking for those personal or communal niches which shelter us from the maelstrom of human misfortune, and

---

11. Cheryl King [pseud.], interviewed by the author, October 18, 2006, Chicago, Illinois. In Reimer-Barry, *Catholic Theology of Marriage*, 31.

instead to enter into the reality of other people's lives and to know the power of tenderness. Whenever we do so, our lives become wonderfully complicated" (AL 308). The pope continues: "No family drops down from heaven perfectly formed; families need constantly to grow and mature in the ability to love. . . . All of us are called to keep striving towards something greater than ourselves and our families" (AL 325). If we take up the pope's challenge to enter into the reality of other people's lives—and I suggest we should—the stories we hear will be messy indeed.

I believe the Christian community is up to the challenge, but we must proceed with caution. Patriarchy has shaped Christian teachings on family life. Christians in the United States today live in a racist, nativist, and heterosexist culture. Christians today must reflect anew on what parts of the tradition can be salvaged and what must change. In order to engage in this broad ecclesial discernment, we need tools for reflecting on where God is (and is not) experienced in family life. Considering the family narratives of Jimena and Diva can provide an initial starting point. The relationship violence Jimena witnessed and experienced is not "of God" because Jimena is a person who deserves respect. Jimena's description of family life lacks justice, grace, stability, love. Her parents may have been married, but Jimena did not experience their relationship as sacramental. Similarly, her experience of being trafficked was not "of God." It is important to name these injustices. In historical perspective, Jimena's story is a story of three generations of family dysfunction and violence. But it is also important to say that Jimena is not a symbol of every Mexican woman; too often rhetoric about "drug lords and rapists" in Mexico are employed in the United States to scare white Americans into thinking that all brown-skinned people are criminals. While parts of Diva's story also demonstrate the realities of structural violence (including underperforming schools that result from the unequal distribution of resources, prevalence of drugs and crime in her neighborhood, and the hyperincarceration of young men of color in the United States), the quality of her marriage relationship with Lamar does foster her integral flourishing and does align with the tradition's understanding of "sacramentality" or the free gift of God's love that can be experienced in intimate human relationships. It is important to name both spaces of grace and spaces of suffering when we look to real people's lives for spiritual wisdom.

Marital Spirituality through an Intersectional Lens

An intersectional lens is critically important when thinking about the theological construct of family. Grace Ji-Sun Kim and Susan M. Shaw define intersectionality as "a lens for understanding how gender, race, social class, sexual identity, and other forms of difference work concurrently to shape people and institutions within multiple relationships of power."[12] These authors remind us that for most of Christian history, the discipline of theological discourse was dominated by men. "Straight white male theologians have spoken for everyone else, as if their theologies do not reflect the bias of their own social positions and power. This has meant that our theologies have been partial, a reflection of only a very small slice of the whole of human experience."[13] By adopting an intersectional lens, theologians today who write about family life will need to do so in such a way that they adequately address the core concepts of social inequality, power, relationality, social context, complexity, and social justice that are at the heart of an intersectional approach.[14] My research with women on the margins has surfaced two key themes for an intersectional marital spirituality. First, married people encounter the living God in the struggle for freedom, wholeness, and life. Second, married people encounter the living God in ordinary actions and seemingly menial tasks.

God in the Struggle

The Christian tradition is full of stories of God's liberating power. A dominant interpretation of the gospel narratives is that Jesus wanted people to live whole, flourishing lives. Womanist theologian M. Shawn Copeland explains that Jesus "was the incarnation of divine compassion" whose life and ministry exemplifies "what it means to take sides with the oppressed and poor in the struggle for life—no matter the cost."[15] But for many married couples, daily reality is a struggle for survival. Without romanticizing suffering, I wish to highlight some of the stories of women and men whose struggles in marriage became an opportunity for Sacred encounter. Struggle toward freedom and resistance to oppression can be seen as avenues of grace. They are opportunities for the believer to claim one's dignity as *imago Dei* (made in the image of God).

Sue, Crystal, and Lettie were research participants in the same study as Diva when I was conducting research in Chicago, Illinois, from 2006 to 2014. Sue explained that there were a lot of times when she and her husband had to choose between paying for her HIV medications or buying food. The experiences of other women in the study were similar. The research participants told of how their family

12. Grace Ji-Sun Kim and Susan M. Shaw, *Intersectional Theology: An Introductory Guide* (Minneapolis: Fortress Press, 2018), 2.

13. Ibid., 3.

14. These are the six core concepts identified by Patricia Hill Collins and Sirma Bilge in *Intersectionality* (Cambridge: Polity Press, 2016), 25–30.

15. M. Shawn Copeland, *Enfleshing Freedom: Body, Race, and Being* (New York: Fortress Press, 2009), 87.

relationships were profoundly altered when they discovered their HIV status, how navigating a complicated and unjust health-care delivery system strained their marriages, and how most of their day is just focused on getting through it. Crystal explained how she had to constantly advocate for herself to get the medical care she needed. Lettie said she felt "stressed out all the time." She worked forty-five hours a week, commuted forty minutes each way, and had four evening meetings each week related to her HIV diagnosis (two support groups, a weekly therapy session, and an alternative medicine session). In their daily practices of self-care including taking medications, eating, sleeping, attending support group meetings, and prayer, the research participants committed to life and to doing the best they could in the struggle for reclaiming their dignity and wholeness. Sometimes, eating fried chicken in the middle of the bed is how a couple nourishes their love relationship and finds God in the midst of their struggle.

Ada María Isasi-Díaz finds in *la lucha* (the struggle) that Latina women are resisting oppression, choosing life, and seeking wholeness.[16] Isasi-Díaz describes this as a daily struggle. Sometimes it is a struggle of the couple against the forces of oppression, but sometimes *la lucha* is one partner's struggle within the institution of marriage. As we saw in Jimena's story, home is not always "safe." The Christian theological tradition has too often failed to name spousal abuse as sin, and some married persons have suffered within their relationships. While men can be victims of domestic violence, it is more common for women and children to suffer from domestic abuse.[17] Resistance to such violence within the home can be confusing, difficult, and even deadly. Christian ethicist Traci C. West explains that the emotional and spiritual consequences of intimate violence and systemic violence "fuse and collide."[18] Male dominance and white supremacy, whether institutionalized through eighteenth-century chattel slavery or the twentieth-century justice system, compound the impact of intimate partner violence. West advocates careful "paying attention to women's anguish" as an essential component of theological methodology. In the stories she recounts, West identifies a pattern by which black women are not heard, not listened to, not permitted to speak out, and censored to the point of losing one's sense of self. But when a married person

---

16. See especially the chapter titled "Elements of a Mujerista Anthropology" in Ada María Isasi-Díaz, *Mujerista Theology: A Theology for the Twenty-First Century* (Maryknoll, NY: Orbis Books, 1996).

17. For recent statistics, see the Rape, Abuse, and Incest National Network (RAINN) website: https://www.rainn.org/statistics/scope-problem.

18. Traci C. West, *Wounds of the Spirit: Black Women, Violence, and Resistance Ethics* (New York: New York University Press, 1999).

is able to claim their human dignity as a child of God and recognize abuse as a violation of their dignity, God is present. In the words of M. Shawn Copeland, "Confession of sin for the wrongs committed against their bodies is a condition for the possibility of engaging the humanizing and reconciling work of Christ on behalf of our redemption."[19] We can start the process of healing by naming the sin and ensuring safety of survivors. God is present in the struggle of truth-telling. God is present when a survivor hears, "I believe you. How can I support you?"

God is present in the myriad struggles of Christian married life. When a couple chooses to sacrifice in order to care for one another and offer mutual support, the living God is present. When a mother practices resilience and hope, creatively finding a way to put food on the table or send her children to school, God is present. God is present when parents teach their children how to recognize racism and when parents empower their children to speak up and speak out against it. White people should not romanticize the pain and difficulty of resisting oppression, especially when that oppression is carried on the backs of communities of color. But it is important to recognize within a spirituality of marriage that God is present in our struggle toward freedom and resistance to oppression. These are avenues of grace. These are opportunities for believers to claim their dignity as *imago Dei*.

God in the Ordinary

A second key theme for an intersectional spirituality of marriage requires attention to the holy in the ordinary. It can seem counterintuitive to say that ordinary life is special. After all, it is ordinary! But Kathleen Norris invites Christians to reject an escapist spirituality and focus on the grace of daily life. "We want life to have meaning, we want fulfillment, healing and even ecstasy, but the human paradox is that we find these things by starting where we are, not where we wish we were. We must look for blessings to come from unlikely, everyday places—out of Galilee, as it were—and not in spectacular events, such as the coming of a comet."[20] Norris reflects on how baking bread, doing dishes, and making time for taking a shower can be moments of grace. Housework "has the power to change us," she says, because she sees in the motions of vacuuming a floor a space for prayer that can "free us, mind and heart, for the workings of the Holy Spirit."[21] Carmen, one of the women in my study, had a home altar with a statue of *La Virgen*, to

19. Copeland, *Enfleshing Freedom*, 130.

20. Kathleen Norris, *The Quotidian Mysteries: Laundry, Liturgy, and Women's Work; The 1998 Madeleva Lecture in Spirituality* (New York: Paulist Press, 1998), 12.

21. Ibid., 82. See also Emily Reimer-Barry, "Finding God in the Dishes," Catholic Moral Theology Blog, https://catholicmoraltheology.com/finding-god-in-the-dishes-gaudete-et-exsultate/.

which she would unload her burdens on a difficult day. She told me that the relief she felt after this daily spiritual practice was immensely helpful for her.

There have been many spiritual writers in the Christian tradition who have emphasized an everyday spirituality. *The Spiritual Exercises* of St. Ignatius of Loyola leads the reader through a four-week journey that ends with a heart open and vision transformed to "find God's presence in all things."[22] Jean-Pierre de Caussade's *The Sacrament of the Present Moment* emphasizes a mysticism of everyday life "based on self-giving (abandonment) to God revealed to each person in the ordinary circumstances of life" and attunement to the "sacrament of the present moment."[23] An intersectional lens invites us to give privileged consideration to voices from communities of color and other historically underrepresented groups when we consider the importance of ordinary life today. Latina, *mujerista*, and womanist scholars have much wisdom on this issue. Latina theologian Carmen Nanko-Fernández explains that *lo cotidiano* ("the daily") refers to "a dynamic mix of sin, grace, and ambiguity, of the perceived presence of God as well as of the perceived absence of the divine."[24] Isasi-Díaz, a *mujerista* theologian, explains that the food we eat, the bus we take, and how we pay for medicine are all part of *lo cotidiano*.[25] Latina feminist María Pilar Aquino emphasizes as well the "spiritual experiences of oppressed women"[26] and their "daily activities" in order to interpret them in the light of faith aimed at transformation toward greater justice.[27] Valerie Torres argues that for Latinoa communities, *la familia* is a privileged context for grace and that the intergenerational and communal nature of family life in Latinoa culture should be identified.[28] Celebrations of life amid struggles, popular religious practices, and the everyday complex realities of family life must be seen as spaces of opportunities for graced encounter. How many children would say, echoing

---

22. As quoted in Sheldrake, *Spirituality: A Brief History*, 126–30.

23. Ibid., 149–50.

24. Carmen Nanko-Fernández, "Lo Cotidiano as Locus Theologicus," in *The Wiley Blackwell Companion to Latino/a Theology*, ed. Orlando Espín (Malden, MA: Wiley-Blackwell, 2015), 16.

25. Ada María Isasi-Díaz, "Mujerista Discourse: A Platform for Latinas' Subjugated Knowledge," in *Decolonizing Epistemologies: Latino/a Theology and Philosophy*, ed. Ada María Isasi-Díaz and Eduardo Mendieta (New York: Fordham University Press, 2011), 44–67, at 50.

26. María Pilar Aquino, *Our Cry for Life: Feminist Theology from Latin America* (Maryknoll, NY: Orbis Books, 1993).

27. María Pilar Aquino, "Latina Feminist Theology: Central Features," in *A Reader in Latina Feminist Theology: Religion and Justice*, ed. María Pilar Aquino, Daisy L. Machado, and Jeanette Rodriguez (Austin: University of Texas Press, 2002), 133–60, at 152.

28. Valerie Torres, "*La Familia* as *Locus Theologicus* and Religious Education in *Lo Cotidiano*," *Religious Education* 105, no. 4 (2010): 444–61.

Matthew 25, "*Mi abuela* gave me food when I was hungry, gave me something to drink when I was thirsty, always welcomed me with a hug, made sure I had clothes to wear and reminded me to bring my jacket, took care of me when I was sick"? When grandparents and extended kinship networks provide care and support of children, family is a locus for encounter of the living God. Everyday contexts like gardening, cooking, visiting sick neighbors, bathing children, and participating in local community institutions like the library, farmers' market, community pool, and recreation center can bring people together and foster solidarity and social bonds.

Conclusion

I have proposed an intersectional spirituality of marriage, one that invites us to privilege the stories of people on the margins as they struggle for freedom and wholeness and find God in ordinary moments of daily life. An intersectional spirituality of marriage is a vision of family and community life that recognizes human interdependence and the importance of solidarity and praxis for justice. It is a hopeful vision because it claims that God cares so much about us that even the "little details" matter.[29]

29. The author would like to thank Neomi DeAnda for valuable feedback on this essay.

Chapter 11

A School for Love
Marriage as Christian Friendship

Richard Gaillardetz

There was a time, but a few generations ago, when it seemed unnecessary to give an *apologia* for Christian marriage. Marriage was widely regarded as a *desideratum* for the vast majority of young adults. Matters are a good deal different today. Some have simply abandoned the institution of marriage altogether, preferring the more flexible relational options afforded by cohabitation. Many others are choosing to delay the decision to marry indefinitely. This may be, in some ways, a welcome development for the church. The cultural shift away from marriage as a presumptive feature of adult life challenges an ecclesial complacency inclined to treat marriage as the default vocation for all but the few called to celibate priesthood or consecrated religious life. This shift away from marriage cannot be remedied by offering the single life as an alternative vocational calling. I am not convinced there is, in fact, a *vocation* to the "single life," if for no other reason than that people are single for such widely divergent reasons.[1] Some are single as an interim state, hoping to one day marry. Others wish to remain single as a permanent lifestyle choice. Still others are single by reason of divorce or the death of a spouse. I am inclined against positing a distinct "single" vocation because from a Christian theological perspective, no one is ever really "single." All of us are called to loving relationship with others. Indeed, all of us are called to a life of friendship. This presumes that human sexuality is not fundamentally oriented toward procreation

---

1. Having said this, there is still much of value in the work of theologians like Jana Bennett who offer rich theological reflections on the experience of singleness. See Jana Bennett, *Singleness and the Church: A New Theology of the Single Life* (New York: Oxford University Press, 2017).

or sexual union, as traditional Catholic teaching has so often put it, but toward the cultivation of friendship. If friendship represents our primordial vocational calling, at least as it relates to a life of holiness, then both consecrated celibacy and Christian marriage represent simply alternative "life-forms" for living a life of friendship. Sandra Schneiders sees marriage and consecrated life as complementary life-forms, both of which have public vows as "the organizational principle of their specific Christian life-form."[2] For Schneiders, consecrated religious life represents a public form of "evangelical friendship."[3] I am proposing here that marriage, in turn, represents a distinct public form of Christian friendship.

Toward a Theology of Christian Friendship

Christians hold that in baptism God invites us into a new way of life, the life of love. Yet love "is transitive," Werner Jeanrond observes. Love requires an object, even if that object is in fact a subject. We do not love in the abstract; we must love someone or something. Jeanrond writes: "Love seeks the other. Love desires to relate to the other, to get to know the other, to admire the other, to experience the other's life, to spend time with the other."[4] Perhaps the most important point to make about the call to love is that love is, from a Christian point of view, less an attitude than an actual relationship.[5] Love in this most basic sense is a call to be with and for another or others in concrete and determinate ways. It means constituting one's life practices within determinate networks of love relationships. As a concrete relationship, love will be accompanied by attitude and affect, but it is the relationship itself that is primary.

This love is realized across multiple relational registers. Central to the Christian message is our commitment to love not only those close to us but also the stranger, the other, and even our enemy. Here love is less something that we are drawn to by desire or attraction; rather, it is elicited by a faith in the other's lovability even when it is not manifest to us. Love of the unlikeable, or even our enemy, is a love based on a commitment to their intrinsic value and dignity.

Such love is basic to our Christian vocation, but it is not sufficient for human flourishing. We need more, for such love often lacks reciprocity and mutuality.

2. Sandra M. Schneiders, *Finding the Treasure* (New York: Paulist Press, 2000), 125.

3. Sandra M. Schneiders, *Selling All* (New York: Paulist Press, 2001), 295–305.

4. Werner Jeanrond, *A Theology of Love* (New York: T & T Clark, 2010), 3.

5. See Vincent Brümmer, *The Model of Love: A Study in Philosophical Theology* (Cambridge: Cambridge University Press, 1993), 33. See also Jeanrond, *A Theology of Love*, 21.

Jeanrond reminds us that not all love relationships are "symmetrical."[6] Children do not love their parents the way that parents love their children. Moreover, although the goal of mature love is an experience of mutuality, the truth is that love of the stranger or love of one's enemy is often a love that will not be returned. Thus, it is natural that we will seek out and cultivate other loves, that is, relationships characterized by fidelity, caring, commitment, tenderness, and intimacy.

Christian baptism does not simply invite us into the life of divine love; it draws into nothing less than friendship with God. In John's gospel, Jesus tells us that he no longer calls us servants but friends (John 15:15). For the Christian, friendship becomes a privileged way of imagining our relationship with God in Jesus and by the power of the Spirit. Our friendship with God grounds our capacity for authentic friendship with others even as, for many, authentic friendship with others becomes, whether noted or not, an encounter with the divine.

Jesus also becomes for us an exemplar of authentic friendship. Although there is no good evidence that Jesus was ever married, neither is there compelling evidence that Jesus formally consecrated his life to celibacy. What we do know is that Jesus needed, valued, and sought out friendships. He gave and received affection. One can assume that his friendships with Mary, Martha, and Lazarus, for example, were marked by mutuality and vulnerability. He gave to them and received from them love and affection. He wept at the news of Lazarus' death (John 11:35). The Synoptic Gospels recount his need for the company of friends during his hour of need on the night before he died (Matt 26:36-46; Mark 14:32-42; Luke 22:39-46). It is this mutual, vulnerable friendship into which Jesus invites us.

The later Christian tradition's consideration of friendship drew on these biblical themes but also on Aristotle's extensive reflections on the life of friendship. The ancient Greek philosopher recognized that there were friendships built simply on pleasure or utility, but he insisted that the most mature form of friendship was a friendship of virtue.[7] Such friendships offer deep solace and partnership; they are also a means for character formation. Through our many engagements with our friends, Aristotle contended, we gradually grow in virtue. He also privileged friendships marked by equality and mutuality. The "friendships" between a master and servant or ruler and subject could only be friendships in an analogous sense. Aristotle would exert considerable influence on later Christian thinkers' consideration of friendship.

One of the most noteworthy treatments of Christian friendship was offered by the English Cistercian monk Aelred of Rievaulx (1110–1167) in his masterpiece,

---

6. Jeanrond, *A Theology of Love*, 19.

7. Aristotle, *Nicomachean Ethics* (Indianapolis: Hackett, 1999), book 9.

Spiritual Friendship.[8] Aelred grounds the possibility of human friendship in the fact that God himself has called us into friendship. It is out of God's love and friendship that we are invited to seek out friendships with those around us. Moreover, Christ always abides in authentic Christian friendship. The monk emphasized that authentic friendship presupposed genuine reciprocity and mutuality. He insisted, then, that while we are called to love all people, we cannot realistically enter into friendship with all, at least not until the eschatological fulfillment.[9]

Like Aelred, a century later St. Thomas Aquinas would also assert that all friendship is love but not all love is friendship.[10] I need to love my enemy, but I do not necessarily need to be friends with them. Why? Because the invitation to friendship is an invitation into a particular kind of affective and vulnerable relationship marked by mutuality and commitment. Aquinas also follows Aristotle in considering marriage as a form of friendship.[11] According to Lisa Fullam, early in his career Aquinas seemed to have viewed marriage as a friendship in a more utilitarian sense, but later he would come to appreciate marriage as a deeper form of friendship, one established by the bond of virtue.[12] This emphasis on friendship as a basic framework for considering marriage would be largely neglected until the twentieth century, when it would reappear in the thought of theologians like Dietrich von Hildebrand[13] and especially in the teaching of the Second Vatican Council. In its treatment of marriage in the *Pastoral Constitution on the Church in the Modern World Today, Gaudium et Spes*, the council explores the character of marital friendship (GS 48).

The fundamental call of the Christian is to a life of generous love, yet our capacity for love requires, it would seem, the sustenance we find in genuine friendship. Christian marriage can best be understood, then, as a call to a public, sacramentally constituted life-form, Christian marital friendship. In the second half of this

8. Aelred of Rievaulx, *Spiritual Friendship*, Cistercian Studies Series (Collegeville, MN: Cistercian Publications, 2010).

9. Here I am following Jeanrond's reading of Aelred; see *A Theology of Love*, 210.

10. ST II–II 23.1c: "I answer that, According to the Philosopher (Ethic. 8.2.3) not every love has the character of friendship, but that love which is together with benevolence, when, to wit, we love someone so as to wish good to him. If, however, we do not wish good to what we love, but wish its good for ourselves, (thus we are said to love wine, or a horse, or the like), it is love not of friendship, but of a kind of concupiscence. For it would be absurd to speak of having friendship for wine or for a horse."

11. St. Thomas Aquinas, *Summa Contra Gentiles* 3, chap. 124, 4.

12. Lisa Fullam, "Toward a Virtue Ethics of Marriage: Augustine and Aquinas on Friendship in Marriage," *Theological Studies* 73 (2012): 663–92, at 682.

13. See Dietrich von Hildebrand, *Marriage: The Mystery of Faithful Love* (originally published in 1929, republished Manchester, NH: Sophia Institute, 1991).

chapter, I would like to explore some of the distinctive contours of this distinctive Christian life-form.

Reflections on Marital Friendship as a Distinct, Public Life-Form in the Church

As a way of entering into an exploration of the distinctive shape of marital friendship as a stable Christian life-form, I focus my reflections on two features of the marriage economy. The etymological root of the word "economy" is taken from the Greek *oikonomia*, a compound of *oikos* (household) and *nomos* (rule). The *oikonomia* concerns how one runs one's household. In this section, I configure my reflections around two artifacts of the marriage economy: the marriage bed and the front porch.

The Marriage Bed

The marriage bed is an obvious symbol of a distinctive feature of marital friendship, one marked by sexual intimacy. It is there that spouses come together to find solace and carnal delight in one another. Their lovemaking can be a time of erotic play and relational healing. There, a couple's mutually self-giving love can bring forth new life. The Catholic tradition has wisely affirmed the deep sacramentality of marital lovemaking. It is sacramental insofar as it serves as an effective sign of God's enduring activity throughout their marriage. But the intimacy couples may encounter there and in the course of their marriage is by no means a given. The pyrotechnics and youthful gymnastics of passionate "hook ups" bear only a distant relationship to the patient habits of marital lovemaking. Moreover, there is nothing automatically graceful and grace-filled about marital sex. Sadly, spouses can and have used sex as a weapon, a lure, a prize, or even a punishment.

The sacramentality of marital lovemaking is exhibited when it is entered into with a shared vulnerability. And that vulnerability happens only when spouses slowly and patiently allow themselves to be known and encountered as they are and not as they would like to be. It occurs when they risk sharing their deepest delights and shadowy fears with one another. The marriage bed is not a training field where one tries to perfect one's sexual moves. Marital lovemaking is not about techniques to be mastered but about the art of tender responsiveness. The risky vulnerability of two imperfect, often sagging, bodies intertwined together in their marriage bed symbolizes the real and rather messy vulnerability that authentic marital friendship itself demands.

The fragile fecundity of marital lovemaking is manifested—for many but not all, and for some determinate span in the life of a marriage, but often not its entirety—in the bringing forth of new life. Here the Catholic intuition has linked the fecundity of marital love with childbearing and child rearing. At the same time, our tradition has recognized that not every sacramental marriage will necessarily bring children into the world. Only some couples, and only for a segment of their marriage together, will be able to bear children. All marriages, however, offer the possibility to render their love generative, fecund, life-giving.

The marital friendship consummated over and over in the marriage bed draws us into the ongoing mystery that is our partner, for we have covenanted ourselves to a person of infinite depths whom we believe we have mastered only at our peril. The writer Andre Dubus insists that actually knowing our spouse, in the sense of figuring him or her out, is not as important as one might think. He observes that "we place knowing and understanding higher than love, and failing at the first two, as we sometimes must, believe we have failed at the third. Perhaps we have not."[14] Only in the space of shared vulnerability and care does the marriage bed disclose something fundamental about marital friendship. This is how we are to be for one another; two lumpy and wounded companions hobbling along a sometimes harsh and forbidding pilgrimage, receiving each other as gift, encouragement, and solace.

We must also acknowledge, however, a real danger within the Catholic tradition, namely, that of so affirming the intimacy and sacramental significance of marital lovemaking that an ideal is offered that seems unattainable to many couples. For even as we recognize the graced significance of marital lovemaking, we must also affirm its essential ordinariness. As David Matzko McCarthy has sagely observed:

> Most sex within marriage is just ordinary, a minor episode in a larger story. One set of sexual expressions may need to be redeemed by another, and can be. One-night stands and passionate affairs, in contrast, need to be earthshaking and splendid because they are the whole story. They are manic attempts to overcome the fact that there is nothing else. The true superiority of sexual intercourse in marriage is that it does not have to mean very much.[15]

McCarthy is not denying the significance of marital lovemaking. He is simply insisting that its significance is embedded in a much larger story.

Finally, the marriage bed serves as a symbol of marital friendship not only because of the intimacy, vulnerability, and fecundity it evokes but also in its invitation to embrace a certain measure of loneliness. As Ronald Rolheiser put

---

14. Andre Dubus, "On Charon's Wharf," in *Broken Vessels* (Boston: D. R. Godine, 1991), 80–81.
15. David Matzko McCarthy, *Sex and Love in the Home* (London: SCM Press, 2001), 8.

it, "It is painful to sleep alone but it is perhaps more painful to sleep alone when you are not sleeping alone."[16] There is no loneliness quite like that of a spouse lying with their partner in a shared bed when earlier that evening their partner had been deaf to their concerns, callous, or demeaning in their interactions. In marriage, from time to time, we feel as if we are sleeping with a "stranger." Marital friendship certainly offers the delight of intimacy and companionship, yet it also brings with it a loneliness, an unbidden solitude.

As I noted above, this too must be a feature of authentic friendship. The occasional experience of marital loneliness is a reminder that there is no creature, including our beloved, who will be perfectly responsive to us. There is no one who can meet all our needs, fulfill all our fantasies, understand all our hopes and fears. This intermittent loneliness, when embraced, reminds those bound in marital friendship of St. Augustine's profound prayer, "Our hearts are restless, Lord, until they rest in you."[17] There is a paschal dying in marital friendship that cannot be avoided. As Rolheiser puts it, "Paschal death is a death that, while ending one kind of life, opens the person undergoing it to receive a deeper and richer form of life. The image of the grain of wheat falling into the ground and dying so as to produce new life is an image of paschal death."[18] The periodic loneliness of authentic marital friendship, of course, is not to be confused with a loneliness that becomes the dominant script in a marriage and that, like a weak acid, slowly dissolves the bonds of love.

I once gave a retreat for priests in which I reflected on celibacy and marriage as complementary paths to holiness. I spoke of both the distinct features of each path and what they shared in common. I proposed to the retreatants that one of the spiritual advantages of authentic married life is that each morning you wake up next to someone telling you to get over yourself! In other words, authentic marital friendship is inevitably a summons to conversion.

In her memoir, *Ordinary Time: Cycles in Marriage, Faith, and Renewal*, Nancy Mairs offers brutally honest reflections on the challenges she and her husband faced in their marriage as they confronted both serious illnesses and serial infidelities. Mairs saw her marriage as, at its core, an invitation to conversion:

> This [the marriage commitment] was, and has remained, the paradigmatic conversion, infinitely more powerful and penetrating than anything connected with

16. Ronald Rolheiser, *The Holy Longing: The Search for a Christian Spirituality* (New York: Doubleday, 1999), 196.

17. St. Augustine, *Confessions*, book 1, chapter 1.

18. Rolheiser, *The Holy Longing*, 146.

exclusively religious conviction or practice. I might have found another way to God. I might have found a better way to God. But I did not. My spirit has been schooled in wedlock.[19]

This linkage of marriage and conversion is striking. The biblical word for conversion, *metanoia*, means not just a shift in one's views or opinions but a fundamental change in direction. Marital friendship, Mairs contends, calls forth change at the very core of one's being. The marriage bed becomes, then, not just a symbol of marriage, intimacy, and fecundity but a concrete expression of the Christian demand for ongoing conversion. A commitment to share a bed with another marks either the acceptance of a summons to lifelong conversion or a sentence to a lifetime of indifference, loneliness, and alienation.

We recalled above Aristotle's conviction that authentic friendship involves two people schooling one another in the life of virtue. This virtuous life extends well beyond the daily interactions among spouses. Christian marital friendship schools us in our engagements with our children, our extended family, our neighbors, and indeed the larger world. It is with this schooling in one's worldly engagements that we can now turn to a second marital artifact illuminating the distinctive shape of marital friendship, the front porch of a home.

The Front Porch as Threshold

One can learn a great deal about the changing contours of North American social life from basic architectural shifts. Once upon a time, in rural and suburban America, it was not uncommon to see homes constructed around a capacious front porch that would serve as an access point to the larger community. Even in urban settings the front stoop would function in a similar way. These familial structures featured the porch or stoop as a kind threshold, a passage way between the security and intimacy of the home and the concerns of the larger community. The front porch allowed one to engage passersby, one and all, and in this way strengthened the fabric of the local community.

Today, the front porch appears less frequently in the new construction of single residence homes. Indeed, in much of suburban America it has been replaced by the fenced-in backyard deck. There, a family is free to be more selective in their social engagement. Invited guests share in a social life conducted within the privacy maintained by tall backyard fences.

---

19. Nancy Mairs, *Ordinary Time: Cycles in Marriage, Faith, and Renewal* (Boston: Beacon Press, 1993), 106.

The front porch, remains, however, an apt symbol for a much-overlooked teaching of the Second Vatican Council regarding the ecclesial character of Christian marriage and family. The council identifies the family as the primary social cell of society. It is to be "a school for a richer humanity" (GS 52).[20] And while there are undoubtedly many Christian families not constituted by marriage, all Christian marriages are, by that very fact, families, that is, domestic churches called to participate in a vital way in the mission of the church:

> Since the Creator established matrimonial union as the starting point and foundation in human society and by his grace made it a great sacrament in Christ and in the church, the apostolate of married people and of families is of the greatest importance both for the church and for civil society. . . . The family received from God the mission to be the primary living cell of society. It can fulfill this mission by showing itself, in the mutual loyalty of its members and in shared prayer offered to God, to be like a domestic sanctuary in the church; when the whole family is involved together in the liturgy; and when it offers generous hospitality and promotes justice and other good works in the service of the needy. (AA 11)

The council recognizes the intrinsic ecclesiality of Christian marriage and family, not only because of the possibilities for shared prayer, or the presence in the home of crucifixes and religious statuary, but because Christian families share in the church's mission in the world. To write of the family as a domestic church, as Vatican II did, risks reducing the Christian household to a kind of spiritual refuge, an ecclesial "oasis" from a hostile world. This is why the image of the front porch as a "threshold" point for married couples and all Christian families is worthy of our reflection. The front porch evokes the essential link between a life of intimacy and vital public obligations. It further highlights the public character of the marital friendship as a distinct life-form. Recalling the front porch as a threshold between home and the larger world summons the married couple away from any narcissistic preoccupation with one another and toward their obligations to put their marital friendship in the service of others. This missional orientation is ritualized in the Catholic nuptial liturgy at the conclusion of which the married couple processes, side by side, through the gathered community and out the church doors in service to the world. This service happens whenever the household remains mindful of

---

20. The English language translations of the Second Vatican Council's documents are taken from Norman Tanner, ed., *The Decrees of the Ecumenical Councils*, vol. 2 (Washington, DC: Georgetown University Press, 1990).

one's deep societal and global belonging through familial habits that encourage solidarity with and care for others.[21]

To speak of the threshold quality of marital friendship, this dynamic movement back and forth between marital intimacy and marital service to society, is not unique to marital friendship. There are many nonmarital friendships, indeed, that are forged in the midst of lives of service and that nourish and sustain that service. The claim here is only that this threshold quality, this movement from interpersonal intimacy to public service is, or should be, an intrinsic feature of Christian marital friendship.

Conclusion

In this chapter, I have sketched out several features of a spirituality of Christian marriage that grounds marriage in the challenges and possibilities of authentic Christian friendship. The distinctive yet primordial drive of human sexuality is not just a drive toward sex and procreation. It is a drive toward authentic human friendship. Within this fundamental calling to a life of friendship, marriage finds its appropriate place as a particular kind of friendship, one that is sacramentally constituted and, much like the evangelical friendship of consecrated religious life, is distinctly configured by public vows. It is a form of Christian friendship that "schools" us by way of ongoing conversion into the life of Christian discipleship. The intimacy, fecundity, and, yes, loneliness of marital friendship are all invoked in the image of the marriage bed. Yet marital friendship has a fundamentally outward-looking character as well. The image of the front porch evokes that aspect of Christian marital friendship that calls the couple out of the safety of the domicile into engagement with the world. As such, the married couple is drawn into the mission of the church to serve the coming reign of God.

---

21. Here Julie Hanlon Rubio's work on family ethics is particularly helpful. See Julie Hanlon Rubio, *Family Ethics: Practices for Christians* (Washington, DC: Georgetown University Press, 2010).

Chapter 12

Learning to Dwell with the Beloved

The Wisdom of the Marriage Liturgy

Timothy P. O'Malley

In Augustine's *De vera religion* (On True Religion), the doctor of grace asserts that Christianity is distinct from pagan philosophy insofar as it unites the pursuit of wisdom and the cultic act. In a sermon to his congregation in Hippo, Augustine develops this line of thought through the eucharistic exhortation "lift up your heart" (*sursum cor*).[1] The *sursum cor* is a summary of Christian philosophy, a confession by the human person that she is made for worshipful wisdom. This worshipful wisdom, for St. Augustine, is the manner in which the Christian reflects on the practice of worship as it relates to every part of human life.

The church refers to this practice of worshipful wisdom as mystagogy. Mystagogy means leading a Christian more deeply into the mysteries of Christian faith through reflection on the rites of the church. As Jean Corbon writes in his *The Wellspring of Worship*, "The search for the meaning of our celebrations is extremely important, for it controls our discovery of the meaning of the liturgy in our lives. If we do not find the meaning of our celebrations, they risk becoming moments that are increasingly meaningless and unrelated to life."[2] Worshipful wisdom or mystagogy has the potential to renew the imagination, changing the way that human beings both interpret and live within the world.

In this essay, I will reflect on the marriage or nuptial liturgy of the church to discern how attention to the rite can inform a way of love that enables the

---

1. Augustine, Sermon 331, in *Sermons—III/9*, trans. Edmund Hill (New York: New City Press, 1994), 331.3.

2. Jean Corbon, *The Wellspring of Worship* (San Francisco: Ignatius Press, 2005), 143.

flourishing of the human person. Love, as many people experience it, is not re-ducible to a fleeting experience of affective intoxication. Instead, love is the slow process by which the human person learns to dwell in fidelity with one's beloved. The worshipful wisdom of the wedding liturgy is a commitment to an abiding friendship with this person, grounded in a relationship with Jesus Christ. Thus, love is not a communion oriented only to the well-being of individual selves. The sacrament of marriage is ordered to the transformation of society through the practice of a mundane love that infuses daily life.

The Discontents of Modern Love

As noted, the experience of love is often overpowering. We know what it means to "fall in love," to have our world shaken to the core by the presence of our beloved. When I first met the woman who would become my spouse, I wanted to spend *every* moment in her presence. When apart, we talked on the phone for hours.

This way of experiencing love is unsustainable over the course of a lifetime. Through the genre of the romantic comedy, we might see this impossibility as a problem. True love should be defined by passionate desire. If married couples find themselves lacking passion, no longer pining for each other throughout the day, then the flame of love has been quenched. This "loveless" couple must reclaim this desire through a romantic vacation or a new commitment to passionate sex. At the very least, they should go out on a date to a fancy restaurant where they can gaze into each other's eyes while dining on *foie gras* and sipping champagne. And there's always lingerie.

Where does this assumption come from? Men and women have not always seen love as an all-consuming passion for one's beloved. In her study of the transforma-tion of love in the modern age, Eva Illouz provides a genealogy of passionate love at least among the upper middle class. Through a careful reading of Victorian novels, Illouz sees love in the nineteenth century as related to the mutual recognition of character rather than two selves engaged in the pursuit of exuberant passion. To fall in love was to recognize the goodness of another person as one entered into the social world of one's beloved. This premodern account of love is characterized by "attachment and habit," unfolding over the course of time and familiarity with the beloved's family.[3]

---

3. Eva Illouz, *Why Love Hurts: A Sociological Explanation* (New York: Polity Press, 2012), 24.

Love takes time because "falling in love" requires an assessment of the character of one's beloved. It is not a private affair because union has implications for family and society. Courtship was a ritual process in premodern love, ordered by rules that facilitated the encounter between the couple, their families, and their friends. In this world, women and men discovered the presence of love through the process of becoming familiar with another person. The goal of marriage was a permanent union where this mutual goodness would be formative of both parties.

In contrast, love in the modern age is characterized by affective epiphanies. To "fall in love" is to share everything with one's beloved. Every thought, every feeling should become an object of conversation. This conversation fans the insatiable passion for one's beloved. This means that love will necessarily include intense friction. In romantic comedies, such love includes arguments, fights, and a passionate tension that often climaxes with a sexual encounter. No one wants to date or sleep with a boring person. If one is in a relationship and discovers a growing passion for another person, then the only responsible thing to do is pursue the new relationship. Commitment be damned! We're talking about happiness, the authentic cultivation of a self in union with another self. It is not character or commitment that is the basis of assessing love but compatibility.[4]

Think for a moment about dating websites or apps. Potential lovers meet through a quantified algorithm dedicated to assessing compatibility. Do you both like to hike? Are you interested in sports or classical music concerts? Are you readers of *The Wall Street Journal* or *The New York Times*? What is your ideal date? If matches don't share these things in common, then the relationship is presumed to be a failure waiting to happen. In modern love, we break up with one another because "we weren't compatible." Such compatibility enters into the bedroom where we have developed tests for sexual compatibility. Do you like how he smells? Do you both like kinkiness? How hot are you for each other's bodies?

The focus on sexual compatibility is related to another facet of modern love—sexual attractiveness. Advertising and film in the mid-nineteenth century created what Illouz calls a "canon of erotic allure."[5] This canon is well known to each of us. If we turn to Hollywood blockbusters and Instagram influencers, we recognize this canon that proposes the ideal male and female bodies. This canon proposes to us that youthful flesh, not the aged body, is the norm for romantic compatibility.

At the same time, popular psychology formed us to presume that a healthy, active sex life was integral to human happiness. The self is happiest when the self is sexually fulfilled. Illouz writes, "Psychology put sex and sexuality on both ends of

4. Ibid., 39.
5. Ibid., 45.

the narrative temporal line constituting the story of a self; one's past and one's future now revolved around sex and sexuality. The self not only told to itself its story as a sexual story, but it made sexuality itself . . . into the *telos* of this narrative."[6] The happy life is the search for the sexually fulfilled life. This is why magazines like *Cosmopolitan* feature article after article presenting the sexual positions that will "blow his mind" (and yours too). It's why drugs like Viagra are so popular among men, advertised during NFL games. What would it mean to be a man or woman who isn't defined by sexual arousal? Is there any worth to our life if every orgasm of our beloved is not mind-blowing?

This approach to modern love has harmed our capacity for commitment. In the premodern era, commitment was part of this mark of character. Commitment, as Illouz notes, "implies a specific capacity to project the self into the future, the capacity to stop the process of searching and decision-making by forgoing the possibility of better prospects."[7] Modern love replaces commitment with the romantic fantasy of the soul mate. There is one person out there in the world, somewhere, who can fulfill every one of my desires. In finding this person, we will find our true selves. The soul mate theory offered by film, television, and music depends not on an external commitment to a person but on the hope that someone can fulfill me forever. The emphasis is on the self, rather than gift of the person.

This reduction of romance to self-fulfilling experiences brackets out the importance of permanent kinship in love. There are no objective, enduring ties between the beloved other than the desiring self. What matters is affinity rather than kinship. Kinship is the recognition that love comes with roles and responsibilities. One now has specific obligations to this person. If the marriage also produces children, then there are additional obligations. When kinship is replaced by affinity, human flourishing no longer involves sticking around or entering into a long-term relationship at all. As Polish sociologist Zygmunt Bauman notes, kinship depends on "the readiness to pay the price . . . in the hard currency of day-in, day-out drudgery. When the willingness . . . is missing, one would be inclined to think twice before acting on the intention."[8]

Is this movement toward love as self-fulfillment a positive or negative development? Perhaps the ties that bound us to one another were sources of oppression rather than liberation? Illouz notes that the transformation of love in the modern age allowed for a newfound freedom in romance, outside the bounds of class

6. Ibid., 46.

7. Ibid., 98.

8. Zygmunt Bauman, *Liquid Love: On the Fragility of Human Bonds* (Malden, MA: Blackwell, 2003), 29.

consciousness. Through a new category of romance—dominated by sexiness—it becomes possible to bypass the class restrictions that once governed relationships. The 1990 film *Pretty Woman* offers an image of this transformation. A young woman hired for sex can enter into the life of a rich, elite businessman and transition from being an object of erotic desire to becoming a beloved partner. Advertising for the film underlined this possibility: "She walked off the street, into his life, and stole his heart." Of course, *Pretty Woman*, like all romantic comedies, must end before Julia Roberts and Richard Gere experience a major disagreement over where to send their kid to kindergarten.

Despite the accompanying freedom of modern love, the transition from ritualized courtship to self-discovery through compatibility has its problems. Illouz writes:

> Social worth is no longer a straightforward outcome of one's economic or social status, but has to be derived from one's self, defined as a unique, private, personal, and non-institutional entity. The erotic-romantic bond must constitute a sense of worth, and modern social worth is chiefly performative: that is, it is to be achieved in the course of and through one's interactions with others. If the lover, preparing to meet the beloved, worries about his smell, his clothes, his hair, his plans for the evening, and *ultimately his worthiness* . . . it is because, in modernity, love has become central to the constitution of worth.[9]

Rejection is no longer a matter of being a poor fit for a potential match. Rejection is related to the very self. If I'm not beloved by this man or this woman, am I worthy of love at all? Such confusion of love and worth has only increased in the digital age. Apps like Tinder enable men and women to present an idealized self to a potential romantic or at least sexual partner. One knows oneself, configures the self, as an object of desire. The mechanics of using Tinder—swiping right when wanting to meet up, swiping left otherwise—fosters this confusion between self-worth and love. The person becomes disposable or swappable if there isn't a match, if there isn't sexual compatibility. They disappear from one's feed, and from one's life, because of a micro-second reaction to a hyper-stylized avatar.

The rejected self enters into a new space of insecurity. The self needs constant signs of love, of desirability, in order to sustain proper self-worth. If something goes wrong in a relationship, if there is rejection, then the blame lies with the spurned lover rather than the one who has left the relationship. "What could I have done differently?" asks the spurned lover.

9. Illouz, *Why Love Hurts*, 119.

Illouz's genealogy of modern love is instantiated in what has become known as hookup culture. In her own work on hookup culture, Donna Freitas argues that a hookup has three dimensions: some kind of sexual intimacy, brevity, and avoiding emotional attachment.[10] Based on the genealogy of modern love above, one may hypothesize that a hookup culture characterized by brief, uncommitted sexual encounters has less to do with changing sexual values and more with the performance of a cultural script that allows men and women to participate in "romance" within the domain of affinity rather than kinship. One has the freedom to relate to another, sort of, without making any commitment beyond the hookup. Sex without the ties that bind allows the self to experience fulfillment without the additional worry of wondering whether this person may be "the one." They're at least "the one" right now. One can feel worthy, become an object of desire, and then quickly move on with the rest of one's life. Whether this is actually how hooking up works is another story.[11] But it does seem to be a strategy of dealing with the perils of love in the modern age.

Freitas believes that the way of addressing hookup culture is through critical engagement with what constitutes "good sex." The "bad sex" of hookup culture teaches men and women "to shove their desires deep down into a dark place, to be revealed to no one."[12] Colleges and universities have a responsibility to challenge the assumption that "bad sex" is the only type of sex that is possible. Through critical engagement with academic literature around sex, one can propose "good sex." "Good sex" is determined by the individual student, who comes to recognize what is "good sex" for the individual self. It could be a hookup, no sex at all, or sex in the context of a long-term relationship.

Notice how Freitas's account of sex depends on the isolated self as described by Illouz. There is dialogue with academic literature, but it is the self who is the determining agent. Illouz demonstrates how much our understanding of love is shaped by social forces that the self cannot recognize with ease. The self is not always free to think critically, without engaging in the difficult task of reforming the imagination.

This renewal of the imagination through practice is pivotal to the philosopher James K. A. Smith's proposal for Christian discipleship. Discipleship is not something that is learned through ideas alone. Rather, it involves new practices,

---

10. Donna Freitas, *The End of Sex: How Hookup Culture Is Leaving a Generation Unhappy, Sexually Unfulfilled, and Confused About Intimacy* (New York: Basic Books, 2013), 25.

11. Jason King, *Faith with Benefits: Hookup Culture on Catholic Campuses* (New York: Oxford University Press, 2017), 5–6.

12. Freitas, *The End of Sex*, 182.

new habits that offer a narrative relative to human flourishing. He writes, "We adopt ways of life that are indexed to such visions of the good life, not usually because we 'think through' our options but rather because some picture captures our imagination."[13] In a hookup culture, the "pictures" that have captured our imagination are drawn from Illouz's account of modern love: the fulfillment of the self through romance, the precarious quality to commitment, and the emphasis on sexual attraction. If one is to move beyond some of the negative features of modern love, it requires learning a new story about sex, love, and dating. The marriage liturgy in Catholicism is one such source for this renewal, moving a person from an understanding of love grounded in passionate desire to one of faithful commitment.

The Wisdom of the Marriage Rite

Having taught a course on the history of the sacrament of marriage at the University of Notre Dame since 2016, I have been surprised to discover interest in Catholicism's nuptial rite. This interest is expressed by students who are not religious, who reject Catholicism's teaching on divorce, homosexuality, and contraception. They're still interested in what the practice of marriage within this religious tradition reveals about love. And they want to use the rite, and its understanding of the sacrament, as a way of offering an alternative vision of love separate from hookup culture.

The *Order of Celebrating Matrimony* has been especially beneficial for the students in class. Many of them enter the course presuming that the church's marriage "ceremony" is the vehicle through which they'll express subjective passion for one another in the presence of family and friends. Yet, there is something about studying the rite that transforms their understanding of love.[14] Students come to see how the various moments of the rite are not about the affirmation of passionate love shared between the couple. Instead, in the rite of marriage, they come to see the gift of an objective bond of love that transcends the couples' subjective affections. They see that the rite underlines a commitment to a concrete, human being through the assistance of God's grace. This grace-filled bond of love now informs every dimension of the couple's life with one another.

---

13. James K. A. Smith, *You Are What You Love: The Spiritual Power of Habit* (Grand Rapids: Brazos Press, 2016), 11.

14. For a fuller account of this rite as a source of worshipful wisdom, see Timothy P. O'Malley, *Off the Hook: God, Love, Dating, and Marriage in a Hookup World* (Notre Dame, IN: Ave Maria Press, 2018).

How does the rite of marriage facilitate this transformation of the student's understanding of love? First, students begin to see how the church views love as connected to society from the beginning. The first public words spoken during the rite are not to the couple but to those gathered to witness the rite:

> We have come rejoicing into the house of the Lord
> for this celebration, dear brothers and sisters,
> and now we stand with N. and N.
> on the day they intend to form a home of their own.
> For them this is a moment of unique importance.
> So let us support them
> with our affection,
> with our friendship,
> and with our prayer as their brothers and sisters.[15]

The communal dimension of love establishes the final end of marriage. The couple has not gathered to profess their unique love for each other. Instead, the rite underlines that marriage is oriented toward the formation of a home. Homes within the Christian imagination are not private spheres, closed communities in which one lives a life apart from one's neighbors.[16] Family and friends have something at stake in the lifelong commitment of the couple.

I often share with my students the great gift of the social dimension to marriage. If my spouse and I were to rely entirely on the category of compatibility, of self-completion, our marriage would have ended quickly after my wife discovered that I leave socks in random places around our home. The opening exhortation of the rite underscores that love is not private but has a public dimension from the very beginning. This is not because the church sticks its nose in private affairs that are none of its business. Instead, it recognizes that to be human is to always depend on other relationships. The myth of the isolated monad, the individual self encountering other selves, is just that—a myth.

Second, students are fascinated with the act of consent, what constitutes the "form" of the sacrament in the Roman Catholic rite of marriage. As college students, they're used to the language of consent. As first-year students at Notre Dame, they receive training in the need to assess sexual consent in every intimate encounter. They're used to asking for consent before any act of intimacy. At the

---

15. *The Order of Celebrating Matrimony: Second Edition* (Collegeville, MN: Liturgical Press, 2016), 52.

16. David Matzko McCarthy, *Sex and Love in the Home: A Theology of the Household*, 2nd ed. (London: SCM Press, 2004), 91.

same time, most are dissatisfied with discussions around consent. They're aware that these conversations presume a cognitive awareness that many individuals involved in sexual encounters do not possess. They're conscious of the complications of consent on college campuses, how they often feel "pressured" to give consent in order to stay in a relationship. They worry about the freedom of any act of consent.

I suspect that this is why they're fascinated with the church's language of consent. In the rite, the church requires that the couple demonstrate the freedom of their consent to one another. Has there been coercion in their decision? Do they know what they're promising? These questions in the rite presume that the couple have had these conversations with each other, with friends, families, and ministers. They're aware that the act of love is not about self-fulfillment but about the affirmation of fidelity to this person for as long as one lives. There is a sobriety to the church's understanding of love that the students find refreshing. They don't need to enter marriage sure that this person is the only human being who could ever fulfill me. They don't need to worry about "perfect" compatibility. They do need to enter into the consent freely, to see that marriage is a lifelong commitment to this person.

The act of consent (or the marriage vows) are of particular interest to the students. In comparison with the often informal and lengthy professions of eternal love presented in film, the church's vows are brief. They say nothing about the interior life of the couple or compatibility. The vows state:

> I, N., take you N., to be my husband/wife.
> I promise to be faithful to you,
> in good times and in bad,
> in sickness and in health,
> to love you and to honor you
> all the days of my life.[17]

In speaking the name of one's beloved, one pledges not to an experiment in self-fulfillment but to the love of *this exact one*. One professes this love not because one's beloved is intelligent, witty, sexy, a good singer, or an excellent mother- or father-to-be. The pledge of love is given simply because this person exists, because this person is worthy of love.

The church is not starry-eyed about this consent. Consent takes place in a world of contingency. There are good times and bad times. Nonetheless, the fidelity that one pledges is not dependent on such contingencies. If one's spouse

---

17. *The Order of Celebrating Matrimony*, 62.

contracts Alzheimer's or pancreatic cancer, you don't just leave. One is to care for one's spouse until the very end.

That these words are given by the church to the couple matters. They're not constructed by independent selves, seeking to express fidelity in their own unique way. They come as gift. Husband and wife must conform their own voices to a pledge of love that comes from outside of their individual affections.

Theologically, the church believes that this act of consent creates an indissoluble bond between the couple. There is something outside the individual wills that now orient the mutual love of the spouses. Such a pledge of love cannot be made through sheer human effort of two individuals who like each other. In this act of consent, it is Jesus Christ who speaks through the words of the spouses. The grace of divine love, the self-giving love shared between Christ and the church, becomes the defining narrative of the couple. This transformation is not automatic. The couple must attune themselves to this love for the rest of their days. The bestowal of a wedding ring, given in the name of the Trinity, is a visible sign of this bond of love. The ring, as it shapes the hands of the couple, changes their very bodily identity. They are "marked" for the rest of their days by this act of fidelity.

Third, the students are often attracted by the lifelong and sometimes mundane dimension of this transformation. The liturgy of marriage is not just a moment along the way but comes to transform every dimension of the couple's lives. As Marc Cardinal Ouellet writes about the moment of consent:

> The mutual "yes" expressed verbally in the liturgical celebration is then translated into the "language of the body," that is . . . into the spouses' shared life, daily fidelity, friendship, reciprocal forgiveness, fecundity, education, etc. The sacramental sign prolonged itself in time. The spiritual act of self-gift "in the Lord" enriched by the redemptive power of God and the salvific action of the Church, establishes the *couple* as a permanent sacrament and transforms its history into salvation history—in other words, into a sign that bears the gift of God to his people.[18]

The language of translation is important. The pledge of fidelity is not given in a moment of exuberant self-expression. It is lived out through the entirety of the couple's life: the formation of a home, the procreation and raising of children, worship and friendship, and the promotion of a more just society.

---

18. Marc Cardinal Ouellet, *Mystery and Sacrament of Love: A Theology of Marriage and the Family for the New Evangelization*, trans. Michelle K. Borras and Adrian J. Walker (Grand Rapids: Eerdmans, 2015), 70.

Of course, sex is part of this "translation" into the language of the body. But, it's not sex understood as a passionate transformation of the self. Sex now exists in a new narrative, a story of fidelity and commitment, in which life is shared in common with one another. Sex is a sign of a bodily commitment to a concrete person that can be expressed in myriad ways. Sometimes it's far sexier to empty the dishwasher than to purchase exotic lingerie.

In this sense, students discover that the worshipful wisdom of the matrimonial rite is the invitation to take up a common life with another person, to become a family through kinship, a communion of love governed not by the logic of power and prestige, fame and fortune, but by the self-giving love of Jesus Christ.

Conclusion

The wedding rite of the church may function as a source of wisdom for the human person seeking to find love in our age. Modern love is characterized by passion, authenticity, compatibility, sexual fulfillment, and a social imagination inspired more by romantic comedies than the mundane life shared in families, homes, and neighborhoods. Deeper reflection on the nuptial rites can provide a new imaginary for thinking about love. This imaginary is based in a faithful, lifelong commitment to a contingent person. Through this sharing of a new form of life, in Christ, the couple becomes a living sign of God's fidelity for the human family.

Chapter 13

Valuing Family Care
Love and Labor

Sandra Sullivan-Dunbar

The Catholic tradition has long understood procreation to be one of the goods of marriage and sexuality. In fact, for most of the history of the Catholic moral tradition, procreation was understood as the preeminent good of marriage and the primary justification for sexual expression. Not every family includes children, of course, and families today as in times past take many different forms. Nevertheless, one widely shared function of families is reproduction and the raising of children. Families are a place where dependent human beings receive needed love and care.

Families, however, are also *economies*. Families are economies *because* they are primary locations for the work of care for children, frail elderly persons, sick persons, and persons with disabilities. Care is an expression of love and compassion, but it is also embodied labor, sometimes very physical labor. And because we are needy, embodied beings, care has a material, economic aspect: care provides others with food, clothing, and shelter.

The idea of the family as an economy may strike some readers as problematic. We are not used to thinking of families in economic terms. The realities of love, sex, and care that are central to families are precisely the sort of things we may wish to protect from commodification. But if we fail to see the economic aspect of the family, we cannot fulfill the vision of Catholic social thought: achievement of the common good, in which every human person possesses the prerequisites of flourishing.[1]

---

1. In *Mater et Magistra* 65, Pope John XXIII defined the common good as "the sum total of those conditions of social living, whereby men are enabled more fully and more readily to achieve their own perfection."

We should shift our view of the family to see it as an economy by taking two steps. First, we should broaden our understanding of "economy" to encompass more than markets. Some economists have suggested that we reclaim aspects of an earlier understanding of economics as "provisioning"—providing sustenance via paid employment and market transactions *as well as* the work of sustaining life that is done within the household and via caregiving relationships.[2]

Second, we must make peace with the reality that much care is mediated through the market—and accept that this flexibility to pay for care, or to provide care for pay, is appropriate and necessary. Today, the family economy intersects in complex ways with the market economy, at local, national, and global levels. Most families purchase most of the goods they need to sustain family members rather than producing them. In addition, domestic tasks and various forms of dependent care are provided through a combination of paid and unpaid work. Most parents have paid for child care. Health care is provided via a complex mix of hospital, outpatient, and home care. Frail elderly persons and persons with disabilities often receive care from paid home care workers, often in combination with care from family members. The care economy is now a global economy: 70.8 percent of paid domestic workers in the United States are migrants.[3]

Once we view the family as an economy, we can ask how to support families in doing the care work that is essential to the common good. I argue that Catholics and Catholic social thought should explicitly acknowledge that, in a marketized global economy, nonmarket caring labor should be subsidized by governments. Otherwise, it will be impossible for all to enjoy the prerequisites of flourishing that comprise the Catholic vision of the common good.

Historical Changes to the Care Economy

Today, when we think of "the economy," we generally think of markets, but the economy was not always understood in this way. Prior to the processes of industrialization and global commercialization that began in Europe in the second half of the eighteenth century, *oeconomy* referred to household stewardship, or managing the resources and labor of the household so that all could have their needs met.

2. Julie A. Nelson, "The Study of Choice or the Study of Provisioning? Gender and the Definition of Economics," in *Beyond Economic Man: Feminist Theory and Economics*, ed. Marianne A. Ferber and Julie A. Nelson (Chicago: University of Chicago Press, 1993), 23–36.

3. International Labour Organization, "ILO Global Estimates on Migrant Workers: Results and Methodology (Special Focus on Migrant Domestic Workers)," 2015, https://www.ilo.org/wcmsp5/groups/public/---dgreports/---dcomm/documents/publication/wcms_436343.pdf.

Most economic production occurred within the household: agricultural work, home-based manufacturing or trades, textiles, and child rearing. In this stage of economic development, children became economic assets at a relatively young age: they could help with whatever activities the family engaged in for sustenance.

As factories were established, more work moved outside the home, and the contemporary distinction between "home" and "work" began to emerge. Economic and political thinkers began to assign different fundamental motives to the home and to the outside world. Home was seen as the place of altruistic other-regard; economics and politics were understood to be driven by regulated self-interest. And these assignments of distinct motives were gendered, as women more often managed domestic labor and men were more likely to work outside the home. Out of these distinctions has grown our discomfort with mixing love and money—a discomfort we must confront if we are to treat caregivers and dependents with justice and dignity.[4]

Today we live in a global market economy. The care economy still exists—care, after all, is central to human life in all periods of human history—but today the care economy takes a more complex form. Arguably, care needs are more demanding today than in the past. To prepare for participation in the contemporary economy, children in the United States and most industrialized nations go to school for many years. If you are an undergraduate reading this chapter, you are well aware that parents and college students themselves make great financial sacrifices to obtain the education necessary to participate fully in our advanced economy. If you lived in a less-developed economy or in an earlier period in economic history, you would likely have finished with your education long ago and already be contributing to the economic support of your family. Children are usually the great joy of their parents, but they are not an economic boon in today's economy! In addition, advances in health care have led to longer life spans: today, more people live long enough to require intensive care in old age.

Our reluctance to view care as economic facilitates injustice to caregivers. We do not include unpaid care in our primary measures of the economy or recognize caregiving as a major contributor to overall social well-being. Because we do not adequately value care, caregivers and dependents are treated unjustly. Responsibility for caregiving is often allocated to marginalized persons under exploitative conditions. While Catholic social thought possesses some resources to recognize and address these injustices, most thinkers in the Catholic moral tradition have

---

4. For more on these historical developments, see Sandra Sullivan-Dunbar, *Human Dependency and Christian Ethics* (Cambridge: Cambridge University Press, 2017), especially chapters 2 and 3.

not, so far, drawn on these resources to develop an understanding of the family economy that promotes a Catholic understanding of the common good.[5]

Measuring the Care Economy

How did we come to neglect care labor in our understandings of the economy? In the late eighteenth century, as more work moved outside the home and more of it was done in exchange for wages, the new discipline of classical economics emerged, and economists tried to understand how to measure economic activity. The easiest way to do this was by measuring the exchange of money—market transactions. But this left questions about how to measure the value of unpaid labor. If money does not change hands, how do we know how much labor is worth? Early economists openly wondered what to do about the fact that the work of a person paid to do household labor would be counted as economic activity, while a family member doing the same work without pay would not be counted.[6]

To grasp this dilemma in contemporary terms, note that if a mother stays home with her child for two years, and then puts him into a day care center, the Gross Domestic Product increases, even though the same amount of labor is being done (the child is receiving care eight hours a day from a paid child-care worker instead of from the mother). Money now changes hands, in the form of the child-care worker's wages, and this transaction is captured in the GDP. When the care was performed by the mother without pay, it was invisible as labor, from the perspective of GDP. For the most part, early economists dismissed this dilemma. They presumed that women were "naturally" suited to and willing to perform the work of care regardless of whether anyone measured it or paid for it. And of course, many mothers are willing to go to extraordinary lengths to care for their children, paid or unpaid. Failing to measure this labor, however, fundamentally distorts economists' accounts of economic activity and growth.

In an international context, the need to recognize unpaid labor may be even more urgent. This is because in less-developed countries, a higher proportion of economic activity is unpaid, whether that be caregiving, subsistence agriculture, or collecting water or firewood. In recent decades, social scientists have developed methods to measure unpaid labor. For example, we now have time-use studies, in which a sample of a population is asked to record their activity in fifteen-minute

---

5. There are a few notable exceptions. See, for example, Christine Firer Hinze, *Glass Ceilings and Dirt Floors: Women, Work, and the Global Economy* (New York: Paulist Press, 2015).

6. See, for example, Alfred Marshall, *Principles of Economics: An Introductory Volume*, 8th ed. (New York: MacMillan, 1948 [1890]), 564.

increments throughout the day. We can then see the time they spend growing food for their own family to survive, or caring for children or a sick or disabled family member, even though neither the food nor care is bought or sold. Such studies can supplement the usual market measures of economic activity to give a better picture of production and exchange in a country.

Unpaid labor is a very large part of most economies. One study found that in twenty-six OECD (Organization for Economic Cooperation and Development) countries and three emerging economies, "between one-third and one-half of all valuable economic activity . . . is not accounted for in traditional measures of well-being, such as GDP per capita."[7] In every one of these countries, the majority of this work was done by women.

Time-use studies have demonstrated problems with current models of development aid. For example, international lending organizations such as the World Bank or the International Monetary Fund make loans to developing countries but have often required that these countries cut back on government spending on education, health care, and child care in order to get the loans. The idea is that reduced government spending and a reduced tax burden will boost the economy—but here the economy is understood only in terms of market transactions. Time-use studies show that after government cuts, the work of education, child care, and health care continues (since it is necessary to life!) but it continues as unpaid labor, and it is primarily done by women, on top of the work they were already doing.[8] Such changes can be counterproductive for a country's long-term economic development. In addition, they are harmful to the people who take on additional work and to those in need of care who may get less care.

Failure to Recognize Unpaid Care Leads to Injustice

The failure to recognize and value such a large portion of human labor causes injustice to caregivers and dependents. I have just described one form of this injustice: when countries cut government support for care activities, those involved in the care economy are harmed. Let me briefly mention three more interrelated forms of injustice.

7. Miranda Veerle, "Cooking, Caring, and Volunteering: Unpaid Work Around the World," *OECD Social, Employment, and Migration Working Papers*, no. 116 (Paris, France: OECD Publishing, 2011), doi: 10.1787/5kghrjm8s142-en.

8. Debbie Budlender, ed., *Time Use Studies and Unpaid Care Work* (New York: Routledge/ UNRISD Research in Gender and Development, 2010).

First, unpaid care performed for other family members makes it more difficult for the caregiver to participate on equal footing in the paid employment market, and this contributes significantly to salary differentials between men and women and significantly lower lifetime and retirement earnings for women.[9] Second, while paid care is very expensive for families as a percentage of their own earnings, care is paid very poorly. When caregivers look to employ a caregiver—whether that be a nanny, a child-care center, or a home care worker for their parents—the payment for this work can generally only be a percentage of the salary that the employer makes in her own paid employment. Otherwise, there is no longer any reason to pursue paid employment at all: the employer may as well stay home and provide the care herself. Because most caregivers can only pay a portion of their take-home pay to a caregiver, care wages are depressed. According to the US Bureau of Labor Statistics, the median hourly wage for child-care workers in the United States in May 2018 was $11.83, which amounts to an annual salary of $24,610.[10] Only 15 percent of these workers received health insurance as an employment benefit.[11] A recent study showed that between 2014 and 2016, more than half of child-care workers received some sort of public assistance to make ends meet.[12] Caregivers for the elderly or disabled receive similarly low wages.[13]

Third, because even care that pays a low wage to the caregiver eats up an enormous portion of the take-home pay of the employer, many families in the United States and other prosperous countries rely for care on already marginalized persons with few employment opportunities, who will therefore work for low wages. Historically, in the United States, care responsibilities were often thrust on people of color through slavery or by restricting other employment opportunities for women of color.[14] Today, many families manage their care needs by employing

9. Erling Barth, Sari Pekkala Kerr, and Claudia Olivetti, "The Dynamics of Gender Earnings Differentials: Evidence from Establishment Data," National Bureau of Economic Research, Working Paper 23381 (2017), https://www.nber.org/papers/w23381.

10. Bureau of Labor Statistics, "Occupational Employment and Wages, May 2018, 39-9011 Childcare Workers," https://stats.bls.gov/oes/current/oes399011.htm.

11. Elise Gould, "Child Care Workers Aren't Paid Enough to Make Ends Meet," Issue Brief #405, *Economic Policy Institute*, November 5, 2015, https://www.epi.org/files/2015/child-care-workers-final.pdf.

12. Marcy Whitebook, Caitlin McLean, Lea J. E. Austin, and Bethany Edwards, *Early Childhood Workforce Index* (Berkeley: Center for the Study of Child Care Employment, University of California–Berkeley, 2018), 6.

13. Bureau of Labor Statistics, "Occupational Employment and Wages, May 2018, 39-9021 Personal Care Aides," https://www.bls.gov/oes/current/oes399021.htm.

14. Evelyn Nakano Glenn, *Forced to Care: Coercion and Caregiving in America* (Cambridge, MA: Harvard University Press, 2010).

migrant care workers. In many cases, these are women who have left their own children behind in the care of aunts, grandmothers, older siblings, or orphanages. Ninety-three percent of migrant workers remit part of their salaries back home, often to pay for food and education for their own children.[15]

Obviously, these remittances are important to families remaining in the country of origin and to the economies of these countries. Nevertheless, for the significant percentage of migrants who leave behind young children, there is a profound cost. Caregiving is exported to wealthy countries at the expense of less-developed countries: there is a "care drain." This is not so different from colonial exploitation of natural resources in the past, but now the commodity that is transferred to wealthier nations is the embodied presence and affection of the caregiver.[16]

We can see the many ways in which failing to account for caregiving as economic labor (which is not to deny that caregiving is an expression of love) leads to an interconnected set of injustices. These interconnected injustices are inconsistent with a Catholic commitment that all persons are entitled to the prerequisites of a flourishing life, including material necessities and care. The care economy is undercapitalized. The solution to this undercapitalization is some form of social subsidy to those doing the important work of care. Such subsidies take many forms: for example, the government can fund high-quality child-care centers, can furnish adequately paid home care services to those in need of them, and/or can provide "family allowances" or direct payments to families of young children, to alleviate the economic burden of the intensive demands of care at this stage.

Resistance to Social Support for Care

In the United States, there is a great deal of resistance to public policies that provide social support for the material demands of caregiving. For example, income support programs such as Temporary Assistance to Needy Families are so underfunded that they meet only a fraction of need.[17] The Supplemental Nutrition Assistance Program (SNAP), colloquially known as "food stamps," significantly reduces the number of families experiencing food insecurity and has clear

15. Tomoko Nishimoto, "Why We Need to Recognize Migrant Domestic Workers' Contributions to Our Economies," International Labor Organization, June 16, 2018, https://www.ilo.org/asia/media-centre/news/WCMS_632454/lang--en/index.htm.

16. Arlie Russell Hochschild, "Love and Gold," in *Global Woman: Nannies, Maids, and Sex Workers in the New Economy*, ed. Barbara Ehrenreich and Arlie Russell Hochschild (New York: Henry Holt & Company, 2002), 15–30.

17. Center for Budget and Policy Priorities, "State Temporary Assistance for Needy Families Programs Do Not Provide Adequate Safety Net for Poor Families," https://www.cbpp.org/state-temporary-assistance-for-needy-families-programs-do-not-provide-adequate-safety-net-for-poor.

positive effects on participating children's health and educational achievement.[18] But SNAP beneficiaries are stigmatized, and there have been repeated attempts to cut the program.[19]

Why is there such resistance to programs that do so much good? Though dependency and care are central aspects of every human life simply by virtue of our human condition, "dependency" has a negative connotation in the contemporary cultural context. We do not like to think of ourselves as dependent. In fact, we stigmatize dependency. Hence, we hear widespread criticism of poor people receiving public assistance as dependent on the government. In addition, we tend to assume that caregiving for dependents is a private activity that is the responsibility of the family. As economist Nancy Folbre says, many of us speak about children as if they were pets.[20] In other words, many people think of having and raising children as a private choice made by parents in order to make their own lives more fulfilling, like getting a dog. In such a conceptual framework, parents should take responsibility for their personal choice by accepting the financial burdens that go along with parenting.

But we need a different conceptual framework. We should recognize parents and caregivers as engaged in the socially essential work of maintaining human life and raising up the next generation of adults. No one would argue that the government should provide financial allowances to care for Fido, or for your pet tarantula, but there are important reasons to support a generous social investment in supporting dependents and caregivers. The Catholic moral tradition has resources for an alternative conceptual framework that would support the family economy, dependents, and caregivers.

Resources in Catholic Social Thought for Valuing Dependency and the Family Economy

The documents of the Catholic social tradition contain some proposals for the material support of caregiving within families. Because the notion of government

18. Food Research and Action Center, "The Role of the Supplemental Nutrition Access Program in Improving Health and Well-Being," December 2017, http://frac.org/wp-content/uploads/hunger-health-role-snap-improving-health-well-being.pdf.

19. Pam Fessler, "More than 750,000 Could Lose Food Stamps Under Trump Administration Proposal," *National Public Radio*, April 1, 2019, https://www.npr.org/2019/04/01/707681965/more-than-750-000-could-lose-food-stamps-under-trump-administration-proposal.

20. Nancy Folbre, *The Invisible Heart: Economics and Family Values* (New York: New Press, 2001), chapter 5, "Children as Pets."

support to the caregivers of young children seems so problematic to many of my students, they are often surprised to learn that John Paul II suggested family allowances (that is, government payments to families of young children) as one way to ensure that families can meet their obligations (*Laborem Exercens* 19). John Paul II framed his proposal in a deeply gendered way, suggesting that these payments would allow mothers to devote themselves primarily to their maternal duties, but, in theory, such allowances might be used to support a range of caregiving strategies (including stay-at-home dads, or hiring a nanny at a more just wage).

More broadly, the Catholic tradition works with a framework that is more hospitable to acknowledging human dependency and interdependency than other, more individualistic frameworks. While not discounting the importance of rights and autonomy, it emphasizes the common good and the interdependence of all members of the human community. Catholic social thought has, since the 1963 papal encyclical *Pacem in Terris*, invoked the language of human rights to say that human persons are entitled to freedom of speech, association, and religion, as well as rights to "the means necessary for the proper development of life, particularly food, clothing, shelter, medical care, rest, and, finally, the necessary social services. In consequence, [each person] has the right to be looked after" when ill, disabled, in old age, or during periods of unemployment that are not the fault of the individual (PT 11). Before we can enjoy rights of speech, religion, and association, we have the need for, and the rights to, care.

Pacem in Terris speaks not only of rights but of corresponding *duties*—if you have a right to housing, for example, then some persons or institutions or the government have a duty to provide housing if you cannot get it on your own (PT 11, 28–33). Thus, the Catholic social tradition offers an account of rights that does not presume purely autonomous individuals fending off intrusion into their choices. Rather, interdependent persons are called on to ensure that each member of the community has what she needs.

There are also seeds in Catholic social thought for a recognition that love and care do not need to be kept sharply separate from considerations of economic sustenance. Paying for care does not "contaminate" the care with self-interest; indeed, reasonable payment for care improves the quality of care and is more just to caregivers.[21] In his 2009 encyclical *Caritas in Veritate*, Pope Benedict XVI called for a more integral understanding of economic development and for a *"further and deeper reflection on the meaning of the economy and its goals"* (CV 32; emphasis in original). He suggested that governments should provide legal structures for

21. Julie A. Nelson and Nancy Folbre, "Why a Well-Paid Nurse Is a Better Nurse," *Nursing Economics* 24, no. 3 (2006): 127–30.

"hybrid forms of economic activity" (CV 36), organizations that aim at both profit and the common good. These combine the self-interested motivations that are generally understood to drive market activity with more other-regarding motives. Benedict also urged that the state should operate with a "spirit of gratuitousness."

Extending this essential insight to the family would seem to be a necessary corollary to Benedict's vision. The view of politics and the market as driven by self-interest, versus the family as the sphere of pure altruism, is a false binary that Benedict wants to challenge. But he is more concerned about injecting altruism into self-interested markets than in ensuring economic justice for family caregivers. Families are (often) places of loving care, but that does not mean that those who give care should have no concern for their own material well-being. It is appropriate for family caregivers to receive social support for the care work they perform. Benedict's insights on economics can be extended to embrace a more integral view of families as a place where love and care respond to embodied needs *and* where an acknowledgment of the embodied needs of caregivers calls for broader social and material support for caregiving.[22]

In short, Catholic social thought offers an overall framework for social justice that can be further articulated to highlight the importance of honoring families as economies and providing material and social support for caregivers. To date, however, the documents of the Catholic social tradition offer few concrete proposals for supporting caregivers, and these have presumed a very traditional family structure and gender roles (*Familiaris Consortio* 23).

Conclusion

Care for dependents is an expression of love, but it is also economic: it is labor, it involves provision for material needs, and it requires material support. Thus families, as a primary locus of care work, are economies. In the contemporary context, there are widespread cultural assumptions that care is tainted when it is done in return for money and that dependent care is the private responsibility of families. Therefore, our society does not provide adequate economic support for care work. This inflicts injustice on dependent caregivers.

The encyclical *Pacem in Terris* articulates a rich conception of human rights, including positive rights to the material prerequisites of flourishing, and articulates corresponding social duties to fulfill these rights for all. At least in part, this

---

22. For an expanded version of this argument, see Sandra Sullivan-Dunbar, "The Care Economy as Alternative Economy," in *Working Alternatives: Studies of Economy and the Human Person*, ed. John C. Seitz and Christine Firer Hinze (New York: Fordham University Press, 2020).

duty is to be fulfilled through our political structures, by government: in Catholic thought, the state exists primarily to promote the common good. Catholic social documents have provided few concrete proposals for social and political support for caregiving, and those that have been put forth usually presume very traditional family structures and gender roles. In order to effectively advocate the social support for caregiving that will be necessary to make the sort of rights outlined in *Pacem in Terris* a reality for all, we must recognize the family as an economy, a place where love and other-regard are central but where caregivers also have needs that demand material support. In addition, Roman Catholic social thought must acknowledge the great complexity of the contemporary social organization of care—with many family forms, gender roles, and a global market for care labor—in order to effectively advocate the sort of social support for caregiving that will be necessary to make the rights outlined in *Pacem in Terris* a reality for all.

Chapter 14

Family Relationships and Incarceration

Kathryn Getek Soltis

It is now common knowledge that the United States incarcerates more people than any other nation on earth. And despite a wide range of perspectives on criminal justice in this country, most people would admit that change of some kind is needed. Most would, however, think about incarceration in largely individualistic terms. As the narrative goes, individuals violate laws. Individuals are found culpable for those violations. Individuals are punished. When we talk about the harms of crime, we readily understand that there is an expanding network of those who suffer loss and trauma; those who are victimized are not only the literal victims but also the victims' family, friends, and the wider community. Yet, when we imagine perpetrators, we usually think about individual wrongdoers; we rarely concern ourselves with the relational networks of offenders. It is for this reason that the family members of incarcerated persons are often referred to as "hidden victims."

The visibility of these hidden victims has increased somewhat over the last couple of decades as researchers have attended to the "collateral consequences" of incarceration.[1] Scholars have started to document the extensive burdens faced

---

1. For example, see John Hagan and Ronit Dinovitzer, "Collateral Consequences of Imprisonment for Children, Communities, and Prisoners," *Crime and Justice* 26 (1999): 121–62; Marc Mauer and Meda Chesney-Lind, eds. *Invisible Punishment: The Collateral Consequences of Mass Imprisonment* (New York: The New Press, 2002); Donald Braman, *Doing Time on the Outside: Incarceration and Family Life in Urban America* (Ann Arbor: University of Michigan Press, 2004); Todd R. Clear, *Imprisoning Communities: How Mass Incarceration Makes Disadvantaged Neighborhoods Worse* (New York: Oxford University Press, 2007); and Megan Comfort, *Doing Time Together: Love and Family in the Shadow of the Prison* (Chicago: University of Chicago Press, 2008).

by families and communities of the incarcerated. In addition, they have called attention to a range of criminal justice practices that create these hardships: the long distances many families must travel to see a loved one in prison, the limiting visitation policies, the high cost of phone calls, etc. The notion of secondary prisonization has also emerged to describe how those close to the incarcerated experience many of the same restrictions and constraints as those behind bars.[2]

The families of the incarcerated, while more present in the scholarly literature, have not received a similar increase in attention from the criminal justice system itself. Contact with loved ones is still viewed as a privilege and often used for incentivizing behavior instead of being regarded as integral to the correctional endeavor. The families of the incarcerated are not prioritized despite evidence that strong family relationships are one of the most important predictors of an inmate's success following release. Even while there may be more programming opportunities (e.g., parenting classes, family days at the prison), the development of family relationships is marginal to the functioning of the criminal justice system.

I argue that to move away from mass incarceration, we need to reflect much more seriously about the families of those behind bars and how they relate to the objectives of punishment and criminal justice. This reflection is necessary both to reform institutions and policies and to think in theologically coherent ways about justice. Recent Catholic theological perspectives on incarceration emphasize that punishment must have a purpose, and restorative justice is regarded as the approach most consistent with Scripture and tradition.[3] A relational understanding of the person anchors this restorative approach, although the full weight of Catholic theological reflection on family has not yet been integrated into the restorative justice framework. Given its assertion that the family is the basic unit of society, the Catholic tradition should offer a prominent voice for reframing criminal justice through the lens of family relationships, challenging the individualistic notions of justice and punishment that have, in part, enabled the scandal of mass incarceration.

In this essay, I examine two key familial relationships as they are impacted by incarceration—parenthood and marriage—and then briefly discuss how race and class bear on which families suffer the most. In the concluding section I consider the implications for a theological response to mass incarceration, a theological account of justice, and official Catholic discourse on families and incarceration.

2. For example, Comfort, *Doing Time Together.*

3. See United States Conference of Catholic Bishops, *Responsibility, Rehabilitation, and Restoration: A Catholic Perspective on Crime and Criminal Justice* (Washington, DC: United States Catholic Conference, 2000), and Amy Levad, *Redeeming a Prison Society: A Liturgical and Sacramental Response to Mass Incarceration* (Minneapolis: Fortress Press, 2014).

Parenthood and Incarceration

An examination of parenting in the context of mass incarceration addresses a social issue that is widespread in scope and an urgent matter of justice. Over half of the men and women behind bars—more than 1.2 million inmates—are parents of children under the age of eighteen. There are 2.7 million minor children with a parent behind bars, which amounts to 1 in every 28 children in the United States. That figure was 1 in 125 in 1980.[4] The ubiquity of parental incarceration is indeed stunning, impacting more than 3.6 percent of all children at a given time. One study puts this in perspective, particularly given the comparative amount of public attention and research, by noting that only about 1 percent of children are on the autism spectrum.[5] The weight of the burden of parental incarceration falls on younger children. Almost a quarter (22%) of children with a parent in prison are under five and the majority (58%) are under ten, with eight years old as the average age.[6]

Conventional wisdom used to be that men and women who went to prison or jail were unfit parents.[7] Studies consistently show, however, that, even while some children may be helped by the removal of a parent, the vast majority are significantly harmed. Prominent effects on children "involve the strains of economic deprivation, the loss of parental socialization through role modeling, support, and supervision, and the stigma and shame of societal labeling."[8] There are particularly strong negative impacts on children's mental and behavioral health, and these are linked with outcomes that continue into adulthood.[9] In addition to higher risks for delinquency and crime, children are at risk for educational failure, premature departures from home, early childbearing and marriage, and idleness linked to joblessness.[10] The stigmatization experienced as a result of a parent's imprisonment can lead to similar problems for children, sometimes setting in motion a chain reaction of antisocial behavior.[11] Even the incarceration of a nonresident parent may have a significant negative effect on children since such

---

4. The Pew Charitable Trusts, *Collateral Costs: Incarceration's Effect on Economic Mobility* (Washington, DC: The Pew Charitable Trusts, 2010). Based on research by Bruce Western and Becky Pettit.

5. Sara Wakefield and Christopher Wildeman, *Children of the Prison Boom: Mass Incarceration and the Future of American Inequality* (New York: Oxford University Press, 2014), 20.

6. Christopher J. Mumola, "Incarcerated Parents and Their Children," US Department of Justice, Bureau of Justice Statistics (Washington, DC: GPO, 2000).

7. J. Mark Eddy and Julie Poehlmann, eds., *Children of Incarcerated Parents: A Handbook for Researchers and Practitioners* (Washington, DC: The Urban Institute Press, 2010), xiv.

8. Hagan and Dinovitzer, "Collateral Consequences," 123.

9. Wakefield and Wildeman, *Children of the Prison Boom*, 6.

10. Hagan and Dinovitzer, "Collateral Consequences," 148.

11. Ibid., 127.

parents often contribute income as well as child care. Research suggests that mass imprisonment creates greater social inequality through its impact on children than from its effects on the men and women actually behind the bars. As a result, even if incarceration rates were dramatically reduced today, the long-term impact of mass incarceration would still be ahead of us since all the children of the prison boom have yet to come of age.[12]

In the wake of mass incarceration, children and their incarcerated parents have not been a priority for correctional systems, social service agencies, or public policymakers. For instance, most states do not have child welfare policies to address parenting issues during imprisonment.[13] Structurally speaking, the realities faced by children of incarcerated parents are invisible. Whether this invisibility is morally justified depends on the theoretical framework used to conceptualize parenting as well as justice. In what follows, I outline two different frameworks and then suggest how they relate to theological approaches to parenting.

The first framework regards parenting as a private, individual activity. The raising of children is the near-exclusive responsibility of their parents and guardians. In this model, parental incarceration is simply an unfortunate reality that some children must face. In other words, the deprivation of parental relationships is among the many deprivations (e.g., of freedom, rights) that characterize an individual's punishment. As a result, the disadvantages conferred on children are the fault of, not the justice system, but the parents. Ultimately, this framework regards the burdens endured by the children and incarcerated parents as unavoidable byproducts of the pursuit of justice.

The second framework, however, regards parenting as a socially significant activity. If children are being deprived of critical relationships of nurture, protection, and education, then the common good is jeopardized. The disadvantages conferred on children are structured into the so-called justice system by a willful negligence of the work of parenting. The harm done to children results from the way society punishes crime, not from the crime itself. Thus, the burdens endured are not unavoidable byproducts but direct obstructions of justice. This is not a private misfortune in the lives of millions of children but an injustice felt broadly within society and shouldered by the most vulnerable.

12. Wakefield and Wildeman, *Children of the Prison Boom*, 12.

13. Creasie Finney Hairston, "Prisoners and Their Families: Parenting Issues during Incarceration," in *Prisoners Once Removed: The Impact of Incarceration and Reentry on Children, Families, and Communities*, ed. Jeremy Travis and Michelle Waul (Washington, DC: Urban Institute Press, 2003), 259–82, at 277.

This second framework demands a reformulation of policies and institutional responsibilities. Were the criminal justice system committed to the support of parents and their children, the impact on these relationships would be strongly considered when deciding between imprisonment or a community-based sentence. There would be a different process for determining the distance at which parents serve their sentences, how time and space are made available for visits and calls, and what sorts of resources were mandated for every facility in this country.[14] In addition, were the care of children a priority, a host of social institutions would be expected to interact with prisons and jails to facilitate parenting relationships. For example, schools could be expected to send report cards to incarcerated parents and facilitate remote parent-teacher conferencing. The Catholic theological tradition offers resources that move in these directions, while also displaying areas in need of development.

Amoris Laetitia, the 2015 post-synodal apostolic exhortation on the family by Pope Francis, is helpful for capturing the basic Catholic approach to parenthood, especially as it is relevant for parental incarceration. Parenthood is understood as a serious responsibility, a duty, and a God-given vocation. The absence of a parent "gravely affects. . . children and their integration into society" (AL 55, cf. 263). Moreover, the education of a child is the parents' "essential and inalienable right . . . of which no one may claim to deprive them" (AL 84). The critical work of parenting, especially in the moral and social formation of children, is a gradual process that requires attention to ordinary, daily living. Thus, the cultivation of habits developed with time and repetition demands a personal, physical presence (AL 263–67).

Extrapolating from this strong language on parenting, incarceration appears to be a severe violation of parents and children alike. The Catholic theological approach to parenthood seems to align itself with the second of the two frameworks identified above, with parenting regarded as a matter of public concern. Echoing similar claims made in Pope John Paul II's *Familiaris Consortio*, Pope Francis suggests that the task of raising and educating children has far-reaching significance for society. Good parenting is a social good and a key foundation for realizing the common good.

There is sufficient theological groundwork in the tradition for a scathing critique of incarceration and its unrestrained disruption of parent-child relationships. No explicit condemnation of incarceration has, however, been made along these

14. See, for example, Ross D. Parke and K. Alison Clarke-Stewart, "The Effects of Parental Incarceration on Children: Perspectives, Promises, and Policies," in Travis and Waul, *Prisoners Once Removed*, 189–232.

lines in any official statements. Despite the generally strong theological defense of parents and children, it is uncertain whether this still applies in the context of crime and punishment.

One challenge is that a theological account of parenting as private emerges from the extensive focus on marriage as the core of family life. The well-being of children is often seen as contingent on the circumstances of individual marriages and the couple's conformity to moral standards.[15] Moreover, when children are referred to as gifts and "the ultimate crown" of marriage (*Gaudium et Spes* 48), children appear to belong to the intimate sphere of the couple. A second challenge is the portrayal of children within individualistic accounts of offenders. The US bishops offer a prime example in their pastoral letter *Responsibility, Rehabilitation, and Restoration*. The children of incarcerated parents are identified as victims of crime and are discussed immediately after the direct victims of the offense. This places blame squarely on the shoulders of the incarcerated parent and undermines support for the possibility of continued-though-limited parenting. Moreover, such a presentation exonerates the criminal justice system and other institutions from responsibility in the child's suffering.

In conclusion, the incarceration of parents results in significant and widespread burdens on children and the parenting relationships on which they depend. A parenting-as-private framework will lay the blame on individual incarcerated parents, but a parenting-as-social framework illuminates the responsibility of the criminal justice system itself. While there are parents who directly harm children, this does not accurately describe the harm of incarceration, which is a socially constructed and imposed hardship. The Catholic tradition offers theological resources to bring attention to this crisis. Even so, private accounts of child rearing—theological and otherwise—obscure the systemic failures that unjustly burden children and their incarcerated parents.

Marriage and Incarceration

The social science literature is clear that incarceration is bad for marriage. One recent study confirmed that incarceration has a "large and immediate" disruptive effect on both married and cohabiting relationships. Within a month of release,

---

15. For echoes of these concerns, see Mary M. Doyle Roche, "Children and the Common Good: Protection and Participation," in *Prophetic Witness: Catholic Women's Strategies for Reform*, ed. Colleen M. Griffith (New York: Herder & Herder/Crossroad Publishing, 2009), 123–31, at 127; and Cristina Traina, "For the Sins of the Parents: Roman Catholic Ethics and the Politics of Family," in Griffith, *Prophetic Witness*, 114–22, at 121.

the odds of relationship dissolution are five times higher than for nonincarcerated individuals. Even short periods of time behind bars are highly damaging, as the study's median incarceration length was just one month long.[16] Scholars have attempted to identify why incarceration has this negative effect, and the answer seems to be found in the experience of separation and marginalization. One study found that—rather than the stigma associated with "doing time"—it was the physical separation of incarceration that best explained why marriages were more likely to dissolve. In particular, the study found a 32 percent increase in the risk of divorce for each additional year of incarceration.[17] Another study argues that the unique experience of marginalization through liminality leads to relationship dissolution. Liminality—the experience of being "betwixt and between"—describes how incarcerated individuals are still members of families and yet are isolated from them.[18]

These findings suggest that marriages end neither because of the criminal conviction itself nor because of the stigma associated with it. Instead, marriages end *because of the way society responds* to a conviction through incarceration. As it is currently practiced in the United States, incarceration deliberately excludes and marginalizes with little if any consideration of the family relationships impacted.

Recalling the two frameworks discussed in the context of incarceration and parenthood, we find two analogous approaches for conceptualizing the burdens on marriage. The first framework would view damaged and destroyed marriages to be private matters outside the scope of concern of the criminal justice system. While perhaps unfortunate, relationship dissolution is a consequence of the choices made by the individual offender. The second framework, on the other hand, would acknowledge a social responsibility for supporting married partnerships. As a result, it would demand extensive efforts to minimize the negative impacts of incarceration on marriage.

A Catholic theological view of marriage resonates with the second framework. Marriage is regarded as foundational for the family, and the family is foundational for society. In her work on family ethics, theologian Julie Hanlon Rubio highlights the social significance of marriage and a couple's relational openness to the wider

---

16. Robert Apel, "The Effects of Jail and Prison Confinement on Cohabitation and Marriage," *The Annals of the American Academy of Political and Social Science* 665, no. 1 (2016): 103–26.

17. Michael Massoglia, Brianna Remster, and Ryan D. King, "Stigma or Separation? Understanding the Incarceration-Divorce Relationship," *Social Forces* 90, no. 1 (2011): 133–56.

18. Kristin Turney, "Neither Here nor There: Incarceration and Family Instability," *Focus* 30, no. 2 (2013–2014): 21–25.

community.[19] In official statements, emphasis is often placed on the unity and indissolubility of married relationships, and there are warnings of widespread consequences when marriages suffer. In *Amoris Laetitia*, Pope Francis asserts that a "crisis in a couple's relationship destabilizes the family and may lead, through separation and divorce, to serious consequences for adults, children, and society as a whole, weakening its individual and social bonds" (AL 41).

Amoris Laetitia features a pastoral response to marriage and family since the threats to these institutions are largely identified with the "frailty of individuals" (AL 38). Of special concern are realities such as narcissism, a fear of commitment, and the treatment of relationships as disposable. Yet, more systemic threats to family and marriage (e.g., lack of employment, poverty, addiction, forced migration) are also mentioned. These latter concerns demonstrate that a Catholic theological account of marriage is capable of promoting the second framework and its concern with the systemic failures of incarceration. Even so, the tradition must resist placing greater emphasis on individual-level threats to marriage since doing so could reinforce the notion that an offender is nearly exclusively responsible for a marriage's dissolution. Given the Catholic tradition's vigorous advocacy for the indissolubility of marriage, there ought to be theological outrage at a criminal justice system that makes little effort to prevent this serious relational harm.

In conclusion, the experience of incarceration significantly increases the likelihood that a marriage will dissolve. Research shows that separation and marginalization are largely responsible for these negative outcomes, suggesting that the harm arises from systemic failures imposed on offenders. A Catholic theological perspective has resources to critique this reality and demand reform, especially given a determined commitment to the indissolubility of marriage. To do so, any tendencies to focus on individual weaknesses must be tempered by greater attention to the systemic, social failures to support these crucial relationships.

Racial and Economic Injustice

Thus far, the familial harms of incarceration have been considered without engaging the racial and economic injustices that are inextricably woven into criminal justice in the United States. Yet it must be asked: *which* families are being harmed by incarceration? The answer is the same as the distorted demographics of the men and women behind our nation's bars. The families being harmed are black and brown families as well as poor families.

19. Julie Hanlon Rubio, *Family Ethics: Practices for Christians* (Washington, DC: Georgetown University Press, 2010). See especially chapter 1, "A Catholic Theological Understanding of Marriage."

To see this clearly, we can consider the children of incarcerated parents. One in 9 black children, or 11.4 percent, have an incarcerated parent. This compares to 3.5 percent of Hispanic children and 1.8 percent of white children.[20] The cumulative statistics are worse. For a white child born in 1990, there was a 1 in 30 chance of experiencing paternal incarceration by the age of fourteen. For a black child, the chance was 1 in 4. If the father dropped out of high school, the chance for a black child to experience paternal incarceration rose to just over 50 percent.[21] It is outrageous that a nation can tolerate such racialized harm, especially against its youngest and most vulnerable members.

Catholic theology proclaims the family to be the "first and vital cell of society" (*Familiaris Consortio* 42). Thus, the reverse makes sense, just as the family shapes society, society shapes families. The racism that sickens society operates in a particular way on the family. Sociologist Bruce Western notes that incarceration inhibits the formation of stable families in the very same communities that supply most of the penal population.[22] This simply compounds negative outcomes since families (and the informal social networks that connect them) can buffer individuals from many of the impacts of social injustice. Thus, when it comes to families and incarceration, the relevant theological resources are those that clarify not simply the importance of parenting and marriage but also the preferential option for the poor.[23] Already vulnerable and marginalized families are made all the more so through incarceration.

Conclusion

There are many more familial relationships beyond simply parenthood and marriage. Even so, the above reflections demonstrate the considerable impact of incarceration on families. It is an impact that must be addressed in theological responses to mass incarceration and ultimately in theological accounts of justice.

Family realities suggest how to conceptualize the burden of confinement. The punitive function of incarceration is typically identified as the deprivation of

20. The Pew Charitable Trusts, *Collateral Costs*.

21. Wakefield and Wildeman, *Children of the Prison Boom*, 33–40.

22. Bruce Western, *Punishment and Inequality in America* (New York: Russell Sage, 2006). See chapter 6, "Incarceration, Marriage, and Family Life."

23. For discussion of the concept of the preferential option for the poor, see, for example, United States Catholic Bishops, *Economic Justice for All: Pastoral Letter on Catholic Social Teaching and the U.S. Economy* (Washington, DC: United States Catholic Conference, 1986), 16, 87–88.

personal liberty.[24] In keeping with an individualistic approach to criminal justice, this view regards the offender's loss of freedom as the most appropriate response to the violation of the rights of others. Yet, in actuality, the primary burden of confinement is not the freedoms lost but the relationships compromised. Separation from community, particularly one's family, is the true source of the pain of incarceration.[25] A theological anthropology that emphasizes the social nature of the person anticipates that this relational burden would be the primary one.

Incarceration is fundamentally social and familial exclusion, and a theological perspective is well equipped to question the legitimacy of using exclusion to serve justice. In Catholic social thought, a person's dignity cannot be realized apart from participation in community. It is for this reason that marginalization is a profound threat to human flourishing. Theological responses to incarceration should reveal how it functions through imposed marginalization and the pain of relational exclusion. In addition, it must be noted that such exclusion is a particularly counterproductive mechanism for addressing those who already suffer from social exclusion. The impact on vulnerable members of the community—children, black families, etc.—shows that incarceration can perpetuate injustice rather than rectify it. It also shows the need for a coherent concept of justice, for which theological voices are crucial.

The harms suffered by children and spouses of the incarcerated demonstrate the danger of retributive notions of justice—theological and otherwise. The realities of human interdependence dictate that punishment cannot be confined to the guilty; the innocent will invariably suffer too. Even if we can persuasively articulate why a guilty individual must "pay," there is no good explanation why, for example, innocent children bear the cost as well. Ultimately, due punishment cannot be assessed in a relational vacuum. This is the failure of the first framework, one that regards parenting and, analogously, marriage in private, individual terms. It is the failure of blaming individual offenders for all the consequences of incarceration. While accountability is necessary, it is society's choice to impose isolation and marginalization as the way to hold offenders accountable.

24. The most influential voice on behalf of this perspective is Gesham M. Sykes who published *The Society of Captives: A Study of a Maximum Security Prison* (Princeton, NJ: Princeton University Press, 1958). See Yvonne Jewkes and Helen Johnston, eds., *Prison Readings: A Critical Introduction to Prisons and Imprisonment* (Portland: Willan Publishing, 2006), 159.

25. For example, see Timothy J. Flanagan, "The Pains of Long-Term Imprisonment: A Comparison of British and American Perspectives," *British Journal of Criminology* 20, no. 2 (1980): 148–56, as cited in Joseph Murray, "The Effects of Imprisonment on Families and Children of Prisoners," in *The Effects of Imprisonment*, ed. Alison Liebling and Shadd Maruna (Portland: Willan Publishing, 2005), 442.

Catholic theological ethics makes clear that family is crucial for society, and, therefore, family must be included in accounts of justice. There can be no true justice that exists *in spite* of injuring children, spouses, etc. The full scope of human relationality must be at the center of justice; the mandate is not simply redress and repair but also positively nourishing all relationships that exist. Theology demonstrates the foundational character of family in particular when we consider human relationality. Family is regarded as a living reflection of the triune God (*Amoris Laetitia* 11, cf. 71). Called to be children of God and sisters and brothers to one another, justice is invariably about getting our family relations right.

A reflection on families and incarceration reveals the powerful resources in Catholic theology in addition to the ways the tradition itself must reframe its discourse. In terms of resources, there is strong language to describe the foundational social roles of parents and married couples, and it is clear that the well-being of a society is intimately connected to the well-being of all its families. Yet at times there is relative silence about the systemic failures to protect and sustain families. In the context of incarceration, it can appear that the burdens endured by families are inevitable hardships caused by the offender. The US bishops imply this when they identify children of offenders as victims of crime. Rather, Catholic theology must assert clearly and often that children, spouses, and others are not hidden victims of crime but hidden victims of *incarceration*. They are victims of a systemic, societal choice to use exclusion and marginalization as a means of achieving justice.

In the midst of mass incarceration, there are millions of families who need a theological voice to speak about justice and its concern for *all* relationships. It is a voice that will prioritize the needs of vulnerable children, demand all means to sustain loving partnerships, and unequivocally condemn that race and poverty determine which families suffer the most. It is a voice that will challenge our individualistic framework for criminal justice, not only because this approach tolerates so much harm, but also because it disguises our own complicity in depriving families of true justice.

Chapter 15

Cohabitation

Part of the Journey toward Marriage?

Kari-Shane Davis Zimmerman

Cohabiting. Living together. Regardless of which description is chosen by a person or couple, this "life stage" has taken on a new level of importance for those dedicated to studying marriage and family relations. The question is no longer who cohabits but rather who does not cohabit. Over half of people aged eighteen to forty-four cohabit at least once. This percentage has increased dramatically over the last twenty years, and cohabitation "is currently the most common first coresidential union among young adults."[1] Given this new situation, what do we currently know about cohabitation? Following that, what does the changing landscape mean for a theology of marriage and family?

Part 1 of this essay provides a general overview of recent research on the topic of cohabitation. Part 2 explores scholars who argue for a recovery of the tradition of betrothal as a way to address cohabitation that is far beyond the "phenomenon" stage. Part 3 offers ways forward at the personal, familial, social, and ecclesial level. For many young adults, the current Catholic approach to cohabitation is either irrelevant or alienating. In response, I offer an alternative approach, treating cohabitation not as a "contemporary moral problem" but as a "contemporary moral dialogue" in which a person's faith community could play an active role in their relationship discernment process.

---

1. Colleen Nugent and Jill Daugherty, "A Demographic, Attitudinal, and Behavioral Profile of Cohabiting Adults in the United States, 2011–2015," *National Health Statistics Report* 111 (2018): https://www.cdc.gov/nchs/data/nhsr/nhsr111.pdf. Most scholarly research on cohabitation does not yet include same-sex couples. Thus, the context for this essay is heterosexual couples only, and the comments made pertain only to this group of men and women.

Cohabitation in the United States Today

There are five key points I wish to make about current research on cohabitation. First, social class plays a large role in why people decide to cohabit and how their cohabiting relationship transpires. As Rhiannon A. Kroeger and Pamela J. Smock note in "Cohabitation: Recent Research and Implications," economically advantaged individuals more often than not find their relationship ending in "marriage."[2] Those less economically advantaged, however, can find themselves in more than one cohabiting union and possibly even with the additional personal identifier of "cohabiting parent." Moreover, for those less economically advantaged, there is an "economic bar" to marriage. So, even if economically disadvantaged people want to move from cohabitating to marriage, money can keep them from doing so.

Second, too often a lot of research attempts to understand cohabitation in terms of how it compares with marriage. Kroeger and Smock argue this approach needs to change. "If we continue to build our knowledge of cohabitation on how it compares to marriage, we will miss some crucial insights."[3] They therefore suggest qualifying relationships even more in order to ascertain what is unique about cohabitation in comparison to other forms of coupling such as "Living Apart Together" and even "Living Together Apart."[4]

This comparison is compounded by the engagement "ritual" that remains the dominant framework for how one goes from dating to marriage. Though proposals and rings can be powerful symbols of commitment, the elaborate contemporary ritual normalizes white, heterosexist, and upper-middle-class socioeconomic practices.[5] The "process" can be riddled with elitist perceptions about what counts (e.g., know your three "Cs"— diamond cut, color, and clarity) or patriarchal assumptions about male and female gender roles. Adding to the "drama" these days is the additional pressure to capture "the moment" in photos and share it on social media.[6] The diamond engagement ring script not only directs marriage practices but also sets up a potentially unreachable bar for exiting cohabiting relationships.

---

2. Rhiannon A. Kroeger and Pamela J. Smock, "Cohabitation: Recent Research and Implications," in *The Wiley Blackwell Companion to the Sociology of Families*, ed. Judith Treas, Jacqueline Scott, and Martin Richards (Malden, MA: John Wiley & Sons, 2014), 227.

3. Ibid.

4. Ibid.

5. Two interesting articles that begin to discuss some of the issues related to cohabitation and debt for young adults and meeting the "economic bar to marriage" are Fenaba R. Addo, "Debt, Cohabitation, and Marriage in Young Adulthood," *Demography* 51 (2014): 1677–1701; and Christina Gibson-Davis, Anna Gassman-Pines, and Rebecca Lehrman, " 'His' and 'Hers': Meeting the Economic Bar to Marriage," *Demograhy* 55 (2018): 2321–43.

6. For example, see The Knot, "How They Asked," https://howtheyasked.com. The Knot portrays itself as the self-help organizational social media website for all things pertaining to weddings.

Third, cohabiting is gendered. As Kroeger and Smock note, in cohabiting households women do more housework than men and men's financial situation usually determines if the couple gets married.[7] Awareness of these double standards is behind Stacy and Wynne Whitman's *Shacking Up: The Smart Girl's Guide to Living in Sin Without Getting Burned.*[8] Stacy and Wynne believe a "girl" needs to be "smart" about making the decision to cohabit because there still are strong cultural and religious traditions operating that deem the decision to cohabit with a male partner before marriage as sinful.[9] Therefore, any female who decides to cohabit must be cautious to avoid "getting burned." Thus, they contend girls should inform family and friends of their intention to cohabit, negotiate boundaries with the person they are going to cohabit with, and discuss finances. Also interesting, they contend the "marriage conversation" is one of those important things to consider before deciding to cohabit. They write, "By creating a time frame for getting engaged or talking about it, you're merely clarifying your hopes and expectations—you're definitely thinking 'marriage' at some point—and ensuring that your partner feels similarly."[10] In short, these kinds of conversations are needed because of the gender inequity so often found in cohabiting relationships.

Fourth, cohabiting couples often "slide" into it rather the decide to enter into it. In his recent analysis of the 2018 NCHS report, Scott Stanley draws attention to the fact that it's harder to break up when one is cohabiting. In Scott's words, some people "get stuck longer." One reason this is the case is because most couples "slide" into cohabiting rather than make a clear decision about motives and future desires. Most disconcerting of all for Stanley is the fact that cohabitation "is increasingly a context for childbearing."[11] Meg Jay echoes Scott's point about "sliding" versus "deciding" in what she calls the "cohabitation effect."[12] She writes, "Cohabitation is loaded with setup and switching costs, the basic ingredients of lock-in. Moving in together can be fun and economical, and the setup costs are subtly woven in. . . .

7. Kroeger and Smock, "Cohabitation," 228.

8. Stacy and Wynne Whitman, *Shacking Up: The Smart Girl's Guide to Living in Sin Without Getting Burned* (New York: Broadway Books, 2003).

9. Not only is the decision to cohabit deemed sinful, but as Elizabeth Peck notes in *Not Just Roommates: Cohabitation After the Sexual Revolution* (Chicago: University of Chicago Press, 2012), cohabitation exists in the "shadows of legal marriage" and remains an unacceptable relationship arrangement in terms of American law and policy.

10. Whitman and Whitman, *Shacking Up*, 87.

11. Scott Stanley, "Cohabitation Is Pervasive," *Institute for Family Studies*, https://ifstudies.org/blog/cohabitation-is-pervasive.

12. Meg Jay, "The Cohabitation Effect," *The Defining Decade: Why Your Twenties Matter—And How to Make the Most of Them Now* (New York: Twelve Books, 2012).

Later, these setup costs have an effect on how likely we are to leave."[13] According to Jay, singles must be aware of what living together truly means, as well as what it doesn't mean. She writes, "I am not for or against living together, but I am for twentysomethings knowing that, far from safeguarding against divorce, moving in with someone increases your chances of locking in on someone, whether he or she is right for you or not."[14]

Finally, there is not one type of cohabitation. As Joshua Gold notes, the professional literature suggests three categories.[15] "Prenuptial" cohabiters intend to marry, but the timing of the ceremony could still be uncertain for a variety of reasons. For example, a couple may have a list of agreed-on accomplishments they want to "mark off" before they get married. According to Gold, cohabitation for this group is understood as the first stage of marriage. "Testers" cohabiters are less certain about marriage. "Marriage remains a possibility, but pre-engagement cohabiting becomes a 'test' of the couple's compatibility."[16] Gold, like others, notes the likelihood of couples "sliding" into cohabitation when they find themselves in this group. As Gold notes, the overall lack of "conjoint clarity on the purpose of the cohabitation and the possibility of future marriage increases the changes for marriage based on financial, pregnancy, or social constraints among those who might not otherwise marry if not already living together."[17] Finally, there are "alternative" cohabiters: those who have no interest in marrying, again for a variety of reasons. "These persons prefer the sexual, domestic, and legal freedoms in cohabiting."[18] And a growing portion of this group happens to be cohabiting adults. "Postdivorce or widowhood, these individuals are wanting companionship and a romantic relationship but not wanting to merge finances or risk marital failure."[19]

---

13. Ibid., 97.

14. Ibid., 99.

15. Joshua M. Gold, "Typologies of Cohabitation: Implications for Clinical Practice and Research," *The Family Journal: Counseling and Therapy for Couples and Families* 20, no. 3 (2012): 315–21. Gold also states that "college-age cohabitors" exist in this model, but given their unique place in life and their mental and emotional development stage this group of men and women should not be mixed with the other three typologies. He notes, however, that college-age cohabiters tend to move into one of these other three categories "as their college careers end and decisions must be faced about the future of their cohabitation" (316).

16. Ibid., 316.

17. Ibid., 317–18.

18. Ibid.

19. Ibid.

Theology and Cohabitation

In 1999, the Catholic bishops issued *Marriage Preparation and Cohabiting Couples: An Information Report.* They concluded that living together before one commits to marriage is a "false sign," as a cohabiting relationship in the eyes of the church "contradicts the meaning of a sexual relationship in marriage as the total gift of one-self in fidelity, exclusivity, and permanency."[20] Moreover, the bishops contend that cohabiting couples face a "high risk for divorce when they do choose to move from cohabitation to marriage." The argument for why this is the case is straightforward: (1) the experience of cohabitation creates risk factors and bad habits that can sabotage a subsequent marriage; (2) persons who cohabit appear to have lower levels of religious participation, education, and earning power—all of which are associated with higher risk of divorce.

The recent research on cohabitation suggests an alternative to the bishops' position from over twenty years ago. In contrast to their prohibitive narrative, some religious scholars approach the topic of cohabitation as part of the marriage journey and an opportunity for engagement with a couple that is discerning marriage. Kieran Scott attends to the "different forms of cohabitation."[21] A person could be engaged in one of three kinds of cohabiting relationships. The first type is temporary or casual cohabitation, and, as the name suggests, the commitment level between the two partners is either very little or absent altogether. A second kind of cohabitation identified by Scott is "conscious preparation for marriage, a trial run as it were." Finally, Scott explains two people might cohabit as a substitute for marriage.

A key point to Scott's argument (and others like him), however, is that the three types are not equal. Couples living together and consciously preparing for marriage are doing something different from two people living together with no future intention to marry. The main reason this is the case is twofold. First, Scott contends the premodern distinction between spousal pledging and nuptial wedding has largely been forgotten today, and yet it contains a significant insight that can better help us understand when the process of marriage begins. It makes room to reconsider the practice of cohabitation. This can take place, however, only if one also admits that, for most couples today, their life together as a married couple has

20. USCCB Report, "Marriage Preparation and Cohabiting Couples: Information Report," in *Perspectives on Marriage: A Reader* (New York: Oxford University Press, 2006), 89.

21. Keiran Scott, "Cohabitation and Marriage as a Life-Process," in *Perspectives on Marriage: A Reader,* 119. Scott draws heavily on the work of English theologian and Christian ethicist Adrian Thatcher. See Adrian Thatcher, *Living Together & Christian Ethics* (Cambridge: Cambridge University Press, 2002).

already begun to take effect when they made the decision to pledge themselves to each other as spouses *with* the intent to marry in the future.

Put in more simple terms, Scott contends marriage is best understood as a journey in which partners travel through life. If this description more accurately captures what committed persons are doing in the process of marriage, then it is easier to understand why the church might think about more openly acknowledging and validating parts of the marriage journey both before and after the official wedding ceremony and deem those "stages" of the relationship as important as the decision to marry. For Scott, the betrothal ceremony of times past was a way in which couples expressed their respect for the sacredness of marriage. Betrothal was not an end in and of itself; it was a practice open to the possibility of marriage.

Scott's point is echoed in the work of Todd Salzman and Michael Lawler.[22] They come to the topic of cohabitation "with a Catholic faith, and we attempt to bring that faith into conversation with the experience of cohabitation and how that experience affects the lives of cohabiting couples."[23] Moreover, like Scott and Adrian Thatcher before them, Salzman and Lawler reiterate that cohabitation is nothing new in the Western and Catholic tradition. Building on this reality, Salzman and Lawler stress that the social sciences indicate that not all forms of cohabitation are equal. Thus, when Salzman and Lawler discuss cohabitation, they are referring to nuptial cohabiters—those already committed to marriage in their future. Relying on the work of marriage researcher Scott Stanley, Salzman and Lawler stress the importance of commitment and its implication of *dedication* to the relationship and *constraints* surrounding behavior. For Salzman and Lawler, this commitment is what ought to be ritualized and celebrated in the form of a betrothal ceremony.[24]

This betrothal ceremony existed before the Council of Trent and its specific decree, *Tametsi*, articulated in 1563. According to Salzman and Lawler, *Tametsi* "transformed the ritual of marriage, namely the wedding, from a simple contract between families, one not circumscribed by any legal formalities, to a solemn contract, one in which certain legal formalities had to be observed for validity."[25] In addition to this contractual change, Salzman and Lawler stress that *Tametsi* also changed the "how and the when" of marriage. It banned the practice of betrothal

22. Todd A. Salzman and Michael G. Lawler, *Sexual Ethics: A Theological Introduction* (Washington, DC: Georgetown University Press, 2012).

23. Ibid., 124.

24. For more on Scott Stanley's ideas related to commitment, see *The Power of Commitment: A Guide to Active, Lifelong Love* (San Francisco: Jossey-Bass Books, 2005).

25. Salzman and Lawler, *Sexual Ethics*, 132.

as a legal part of marriage. While the first sexual intercourse between the couple (spouses) usually followed the betrothal, this "fact of the Catholic tradition" was obscured after the Council of Trent.[26]

Discussion Points Going Forward

In this essay, I have tried to highlight what we know about cohabitation in the United States. There is no single form of cohabitation, and predicting divorce risk is more complicated than researchers originally thought. In addition, this essay has explored the possibility of betrothal offered by some theologians as a way faith communities, in this case the Catholic Church, can respond. In this final section, I argue that we need to move the betrothal ritual beyond the pages of theological textbooks and into the real lives of couples and families and, more importantly, into the sacred space of our faith communities. This move needs to happen on four different levels—the personal, familial, social, and ecclesial—so that we may be able to respond to the exponential uptick in cohabitation witnessed over the past two decades.

First, at the individual level, young adults and couples thinking about possibly cohabiting must understand that a discernment process is a necessary step before moving in together in order to avoid the "sliding versus deciding" dilemma that both Stanley and Jay discuss in their research. To discern whether or not cohabitation is an option, families and faith communities need to be leaders in helping young people articulate their nonnegotiables when it comes to healthy personal relationships. What are the values, ideas, principles, beliefs, or practices that they hold close to their heart and do not want to give up just because they are now in a relationship? Discernment needs to happen early in high school youth ministry venues and religious classrooms. We need to help young adults understand, create, and sustain healthy personal relationships so that when they progress in personal and intimate relationships later on in life (usually in their twenties), they already have been practicing what it means to discern and reflect on their relationship "nonnegotiables." The more practice young adults have in participating in active discernment about their personal relationship, the more they will be able to reflect and actively decide if they eventually want to cohabit because they will have practiced what it means to actively "decide" about a relationship.

Second, at the familial level, families need to talk more openly and honestly about "all-things relationships." This will neither be easy for every family nor

26. Ibid., 131.

necessarily look the same. Nonetheless, families should carve out space in which young adults and the adults they have come to trust can begin to think through the complexities of being in an intimate relationship with another person. There must be at least one community to which both the individual and the couple can turn for help. Active conversations need to happen between couples and their families when making the decision to cohabit. While these kinds of conversations can be fraught with different expectations, familial communities have the power to shape a couple's relationship well into its future. Conversations need to take place (and theologians need to be on the front lines assisting) because there is an opportunity for discernment to be practiced by all involved.

Third, at the social level, there are socioeconomic and gender dynamics that require further study and consideration. Gold points out that those in cohabiting relationships "lack formal recognition by the legal system, medical care, and health insurance companies." Thus, when a cohabiting relationship dissolves, "there are no legal safeguards for either party or no legal recourse for how to divide assets, address any childcare issues, and so on."[27] Compounding matters, Fenaba R. Addo argues that total debt, credit card debt, and educational debt "all increased the odds of cohabitation for women."[28] It is unsurprising, then, that Kroeger and Smock highlight in their analysis that recent data "suggests that women experience more severe economic consequences when exiting cohabitating relationships than do their male counterparts."[29] Since marriage has moved from being first on a couple's timeline to the capstone of people's personal, professional, and economic goals, Addo argues for the need to revisit "the relationship between economic resources and early union formation, particularly during a period when cohabitation has become more common and rising inequality has contributed to a new marital divide in America."[30] In what ways can theologians be a part of this discussion and help reshape a couple's socioeconomic views of "what counts"? In addition, can theologians articulate a "marriage journey" that conceives of marriage not as a luxury good or capstone event attainable only by those who can afford expensive weddings? More pointedly, with respect to the love that animates current engagement rituals, can faith communities become the new locus for couples thinking about progressing in a relationship, providing an alternative to the diamond store?

Finally, it is time for the betrothal ritual to move from the pages of textbooks into the sanctuary so that faith communities can be a part of a couple's discernment

---

27. Gold, "Typologies of Cohabitation," 318.

28. Addo, "Debt, Cohabitation, and Marriage in Young Adulthood," 1697.

29. Kroeger and Smock, "Cohabitation," 228.

30. Addo, "Debt, Cohabitation, and Marriage in Young Adulthood," 1698.

process. I stress this point because if we are to develop an "ethics of encounter," as Pope Francis has recently suggested, faith communities need to be another place (in addition to the family) in which individuals and couples do the hard work of asking themselves all kinds of questions about their current personal relationship and discerning what the future may or may not look like. This also means faith communities need to become more comfortable with couples discerning, perhaps, that a relationship should not go forward into the next step of marriage (whatever the reasoning), regardless of the living situation of the couple. A marriage agenda should not be pushed onto a couple, but neither should a cohabitation agenda. Rather, a betrothal ritual should be introduced and a couple should be invited to participate in the *guided* ritual. Such a move can enable the couple to begin practicing what it means to infuse the relationship with more commitment and responsibility. At the same time, this betrothal ritual could include space for a couple to articulate their desire to move ahead in front of familial and faith communities. They are asked to enter into a structured and guided discernment process that allows them to begin to experience what it's going to mean to make a more permanent commitment. Young adults discerning their relationship future need something similar, especially if they have decided to cohabit. What exactly this ritual looks like can be different for each faith community. But, the longer we wait for a ritual to appear, the more people will slide into cohabitation without reflecting on it or be prevented from moving on to marriage because of the dominance of the engagement ring script (followed by a "let's plan the wedding day" script). Instead, family and faith should take the lead in helping couples on their relationship journey.

Conclusion

This essay has attempted to demonstrate that the question is no longer "Who cohabits?" but rather "Who is not cohabiting?" Moreover, we know not all forms of cohabitation are the same, and persons enter these unions for various reasons. People of faith do not have to compromise their beliefs about marriage in order to address this issue and respond proactively. Christians have a theological ritual at their disposal that served as a guidepost for couples and families in times past. Today, the "signs of the times" indicate strongly there is every good reason to return to the ritual of betrothal not to undercut the sanctity of marriage but rather to reinvigorate it. Cohabitation directed toward lifelong commitment could become serious and effective "preparation for" marriage if discerned and practiced within a ritual framework of betrothal that requires individual discernment and includes familial participation.

Chapter 16

Singleness as a Vocation of Love

Jana Marguerite Bennett

In the latest US Census report on singleness for adults eighteen and older, 45.2 percent of all people over the age of eighteen were single; 63.5 percent were "never married" (which may still mean living with a partner); 23.1 percent were divorced; 13.4 were widowed; 35.7 percent had children currently living at home; 53.2 percent were women, of whom a little more than a third had given birth in the previous twelve months.[1] There are several important stories that need to be told about these statistics. Moreover, there are some important questions Christians need to address in relation to singles, who make up almost half of the US population.

While most people, including Christians, are familiar with the never-married category of singleness, which includes cohabitation, far fewer people think of singleness in terms of the other statistics: divorce, widowhood, and single parenting. In media, television shows, and novels, these states of life are seen as sometime tragedies for a few unlucky people who experience divorce or death of a spouse. Likewise, Christians often overlook these less-well-known states of life. Divorce is the state of life that has been most often written about by contemporary theologians, typically described in terms of disintegration of families, except perhaps in cases of spousal abuse. Widowhood is written about much more rarely, and single parenting is hardly mentioned. These less-well-known states of life are, however, singularly important in the Christian tradition. Moreover, these states of

---

1. US Census Bureau, "Unmarried and Single Americans Week: Sept. 17–23, 2017," https://www.census.gov/content/dam/Census/newsroom/facts-for-features/2017/cb17-ff16.pdf.

life are integral to our having a full, robust understanding of Christian discipleship for all people—whether they are married or not.

In this essay, I give some depth to the statistics about divorce, widowhood, and single parenting. I name the largely negative ways that society, generally, and Christians, more specifically, have spoken about them. I describe how these states of life show up in Scripture and Catholic tradition, including how they've been incorporated into Christian life in previous centuries. I conclude with a discussion of Pope Francis's recent exhortation, which asks all Catholics to see these states of life as part of the whole Christian community.

Divorce

Divorce used to be a shameful secret that didn't get discussed in polite society but is now considered simply a part of the fabric of contemporary life. Although divorce rates are at their lowest levels since the 1980s, best estimates still put the rate around or slightly above 40 percent.[2] In addition, fewer people are getting married, especially among young adults. Thus, socially, fewer people understand marriage as a "forever" partnership but instead see it as an institution with some flexibility.[3] In recognition of these social changes, some Christian traditions have even developed divorce rituals, such as a prayer service that marks the end of a marriage.[4]

Although researchers note a greater social acceptability of divorce in recent decades, they still note negative impacts of divorce. When most people get married, they do not tend to consider that, one day, they might end up divorced. Statistics never tell a whole story: they don't indicate the name calling, fights, years of anger or coldness, long-term illnesses, or abuse that might factor into couples' decisions to get divorced. Statistics don't quite account for the stigmas that remain (even today) of divorce or its aftereffects. For example, women are more likely to experience negative impacts of divorce, especially financially.[5] Both

---

2. Betsey Stevenson and Justin Wolfers, "Marriage and Divorce: Changes and the Driving Forces," *Journal of Economic Perspectives* 21, no. 2 (2007): 27–52; Sheela Kennedy and Steven Ruggles, "Breaking Up Is Hard to Count: The Rise of Divorce in the United States, 1980–2010," *Demography* 51, no. 2 (2014): 587–98.

3. Judith Treas, Jonathan Lui, and Zoya Gubernskaya, "Attitudes on Marriage and New Relationships: Cross-National Evidence on the Deinstitutionalization of Marriage," *Demographic Research* 30 (2014): 1494–1526.

4. Laura Arosio, "A Ceremony for Divorce? Emerging Practices for a New Rite of Passage," *INTAMS Review* 17 (2011): 14–24.

5. See, for example, Christopher Tamborini, Kenneth Couch, and Gayle Reznik, "Long-Term Impact of Divorce on Women's Earnings Across Multiple Divorce Windows: A Life Course Perspective," *Advances in Life Course Research* 26 (2015): 44–59.

partners may sometimes experience heightened depression, anxiety, and stress.[6] Moreover, friends and the surrounding community are likely to experience some senses of loss and grief.

In addition (as with all states of singleness), divorce does not merely affect one person or even merely the couple. We should never think that "singleness" really only means "one person's life." Divorce affects a whole host of people, especially any children involved in a couple's life. Children of divorce are a particular concern. Most research has suggested detrimental effects on children's emotional health, behavioral concerns, relationship with one or both parents, and success in school. There may be some benefits of divorce for children of couples in high-conflict marriages (about one-third of all marriages) that display poor communication skills, aggression, abuse, or other high-risk situations.[7]

Into this social context, Christian theologians have written quite a bit about divorce. Christian tradition as a whole has mixed responses to ending relationships that were forged by the lifelong vows of marriage, the promises to remain with another person in sickness, health, good times and bad, as long as life lasts. If marriage is to mean something—if those lifelong vows are to mean something at all—then we must take very seriously the times when those vows are broken. Perhaps that is why many Christians who have written about their divorces have told the story of their divorces using the language of tragedy. Lauren Winner, contemporary spirituality author, describes the ways she thought of her own divorce as a personal failure: "In Christianity there's this script of, you do the right things and you will not come to that place of despair, and something is wrong with you if you do."[8] In other words, she thought that Nice Christians Don't Divorce. So how, then, should Christians think about the fact that human relationships fail, for a variety of good and not-so-good reasons?

Christian tradition has long named concern about divorce because Jesus' own words about divorce in the gospels are strongly worded. In Matthew's gospel, Jesus addresses someone who asks him, "Is it lawful for a man to divorce for any cause whatever?" (Matt 19:3). Jesus replies by quoting a passage from Scripture (Gen 2): "'For this reason a man shall leave his father and mother to be joined to

---

6. David Sbarra, Karen Hasselmo, and Kyle Bourassa, "Divorce and Health: Beyond Individual Differences," *Current Directions in Psychological Science* 24 (2015): 109–13.

7. See, for example, Judith Wallerstein, Julia Lewis, and Sherrin Packer Rosenthal, "Mothers and Their Children After Divorce: Report from a 25-Year Longitudinal Study," *Psychoanalytic Psychology* 30 (2013): 167–84.

8. Yonat Shimron, "Historian Tackles Doubt, Divorce, and the Priesthood," *Washington Post*, February 15, 2012, https://www.washingtonpost.com/national/on-faith/historian-tackles-doubt-divorce-and-the-priesthood/2012/02/15/gIQAoOTKGR_story.html?noredirect=on&utm_term=.82a28f4c820f.

his wife, and the two shall become one flesh.' So they are no longer two, but one flesh. Therefore what God has joined together, no human being must separate" (Matt 19:5-6). The Pharisees push Jesus on the point, however. They ask him why Jesus should think no couple should separate, given that Moses' own law permits divorce. Jesus links Moses' law to "hardness of hearts." This Scripture might therefore even suggest that divorce can be equated to refusal to listen to God truly, refusal to display the kind of love that God offers.

In his first letter to the Corinthian church, Paul writes about divorce as well. He states that a wife should not separate from her husband and "a husband should not divorce his wife" (7:11). If a wife does separate from her husband, however, she should not remarry but either live singly or seek reconciliation. Paul seems especially to permit divorce in cases where believers have married unbelievers. From New Testament scriptural accounts, then, divorce seems permissible but certainly not preferred.

Catholic tradition about marriage and divorce reflects these, and other, Scriptures. In order to appreciate Catholic thinking about divorce, we first must recall that the church names marriage as a sacrament, that is, as a sign of God's presence and action in our world. The couple themselves represent this sign of God's presence. Both members of a couple must freely consent to a marriage, without coercive action on the part of either person or of any friend or member of the couple's family. Such free consent gives witness to God's own gracious assent to human free will. In addition, the sacramental signs of marriage include the unity and fidelity of the couple to each, just as God has steadfast love for us (Pss 136–39). Finally, the sacramentality of marriage also reflects that God is a God of life; so too, the married couple is asked to be open to life, specifically through children. Based on Paul's words about marrying unbelievers, the church also may permit particular kinds of annulments for interfaith marriages.

Because marriage is a sign of God's grace in all these ways, and exactly because God is eternal and ever-loving, Catholic tradition holds that the sacramental aspect of a couple's relationship therefore remains present even if a couple decides to break up a marriage in a legal sense. Catholics' main remedy for marriages that break apart is annulment. Contrary to popular belief, annulment is not "Catholic divorce" but rather a process of discernment that asks whether the sacramental signs of marriage were present at the beginning of a relationship. Were free consent, unity, and openness to life present? If the sacramentality was not present from the beginning, then the church may determine that the marriage is annulled. Couples seeking annulments must first have gone through the process of civil divorce. Divorce is the legal process that makes determinations about the end of a relationship, specifically about the ways that property might be divided and custody of children apportioned. Annulment, by contrast, focuses on the relationship's beginnings. Annulment does *not* make any children of the relationship illegitimate.

The other aspect of divorce that Christians need to be concerned with is compassion for people who are in the midst of divorce. The church allows that people who have divorced still have a full place in Christian life, including participation in the sacraments. More than that, Christians need to provide support for couples and families going through divorce. As Pope Francis writes in *Amoris Laetitia*, "Seeing things with the eyes of Christ inspires the Church's pastoral care for the faithful who are living together, or are only married civilly, or are divorced and remarried. Following this divine pedagogy, the Church turns with love to those who participate in her life in an imperfect manner: she seeks the grace of conversion for them; she encourages them to do good, to take loving care of each other and to serve the community in which they live and work" (AL 78).

More than that, Christians need to recognize that the divorced people in their midst remind us of God's presence to each one of us, even and especially in the midst of our own brokenness. God does not love any of us, let alone love us more or better, because we are perfect or because we are part of relationships that perfectly reflect who God is. Rather, Catholic tradition expects that we behave humanly, which is to say, we shall all fail in our relationships, likely on a daily basis. I will be annoyed, irritated, or just plain tired and yell at my husband or my kids. I will say precisely the wrong thing in precisely the wrong moment and be horrified that I did so. They will do the same. I think a real difficulty for many people, when it comes to Christianity, is that Christians propose idealistic visions of marriage and family. The ideals are necessary; we need a vision for who God means us to be. Yet just as necessary is the reminder that God is with us in it all. Those who are divorced are shining examples of faith in God's grace in all the moments of our lives.

Widowhood

Across the whole adult population, about 8.6 percent of women fifteen and older, and 2 percent of men fifteen and older, are widowed.[9] As we would expect, most people who are widowed are older; 79 percent of women and 35 percent of men over the age of eighty-five are widows or widowers, compared with 34 percent

---

9. US Census Bureau, "American Families, 15 Years of Age and Older," *US Census Bureau*, https://www.census.gov/data/tables/2016/demo/families/cps-2016.html.

of women and 6.4 percent of men between the ages of sixty-five and seventy-five.[10] It is also worth noting that between 1 and 5 percent of Americans experience death of a spouse at younger ages. Both widowed and divorced women suffer economic consequences from losing a partner. The economic effects of widowhood are not as dire as they were in past times, especially since women are now more likely to hold jobs that enable self-sufficiency. Nonetheless, financial concerns remain an issue for single widows who have not remarried.[11]

Financial concerns, especially of widowed women, feature heavily in Jewish and Christian traditions. Both have histories of valuing widows in their midst, though that history often goes overlooked these days. Compared with divorce, widowhood is far less often written about in contemporary society. Some of that may be due to the fact that marriage relationships have often been connected to economic necessity; in an era where most women work jobs that provide livelihood, the kind of economic devastation widows felt in earlier centuries is mitigated.

Scriptures are clear, however. God commands people to care for the widows and orphans in their midst. (I will come back to the points made about orphans in my next section on single parenting.) God's law given to the ancient Israelites, as stated in Exodus 22:21-22, says: "You shall not wrong any widow or orphan. If ever you wrong them and they cry out to me, I will surely listen to their cry." Elsewhere, God is proclaimed as a God who is "mighty and awesome . . . who executes justice for the orphan and widow" (Deut 10:17-18). Psalm 68:6 proclaims that God is "Father of the fatherless, defender of widows." These are just a small sampling of the places where God is so named. In other words, Jewish and Christian heritage names a significant part of God's identity as One who stands with people who have no families—most especially with those who have lost their husbands.

Christian Scriptures specifically mention the ways that the earliest Christian communities cared for widows. One of the earliest disputes is recorded in the Acts of the Apostles, where: "At that time, as the number of disciples continued to grow, the Hellenists complained against the Hebrews because their widows were being neglected in the daily distribution. So the Twelve called together the community of the disciples and said, 'It is not right for us to neglect the word of God to serve at table'" (Acts 6:1-2). This Scripture alludes to the importance of

10. Andrew Roberts, Stella Ogunwole, Laura Blakeslee, and Megan Rabe, "The Population 65 Years and Older in the United States, 2016," *US Census Bureau*, https://www.census.gov/content /dam/Census/library/publications/2018/acs/ACS-38.pdf.

11. Elliot Raphaelson, "Widows Face Hard Financial Planning Decisions," *Chicago Tribune*, April 24, 2019, https://www.chicagotribune.com/business/sns-201904241302--tms--savingsgctnzy -a20190424-20190424-story.html.

two practices in Christian life: preaching the word of God but also distributing food and other goods to those in need, such as widows. The ideal Christian community considers the material needs of all those in its midst.

In addition, Paul's letter to Timothy suggests that churches should institute an "Order of Widows"—that is, a holy group of widowed women who were responsible for some of the rites of the church. Paul writes about "enrolling widows" in a group of widows that appear to take vows. These widows practice hospitality, do good works, and otherwise participate in the life of the church (see 1 Tim 5:3-16). Christian practice included such orders from the earliest days, and these orders continue to exist down through the centuries, though in lesser numbers today than in previous centuries.

Pope Francis calls on Christians to take up care of widows, particularly those who are elderly, in his apostolic exhortation on the family. Importantly, it is not only that Christians are called on to "help" widows, but Christians must recognize the integral value that widows have for Christian community. Most especially, elderly widows and widowers offer insights and connections to our history, as well as to wisdom that our culture needs: "A family that remembers has a future," Pope Francis writes (AL 193). If we do not know who we are, what troubles we have been part of, we cannot move forward to a future. Moreover, the way we treat the elderly shapes who we become in the future. If people are always worried that they will be forgotten when they are no longer "young," there is no impetus for having a future beyond the few short years of youth and young adulthood. There is literally no future for people if they cannot envision themselves as active and contributing members of society even in times and places when they might lose their spouses, be older, or both.

Single Parenting

Christians, and others, ideally *should* understand single parenting as including divorced and widowed single parents but also never-married women who have chosen to have children without being married, never-married parents who are not living with a partner, and parents who are parenting solo for a significant length of time (as when military spouses are deployed overseas or a parent is in prison). In other words, there are multiple ways in which single-parent households exist for significant lengths of time and therefore multiple opportunities for people to help others in what can be trying circumstances. Yet, theologians and others largely overlook these various single-parent households in order to focus on one single-parent household type: the household that is run by a single mother. To be fair, the number of women-run single-parent households is significant. About 1 in

5 children today live in single divorced/widowed/unmarried parent households headed by women while only 4 percent live in such households headed by men.[12]

The contemporary American political scene as well as contemporary Christian communities have been suspicious of single parents in general. Sociological research suggests that about two-thirds of Americans stated "unmarried parenthood—solo mothering especially—as a negative trend for society."[13] Moreover, "[a]cceptance of unmarried parenthood tends to be particularly low among whites, college graduates, and Republicans."[14] These mothers become vilified on several counts. First, they dared to have sex and children before getting married. Second, they depend on the larger community to support and sustain them. Child care is expensive, so single parents may find it quite difficult to pay for child care, which costs more than housing in many parts of the United States.

Yet, life for many single parents is, in fact, real poverty rather than some kind of free cash gift from the government. Money remains a significant concern for many single parents. The Pew Research Forum observes that "among solo parents, mothers are almost twice as likely as fathers to be living below the poverty line (30% vs. 17%)," and about a quarter of solo parents, men and women, live below the poverty line, compared with 16 percent of unmarried cohabiting parents.[15] This is despite the fact that the same percentage of single parents and cohabiting parents work (72%). The effects of welfare reforms are disputed, typically across political ideological lines. Welfare has decreased, yet there has been a sharp increase in the number of families living on two dollars a day for at least three months of the year.[16] Statistics show that half of all SNAP recipients work but have difficulty finding jobs that pay enough to cover the cost of food and housing. Additionally, 44 percent of SNAP recipients are children under the age of eighteen, 12 percent are over the age of sixty, and 9 percent are disabled. A recent study of the impact of welfare reforms, including work requirements, suggests that there was an unintended highly negative consequence for children of those on welfare, including that they are more likely not to graduate from high school and

12. Gretchen Livingston, "About One-Third of US Children Are Living with an Unmarried Parent," Pew Research Center, April 27, 2018, https://www.pewresearch.org/fact-tank/2018/04/27/about-one-third-of-u-s-children-are-living-with-an-unmarried-parent/.

13. Ibid.

14. Ibid.

15. Gretchen Livingston, "The Changing Profile of Unmarried Parents," Pew Research Center April 25, 2018, https://www.pewsocialtrends.org/2018/04/25/the-changing-profile-of-unmarried-parents/.

16. Kathryn Edin and H. Luke Shaefer, "20 Years Since Welfare Reform," *The Atlantic*, August 22, 2016, https://www.theatlantic.com/business/archive/2016/08/20-years-welfare-reform/496730/.

to have behavior problems. A difficulty may be that the job requirements did not come with additional child-care support, after-school programs, or other means of helping care for children while a mother or father was at work.[17]

Despite the contemporary attitudes toward younger single mothers in particular, Jewish and Christian Scriptures have both emphasized a need to care for the single-parent households in our midst. Some of the Scriptures about widows, quoted in the above section, also mention "orphans" or the "fatherless." In scriptural language and custom, orphans are not necessarily people who have lost both parents; they might still have had a mother but had lost a key source of economic security. Thus, along with widowhood, single parenting has been called out by God as a particular status in need of support from the community. The link between economic security and the well-being of mothers (in particular) and their children has not lessened with the passage of millennia.

Catholics are beginning to reclaim care of the "fatherless" in their contemporary practice. Pope Francis specifically notes instances about single-mother households in his apostolic exhortation on the family:

> In such difficult situations of need, the Church must be particularly concerned to offer understanding, comfort and acceptance, rather than imposing straightaway a set of rules that only lead people to feel judged and abandoned by the very Mother called to show them God's mercy. (AL 49)

The pope thus asks us both to respond to the needs of single parents and their children and to desist from making presumptions about single parents that are detrimental to the gospel.

In addition, we should consider the gifts that single parents bring to the church. Single parents offer as many and varied gifts as there are people; some of their individual gifts may include determination and grit, patience, flexibility, and more. In addition, single parents so often demonstrate a willingness to depend on others for help at times, something that everyone should learn better. We are all dependent on each other, and we need each other. A great sin of the contemporary nuclear family may be that it sees itself as self-sufficient, when sufficiency taken to extremes is actually detrimental to the growth of individuals, couples, and children. We need each other to reflect back to us ourselves and offer a listening ear or a helping hand. Single parents show us that grace very often.

---

17. See Fred Wulczyn, Richard Barth, Ying-Ying Yuan, Brenda Harden, and John Landsverk, *Beyond Common Sense: Child Welfare, Child Well-Being, and the Evidence for Policy Reform* (New York: Routledge, 2005).

The "Larger Family"

So far, we have discussed common negative attitudes, both from broader culture as well as from Christians, toward the divorced, widowed, and single parents. We have also seen a few Scriptures that suggest Christians not only ought to be caring directly for the divorced, widowed, and single-parenting households but see these families as integral to our Christian life together. Part of our vision about love and families needs to be reformed to include what Pope Francis, among others, has named as the "larger family." Current church teaching suggests that families need to understand themselves as part of a "larger family," that is, the church community. Pope Francis writes in *Amoris Laetitia*:

> In addition to the small circle of the couple and their children, there is the larger family, which cannot be overlooked. Indeed, "the love between husband and wife and, in a derivative and broader way, the love between members of the same family—between parents and children, brothers and sisters and relatives and members of the household—is given life and sustenance by an unceasing inner dynamism leading the family to ever deeper and more intense communion, which is the foundation and soul of the community of marriage and the family." Friends and other families are part of this larger family, as well as communities of families who support one another in their difficulties, their social commitments and their faith. (AL 196)

Pope Francis here highlights that Christian families are never solely nuclear families—that is, married parents with children. If the love between a husband and wife is properly realized, that love must extend not only to children of the couple but to all those people who are part of that family's reach and circle. More than that, the married couple *needs* the "life and sustenance" that others offer to them. Married relationships need the strong support of other people, and married couples need to be able to offer reciprocal sustenance to others. Neither individuals nor couples can survive in a vacuum, devoid of the love and life that communion with others offers. Indeed, community as a whole requires the "deeper and more intense communion" that provides its "foundation and soul" only when the reciprocal relationship between the married couple and the larger family exists to its fullest extent. Both individuals and married couples are fragile entities; we encounter this fragility every day. The very fact that divorce exists, or that widows suffer, or that single-parenting households struggle points to the fact that we humans make up a fragile communion with each other. Yet we need each other.

So Pope Francis exhorts us: this "larger family" is meant to help provide the kind of care that many overlooked and forgotten people need. We all, as the Body of Christ, should be caring for others, especially those who are not members of our immediate families. We should check in with the elderly among us, offer help to others in our parish regardless of state of life, be present to the teenager in need of a listening ear, or people with disabilities who need more accessibility.

What is more, our charge to care for others is meant to be reciprocated toward us. We have a charge to accept others' generosity and hospitality. For we must all realize that, even if we get married, it is likely that we shall find ourselves in "seasons of singleness." We shall find ourselves in need of support from our Christian "larger family" in ways we did not anticipate. We shall find ourselves in need of bearing Christ for others and being Christ for others.

PART III
FAMILIES

Contemporary family ethics emerged in the last few decades as more laymen and -women became Catholic theologians and began to write about the ordinary lives of families. Pope John Paul II's 1981 apostolic exhortation *Familiaris Consortio* inspired scholarship and pastoral care in the 1980s. University of Chicago professor Don Browning brought theologians together with scholars in biblical studies, history, and the social sciences with his Religion, Culture, and Family project in the 1990s and early 2000s to produce an important set of resources that brought intellectual weight to academic work on families. Two dominant strains mark the field of family ethics today: social ethicists analyze the impact of social structures on families and virtue ethicists write about practices with power to shape families from the inside out. Pope Francis's recent apostolic exhortation *Amoris Laetitia* is central to contemporary debates. Supporters build on the pope's focus of welcoming all families and his insistence that the church is called "to form consciences, not replace them" (37). Critics worry that the pope has strayed too far from traditional moral norms.

We include in this section essays that analyze social structures and cultural changes that challenge families and offer a range of structural and personal ways to respond. Catholic theology on marriage and family in earlier eras often presumed an intact family of faithful Catholics. Victor Carmona's moving essay challenges this assumption by focusing on mixed-status families in the United States, families where one spouse is undocumented. Gemma Cruz complements this essay by her research on global migration which leads to family separation and adaptations in gender relations and parenting. Attentive to the diversity of households where Catholics reside, we include an essay by Daniel Olsen on interchurch families where Christians of different denominations come together, and a piece by Tom

Beaudoin on rising numbers of "secular" Catholic families that claim "Catholic heritage" but not traditional faith practices. Both ask what Catholic theology has to learn from families like these. We also include essays on struggles with work (Christine Firer Hinze), time (Marcus Mescher and Tim and Sue Muldoon), and money (David Cloutier) that engage rich resources from Catholic theology and ethics. Rounding out the section, Mary Doyle Roche's essay on youth protest challenges conventional ideas of parenting and family ethics by lifting up young adults as role models who are embodying the best of the Catholic social justice tradition.

Chapter 17

Mixed-Status Families, Solidarity, and *Lo Cotidiano*

Victor Carmona

Early in our marriage Astrid and I felt the tremendous weight of the US immigration system. At our interview for her permanent residency visa (her "green card"), the officer informed us that she would be deported. Apparently, we had submitted the wrong paperwork in an incorrect sequence. We were stunned. Astrid was other-than-documented for less than a year, but it felt like a lifetime. During those tense months, the threat of her deportation brought with it a constant state of fear that neither of us had experienced before and hope to never feel again. We were afraid of driving, especially near the neighboring county, because the community knew police officers there targeted Latinx drivers, and they could question our legal status during a routine traffic stop.[1] We were fearful of visiting family because of immigration checkpoints that the government sets up within one hundred miles from the US border. We were powerless. Though I was born in the United States, it was highly likely that, since I am a bilingual Mexican-American US citizen, the government would not grant us a hardship waiver were it to deport Astrid to Mexico. It was hard for us to leave home each morning, knowing that we might not be with each other at the end of the day. That is how our marriage began. That experience shapes it to this day.

Our experience was—and remains—a common feature of family life for many Latinx families. We had joined the nearly two million married couples whose

---

1. While it is a contested term, in this chapter I use the gender-neutral "Latinx" to describe communities in the United States that have ties to Latin America. I acknowledge that many in our communities are ambivalent about the term and prefer to use others instead, including Latino, Latinoa, Latina/o, Latin@, and LatinaXo.

marriages suffer under the strain of our country's broken immigration system because one of the spouses is undocumented.[2] When our first of two daughters was born, we became part of the nearly nine million undocumented immigrants, permanent residents, and citizens living in mixed-status families across the United States.[3] Attention to reality in daily life—to *lo cotidiano*[4]—sheds light on two kinds of ordinary dilemmas that mixed-status families face: those having to do with familial relationships and those having to do with the family's mission in broader society. Attentiveness to these dilemmas offers insights into solidarity that challenges and nurtures acts of love amid a society that struggles still to understand that immigrants and citizens don't lead separate lives but are, instead, bound together in the struggles of daily family life.

Ordinary Life

Ordinary life or *lo cotidiano* is an essential time and place from which to reflect on the meaning and implications of personal and communal faith in God, including in the context of family life. As Carmen Nanko-Fernández explains, in Latinx faith communities *lo cotidiano* is a source for divine revelation in terms of "the perceived presence of God as well as . . . the perceived absence of the divine."[5] While we have a shared ethnicity and ancestry from Latin America, Latinx communities are diverse. We are Catholic and Protestant. We practice other religions or none at all. We espouse a rich array of social and political views that speak to each Latinx's age, gender, race, sexual orientation, income, and national origin. We also belong to all kinds of families, including those with single parents and those divided by international borders. Therefore, our families live *lo cotidiano* in a variety of ways; the perceived presence or absence of God may be discerned accordingly.

---

2. This data includes married couples between 2012 and 2016. It includes 1.2 million undocumented immigrants married to a US citizen and 0.75 million married to a legal permanent resident. See Migration Policy Institute, "Profile of the Unauthorized Population: United States," https://www.migrationpolicy.org/data/unauthorized-immigrant-population/state/US#parental.

3. See Jeffrey S. Passel and D'Vera Coh, "A Portrait of the Unauthorized Immigrants in the United States, 2010," Pew Research Center, 11–12, https://www.pewresearch.org/wp-content uploads/sites/5/reports/133.pdf.

4. For the term *lo cotidiano*, see Ada María Isasi-Díaz, *La Lucha Continues: Mujerista Theology* (Maryknoll, NY: Orbis Books, 2004), 95.

5. Carmen Nanko-Fernández, "*Lo Cotidiano* as *Locus Theologicus*," in *The Wiley Blackwell Companion to Latino/a Theology*, ed. Orlando O. Espín (Malden, MA: Wiley Blackwell, 2015), 16.

As a Mexican-American Catholic Latino theologian, I am convinced of the insights into the meaning of solidarity that the experiences of mixed-status families offer other Christians. The US–Mexico borderlands and the fluidity of the peoples who have lived there for generations have nurtured Mexican-American and borderlander/*fronterizo* identities that are culturally distinct from the dominant cultures of the United States and Mexico. Historical memories of the border, whether they be of shifting boundaries that cross a people or of people who cross those boundaries, shape Mexican-American theological-ethical reflections on migration, including this one. Cuban-American scholarship on migration tends to advance perspectives that are shaped by the painful experience of exile, of families that have faced the challenge of being cut off from one another by the actions of the US and Cuban governments. Puerto Rican perspectives reflect the lived experience of families that belong to a diaspora that enjoys the benefits of US citizenship while suffering the consequences, as the aftermath of Hurricane Maria makes clear, of being from a US territory with limited self-determination. Honduran- and Salvadoran-American reflections speak to the refuge and sanctuary that families seek in their attempt to escape the violence that US actions in Central America have unleashed since the Cold War (if not earlier during the Banana Wars). Thus, while our communities have produced reflections on exile, diaspora, refuge, and sanctuary, my perspective highlights the reality of border enforcement on *lo cotidiano*, in daily life.

The centrality of daily life for Latinx theologies emerges from reflections by Latinas on their struggles against oppression. Already in 1986, Cuban-American *mujerista* theologian Ada María Isasi-Díaz had begun honing our communities' attention to the importance of *lo cotidiano* to understand and enact the task of liberation. Years later, she described that task after doing ethnographic work with Mexican-American and Cuban-American women, some of them immigrants:

> For us Latinas, salvation refers to having a relationship with God, a relationship that does not exist if we do not love our neighbor. Our relationship with God affects all aspects of our lives, all human reality. As Latinas become increasingly aware of the injustices we suffer, we reject any concept of salvation that does not affect our present and future reality. For us, salvation occurs in history and is intrinsically connected to our liberation [. . ., which] has to do with becoming agents of our own history, with having what one needs to live and to be able to strive for human fulfillment.[6]

---

6. Ada María Isasi-Díaz, *En La Lucha = In the Struggle: Elaborating a Mujerista Theology* (Minneapolis: Fortress Press, 2004), 53.

The struggles of daily life speak prophetically to the in-breaking of the kin-dom of God that is unfolding in the midst of the present day.[7] The actions that neighborly love entails amid injustices that grate against the human dignity of Latinas and other marginalized members of our communities thus have an epistemological *and* a hermeneutic function. They are both necessary to attain firsthand experiential knowledge of the ways in which God acts in history to end oppression *and* to interpret how oppressive structures stand in the way of such liberation—structures that we must therefore oppose.

Not Separate

Attention to *lo cotidiano* points to a simple yet powerful fact: immigrants and citizens don't lead separate lives. In 2017, the United States had a population of about 325 million people; around 44 million of them were immigrants, making up just under 14 percent of the country's population.[8] Immigrants are an integral part of family life in the United States. That same year, 70 million people in the United States were children under eighteen; a bit over 18 million of them lived with at least one parent who is an immigrant, nearly 25 percent of our country's youth.[9] Of those 18 million children, about 5 million lived with at least one parent who is an undocumented immigrant.[10] Just over 4 million of those children, roughly 80 percent, were born in the United States and thus attained citizenship at birth; 33,000 were naturalized citizens, nearly 1 percent; 167,000 were permanent legal residents, about 3 percent; and 809,000 were undocumented immigrants themselves, or approximately 16 percent.[11] While some families include only US citizens and other families only include immigrants, many more are mixed-status families that bind immigrants and citizens together.

Parents and children can fall under different legal categories within the US immigration system. Some may be citizens by birth or through naturalization, others may be legal permanent residents, and others may be undocumented.

---

7. See Isasi-Díaz, *La Lucha Continues*, 248.

8. Claire Felter and Danielle Renwick, "The U.S. Immigration Debate," Council on Foreign Relations, https://www.cfr.org/backgrounder/us-immigration-debate-0.

9. Ibid.

10. Julia Gelatt and Jie Zong, "Settling In: A Profile of the Unauthorized Immigrant Population in the United States," Migration Policy Institute, 4, https://www.migrationpolicy.org/research/profile-unauthorized-immigrant-population-united-states.

11. Jie Zong, Jeanne Batalova, and Micayla Burrows, "Frequently Requested Statistics on Immigrants and Immigration in the United States," Migration Policy Institute, https://www.migration policy.org/article/frequently-requested-statistics-immigrants-and-immigration-united-states.

That is partly the case because the Immigration and Nationality Act of 1965 and the Immigration Act of 1990 determine how the federal government distributes visas. The government may use one of two visa categories to allow foreigners legal entry into the country: temporary visas (also known as nonimmigrant visas) and permanent ones (also known as permanent immigrant visas or "green cards"). Temporary visas are for foreigners who intend to visit the United States to travel, work, or study for a limited time. Permanent visas are for foreigners who intend to settle in the United States for one of three main reasons: to join family, to work, or to seek asylum/refuge. After three to five years, those legal permanent residents may apply for US citizenship. Undocumented immigrants are those who cross the border illegally, overstay their nonimmigrant visa, or no longer meet the requirements of their permanent visas.

The current immigration system requires, for the most part, that citizens and foreigners have an existing familial or employment relationship. Before a foreigner can apply for a family or employer-sponsored permanent visa, a US citizen, permanent resident, or business must petition the government for a visa by establishing their relationship with that person. Without that petition, a foreigner may not apply for one. United States citizens who are twenty-one or older may petition a visa for immediate family members: their spouse, parent, or unmarried child under twenty-one. Those visas are not numerically capped, though the government does charge those it approves against a per-country annual cap. Most other family and employer-sponsored visa categories (over ten of them), however, are capped. As Julia Gelatt explains, "U.S. law imposes a limit on how many immigrants from any particular country can receive green cards in a given year. Under the per-country cap set in the Immigration Act of 1990, no country can receive more than 7 percent of the total number of employment-based and family-sponsored preference visas in a given year."[12]

As a consequence, no single proverbial "line" exists to apply for a permanent visa for entering the country legally, a fact that illustrates how parents and children can come to have a different legal status from one another. Instead, there are at least nine lines for immigrants from each country in the world as each line moves through the annual caps—lines that include the US citizens, permanent residents, and businesses who petition for those visas. Some lines have extremely long wait times. Siblings can also be waiting in different lines or different officers may approve a visa for one but not the other. For example, as of July 2019, the wait for a US citizen who petitions the government for a family visa to become available for

---

12. Julia Gelatt, "Explainer: How the U.S. Legal Immigration System Works," Migration Policy Institute, 5, https://www.migrationpolicy.org/content/explainer-how-us-legal-immigration-system-works.

their adult unmarried child from Mexico is nearly twenty years long, six months longer if the petitioner is a US permanent resident.[13] Thankfully, there are no wait times for a visa to become available if a US citizen petitions a permanent visa for their unmarried minor child from Mexico (though the immigration process itself might still take several months and cost thousands of dollars). Also, thankfully, for petitioners who are permanent residents, the wait time for a visa to become available for their unmarried minor child from Mexico is three months. If backlogs increase, those children may age-out of their line when they turn twenty-one. They must then go to the back of a twenty-plus-year line. If they marry, they must join another line that at present is eighteen years long for adult married children of US citizens. There are no permanent visas allotted to adult married children of permanent residents.

The reality of mixed-status families also points to the main ways in which one or more of its members may become undocumented, at times for long periods of time.[14] Some become undocumented by crossing the border illegally, even without their full knowledge, to be with family (as in the case of small children). Others, nearly 4.5 million people, about 42 percent of the country's undocumented population, entered the US with a nonimmigrant visa and then lost their legal status once they stayed beyond its expiration date (as in the case of some tourists, or college students who stay in the US after they have graduated).[15] Others still may become undocumented as they go through the process of asking the government to grant them a change from a nonimmigrant visa to a permanent one (for instance, a college student who would like to stay in the US to work after they have graduated) or by submitting the wrong paperwork in an incorrect sequence.

Dilemmas of Mixed-Status Families

Mixed-status families live under the constant threat of deportation that has created a culture of fear that affects individual family members in different ways. In *Everyday Illegal*, sociologist Joanna Dreby studies how illegality undermines

13. Bureau of Consular Affairs, "Visa Bulletin for July 2019," United States Department of State, https://travel.state.gov/content/travel/en/legal/visa-law0/visa-bulletin/2019/visa-bulletin -for-july-2019.html.

14. In "Profile of the Unauthorized Population: United States," the Migration Policy Institute notes 62 percent of undocumented immigrants in the United States have lived in the country for ten or more years.

15. Robert Warren and Donald Kerwin, "The 2,000 Mile Wall in Search of a Purpose: Since 2007 Visa Overstays Have Outnumbered Undocumented Border Crossers by a Half Million," *Journal on Migration and Human Security* 5, no. 1 (2017): doi: 10.1177/233150241700500107.

families in New Jersey and Ohio.[16] Women she interviewed point to a sense of powerlessness toward the government's ability to transform them into "suddenly single mothers, and not of their own choosing."[17] The threat of deportation that weights over their families negatively impacts their sense of self-determination and autonomy. As for the men in her study, that threat undermines their sense of fatherhood. They often center their relationship with their children on their ability to provide, something difficult to do if the government deports them. As for the children she observed and interviewed, the culture of fear sows instability in their lives. Regardless of whether they are citizens, the threat of deportation has taught them to associate stigma with being an immigrant.

The constant state of fear doesn't just affect family members individually. It also impacts a mixed-status family's ability to relate with others in broader society *and* undermines the relationships between spouses, parents and children, and siblings. Dreby writes:

> [For] children and families, legal status has begun to accrue the power of social status distinctions. Under restrictive immigration policies, the social consequences of legal status intensify, especially for children and for families, calling for a re-framing of our understanding of illegality. Rather than an administrative category that one must wait in line to achieve, legal status is a source of social inequality. Restrictive policy environments heighten the social consequences of legal-status differences, so that children and families experience these differences much as they experience the effects of race, class, and gender.[18]

The social consequences that Dreby references above are well known by mixed-status families in Latinx communities because they have to do with *lo cotidiano*. Until the Obama Administration began, driving to school without a license or working without authorization created inconveniences ranging from one's car being towed to risking exploitative situations. Since then, the consequences of undocumented status extend to losing a loved one. The pervasive threat of deportation is such that it has as profound an impact on the ability of each family member (be they a citizen, permanent resident, or undocumented) to live in society. Every contact with nonfamily members is fraught with danger. These are the kinds of ordinary dilemmas that immigrants face in broader society. As a consequence,

16. Joanna Dreby, *Everyday Illegal: When Policies Undermine Immigrant Families* (Oakland: University of California Press, 2015).

17. Ibid., 52.

18. Ibid., 12.

some parents teach their children to keep their undocumented status or that of their siblings or parents a secret. Other parents never tell their children.

Members of mixed-status families are not immune to the social consequences of legal uncertainty within the family. The threat of deportation affects their relationships in distinct ways as well. In the case of spouses, Dreby finds that when they do not share the same status, "imbalances heighten existing gender inequalities."[19] In abusive marriages, a husband may use a wife's lack of legal status to exert power over her. In healthy ones, legal status may determine which spouse's job takes priority when allocating a family's limited resources. When it comes to parents and children, Dreby observes that "US citizen children's full legal rights may give them an advantage over unauthorized parents, who do not feel at liberty to exert their authority in certain situations."[20] At times, children help their parents by interpreting and mediating for them when they interact with school officials, police, or health-care providers, but such parental dependence alters family life. When it comes to the relationship between siblings, for instance, US citizen children in the families that Dreby interviewed tended to negotiate to do less housework. Her research also suggests that "parents may find themselves unknowingly investing more in their US citizen children's activities outside the home because their US citizen children have opportunities that their unauthorized children cannot access. Unauthorized children, at home and available, pick up the slack."[21] If a sibling doesn't know of their undocumented status or if they do but do not fully comprehend the implications, experiences like these awaken and raise their awareness. Ultimately, most undocumented children will learn of their status or fully grasp its impact by the time they are about to graduate high school and cannot apply to most colleges while their US citizen siblings can. These are the kinds of *ordinary* dilemmas that mixed-status families face at home.

Solidarity

In light of *lo cotidiano*, mixed-status families speak prophetically to the in-breaking of the kin-dom of God amid our communities' ongoing pursuit of immigration reform. That claim does not aim to justify their suffering but rather echo Isasi-Díaz's insight that the actions that neighborly love entails—even within families—have an epistemological *and* a hermeneutic function in discerning the ongoing unfolding of the kin-dom of God. The daily struggles of mixed-status families reveal God's continuing action, in the unlikeliest of places, to end op-

19. Ibid., 175.
20. Ibid.
21. Ibid., 112.

pression from sin and its structures in and through the lives of those who suffer under its weight. Those actions also disclose how oppressive structures stand in the way of liberation. From that perspective, the invitation is to discern God's presence in the relationships between spouses, parents and children, and siblings in mixed-status families. Doing so suggests how mixed-status families take up the practice of solidarity.

Love is at the heart of each family's struggle to make it through each day, together. Catholic social teaching on the family suggests why that may be so. As Pope Francis writes in *Amoris Laetitia*: "we were made for love. . . . The most intense joys in life arise when we are able to elicit joy in others, as a foretaste of heaven" (AL 129). The love of spouses and their family can elicit such joy because God created human beings accordingly. For Thomas Aquinas, whose insights partially undergird Francis's claim, human beings perceive or apprehend the good through love in a way that speaks to all of creation's relationship with God. That is because he conceives of creation as being ordered in such a way as to incline all creatures to seek external goods because they need them to survive and flourish. No creature is self-sufficient. Thus, human beings are embodied rational souls that naturally feel an inclination to love and know the good. In the context of a relationship between lover and beloved, the good the lover apprehends in the beloved arouses love. Desire keeps the lover's appetite moving toward the beloved, and it is joy that he or she experiences once that movement reaches its destination. Only then do lover and beloved rest in the joyful love that unites them; a love that is analogous (if imperfectly so) to the joyful love of union with God that Aquinas believes awaits in the beatific vision. Actions of neighborly love give witness to a joy that speaks to the undergirding relationship with God that sustains human beings.

Francis and Aquinas thus offer some insights into why it is fitting to love one's spouse, parent, child, or sibling, regardless of their legal status or one's own. The weight of illegality cannot snuff out the capacity of neighborly love to speak to a human being's undergirding relationship with God. While the effects of the US immigration system are real, and painfully so, no society or government, including the United States, has the power to contravene the natural inclinations driving citizens, permanent residents, and undocumented immigrants—all of whom are God's creatures—to love one another as a spouse, parent, child, or sibling. From that perspective, attempts to use immigration law for such a purpose contravene the created order; in doing so they transform the immigration system into a structure of sin. In *Reconciliatio et Paenitentia*, Pope John Paul II deepens the tradition's understanding of sin by teaching that sinful structures, or those that "by their very matter constitute a direct attack on one's neighbor," come about from social sin, which is a "collective behavior of certain social groups, big or small, or even of whole nations" that are "the result of the accumulation and concentration of many personal sins" (RP 16). Francis's and Aquinas's insights on love do not negate, diminish, or explain away the pain and suffering that mixed-status families experience. They do suggest, however, that relationships within mixed-status families speak still to God's presence in the very fiber of their beings, through their love for one another, even in the midst of suffering under the weight of illegality. John Paul II's teaching on sin invites us to question whether US citizens are acting sinfully in granting explicit or tacit support to an increasingly harsh and inhumane execution of immigration law to preserve the rule of law *at any cost*.

Attentiveness to *lo cotidiano* also demands recognition that differences in legal status have ethically significant effects within mixed-status families in ways that also speak to the reality of personal and social sin. Our families are no different. Personal experience suggests, and sociological research confirms, that they also muddle through the dilemmas of daily life as each member pursues the good they and their families need to survive and flourish. Like other Christian families, at times we struggle to love one another through actions that correctly apprehend and live up to the demands of right relationship, be it with one's spouse, parent, child, or sibling (as the kin-dom of God calls for). Mixed-status families, however, do so under the added strain of illegality. Differences in legal status add a power dimension that is absent from citizen-only families. When mixed-status families are Latinx (as most are), they also do so under the further strain of *familismo*, which Latinx behavioral scientists explain as "a cultural value that defines the family as a system of support and emphasizes the importance of family obligations and involvement with kin."[22] Thus, *familismo* is the value that explains why undocumented siblings would pick up the slack of their citizen siblings. Perhaps, at times, they do so out of love, but other times they do so because they are expected to and are given no choice in the matter. *Familismo* places demands and expectations on vulnerable family members (mothers, the youngest daughter, sisters, LGBTQ children, and the undocumented) who are expected to sacrifice their flourishing for the common good of the family. The demands of right relationship require justice within familial relationships precisely out of love. As Nichole Flores shows through her research, Latinx theologians are increasingly raising this critique of Latinx families, which bears "affinity to Aquinas's articulation of general and particular justice [and] suggests that the good of the community hinges upon the good of its particular members."[23] Solidarity demands no less.

22. Ana Romero Morales and Andrés J. Consoli, "Mexican/Mexican-American Siblings: The Impact of Undocumented Status on the Family, the Sibling Relationship, and the Self," *Journal of Latinx Psychology* (2019): 3, doi: 10/1037/lat0000133.

23. Nichole M. Flores, "Latina/o Families: Solidarity and the Common Good," *Journal of the Society of Christian Ethics* 33, no. 2 (2013): 62.

Practices of solidarity challenge and nurture the love that mixed-status family members have for one another. John Paul II defines solidarity as a virtue precisely because it is "a firm and persevering determination" that persons, and indeed entire communities, need to nourish so they may commit to the pursuit of the common good; "that is to say to the good of all and of each individual because we are *all* really responsible for all" (*Sollicitudo Rei Socialis* 38). In that light, the practice of solidarity within mixed-status families creates ongoing opportunities for personal conversion through the smallest of acts of neighborly love. Whenever US citizens use the privilege of attending college to learn about ways to support, strengthen, and amplify the voice of their undocumented sibling, they do so in solidarity. Their decision may require the humility of acknowledging that an unjust immigration system may have favored them, particularly during childhood, while it hindered their sibling from attending college, exerting their voice freely, being without fear in pursuit of their legal status, or flourishing. Whenever siblings make those decisions, in *lo cotidiano* of college life, their conversion helps heal the effects of personal and social sin in ways that give witness to the unfolding kin-dom of God within their families, even as they suffer under the weight of illegality.

Solidarity also challenges and nurtures mixed-status families to pursue the common good, following what Pope Francis says in *Amoris Laetitia*: "Families should not see themselves as a refuge from society, but instead go forth from their homes in a spirit of solidarity with others" (AL 181). Instead of withdrawing under the weight of illegality, mixed-status families remain as active as they can in the pursuit of the common good in the communities where they live. One of the ways that Latinx families do so is by having a permeable boundary between family and nonfamily. As Flores observes, through baptism a *compadre* and/or *comadre* (the child's godfather and/or godmother) are "grafted on to the family tree through a sacramental responsibility to serve as coparent to a particular family."[24] This responsibility effectively extends to fostering the social, political, and economic well-being of a *compadre's* or *comadre's* family in *lo cotidiano*. It may include facing the effects of illegality, from driving a *compadre* to the hospital because he doesn't have papers while you do, to being willing to support a *comadre's* children if she is deported. Through acts such as these, most unknown beyond the communities where they take place, mixed-status families serve the common good. They transform US society in simple yet profound ways that give witness to the kin-dom of God that is unfolding in their midst, even under the weight of illegality.

24. Ibid., 61.

Chapter 18

It Takes a Global Village

Families in the Age of Migration

Gemma Tulud Cruz

With an estimated 258 million migrants, 25 million refugees, and 3 million asylum seekers scattered across the world, cross-border movements have indelibly changed the way people live, work, and relate with one another. Not surprisingly, the *Instrumentum Laboris* for the Synod on the Family includes "the impact of migration" and "the plight of displaced peoples" (66–79) in the list of critical challenges facing families today.

When the family is touched by international migration, it immediately becomes a geographically split household and, in most cases, a transnational family. A transnational family is different from an ordinary migrant's family in that the defining factor is not the act of border crossing but the dispersion of the family across international borders where different family members spend time in one or the other country depending on various factors.

There are terms for certain types of transnational families. "Astronaut families" refers to mostly East Asian middle-class families in which the husband/father returns to the source country to pursue his career while the wife and children remain in the destination country. Only the husband who is left behind travels for brief family visits whenever his schedule affords him the opportunity (hence the term "astronaut"). In South Korea, families that send young children to English-speaking countries to learn English in the hope of giving them the best chance of getting ahead later on are called "wild geese families," a term given by the Korean media to refer to the lengths the parents will go for the educational well-being of their children.

Migration also sometimes leads to the creation of the "stepfamily," when the husband or wife engages in extramarital affairs, or the marriage ends in separation or divorce, and one or both spouses have children with another partner. For an increasing number of families from the Global South, the search for bare life, which fuels unauthorized migration, also results in a family identity and membership that is peculiar to international migration, that is, the mixed-status families. In the United States, where over 16.5 million households are home to mixed-status families,[1] often unauthorized parent(s) and citizen child(ren) live constantly with the fear and nightmare of arrest, detention, separation, and deportation. Another beleaguered type of mixed-status family includes members who are among the estimated 10 million stateless people worldwide. A related and perhaps more tragic type of family is those whose members are all stateless as a result of past and present forced movements in history.

Family in the context of migration also transcends blood as migrants build and maintain family-like relationships on the basis of race, ethnicity, or, in the case of migrant workers, occupation. For instance, in associations of migrant women domestic workers in Hong Kong, everyone looks after the welfare of one another as families do. The same story is repeated in numerous formal and informal migrant associations worldwide. Oftentimes, migrants' faith, coupled with their own experience of hardships, also imbue them with an even larger sense of what family means. When asked why she thought the church should be involved in helping immigrants, Claudia, a Salvadoran Catholic in the United States responded, "There's a simple reason for that. Our faith tells us that we have to help our *prójimo* (fellow human beings), our brothers and sisters, and we are all brothers and sisters."[2]

In what follows, I explore the impact of global migration on family life and the questions this raises for Christian theology, particularly Catholic teachings. I endeavor to do this by considering the ways in which migrants and their families maintain family relationships and responsibilities in the context of global migration and critically reflecting on how Christian theology may be responsive to these kinship practices. I argue that Christian theology on the family in the age of global migration necessitates cross-cultural, transnational, intergenerational, and gender-sensitive perspectives.

---

1. Kristin Heyer, "Legalization and the Undocumented According to Catholic Social Teaching," in *On "Strangers No Longer": Perspectives on the Historic US-Mexican Catholic Bishops' Pastoral Letter on Migration*, ed. Todd Scribner and Kevin Appleby (New York: Paulist Press, 2013), 95.

2. Cecilia Menjivar, "Religion and Immigration in Comparative Perspective: Catholic and Evangelical Salvadorans in San Francisco, Washington, D.C. and Phoenix," *Sociology of Religion* 64, no. 1 (2003): 33.

Family Roles and Practices in the Context of Migration

Families provide our most intimate relationships such that protracted or, worse, violent separation threatens our well-being and subjectivity as human beings. In itself, physical separation poses immense difficulties. Globally diversified social and cultural realities that affect families and increasingly restrictive migration policies of destination countries compound the difficulties. In this context, how do families of migrants maintain family relationships and responsibilities?

One way is cyber parenting that uses information and communication technologies (hereafter ICTs). In fact, ICTs are a crucial aspect in the configuration of new communication processes and practices among transnational families by serving as conduits for maintaining family ties and interactions, strengthening cultural values and forms of expression, and providing affective support to the family. Social networks and other instant multiplatform digital forms of social connection such as Facebook, Twitter, Weibo, Instagram, Skype, WhatsApp, and Viber are particularly valuable.

Chain migration could also be considered a way of being and doing family. For family members left behind this means giving and doing all they can to enable the first or subsequent family member(s) to migrate. The family members who are overseas will then be somewhat expected to eventually help facilitate the migration of other family members. Some children of migrants even study, or are made to study, for university degrees that are in demand for overseas work in order to stand a better chance of following the path of, and/or being reunited with, family members.

In the context of temporary labor migration, maintaining family relationships and responsibilities on the part of migrant parents could mean shortening the time until the migrant must again sign a contract, or (over)compensating for one's absence through material things such as money or gifts. The latter is often a quick fix, or knee-jerk response, among migrant parents who are eager, if not desperate, to (re)establish emotional connection with their children, some of whom may be, at best, indifferent or, worse, distant and angry for various reasons connected to the parents' migration. Younger children may not even know or remember the returning parent(s), which in itself is hurtful and demands more efforts at reestablishing a relationship of trust.[3]

3. Christine Gudorf, "Temporary Migrants, Their Bodies and Families," in *Living (With)out Borders: Catholic Theological Ethics on the Migrations of Peoples*, ed. M. T. Davila and Agnes Brazal (New York: Orbis Books, 2016), 106.

Because migration is gendered, families of migrants reconstitute and rearrange motherhood to accommodate the temporal and spatial separations forced by migration[4] as a means of maintaining family relationships and responsibilities, a phenomenon known as transnational motherhood. Transnational mothers reconstitute mothering by providing acts of care from afar and overcompensating for their physical absence through more regular communication. Unauthorized mothers engage in even more intense transnational communication and gift-giving practices since they cannot easily visit their family back home. For example, with Zimbabwean women in South Africa what happens is not only a "complexification of motherhood" but, in some cases, the "othering" of migrant wives and mothers.[5] It is not uncommon for migrant wives and mothers to get the blame for spousal abandonment, separation and divorce, teenage pregnancies, children's poor school performance, delinquency, and even child suicide.

For some families, (temporary) physical separation is reluctantly embraced as a means of expressing family responsibility. One could see this in the situation of unaccompanied minors such as those sent by parents from Central America's Northern Triangle (Guatemala, Honduras, and El Salvador) to the United States by paying human smugglers in a desperate bid to spare their children from gang violence, or those sent by their parents to join the wave of migrants who crossed into Europe in 2015 to escape the conflict in Syria.

Language brokering among immigrant children as young as eight or nine years old is another unique expression of family responsibility in the context of migration. It occurs when only the child(ren) can communicate fluently in the host country's language. In such cases, even minors are forced to take on much of the burden of being the spokesperson at the doctor's office, at the real estate agent, or with lawyers, all of which are complicated interactions and transactions that are way beyond their cognitive thinking and ability. The experience of Anne Chiew, a Chinese Australian, sheds light on how this practice works:

> All the mail, any forms, any newsletters from school—I would not only have to translate for them but fill out the forms for them as well. Any word I didn't know I would have to look them up in the dictionary and try and work out what the hell it meant. I would go to the bank with them and open term deposit accounts with them standing next to me and I did all the talking. But I remember being

4. Pierette Hondagneu-Sotelo and Ernestine Avila, "'I'm Here, But I'm There': The Meaning of Latina Transnational Motherhood," *Gender and Society* 11, no. 5 (1997): 562.

5. Lesley Moorhouse and Peter Cunningham, "'We Are Purified by Fire': The Complexification of Motherhood in the Context of Migration," *Journal of Intercultural Studies* 33, no. 5 (2012): 493–508.

on my tippy-toes, trying to see over the teller counter, that's how small I was still. Translating naturally moved on to making decisions. I wasn't only telling mum and dad what the letter said, I was telling them what they should be doing with it and what the next steps were. They say as you get older you end up looking after your parents and the role of carer is reversed. I felt like that happened to me since I was in grade four. It did cause a lot of stress, because if I didn't know something I didn't know who to turn to for help. I felt responsible for them and it all rested on me.[6]

Transcultural mediation, another family practice in the context of migration, is also strong among families on permanent migration. This is particularly true for parents born and raised (even married) in completely different geographic and religio-cultural contexts, who have to contend with the challenges of maintaining their religio-cultural identity and reproducing it in and through their children while raising them in a host country with entirely different culture. Ifeyinwa Mbakogu illustrates this in the case of African families in Canada. Children, like the parents, find themselves pitched between two worlds, the Canadian and African, with the parents enforcing African practices that may be acceptable in the old country but a violation of the law in the Canada (e.g., what may be called "discipline" for African parents is considered physical abuse in Canada). The situation is complicated when parents deal with two sets of children: children who were born and perhaps raised in Africa and are now Canadian citizens and children born in Canada.[7]

There are, of course, some positive aspects to the changes in family roles and practices as a result of migration. Research shows that female transnationalism alters some family roles and practices, as when care arrangements become means to mute or transform oppressive conditions that are gender-based.[8] As Kristin Heyer notes in *Kinship Across Borders*, migration to the United States might not only disrupt family life but also make room for the agency of women

---

6. Cathy Pryor, "Language Brokering: When You're the Only One in the House Who Speaks English," ABC News, August 9, 2017, https://www.abc.net.au/news/2017-08-10/when-kids -translate-for-their-migrant-parents/8767820.

7. Ifeyinwa Mbakogu, "Who Is the Parent and Who Is the Kid?," in *Engaging the Diaspora: Migration and African Families*, ed. Pauline Ada Uwakweh et al. (Lanham, MD: Lexington Books, 2013), 41.

8. Theodora Lam and Brenda Yeoh, "Migrant Mothers, Left-Behind Fathers: The Negotiation of Gender Subjectivities in Indonesia and the Philippines," *Gender, Place and Culture* 25, no. 1 (2018): 104–17.

within families.[9] As people migrate, they confront a new social context that also impacts gender relations, especially in Western countries where social policies and practices tend to be geared toward gender equality.

More specifically, female migration has been shown to initiate the reconstitution of gender relations as it forces the rearrangement of household labor in transnational families by distributing a portion of women's household chores, including child care, to men. While some men may directly or indirectly avoid housekeeping, the vast majority perform at least some of the work traditionally performed by their wives. Traditional concepts of the value of women's work are significantly altered by the economic contribution Sri Lankan migrant domestic workers make to their households.[10] Female migration, in other words, could result in the destabilization of the power structure within the family as women migrants are given, or claim for themselves, some authority in the family by virtue of their roles as breadwinners. Pierette Hondagneu-Sotelo and Ernestine Avila point to how transnational mothering may be expanding the meaning of mothering to encompass breadwinning.[11]

In what amounts to a male equivalent of role expansion, Jason Pribilsky shows how the men's new priorities of budgeting and saving money, which are necessary for generating remittances, conflict with their practices of consumption back home but also provide space for new models for fatherhood to emerge. In this case, men's experience of migration led them to new consumption practices, which lead them to confront entrenched ideas of masculinity and money use.[12]

Nevertheless, while the maintenance of transnational families holds tremendous promise for the transgression of gender boundaries, some research shows how it simultaneously upholds gender boundaries. The double-edged changes in gender roles and relations has been called a gender paradox.[13] Still, family roles and practices such as transnational motherhood, (cyber)parents, and "other carers" (more commonly known as "other mothers") across borders provide impetus for thinking about theological questions on gender, the ethics of care, and what it means to be a family today.

---

9. See Kristin Heyer, *Kinship Across Borders: A Christian Ethic of Immigration* (Washington, DC: Georgetown University Press, 2012).

10. Michelle Gamburd, *The Kitchen Spoon's Handle: Transnationalism and Sri Lanka's Migrant Housemaids* (Ithaca, NY: Cornell University Press, 2000), 241.

11. Hondagneu-Sotelo and Avila, "I'm Here, But I'm There," 562.

12. Jason Pribilsky, "Consumption Dilemmas: Tracking Masculinity, Money and Transnational Fatherhood between the Ecuadorian Andes and New York City," *Journal of Ethnic and Migration Studies* 38, no. 2 (2012): 323–43.

13. Rhacel Salazar Parreñas, "The Gender Paradox in the Transnational Families of Filipino Migrant Women," *Asian and Pacific Migration Journal* 14, no. 3 (2005): 244.

Enlarged Ideas of Family Identity and Membership

How is Christian theology responding to migration's effects on the shape of families and gender roles in marriage and parenting? Recent church teaching on the family falls short. *Amoris Laetitia* provides some useful starting points with terms such as "wider family," which includes "parents, aunts and uncles, cousins and even neighbours" (AL 187, 197), and "larger family," which includes "friends and other families . . . as well as communities of families who support one another in their difficulties, their social commitments and their faith" (AL 196) and "fathers-in-law, mothers-in-law and all the relatives of the couple" (AL 198). These terms, however, do not fully take into account the complex character of kinship arising from global migration.

Amoris Laetitia also talks about the "tranquil home with its family sitting around the festive table" with "the father and mother at the center" (AL 9) and the parents as the "foundations of the home" (AL 14). It focuses on the traditional ideal of the nuclear family by speaking of the family as "entrusted to a man, a woman and their children" (AL 29) and uses the Holy Family of Nazareth as a model (AL 30, 66). In itself, the nuclear family model is problematic because it has middle-class underpinnings.[14] Moreover, it is heavily Western in character and overlooks how migrants transform the meanings of motherhood and fatherhood to accommodate spatial and temporal separations. Further, this model overlooks how migration creates new family forms (e.g., transnational family, cross-border/ cyber parenting) and how state and global apparatus, particularly labor market policies and family politics, make necessary new ways of being a family. Last but not least, the abovementioned tranquil image of a nuclear family is not the reality of transnational families who have members who are absent not only during the quintessential family ritual, that is, the family dinner, but even during special occasions such as graduations or critical moments such as births and deaths. Whether it is the migrant workers' families, astronaut families, stateless families, mixed-status families, families forcibly separated by detention or deportation, or ordinary immigrant families dealing with racism or nativism, the experience of families on the move today is often far from tranquil.

The experience of families in the context of migration calls for a more expansive understanding of what a family is. Transnational families drive home the point that the family is not just a biological nuclear activity but one in which formative relationships operate on a vertical axis. Transnational family life in the age of (feminized) global migration challenges dominant discourses, which generally frame gender relations within households or families and ignore how physical

14. Lisa Cahill, *Family: A Christian Social Perspective* (Minneapolis: Fortress Press, 2000), 96.

separation and state policies influence family politics and the political economy of emotions. Approaches that ignore the role of the state in family politics often promote the view that a return to the nuclear family is the only viable solution to the emotional difficulties of children and transnational families. This approach runs the risk of vilifying migrant fathers and, in particular, mothers and downplays the sacrifices and contributions they make to the family and society.

If the role of the church is not only to protect but also to empower families, church teaching and messaging need to be informed by practical realities. The teaching on the Christian family as a domestic church, for example, has practical liabilities, especially when it is contextualized by the glorification of motherhood and the delineation of a female sphere devoted primarily to domestic duties.[15] "We read about *the* mother, *the* father, *the* child, and *the* family as if they were static stereotypes."[16] Even the discourse of *broken* families fails to capture the flexible strategies transnational families accomplish.[17] What is needed is a theology that is "liberated from its 'precisions' and 'categorizations' . . . ready to move away from its 'comfort zones' in its quest for more relevance" and "to a theology that is built on companionship and dialogue."[18]

Scripture offers a good basis for articulating such a theology in relation to family identity and membership. In the final interaction between Jesus and a family member (John 19:26-27 when Jesus told Mary, "Woman, here is your son," and to the Beloved Disciple, "Here is your mother") at the cross, a new family comes into being. Family of birth gives way to family of creation. It is specifically at the cross that this family is created, and it is our relationship to Jesus that forms our filial, maternal, fraternal, and sisterly bonds.[19] Jesus' words in Matthew 12:50 ("Whoever does the will of my Father in heaven is my brother and sister and mother") refer to the need to understand the family not just literally but also metaphorically, and this is made real at the foot of the cross. It is not that Jesus divests himself of kin but rather that the kinship bonds are transformed. The resulting new understanding of the family is certainly more attuned to the experience of families in the

---

15. Ibid., 95–96.

16. Cristina Traina, "For the Sins of the Parents: Roman Catholic Ethics and the Politics of the Family," in *Prophetic Witness: Catholic Women's Strategies for Reform*, ed. Colleen Griffith (New York: Crossroad, 2009), 121. Italics in original.

17. Kristin Heyer, "*Familismo* Across the Americas: En Route to a Liberating Christian Family Ethic," in Davila and Brazal, *Living (With)out Borders*, 127. Italics in original.

18. Frances Camilleri-Cassar, "Trapped at the Periphery? Interdisciplinary Perspectives on African Migrant Women in Malta," *Melita Theologica* 67, no. 1 (2017): 102, 112.

19. Margaret Wesley, *Son of Mary: The Family of Jesus and the Community of Faith in the Fourth Gospel* (Eugene, OR: Wipf and Stock, 2015), 283.

context of migration insofar as: (1) Jesus directly points to the notion of family beyond biological ties; (2) kinship beyond biological connection is forged at the foot of the cross, which is symbolic of pain, suffering, and injustice and; (3) love and discipleship, not necessarily biological kinship, are revealed as key to being a family and being a member of a family.

A More Wholistic Approach to Parenthood

Migration clearly creates new avenues for reconfiguring gender relations. Patriarchal structures, however, are not completely dismantled. What is taking place is the "reinvention and transformation of patriarchy . . . a kind of soft patriarchy that makes men assume full responsibility for their lives and their families but with room to conceive the possibility of seeing their spouses as equal partners."[20] These changes call for a reconsideration of the ethics of family care, particularly the value of caretaking.

The problem is that church teaching on this matter has been, and continues to be, mired in the often-contested stance of complementarity and its various expressions. Ivy Helman notes the dueling reception of these teachings among Catholic women theologians.[21] "Too often Vatican documents on women contain stereotypes (like the nurturing mother), platitudes (like the feminine genius), or unsubstantiated claims (e.g., regarding women's supposed greater sensitivity and intuition)."[22] Even *Amoris Laetitia* reminds us that women's "specifically feminine abilities—motherhood in particular—also grant duties, because womanhood also entails a specific mission in this world, a mission that society needs to protect and preserve for the good of all" (AL 173). Moreover, the document speaks of fathers almost exclusively in terms of masculine roles (AL 175, 177) and continues a stereotyping of the father as worker and breadwinner (AL 176). Feminist theologians find complementarity problematic because the roles played by the sexes occupy very different social locations and are unequally valued.[23] While Catholic social

---

20. Nestor Medina, "Being Church as Latina/o Pentecostals," in *Church in an Age of Global Migration: A Moving Body*, ed. Susanna Snyder et al. (New York: Palgrave, 2016), 75.

21. Ivy Helman, *Women and the Vatican: An Exploration of Official Documents* (New York: Orbis Books, 2012).

22. Emily Reimer-Barry, "Constructing a New Theology of Women," *U. S. Catholic*, http://www.uscatholic.org/articles/201501/constructing-new-theology-women-29662.

23. Kochurani Abraham, "The 21st Century Challenge to Marriage and Family: Re-defining Gender Relations and Power Equations," in *Reimagining Marriage and Family in Asia: Asian Christian Women's Perspectives*, ed. Sharon Bong and Pushpa Joseph (Petaling Jaya: Strategic Information and Research Development Centre, 2008), 146.

teaching traditionally regards all members of society as having reciprocal rights and responsibilities, the ways in which this is true for women and men differ.[24]

The experience of migrant mothers, such as those who blur the traditional male role of worker/breadwinner, and migrant or left-behind fathers, such as those who embrace domestic and nurturing roles, opens up spaces for a more wholistic look at parenthood, gender roles, and family practices. A more nuanced retrieval and renewal of the theology on Mary and God as Father, the most powerful symbols of the feminine/motherhood and masculine/fatherhood in Christian theology, respectively, is helpful in this regard. A more generic, less binary approach to parenthood that looks at men and women as parents, individually and together, without simply and exclusively labeling what they do as practices for "mothers" and "fathers" is also beneficial. The myopic and binary preoccupation with gender roles in theological and secular literature, which tends toward women and motherhood, has lamentably entrenched positions on gender issues, resulting in the impoverishment of perspectives on parenthood. It does not help that this preoccupation, prompted by legitimate moral questions, has resulted in the institutionalization of motherhood that has gone as far as calling other carers "other mothers" or "spiritual mothers" in ways that reinforce the stereotyping of women as more caring and nurturing. These could make migrant mothers feel (more) guilty. Love in the family is "not simply of the love of father and mother as individuals, but also of their mutual love, perceived as the source of one's life and the solid foundation of the family" (AL 172). Julie Hanlon Rubio, who approaches family ethics "beyond sex and controversy," drives home this more constructive perspective to parenthood. She writes, "The dual vocation of parenthood belongs to everyone. Christian mothers must ask themselves if they are fulfilling the public side of their vocation, while Christian fathers ought to challenge themselves to participate more fully in the private lives of those they love most."[25]

A more specific challenge that emerges as far as the experience of parenthood among migrant families is concerned is twofold: (1) parenthood in the context of physical separation and (2) parenthood beyond biological parents, relatives, and, as per experience of language brokers, adults. Heyer argues that the realities that migrant and mixed-status family members endure contest idealized family values and dominant forms of Christian family ethics. A more constructive Chris-

---

24. Lisa Cahill, "Commentary on *Familiaris Consortio*," in *Modern Catholic Social Teaching: Commentaries and Interpretations*, ed. Kenneth Himes (Washington, DC: Georgetown University Press, 2005), 373.

25. Julie Hanlon Rubio, *A Christian Theology of Marriage and Family* (New York: Paulist Press, 2003), 144.

tian family ethic needs to be grounded in a profoundly relational anthropology, covenantal love, and the social mission of the family in such a way that families become *schools of deeper humanity*.[26] Assumptions about the complementarity of the sexes often lurk beneath the surface in family ethics and bolster uneven burdens for the work of social reproduction and caregiving rather than calling forth intergenerational solidarity marked by shared responsibility and adequate compensation. An alternative is a political economy in which being in need of care and being responsible for the care of others are the human norm.

Conclusion

Migration clearly has implications for the ongoing identity development and relationship dynamics within the family. Indeed, whether it is the ones who are away or the ones who are left behind, families touched by migration face old, as well as new, challenges and opportunities that require a wholistic and far more nuanced approach to the moral economy of kinship. The family in the age of migration is in flux and, as is characteristic of the processes of globalization, is experiencing detraditionalization insofar as there are changes occurring to its locus of identity and, to a certain extent, authority. Ultimately, a theology of family in the age of migration needs to take into account not only political economy in its various manifestations but also kinship ideology. At play is a struggle between forces of tradition and change, between old forms of oppression and, to a certain extent, new forms of empowerment. The outcome will depend on issues that need further research and reflection (like how migrant men adjust and change their care practices and domestic roles to accommodate challenges brought about by migration and how "other carers," including grandparents and children in the left-behind family, provide care in the context of migration). There is a well-known African proverb that says, "It takes a village to raise a child." The experience of families in the context of migration shows that it takes a global village to raise a family.

---

26. Heyer, "*Familismo* Across the Americas," 121–31. Italics in original.

Chapter 19

Signs of Union

Interchurch Families in a Fragmented World

Daniel Olsen

Mixed marriage families have the duty to proclaim Christ with the fullness implied in a common baptism, they have too the delicate task of making themselves builders of unity.

—*Directory for the Application of Principles and Norms on Ecumenism* 66

It is difficult to find an American Christian today who does not have a relative, friend, or colleague who is dating or married to a member of another Christian church, if not another religion. As religious intermarriage rates climb in North America[1] and church pews begin to reflect this growing diversity, questions of Christian identity and religious belonging are becoming more prevalent for these couples and their churches. Will these mixed-marriage[2] couples be able to sustain their Christian identity while connected to two different churches? Will they be able to raise their children with a coherent understanding of either church or of Christianity itself? Will they be able live out their commitment to Christ and one another in unity and love? Clear answers to these questions remain elusive,

---

1. See Robert D. Putnam and David E. Campbell, *American Grace: How Religion Divides and Unites Us* (New York: Simon & Schuster, 2010), 148–49.

2. The term "mixed marriage" or "religiously mixed marriage," unless otherwise specified, refers to a marriage between two Christian spouses from different churches/denominations, without differentiation between religious belonging and practices.

and it is often the couples and their children who bear the brunt of figuring out on a case-by-case basis how to answer them.

Drawing on the framework for accompanying Christian families outlined in Pope Francis's apostolic exhortation *Amoris Laetitia*, this essay offers a sustained reflection on why and how the Christian community should better minister to mixed-marriage couples at the local level. I begin by describing recent shifts in religious affiliation and marriage practices in the United States, then outline pastoral challenges for mixed-marriage couples, before offering ways to welcome and support these couples in Christian parishes/congregations. I focus on those couples that include one spouse who is Catholic, while hoping my work will also be helpful for other mixed Christian families. I conclude by briefly considering how the Christian community can benefit from the witness of interchurch families. As trends reveal that young Christians are finding less resonance with their churches of origin, dedicated mixed-marriage families provide a counternarrative to pervasive social divisiveness by modeling in their homes the unity the church seeks.

The Changing Context of Christian Marriage in the United States

Catholics and other Christians are marrying in their churches much less frequently than they did just a generation ago.[3] Cohabitation rates have also sharply increased.[4] Many young adults in the United States, Christians included, are choosing to live together for years or even decades without being married, such that cohabitation is no longer predominantly viewed as a stage on the way toward marriage. Christians are also switching religious traditions at an increasing rate. In *American Grace*, Robert D. Putnam and David E. Campbell note that "roughly 35-40% of all Americans and 40-45% of white Americans have switched at some point away from their parents' religion."[5] Religion is becoming less of an inheritance and more of a choice. Trends also reveal a growing secularism in the United States. As the category of "formerly Christian" and "formerly religious" grows, fewer Christians are available to marry at all.

3. See the Pew Forum, "Religious Landscape Study," https://www.pewforum.org/religious-landscape-study/marital-status/.

4. Renee Stepler, "Number of U. S. Adults Cohabiting with a Parenter Continues to Rise, Especially Among Those 50 and Older," Pew Research Center, April 6, 2017, https://www.pewresearch.org/fact-tank/2017/04/06/number-of-u-s-adults-cohabiting-with-a-partner-continues-to-rise-especially-among-those-50-and-older/.

5. Putnam and Campbell, *American Grace*, 137.

These sociological trends have alarmed Christian leaders in the United States. What will happen when the basic living cell of the church, the Christian home, becomes less and less the norm for American Christians? What will become of the children of couples who are no longer marrying and who have little or no intention of raising their children "in a church" as they grow up? These trends are game-changers in framing pastoral outreach to Christian couples. Given rapid changes in marriage, US churches have struggled to match pastoral programs with the shifting needs, especially for mixed-marriage couples. Pastors and pastoral ministers are in the process of reconceiving who they expect to arrive at their doorsteps and how to respond to those who do show up.

In terms of mixed-marriage couples, just fifty years ago these marriages were strongly discouraged by most Christian churches[6] and, unsurprisingly, quite few in number. Given recent advances in the movement for Christian unity and shifts in church teaching, such as those seen at the Second Vatican Council, mixed marriages are much more common and welcomed in Christian congregations and parishes today. In some parts of the United States half (or more) of all marriages now celebrated in Catholic churches are religiously mixed, with most Catholic dioceses having 20 percent or more of marriages celebrated in the church being mixed or interreligious. These numbers are even higher in most Protestant denominations. As these marriages grow in number, perceptions about their place in their local churches have shifted; however, several unique challenges remain for these families, particularly if one spouse is Catholic. Understanding these challenges will provide further context for thinking through the unique pastoral support that mixed-marriage families require.

1. Eucharistic sharing: Catholic Christians, outside of exceptional circumstances and with express permission from the local bishop,[7] are not lawfully able to receive Eucharist/Communion in the Christian church of their spouse. Alternately, when their non-Catholic spouse comes to a Catholic church for Mass, s/he is also asked not to receive Communion, again outside of exceptional

6. For one notable example, see the *Code of Canon Law of the Roman Catholic Church* (1917), canon 1060. "Most severely does the Church everywhere prohibit marriage to be entered into by two baptized persons, one Catholic and the other belonging to an heretical or schismatic sect; if there is danger of perversion for the Catholic party or the children, the marriage is likewise prohibited by divine law itself."

7. *Code of Canon Law of the Catholic Church* (1983), canon 844. For further clarity on how to interpret this "exception," see The Pontifical Council for Promoting Christian Unity, *Directory for the Application of Principles and Norms on Ecumenism*, 125, 129–32, 143–60.

cases.[8] Many mainline Protestant churches welcome all baptized Christians to the Lord's table, but current Catholic teaching does not permit reciprocity in this regard. This reality leads to tensions and pain for interchurch couples who often express a deep spiritual need to receive Eucharist together.

2. Promises: Before entering into a mixed marriage, the Catholic spouse is required to affirm that "he or she is prepared to avoid the dangers of abandoning the faith and to promise sincerely to do all in his/her power to see that the children of the marriage be baptized and educated in the Catholic Church" (*Directory for the Application of Principles and Norms on Ecumenism* 150). This promise does not need to be made by the non-Catholic Christian spouse, but she or he needs to be informed of it. "To do all in one's power" does not mean that the promise is a requirement that the children become Catholic, but it is a very strongly worded declaration that presumes the child is raised Catholic unless a strong reason emerges not to do so.

3. Baptism: While most churches mutually recognize the validity of one another's baptism, the reality is that one is baptized into a particular church, whether it be Catholic, Presbyterian, Lutheran, Methodist, Greek Orthodox, etc. Deciding which church to baptize one's child in can become a stressor for mixed-marriage couples and their extended families and churches. Beyond this, many Christians do not practice infant baptism, thus making even the decision of when one's child is baptized challenging for some.

4. Christian formation: Either prior to or following baptism, young Christians regularly enter programs of formation in their churches. It is a challenge to form the child in one parent's tradition while being respectful and knowledgeable about the other. This is all the more challenging when one hears from a preacher or classroom teacher the false claims that "only Catholics believe in the real presence of Christ in the Eucharist," or "we don't worship Mary like Catholics do." Tension can quickly emerge as interchurch children are formed in their confessional identity in a comparative, sometimes pejorative, manner. Finding ways to form children in one Christian church while growing in esteem for another remains a challenge.

5. Extended families and churches: Interchurch couples and their children often deal with pressures from their extended families, fellow congregants, and clergy/ministers regarding how they should remain connected to their churches of origin. One side of a family may presume that the child will be raised Catholic, while the other assumes the child will be raised Lutheran. Respective clergy often

---

8. See United States Conference of Catholic Bishops, *Guidelines for the Reception of Communion*, http://www.usccb.org/prayer-and-worship/the-mass/order-of-mass/liturgy-of-the-eucharist/guidelines-for-the-reception-of-communion.cfm.

have similar assumptions. These expectations can bring anxiety for couples as they make decisions for their young families.

Outlining these potential challenges should not be read as a critical assessment of either the couple for deciding to wed or of Catholic (or any other Christian church's) teachings and practices regarding mixed marriages. Christian disunity is the root problem, not the couples themselves or any one church's policies or practices. Properly naming the sin of division, however, does not mitigate the pain that ongoing Christian disunity brings. These directives and recommended pastoral practices, as theologically coherent as they may be, are not easily lived out in interchurch homes.

The challenges noted above likely have some connection to the fact that studies continue to show that those who are religiously intermarried are more likely to divorce and to leave their churches as they age than those who marry someone from their own tradition.[9] This general statistic does not, however, differentiate between the level of religious belonging and commitment of the involved couple. Along with the Christian diversity that mixed-marriage couples bring, these couples, like all couples, will come with a diversity in strength of religious belonging. Some couples will be deeply immersed in their respective traditions, bringing strong roots from years of intentionally practicing their Christian faith. Given the declining rates of religious belonging among young American Christians, however, it is more likely that one or even both partners will be loosely affiliated with their church. It is these couples, studies show, who divorce more than their same-church counterparts.

Beyond the couples' religious commitment, I would suggest that one reason for these uncomfortable statistics about religiously mixed couples is that Christians have not yet provided adequate resources for addressing their unique needs at the congregational level. How many parishes have distinctive programs of welcome and ongoing enrichment for mixed-marriage families? How many congregations have mentoring programs for these couples? Might some of these families be departing because they don't feel welcomed and supported by their communities? Or perhaps they are fed up with the intra-Christian squabbles that prevent them from fully exercising their marital union while at their churches?

The onus of responsibility for caring for interchurch couples needs to shift onto the churches themselves. The churches are divorced, not the couples. These communities should be striving through all possible means for full, visible unity

---

9. See Naomi Schaefer Riley, *'Til Faith Do Us Part: How Interfaith Marriage Is Transforming America* (Oxford: Oxford University Press, 2013); Darren E. Sherkat, "Religious Intermarriage in the United States: Trends, Patterns, and Predictors," *Social Science Research* 33, no. 4 (2004): 606–25.

so that the tensions themselves will dissipate. In the meantime, there are countless interchurch families who need immediate pastoral support that they are not, by and large, receiving. It is past time for Christians to respond with urgency to a problem of their own making. Finding ways to welcome and support interchurch Christian couples is essential for the future health of the Christian community in the United States.

Revisioning Ministry to Mixed-Marriage Families

The reasons for an interchurch couple to decide to approach a church for marriage will vary widely from the superficial to the mundane to the traditional to the deeply spiritual, sometimes all at once. No matter their reason for coming, it is important to welcome them as inquirers who are approaching this community of faith with an interest in deepening a relationship. Radical welcoming of all couples, rooted in a posture of listening, is a needed starting point for parishes looking to begin effective outreach for interchurch couples.

These initial moments of welcome, however, need the backing of well-planned preparation programs for mixed marriages along with ongoing marriage enrichment programs. Early in their marriage, Christian couples, perhaps especially mixed-marriage couples, need to be supported by the parish as they develop the skills needed to live out the promises they make on their wedding day. Rooted in baptism, Christian marriage requires a lifelong vocational commitment to union with one's spouse. The right habits (virtues) needed to live out this commitment in Christ, however, are not magically conferred on the couple at their wedding. If couples are not accompanied on their Christian journey by, with, and through their congregations, how can they be expected to find the way on their own with a high level of success? This question is especially relevant when you factor in the added pressures brought about by belonging in two different churches.

Pope Francis claims in his apostolic exhortation *Amoris Laetitia* that the "main contribution to the pastoral care of families is offered by the parish, which is the family of families" (202). Taking this insight as a starting point, some Catholic pastoral staffs are beginning to map out how their parishes can become hubs of support and accompaniment for interchurch families. Since "married life is a process of growth, in which each spouse is God's means of helping the other to mature" (221), our parishes are called to walk with families in this process of maturation. In a wonderful image to explain further this understanding of growth in marriage, Pope Francis invites couples to think of themselves as artists who continually shape their spouses, through grace and love, into the identity God calls them to be. "Each marriage is a kind of 'salvation history' which from humble beginnings—thanks to God's gifts and a creative and generous response on our part—grows over time into something precious and enduring" (221). This image of active growth in Christian marriage, and the decisive role that spouses, parishes, and congregations have to play in it, guides the following suggestions on how congregations can accompany mixed-marriage families, grounded in a model of accompaniment outlined in *Amoris Laetitia.*

Parishes can be viewed as gateways into the lifeblood of the Christian community. Parish staffs and volunteers are often the people first encountered by those seeking to know more about these places of Christian communal life. As such, an important first step for a parish-based program of pastoral accompaniment is to train the parish staff on how to welcome interchurch couples. Knowing what the Catholic Church teaches about mixed-marriage couples is helpful, but even more decisive for these first visits is being able to welcome them well. Everyone from the pastor and pastoral staff to the receptionists and greeters at Sunday Mass can benefit from a standardized script of welcome for young adults who are seeking knowledge about getting married in the parish. For various reasons, church ministers often lack the training and knowledge required to meet the growing needs of mixed-marriage couples. Beginning with a commitment to radical hospitality is a crucial first step of accompaniment.

After welcome, the parish staff can identify and refer couples to appropriate support services (marriage prep, marriage enrichment, pastoral care, etc.) to meet their unique needs. If there is a school associated with the parish, a "school-centered" session should be offered to welcome and listen to the distinctive needs of interchurch parents. Teachers and catechists will be asked to become more attentive to ministry to interchurch children. It is important that they consider such questions as: How do we describe other Christians in our classrooms? How do we present Catholic teaching in a non-triumphalist manner? How do we include non-Catholic students in religion classes or formation programs?

Within the life of the parish, it will become important to host gatherings specifically for interchurch couples, perhaps even inviting those who are dating, engaged, and/or newly married to someone from a different Christian tradition. These listening sessions may not even be on church property, but at local coffeehouses, bars, or restaurants. In directly reaching out to these young couples, parishes exhibit a missionary impulse that seeks to minister to couples where they are (AL 230). Providing forums for them to share, even informally, with their peers, parish staff members or professionals can begin a dialogue whereby all learn of the unique pressures these couples may be facing. As they are conversing, they will also be establishing trust and collegial bonds that may prove fruitful in the future. If nothing else, these forums can demonstrate to mixed-marriage couples that they are being recognized and their concerns are being heard and taken seriously by their congregation.

When trust and shared concerns become apparent, ongoing "discussion" or "support" groups for interested couples may form. Seeing themselves as part of an intentional community that regularly prays together and seeks ways to extend communion inside and outside of their homes can greatly enhance the ability of these couples to navigate their faith lives constructively. These couples will also come to understand better Pope Francis's claims that newly married couples need to complete the process of growing into their loving union with the assistance of parish resources well after the vows are exchanged (AL 217–18).

Marriage is a lifelong "project" that requires the support and pastoral accompaniment of trusted guides and fellow travelers (AL 223). To best ensure that couples will progress along this path fruitfully, it is essential to identify strong interchurch couples who can serve as mentors for young interchurch couples in the parish. Pairing them together to provide insights for young couples as they first encounter various issues in their relationship can be quite impactful. This level of mentoring and partnering may take some time to develop in a parish/congregational setting, but it could become a tremendous resource to provide the needed accompaniment that mixed-marriage families should expect to have from their churches.

Identifying these overlapping areas of outreach to interchurch couples at the parish level is just the beginning of what can be viewed as a concerted response to the call of Pope Francis in *Amoris Laetitia* to minister to mixed-marriage couples in light of the challenges that they face. Implicit in the plan noted above is regular dialogue with other local Christian pastors, integrating their insights into the program's goals and mission. By giving these couples options for integration into the parish, the goal is to invite them beyond the relatively anonymous status that many of them choose for themselves in their churches at present. Moreover, these efforts at pastoral ministry, as the concluding section argues, might simultaneously provide Christians with new bridges for Christian unity.

Living Signs of Union

An argument traditionally employed to discourage mixed marriages is that the disunity of their churches of origin invites inherent discord into the fabric of the Christian home. This reality all too often prevents them from growing into the unity Christ desires for them as a couple and family. This argument often centers on the negative impact of what couples cannot share. Acknowledging that the challenges interchurch couples will face remain painful, however, cannot cover up the truth that they are not insurmountable. These families can grow into unity together through their mutual love and God's grace, while providing living signs of union in Christ that all Christians seek.

In *American Grace*, Putnam and Campbell find that a variety of diverse and cohesive social networks allow Americans to foster a peaceful coexistence unique in the world, despite much societal difference in the United States. Religious intermarriage, in particular, binds Americans in ways that increase the positive assessment they hold of others. Claiming that "it is difficult to damn those you know and love,"[10] they draw on social contact theory to show the importance of living with diversity. This theory holds that four conditions are required before social contact will lead to a reduction in prejudice: "all parties must have equal status, share common goals, have intergroup cooperation, and have the support of authorities."[11]

Let us assume equal status and common goals among interchurch couples. If we can enhance intergroup cooperation through programs of support and mentoring, as proposed above, while garnering the support of local church leadership and their families of origin, interchurch spouses can become bridges between their respective churches. Reducing prejudice and increasing tolerance by enhancing one's assessment of another group through interactions with a friend, colleague, or spouse is a small piece of the puzzle of achieving full Christian unity, but when one factors in how many people will be influenced by one marriage, the impact can be immense. The social cohesion produced by working together to support couples who intermarry can also provide a sort of glue for our respective churches that positively binds us to one another, changing perspectives while opening us up to seeing one another as gifts rather than enemies or distractions.

Another element to consider is that these couples have sought to marry in a church, which increasingly sets them apart from their peers. They have chosen to begin their marriage through a local Christian community, committing themselves to a life of joint Christian discipleship. In making this commitment, their marriage vow is also a simultaneous promise to become part of the movement for Christian unity, even if they don't recognize it at the time. As they live into their Christian marriage, they will be required to make decisions for the good of their unified Christian household in the face of disunity. Okay, we'll baptize Abby in the Episcopal Church, but she is going to experience Catholic worship as well. Okay, Matthew is going to enter the Catholic school and join the preparation program for First Communion in second grade, but we are also going to attend

10. Putnam and Campbell, *American Grace*, 517.
11. Ibid., 527.

Bible study as a family at my Evangelical church. Our normal practice will be to attend the early Mass on Sunday and then go to the contemporary Lutheran worship service. Whatever decisions that each couple make for the good of their family are also intentional acts designed to help them live out a Christian life in connection to their churches. In their everyday existence, they feel the effects of Christian disunity but also become living signs of union as they witness the riches of other Christian churches in ways same-church couples do not.

The ecumenical movement, the movement for full, visible Christian unity, is an organic and ever-changing reality that has only gained solid traction in the past several decades. In just the past century, churches have moved from condemnation and outright distrust to deep levels of cooperation, mutual understanding, and friendship. In the past generation several Christian denominations have even established full communion agreements, which allow for unprecedented levels of participation in one another's churches. These agreements are producing fruit, but they are only steps along the journey toward the full, visible union Christians hope to achieve in the future. As these Christian churches live into these new realities, further insights will surely emerge for the benefit of all Christians.

What is often ignored, however, is that we already have countless full communion agreements in our midst. In interchurch homes, understood as domestic churches in Catholic theology, we have rich examples of how intentional disciples are finding ways to fully commune with Christ and one another despite their churches' inability to do so at present. Many of them feel the pain of not being able to share at the Lord's table on Sunday, even as they share at the family table every other day. This painful reality, however, does not prevent them from studying Scripture together, praying together, and witnessing together on mission trips or at food pantries. In these moments of communion, embedded in the everyday living out of the covenantal reality of their marriages, they offer signs of union and hope for Christians longing for a visibly unified community.

Many hurdles remain to actualize Christ's prayer that Christians be one as he and his Father are one (John 17:21), but the movement for Christian unity is alive and well in the homes of interchurch families. The daily experience of the pain of Christian division, paired with their growing love of Christ and one another, fuel their desire to live as "laboratories of unity."[12] When these laboratories do their work unconnected to their local communities, however, who knows what results their experiments are yielding? The need to do more to welcome and support

---

12. Pope Benedict XVI, "Warsaw Address," found in Ruth Reardon, "Pope Benedict XVI on Interchurch Families: 'Laboratories of Unity,'" *One in Christ* 41, no. 2 (2006): 85–86.

these couples in living out their Christian marriage is not just for the benefit of these couples; it is for the benefit of all Christians.

Christian married couples share in the same mission as the ecumenical movement, namely, to respond faithfully to God's grace in order to participate in and model themselves after the union that Jesus Christ has with God, his Father, through the Holy Spirit. Like the search for Christian unity itself, Christian marriage is a communal endeavor. Couples need the support found in remaining connected to the religious life of their churches, especially including communal worship opportunities where they uniquely encounter God's word and the sacraments. When diverse Christians come to know their places of worship as life-giving fonts of grace, where they regularly encounter the triune God's outpouring of grace, lived communion becomes more than just a hoped-for future. The living signs of union that these families exhibit today offer new and potentially fruitful ways forward for the ecumenical movement, whose success is required to remove the biggest impediment for the evangelizing mission of the church, namely, the unseemly persistence of Christian division. Christians should do all in their power to see that these couples find the support they need from their churches, while recognizing their living out of Christian unity as a gift for all.

Chapter 20

Secular Catholic Families

Inheritance and Invention

Tom Beaudoin

Catholics are more likely to be modestly affiliated, marginally affiliated, and unaffiliated with church than to be highly affiliated. It is also well known that declining overall numbers of children are presented for baptism and confirmation, fewer adults for church marriage, and fewer men for ordination, while the sacrament of reconciliation ("confession") is rarely elected. The practices of affiliation in Catholic families are not generating the sustaining mass of lifelong adult adherents to which the church had been accustomed—and on which its institutional life depends. The call of the Second Vatican Council for the "full, conscious, and active participation" of the whole church, while inspiring monumental strides in lay empowerment, including durable classes of lay pastoral leadership and lay Catholic intellectual life in ethics and theology, has not broadly come to pass in the United States. The crisis of participation is the space in which secular Catholic families have grown.

What is known is that disaffiliated persons now outnumber Roman Catholics in the United States and that within Roman Catholicism there is considerable religious pluralism.[1] Marginally affiliated (for whom "normatively" defined church belief and practice are not that important), disaffiliated (for whom it is not important at all), and nonaffiliated (who left for something else) persons and families are widespread. Those without any professed religious affiliation are an

---

1. Tricia Bruce, "Cultural Catholics in the United States," in *Annual Review of the Sociology of Religion: The Changing Faces of Catholicism*, ed. Solange Lefebvre and Alfonso Pérèz-Agote Poveda (Leiden: Brill, 2018), 83–106. See Stephen Bullivant, *Mass Exodus: Catholic Disaffiliation in Britain and America Since Vatican II* (New York: Oxford University Press, 2019).

even more specific part of the population than unaffiliated persons and are called "Nones" by researchers. Whereas Nones have received attention for approaching more than one-quarter of the US population, most Americans do not practice active, high affiliation in their religion.[2] Catholic heritages are well represented in these groups. Many of the Nones or marginally/unaffiliated persons were baptized Catholic, raised in a Catholic family, or raised in a family with Catholic influences. In a notable development, Nones are numerically eclipsing Catholics in the United States. This does not mean that atheism or agnosticism have won the day. Many marginally affiliated, unaffiliated, and Nones describe themselves as spiritually invested. Amid most Catholic families, however, it seems that the beliefs, practices, and needs considered sacred, spiritual, or religious are not largely satisfiable within the church. Seen from the vantage of official expectations, Catholicism's "margins" and "outside" keep growing.

Reasons for the "secularity" of Catholic families are complex. Some move toward secularity due to dissatisfying interpersonal or ministerial relationships in the church. Others grow weary of disconnected ritual. Many feel a lack of church teaching's relevance to life, compounded by the sexual abuse crisis and cover-up eroding the church's credibility. The deepest reasons for the fortunes of Catholic affiliation are changing cultural assumptions about being religious. The benefits and penalties for staying "in line" for Catholics and other established religious traditions no longer motivate as broadly and deeply as they once did. Lesser-appreciated conditions for generating secular Catholic families are also important: economic insecurity preventing people from getting to church; racism in white churches deterring Catholics of color from participating; class biases in active Catholic life preventing outreach and hospitality toward, or conditions of "acceptability" pertaining for, working-class and poor Catholic families; parish closings alienating members or making travel to another parish difficult.[3]

Neglect of Secular Catholic Families

Secular Catholic families are a rich, complicating reality for the Roman Catholic Church, opening a substantial range of new considerations and questions.

---

2. See Pew Research Center, "The Shifting Religious Identity of Latinos in the United States" (2014), https://www.pewforum.org/2014/05/07/the-shifting-religious-identity-of-latinos-in-the-united-states/, and Religion News Service, "Pew Report: Older US Christians Being Quickly Replaced by Young 'Nones'" (2019), https://religionnews.com/2019/10/17/pew-report-older-u-s-christians-being-quickly-replaced-by-young-nones/.

3. For example, see Robert McCarty and John Vitek, *Going, Going, Gone: The Dynamics of Disaffiliation in Young Catholics* (Winona, MN: Saint Mary's Press, 2018).

Secular Catholic families are not actively affiliated with Catholicism as defined by official expectations about belief and practice, making something other than the "normative" Catholic Church central to their lives. Such families can come from any racial-ethnic identification or social class. They usually include at least one adult presence—a partner, parent, guardian, or formative caregiver—with a Catholic heritage. It is not only families who do not take up Catholicism as a central concern who can be considered secular Catholic families for the purposes of this chapter; so too can families who are divided about the place of Catholicism in the family or families who value, make explicit, and integrate Catholicism but whose Catholicism differs from what is taken to be normative by ecclesial authorities in their context, such as families for whom Catholic identity is salient and who favor contraception or abortion rights or who embrace intermarriage and raising children in other-than-Catholic traditions. To speak of secular Catholic families is constantly to risk overgeneralizing. This is what happens when we try to look to the "other" of normative Catholic affiliation—we begin to see the complex universe of all who do not fit what mainstream church and ethical discourse takes to be a good Catholic family.

Substantive research on secular Catholic family life is scarce. What do parents or guardians and children in such families do that is distinctive? What are the ecologies of their lives and the webs in which they are embedded? What do they value and how do they make decisions? Though we currently lack a critical mass of research, personal testimonials and ministry experiences are legion, animating Catholic conferences and church publications. Most Catholic families have their own store of narratives about it—as well as zones of silence. Because so much of academic Catholic theology has presumed, prescribed, and preferred a higher degree of affiliation than most Catholic families can manage, the actual lives and practices of secular Catholic parents and children, their friends and coworkers, their social worlds and desires are undervalued. This undervaluation in theology and ethics runs alongside institutional angst about the participation of Catholic families in church and the rise of nonparticipating younger generations.

Moreover, too little is known through Catholic theology and ethics about the intersectional dynamics at work in secular Catholic families. How are African American secular Catholic families similar to or different from Latinx, white, and Asian American, or from interracial and interethnic secular Catholicisms? What about straight and queer secular Catholic families, or wealthy, middle class, working class, and poor? Theologians and ethicists should presume that it is all happening, yet little of it is well understood.

The overwhelmingly white, European-descended, male high-level leadership of the Roman Catholic Church in the United States has shown little interest in meeting these developments with curiosity, careful listening, and depth of reflection. Catholic academic theological discourse, strongly white in its heritage and still predominantly white in its makeup, has resisted making secular Catholicism a "normative" center of gravity for theological research and teaching in a way that would challenge the "normativity" of what is taken as given for academic theology in tradition and Scripture. There is a certain holding on to the picture of the church as it must or should be among both ecclesial and academic theological leadership.

If the popular picture of secular Catholic families is usually a white, European-descended image, that has to do with the disproportionate visibility of white Catholicism in the US social imaginary. Due to the racialized legacies of US Catholicism, white Catholic-heritage families, by and large, are the default image for the prerogative of being the "typical" Catholic identity. Such families can therefore, distinct from any intention to do so, "afford" to take more liberties with affiliation and suffer fewer cultural penalties. This is particularly so for white families that have become "de-ethnicized" over generations. Academic and pastoral leaders in minoritized and marginalized Catholic groups rarely report, promote, or theologize from the presence of secular Catholics, even as such numbers are rising. This may be in part due to institutional pressures to perform and narrate Catholic loyalty. Narratives of enduring fidelity are unfortunately an ingredient to being recognized as worthy of full inclusion by white-dominant Catholic structures and governance in ecclesial and academic contexts. There is little sense a of noble "unfaithfulness" to Catholicism. Grounding underrepresented Catholic theologies partly in their secular Catholicisms would threaten the already-precarious visibility and standing of these communities.[4]

Secular Families as a Challenge to Catholic Theology

One touchstone for Catholic family ethics is Pope Francis's *Amoris Laetitia*. This Roman Catholic teaching document from 2016, referred to as an "apostolic exhortation," is a pastorally sensitive outline for addressing Catholic families. It shows that the world's Roman Catholic bishops, who gathered in 2014 and 2015 collectively (in "synod") to discuss families, are aware of some challenges and realities of secular Catholic families. Part of this awareness comes from a remarkable innovation for generating Catholic teaching through the synodal process: a global

---

4. For example, Natalia Imperatori-Lee names disaffiliation as a Latinx reality (for which "personal parishes" inspired by Latin American base communities might be a way to keep people involved with the church). Note that the "key" remains "sustaining the Catholic identity and practice of this population and stemming the tide of disaffiliation." See Imperatori-Lee, *Cuéntame: Narrative in the Ecclesial Present* (Maryknoll, NY: Orbis Books, 2018).

survey sent by the Vatican to bishops to gather information about Catholic family life. One need not agree with sociologist Michele Dillon's historical point to appreciate the importance of Dillon's claim about this survey process: "For the first time in history, Church officials were publicly asking questions about Catholic phenomena they had previously either marginalized or framed as contradictory of Catholicism."[5] For a tradition not known for careful empirical study as a condition for generating official teaching, this is a notable step forward.

Theologian Brian Robinette argues that *Amoris Laetitia* profitably engages the spiritual aspirations of the marginally affiliated, suggesting Francis read the signs of the times well regarding the affiliation crisis. *Amoris Laetitia*, Robinette proposes, provides an "invitation" and "argument" for Catholics to model the family as a place of loving growth, for the family members themselves and for society as a whole. Robinette has creatively identified a key correlation between Francis's values and those of many disaffiliated persons: that familial love is a personal and social good.[6]

Such a capacity to interpret innovatively back and forth between official church discourses and living values among secular Catholics is surely an essential requirement for any effective theology in society today. Yet the presumption here seems to be that marginalized Catholics have not known enough such goods and need a pope or affiliated Catholic families to teach them. Such a presumption continues the academic and pastoral "loss" narrative of disaffiliation—that secular Catholic families are deficient or lost, needing the church's beneficence.

Moreover, this apologetic approach suggests that church teaching lacks nothing important that secular Catholic families might provide. For example, *Amoris Laetitia* nods to secular Catholic families, and proposes medicine for them, in its claim that "children who grew up in missionary families often become missionaries themselves," in contrast to those who have turned to "giving up their faith or their convictions" (AL 289). This acknowledgment is a mixed blessing. While some secular Catholic families have surrendered or exchanged one set of faiths or convictions for another, it is simplistic to present the options in a binary way, as keeping or giving up faith or convictions.

5. Michele Dillon, *Postsecular Catholicism: Relevance and Renewal* (New York: Oxford University Pess, 2018), 131.

6. Brian D. Robinette, "*Amoris Laetitia* and the Nones," in *Amoris Laetitia: A New Momentum for Moral Formation and Pastoral Practice*, ed. Grant Gallicho and James F. Keenan (Mahwah, NJ: Paulist Press, 2018), 86–94.

Complicated Choice, Freedom, and Hope

This is not to say that there are not questions to be raised about secular Catholic families. After all, it does not help to suggest that there is any situation or intention for family practices—whether "secular," "religious," or otherwise—that is not ideological, in the sense of being embedded in historically contingent power relations. (In this sense, no "religious" or "nonreligious" identity for a Catholic-heritage family is *ipso facto* always best, because the terms make sense only relative to their situation.) One of the most evident costs to families of being secular Catholics might be the elevation of choice in taking on a religion, spirituality, or life philosophy.

Sociologist Phil Zuckerman's research on secular families emphasizes the centrality of the value of self-determining choice. He reports that "secular families perform rituals, celebrate holidays, and partake of traditions only if they want to," affording "a greater sense of the reasons, purposes, and benefits of doing so."[7] Such a perspective, however, can be celebratory to the point of sounding naïve. It is not that being selective about festivities is wrong, but characterizing secular families as unencumbered in those choices is misleading. Zuckerman helpfully notes that secular families may lack a sense of "heritage" due to the novelty of their secular identity, having left active religious practice or affiliation behind, perhaps surrendering an inherited family religious legacy. Zuckerman argues that such families can create a new sense of heritage in the family by valuing and ritualizing customs around "personal freedom, individual proclivity, ongoing choice."[8] While it would be easy to wonder whether this is a retreat into a cocooning familial individualism, this is not far from what *Amoris Laetitia* calls the crucial qualities to cultivate in children of "prudence, good judgment, and common sense." We could even say that secular Catholic families often try—in practice—to honor Francis's observation that "inevitably, each child will surprise us with ideas and projects born of [their] freedom, which challenge us to rethink our own ideas" (AL 262). The question Zuckerman and Francis implicitly pose is what freedom around affiliation means in Catholic-heritage families.

Religionist Christel Manning's study of secular parenting, including formerly affiliated Catholics, also found choice of a way of life to be a prime parenting value. Manning found that participants in parenting interviews wrapped the explanations of their child-rearing decisions around a "choice narrative." Although

---

7. Philip Zuckerman, *Living the Secular Life: New Answers to Old Questions* (New York: Penguin Books, 2015), 104.

8. Ibid., 106.

secular parents make a range of choices about whether or what kind of religious upbringing to allow, they tend to emphasize individual agency and the power of having options. Writing specifically of parents who claim no affiliation, Manning writes that when they become parents, "some go back to church, some join a community that welcomes doubters, some self-provide knowledge about religion or a secular philosophy [to their children], some outsource religious instruction, and some do nothing. Yet regardless of which path they choose, the decision is always framed as a way to help the child make his or her own choices."[9]

Manning observes how neatly this narrative fits with American individualism and market commodification. Wanting the best for children, parents inadvertently school them in self-centered capitalistic valuation about the most important perspective in their lives: their (religious and/or secular) basic horizon of understanding about reality. For Manning, secular parents seem unaware of these risks, of how small an ethical space this actually is compared to how large they imagine it to be. Secular parents impart the same message as consumer culture: "We always have a choice."[10]

This choice narrative can be "illusory" for those whose life prospects are markedly circumscribed, such as by abuse or personal and structural discrimination. Choice can be "tyrannical" when it generates anxiety about which choice is best or what one might be missing by not making other choices.[11] Far from retreating from these risks, however, and falling back into an apology for an idealized religious nest that would be free of its own ideologies, Manning sensibly concludes that the "choice narrative" is best characterized as "ambiguous." It both opens and closes reality to secular parents; it allows and compromises freedom at once. "It has fractured our society, to be sure, but it has also liberated some of us."[12]

A secular Catholic ethic, then, can be construed that contests the commonplace Catholic bias toward normative affiliation articulated in *Amoris Laetitia* (and almost everywhere else in US Catholic theology and ministry). This secular Catholic familial ethic facilitates Catholic-heritage parents encouraging children to make choices about what they want to be when they grow up, doing so with the above

9. Christel Manning, *Losing Our Religion: How Unaffiliated Parents Are Raising Their Children* (New York: New York University Press, 2015), 138–39.

10. Ibid., 148.

11. See ibid., 154–61.

12. Ibid., 152. I would add that the ambiguity of the choice narrative is not a sufficient reason to valorize the "religious reproduction" approach, the presumption that children should be raised expecting to share their parents' religion. On "religious reproduction," see F. LeRon Shults, *Theology After the Birth of God: Atheist Conceptions in Cognition and Culture* (New York: Palgrave Macmillan, 2014), 13–16, *inter alia*.

risks in mind. Just as one would with adult work or vocation—believing that there is time to "figure that out when you are grown up"—so one can do with religious or nonreligious identification. Of course, parents can prepare children with life skills for a choice of religion or way of life as they would for work or vocation. A clutch of commitments can sit alongside (or take the place of) appeals to God or church in the familial ethical imagination: empathy, fairness, equity, happiness, integrity, service, and love of children for their own sake, whatever value system they take on religiously. Family practices can be responses to questions like: What do I need in order to say yes to my own life in a way that facilitates a yes for others? Have we really said yes to our own lives irrespective of whether we are meeting secular or religious admonitions? Can this family be one that will discover what family means as much as it tries to fulfill an expectation? Holding open the door for these paths, insofar as it lies in their freedom, is something family members can give each other. Psychologist James Hollis describes the psychological maturity involved in such parenting: "The desire to replicate our value system is not love; it is narcissism and impedes their journey. It is difficult enough to individuate. Why should they carry our needs as well?"[13]

To parent in a way that encourages children's discretion about identifying with religion and/or secularity is still to form children in particular ways with specific biases about religion. Again, there is no such thing as nonideological family life in regard to religion, ethics, spirituality. Although not conclusive, there is evidence that children are likely to maintain little to no religious affiliation if they are raised without such affiliation. This suggests that there is no "neutral" parenting when it comes to religious or nonreligious affiliation in adulthood.

Acknowledging this dimension of secular Catholic families' new ethical postures is a way of realizing what *Amoris Laetitia* calls "most important" regarding children in the family: "the ability lovingly to help them grow in freedom, maturity, overall discipline, and real autonomy" (AL 261). The church needs a more fitting appreciation regarding in what this freedom, maturity, discipline, and autonomy consists. Indeed, once affiliation is recognized as a stake in Catholic ethics of family, tied deeply to nearly everything that has been written on the topic, we realize what a difference a change of course can make. Ethics of family and relationships from a stance that includes nonnormative affiliations will be substantially transformed.

As a lived ethics, it will not be easy. It can be a dance for family members to relate to each other around affiliation. As Zuckerman writes of secular families

---

13. James Hollis, *The Middle Passage* (Toronto: Inner City, 1993), 65.

relating to religious relatives, "It is difficult to be honest while at the same time seeking not to offend, to be respectful while simultaneously not obsequious, to be genuine and open even in the face of that which mystifies or even offends, to be loving while strongly disagreeing about very important personal, political, and existential matters."[14] These lived complications point to one challenge of secular Catholic parenting: being "out" among more affiliated Catholic relatives. This is not only a matter of appeasing the "good Catholics" in the family, whose equanimity may be tested by the difference in belief and practice that the "bad" or "fallen away" Catholics live and are teaching their children, and modeling for relatives, and putting on display at family events, especially official sacramental events like weddings, First Communions, baptisms, ordinations, and the like. It may also be a matter of not spoiling the silence of the other "bad Catholics" in the family, not stirring up the underdiscussed topic of what kinds of beliefs and practices are actually going on in the family.

One part of the family being public about "nonnormative affiliation" can create discomfort for everyone else who does not feel ready or safe about being public within the family. On the other hand, letting one's secular Catholicism be known in the family, at one's own pace and with consideration for the feelings of others, can be the beginning of solidarity with others in the family who are harboring such thoughts and not sure how to express them. Anticipating that this can happen in Catholic families is an important disposition; expecting it is even better. Mature hope for the secularity of one's Catholic family members will be for many a challenging ethically minded space-making. This hope means the courage to live with and into the outside of one's affiliation, to not let given ins and outs of being Catholic become decisive for what we are and what we can become.

We can talk about such hope as family practices that are drawn from secular Catholic families but are not limited to them. The practices include centering the family in the worthiness of life in its manifold natural and social manifestations. This means modeling that friendship, love, and commitment can occur across lines that seem threatening: children should be free to befriend and eventually partner outside of the "religious" (or "nonreligious") fold. Parents model this in their own committed relationships. This is freedom to love and be loved. This is also responsibility for the social commons. The invented and frangible character of how we imagine our religious affiliations suggests that, however much they serve to stabilize our values at formative stages of life, they must also give entry to sharing life with others who were raised differently and with whom we share

14. Zuckerman, *Living the Secular Life*, 81.

social responsibility for access to the goods of life. This suggests a coalitional family who learns about participating in coalitions, where the family's acknowledgment of the unequal world into which all are born is an index of its coming to terms with unearned advantage. For such family practices, religions or ways of life are not good in themselves but only insofar as they place one well into coalitions with other families, where we depend on each other for the privilege of being alive, according to the measure of our freedom. This vision for family practice potentially puts secular Catholic and affiliated Catholic families in a shared space. This vision draws from historic Catholic values, like the common good and the dignity of the person, but makes them answer to secular exigencies that widen the familial circle of inclusion beyond the question of who is affiliated and who is disaffiliated. All this is what is meant by hope for secularity or deconversion in the Catholic-heritage family: a felt responsibility for difference out of the quest to identify with and as the different.

Such hope, in practice, is frankly beyond the pale for many Catholic families, but it represents the most daring and most confident stance. This is because mature hope for the secularizing or deconversion of Catholic family members says that we want "them" (starting with "us") to experience the possibility of not being Catholic, the contingency of their Catholic identity, a difficult but ultimately manageable de-idealization of inherited or cherished self-stabilizing supports, a consideration that one's life could genuinely be otherwise, whether or not one finally chooses to define oneself as Catholic and how one chooses to do so. Mature hope for the deconversion of one's Catholic family is a desire for "spiritual indifference" in the other, wise and radical openness, with the knowledge that such freedom may lead in unexpected directions, including deeper down the road of what is taken to be normative Catholicism. Such an ethics can contribute to awareness and integration of affiliational diversity in families.

Toward a New Catholic Family Ethics

The 2014–2015 Synods of Bishops on Families innovated a model of engagement with secular families that Dillon summarizes as a "willingness to reflexively examine its teachings on marriage and family life, [an] openness to Catholics' secular experiences, [and] deliberate dialogical engagement with the mutual relevance of doctrinal ideas and Catholic realities."[15] Crucially, Dillon characterizes the stakes for Catholic teaching on the family: "The living tradition of Catholic

---

15. Dillon, *Postsecular Catholicism*, 154.

doctrine both absorbs and is integrated into the secularization of the Church and of everyday Catholic life."[16] For Dillon, this is a positive "postsecular" development in Roman Catholicism because it recognizes the value of both Catholic teaching as well as worthy developments in secular Catholic life.

More intensive, practice-based studies of secular Catholic family ethics are an important research domain for the next stage of research and pastoral attention. Ethics can work from the Catholic-heritage religious and nonreligious pluralism within, on the margins of, and outside the church, from Catholicisms in practice. Ethics can anticipate and advocate such Catholicisms, following the lead of the Second Vatican Council in commending Catholics to "recognize, preserve, and promote" the "good things, spiritual and moral, as well as the socio-cultural values found among" religiously diverse persons, not only in "dialogue," but also in "collaboration" (*Nostra Aetate* 2). This is what, I imagine, Catholic ethicists and theologians often quietly do already when they are so positioned by their own family life. This quietness maintains the affiliational bias.

Ethics as an academic field aspires in a unique way among theological fields to the business and status of normative discourse in the Roman Catholic tradition. It can leverage this aspiration in support of lived Catholicisms by normalizing such diversity, which entails working from such categories and treating them as morally substantial. This, however, will reframe the aspiration to normativity because it means acknowledging the limits of Catholic in-group speech about the good life. It means opening to an outside to Catholic ethics—within "Catholicism" itself. Dealing adequately with secular Catholic families means that Catholic ethics will be more like interreligious or comparative ethics, but "within" the Catholic community, where "Catholic community" is understood as largely constituted by secular Catholic families who occupy a range of habitations in relation to what actively affiliated insiders consider to be the heart of the tradition. Thus, this advocacy of secular familial Catholicisms is a considerable challenge to official versions of Catholic ethics' self-understanding.

Ethicist Julie Hanlon Rubio's recent acknowledgment that her Catholic ethics of family could not address the spiritual diversity within her own family is gutsy because it is so rare.[17] There is something beautiful to be honored in what all Catholic-heritage families—however affiliated—actually are and become, but such narratives are too-seldom told and even more rarely a basis for Catholic ministry, theology, and official teaching.

---

16. Ibid., 155.

17. Julie Hanlon Rubio, "Practices of Love and Solidarity: Family Ethics," in *Invitation to Practical Theology: Catholic Voices and Visions*, ed. Claire E. Wolfteich (New York: Paulist Press, 2014).

Chapter 21

Catholics and Feminists on Work, Family, and Flourishing

Christine Firer Hinze

As we move through our busy days, few of us spend much time pondering the deeper purposes of work, family, and economic life. Our institutional leaders and policy makers also tend to take for granted their meanings and aims. But in times of great historical disjuncture and change, what has long appeared obvious and settled about family, work, and economic life is called into question, and long-held self-understandings and ways of proceeding are rethought and reformed.

The nineteenth-century ascendance of modern industrial capitalism was one such period of disruption. In response, there arose public voices and social movements concerned to secure justice for vulnerable workers and families in the new economic regime. In the United States, leaders, thinkers, activists, and average citizens all played important roles in reshaping laws, institutions, culture, and customs to improve wage earners' lots and to ensure families the economic resources needed to perform their irreplaceable functions.

In the twenty-first century, the work, family, and economic waters continue to shift and churn, and we must navigate our courses through these waters amid larger, crisscrossing social currents we neither fully understand nor control. Most of us find our energies and attention absorbed in the day-to-day piloting of our personal "life rafts" through often unpredictable and choppy social and economic seas. Yet not far below the surface, deeper questions—about our relationships, our aspirations for work and family, and the ways our economic institutions shape and support these—continue to beckon. Pausing to reflect and getting a handle on such questions, we sense, could help guide us toward the kinds of work, relationships, and living we desire for ourselves, our loved ones, and our larger communities.

This essay invites that opportunity, in conversation with two modern wisdom traditions: Catholic social thought and feminist ethics and economics.[1] Modern social Catholicism and feminism offer illuminating perspectives, critiques, and transformative proposals concerning economy, work, and family today. Born amid the tectonic economic and social shifts of the nineteenth century, today these two modern traditions continue to develop as rich alternative resources for economic thought and practice. Amid major disagreements, Catholics' and feminists' surprisingly overlapping critiques of dominant economic ideologies and countercultural visions for work-family justice make them potentially powerful conversation partners and edgy allies. Exploring their contributions can help expand our imaginations and hone our directional skills as we map present coordinates and plot directions forward in these key life arenas.

Catholic Social Thought on Economy, Family, and Work

A thumbnail sketch of modern social Catholicism's approach to economy, work, and family comprises eight foundational affirmations.

Family, work, and economy are essential, "natural," human relations and activities that exist to serve people's survival, sustenance, and flourishing. In every time and culture, people form families and engage in labor and economic activities to meet material needs, to develop and employ their skills and capacities, and to serve their wider communities. These human activities also carry moral and spiritual significance.

Inclusive provisioning is economy's defining purpose. God intends the world and its resources for the sustenance of all; families, work, and markets are institutions responsible for stewarding this divine intention. Inclusive provisioning—making the requisites of material well-being available to all members—is, therefore, economy's purpose and primary *raison d'être.* Is everyone's dignity respected? Can everyone meaningfully participate? Does everyone have access to enough? These are the criteria on which the success of any economic system must be judged—criteria that firmly oppose the value-neutrality and metrics of currently dominant neoclassical economics.

Work is a humanly valuable personal and communal activity. In a properly functioning economy, people ordinarily provide for their family's material needs by working. Though it can be toilsome and wearying, work is a necessary and salutary human activity. When performed under free, fair, and just conditions,

---

1. For a similar approach, see Christine Firer Hinze, *Glass Ceilings and Dirt Floors: Women, Work, and the Global Economy* (Mahwah, NJ: Paulist Press, 2015), 75–101.

our work advances moral goods by enabling material sustenance, developing and employing talents and abilities, and contributing to the common good of families and communities. The dignity of the persons performing it confers on all honest labor, even the most menial, its own dignity and worth.

Provisioning in modern market economies requires the combined labors of the unpaid, household sector and the formal, waged sectors. While operating according to different logics and reward systems, these economies depend on and influence one another. In contrast to modern tendencies to identify "economy" and "work" solely with the market arena, Catholic teaching emphasizes the equally important economic role of the household economy. "The economy (*'oiko-nomia,'* household management) was born from domestic work. The home has been for a long time—and in many regions still is—a place of production and the center of life." Work, both waged and unpaid, is essential to establishing and supporting a family, and families are "the first schools of work," where the young learn and practice the skills and virtues of being a good worker and doing good work (*Compendium of the Social Doctrine of the Church* 248–49). The family is thus "an essential agent of economic life" but retains its distinctly nonmarket identity and code. In particular, family relations are "guided not by the market mentality but by the logic of sharing and solidarity among generations" (*Compendium* 249).

Economy and work serve families' sustenance and support their larger purposes and mission. Catholic social thought esteems the family as the "first and vital cell of society." Grounded in marriage, families are "bound by blood or adoption for the whole of life," comprise multiple kin relationships, and can take a range of forms (cf. *Apostolicam Actuositatem* 11). Families, writes Pope John Paul II, are charged with four fundamental tasks: to form intimate communities of life and love; to serve, nurture, and protect life at all its stages; to contribute to society through education and hospitality, social involvement, and action; and to embody Christian life and mission as "domestic church"—as believing and praying, evangelizing, and neighbor-serving communities (*Familiaris Consortio*, part 2; *Amoris Laetitia*, chapter 5). Waged and household work serve the sustenance and well-being of each family member and the family as a whole, enabling families to "be who they are" by living out their fourfold calling (cf. *Compendium* 251).

Adults have rights to work in just conditions, whose pay and benefits yield a sufficient, secure, and dignified livelihood for themselves and their households/families. Worker justice has been a central theme in modern Catholic social teaching. While cautiously supporting market economies, popes have unwaveringly declared human labor's non-commodifiability and dignity; families' rights to economic sustenance; and workers' rights to "living wages" that support the family in return for honest work, with conditions and hours of work conducive to a dignified and decent livelihood and family life. Workers' rights to status, voice, and influence in their workplaces, and to social insurance in the event of illness, disability, and old age, are championed. To attain all these, laborers' rights to unionize and, when necessary, to strike are also consistently supported.

When jobs are lacking, or when wage work does not yield remuneration or benefits sufficient for family livelihood, Catholic thought regards it as society's duty, usually through government, to ensure their delivery through other means.[2] This can involve various arrangements—mandated living wages, family living wages for household heads, family allowances, public or private insurance plans, etc. But economic and government policies must see that all families have fair access to work and to necessary resources.

Men and women are created distinctive, equal, and complementary, with implications for family, work, and economic life. Official papal social teaching in particular depicts men and women as playing differentiated and complementary roles in waged and familial economies. To accomplish the labor necessary for livelihood, official teachings have assumed and favored a gendered division of labor between a masculine-keyed waged economy and a feminine-keyed family economy. Since the later twentieth century, social teaching has also underscored the value of women's active participation in all spheres of public life and the importance of husbands' and fathers' family engagement.[3] But one caveat endures: that waged work and public engagement not require women—especially mothers, and mothers of young children most of all—to curtail or forsake their special role in the family household. A well-ordered economy will "make it possible for a mother . . . to devote herself to taking care of her children. . . . Having to abandon these tasks in order to take up paid work outside the home is wrong from the point of view of the good of society and of the family when it contradicts or hinders these primary goals of the mission of a mother" (*Laborem Exercens* 19).

Feminists have roundly criticized the inequitable consequences of the gendered division of labor that both secular and Catholic family living-wage agendas assumed. Yet this arrangement's wide appeal was not due solely to patriarchal interests in relegating women to "pregnant, barefoot, in the kitchen" status. As industrialization, urbanization, and individualist market competition were rapidly displacing traditional home-based and local economies, gendered separate-spheres

---

2. See, for example, *Amoris Laetitia* 44 (quoting Pontifical Council for the Family, *Charter of the Rights of the Family*): "Families have the right 'to be able to count on an adequate family policy on the part of public authorities in the juridical, economic, social and fiscal domains.'"

3. See, for example, Christine Firer Hinze, "Women, Families, and the Legacy of *Laborem Exercens*: An Unfinished Agenda," *Journal of Catholic Social Thought* 6 (2009): 63–92.

ideology functioned as a strategy for *sustaining and supporting crucial adult presence and caring labor in the familial household.* Against modern markets' power to disrupt traditional family and community relations, breadwinner-homemaker ideology deployed gender in service of a profound social intuition: that familial households and face-to-face communities cultivate extra-market and market-resistant relationships and values critical to human sustenance and well-being and urgently in need of protecting and nurturing. For achieving this, assigning one adult family member per household to this full-time task based on gender proved an emotionally potent and culturally efficient strategy.

It was not, however, the only possible strategy. The biological realities of child-bearing and lactation have long reinforced cultural connections between women and domesticity; yet Catholic treatments of men's and women's economic roles retain a certain elasticity insofar as these roles are not strictly ends in themselves but serve larger socio-moral purposes. Families might also—and in practice often do—fulfill these purposes by employing nongendered or diversely gendered strategies for organizing home and waged labor.[4]

Work and economic activity, whether waged and household-based, are necessary, important, but limited and instrumental human goods. For social Catholicism, people do not live solely to work at even the most satisfying jobs or meaningful professions. Money isn't everything, and there are more important things than work. Today, these truths are perhaps recognized more readily by working-class families than by professional elites. Though significant, work and economic activity (producing, trading, earning, spending, consuming) are not ends in themselves. Instead, they are meant to serve the sustenance and well-being of embodied and enspirited persons and families, provide supportive conditions for our non-commodifiable intellectual, moral, and spiritual development and communal pursuits.

By subordinating work and economy to larger human purposes Catholicism presses against strong currents in modern market societies toward a 24/7 open-for-business culture, reductive materialism, competitive consumerism in pursuit of continually rising standards of living, and a dystopic "world of total work" for "a people without rest" for both workaholic professionals and lower-skilled job-holders working erratic hours at precarious or poorly paid jobs. In our culture of busyness and overwork, social Catholicism's insistence on limits to work hours; weekly pauses from labor for rest, worship, and family time; and temperance in spending and consumption sound almost subversive.[5]

---

4. Cf. Christine Firer Hinze, "U.S. Catholic Social Thought, Gender, and Livelihood," *Theological Studies* 66 (2005): 568–91.

5. See Bernard Häring, *The Law of Christ*, vol. 2 (Westminster: Newman Press, 1961), 325.

Thus, Pope Francis, who frequently decries the curse of unemployment and extols work's value, also insists that "a person is not just about work." Addressing labor unionists in 2017, he called for "a healthy culture of idleness, of knowing how to rest."

> This is not laziness; it is a human need. . . . When I ask a man, a woman who has two, three children: "Tell me, do you play with your children? Do you have this 'idleness'?"—"Well, you know, when I go to work, they are still asleep, and when I get back, they're already in bed." This is inhuman. That is why, along with work, the other culture [of healthy idleness, rest, and play] must also be present.[6]

In this same countercultural vein, Catholic living-wage teaching's assumption— that one full-time job, or no more than fifty hours per week of adult waged labor should be needed to provide a modest, dignified living for a household of two adults and several children—points to an ethos of limited hours of waged work and what we today would call work-life balance.[7] It's worth imagining how this quite radical agenda for shorter hours of work and a modest standard of living, disentangled from problematically gendered economic dependencies and role constrictions, might challenge and inspire family-work values, practices, and policies today.

Feminist Contributions and Challenges

Feminist ethicists and economists approach economy, work, and family from a perspective committed to the holistic well-being of all women, along with children, men, and families.[8] As noted, feminist treatments of these subjects share much common ground with social Catholicism. Both feminists and Catholics share a normative understanding of economy and its inclusive provisioning purposes. For both, economic provisioning requires market and household labor, with the former serving the latter. Both insist that the key criterion for an economy's success is not GDP, profits, or growth but access to livelihood for all families

6. Pope Francis, "Address to Delegates from the Italian Confederation of Workers' Unions," June 28, 2017, http://w2.vatican.va/content/francesco/en/speeches/2017/june/documents/papa -francesco_20170628_delegati-cisl.html.

7. See Martha Starr, "Consumption, Work Hours and Values in the Writings of John A. Ryan: Is It Possible to Return to the Road Not Taken?," *Review of Social Economy* 66, no. 1 (2008): 7–24.

8. See, for example, Alison Jaggar, "Feminist Ethics," in *Encyclopedia of Ethics*, 2nd ed., ed. L. Becker and C. Becker (New York: Garland Press, 2001); Marilyn Power, "Social Provisioning as a Starting Point for Feminist Economics," *Feminist Economics* 10, no. 3 (2004): 3–19; and works by feminist economists Deborah Figart, Nancy Folbre, and Julie Nelson.

through free and dignified economic participation. Both appreciate work's value and advocate for workers' rights in both waged and household arenas. Both support government action and policies to ensure workers' rights and access to livelihood. Both oppose the incursion of market values and relations into family and other nonmarket spheres. Both embrace convictions about human flourishing that lead them to decry the ways current economic culture fosters materialism, individualism, and the absorption of time, attention, and energies into what Juliet Schor calls the work-spend-consumption cycle.[9]

Feminist scholarship on family, work, and economy also adds to and challenges social Catholicism in a variety of ways. Three especially significant contributions are feminism's ideological and structural analysis of the care economy; its critical exposure of the ways that gender functions, along with class and race, to entrench systemic inequalities; and its advocacy for reforms to enable and support both gender-equitable economic *stability* for workers and families and *fluidity* in ways that gender, work, households, and families are being formed, organized, and related today.

Care Economy

For feminist thinkers, "care work" comprises "the relationships and activities involved in maintaining people on a daily basis and inter-generationally."[10] Care work involves a number of intertwined activities, including direct caring for persons; maintaining physical surroundings for living; and the "kith and kin work" of fostering and sustaining relationships and social connections in homes, families, and communities.[11] The "care economy" comprises the networks of relationships and activities that arise to address humans' needs as embodied, (inter)dependent, and vulnerable beings.

A functioning care sector, in which familial households are primary sites, is indispensable to human survival and flourishing; without it, the formal economy, indeed, every public institution, would collapse. Mainstream economics depicts households as dependent units of consumption. Feminist analysis suggests the reverse: the formal economy is dependent on the resources and supports produced daily by those who labor in the economy of care.[12]

---

9. Juliet Schor, *The Overworked American* (New York: Basic Books, 1991).

10. Evelyn Nakano Glenn, *Forced to Care: Coercion and Caregiving in America* (Cambridge, MA: Harvard University Press, 2010), 5.

11. Ibid.

12. For more on dependency and care, see works by feminist philosopher Eva Feder Kittay; and Sandra Sullivan-Dunbar's essay "Valuing Family Care: Love and Labor" in this volume, along with her *Human Dependency and Christian Ethics* (Cambridge: Cambridge University Press, 2017).

Systemic Inequities

While they need and benefit from the care economy, however, economic and other public institutions consistently underacknowledge and underreward care work and those who perform it. And overwhelmingly, those who perform it in both household and waged economies are women, whose appointments as CEOs of the care economy come with the "status obligations" that being female confer.[13]

As more and more married women and mothers moved into the formal work-force after the 1960s, they continued to feel disproportionately responsible for, and to perform a disproportionate share of, the caring labor of the home.[14] What amounted to a massive collective transfer of adult time and energies from domicile to workplace during these decades inevitably subtracted time for the work of the household and care economy. Wage-earning women's greater commitments to household care work disadvantaged them in relation to male peers, who were better able to perform the role of the "ideal worker" by devoting full time and attention to the job seemingly unencumbered by outside concerns or responsibilities. The upshot for working families, exacerbated by a culture "with an affinity for busyness," has been a well-documented time squeeze, felt particularly by the majority of wage-earning women who put in a daily second shift of household care work. Upper-class professional families can alleviate "time famine" by purchasing many care services, but most other families cannot.[15]

The labor of care and social reproduction is "the work that makes all other work possible."[16] But the current social organization of care embeds a gendered pattern of injustice that amounts to "a systemic transfer of hidden subsidies" from the unpaid care sector to the waged economy. The daily time, energy, and attention expended by unpaid and underpaid care workers (the latter, disproportionately immigrant women of color) yield economic value that gets reallocated from these workers'

13. Glenn, *Forced to Care*, 7. Linking manhood and womanhood to work- and family-related *status obligations* helps communities ensure that critical social tasks will be performed, even in the face of difficulty or inconvenience.

14. The twentieth century saw massive rises in women's labor-force participation, from 19 percent to over 70 percent. By 2012, 71 percent of women with children under eighteen years of age, including 61 percent of women with children aged three and younger (versus under 35 percent in 1970) were in the paid labor force. US Department of Labor Women's Bureau, "Facts Over Time: Women in the Labor Force," https://www.dol.gov/wb/stats/NEWSTATS/facts/women_lf.htm.

15. On "ideal worker–marginalized caregiver" ideology, see Joan C. Williams, *Unbending Gender* (New York: Oxford University Press, 2000); on busyness culture, see Lonnie Golden, "A Brief History of Long Work Time and the Contemporary Sources of Overwork," *Journal of Business Ethics* 84, Supplement 2 (2009): 217–27.

16. For this phrase, see National Domestic Workers' Alliance, https://www.domesticworkers.org/.

pockets, clocks, and lives to the pockets, clocks, and lives of those who benefit from their cheap, or free, labor. These unrecorded transfers impose time, opportunity, and monetary "taxes" across caregivers' life cycles. Insofar as this analysis is accurate, current business as usual sustains an exploitative system, one that relegates care workers to greater economic vulnerability, marginalization, and inequality.[17]

Strikingly, neither this devaluation of care work and workers nor the obvious problems posed by moving domestic caregivers into the wage economy without reorganizing responsibilities and resources to secure the work of the household have been widely recognized as public or structural issues. Instead, they continue to be framed and experienced as hard choices facing individual women, men, and families. But feminist scholars point out that the masculine-keyed fiction of the autonomous, "ideal worker" is part of a *system* that marginalizes and undervalues the feminized, backstage care work and workers that it depends on. This setup ensures that caregivers will fall short as ideal workers and that our whole care infrastructure remains largely invisible, inadequately rewarded, and excluded or underreported in most measures of economic productivity.

By bringing structural dynamics into focus, feminist critical analysis reveals how beliefs and practices surrounding gender, race, and class exacerbate and entrench disparities in economic and social resources, opportunities, and power. For impoverished or precarious workers and people of color, these disparities are compounded. Finally, with Catholics, feminists decry two additional contemporary trends impeding inclusive livelihood: steeply increasing wealth and income inequalities, and the Sisyphean quest to attain "enough" within a mass consumer culture that evaluates economic sufficiency and standards of living against ever-receding horizons of "more, newer, and better."[18]

Stable Livelihoods; Fluid Genderings

Both social Catholics and feminists champion access to economic livelihood and security for all workers and families. But most feminists support, in ways Catholic teaching does not, contemporary trends toward fluidity, pluralism, and

17. Rania Antonopoulos, "The Unpaid Care Work–Paid Work Connection," International Labor Office, Policy Integrations and Statistics Department, Working Paper no. 86 (Geneva, Switzerland: International Labor Organization, 2009); Firer Hinze, *Glass Ceilings*, chap. 3.

18. On competitive consumption, see Robert H. Frank, *Luxury Fever: Weighing the Cost of Excess* (Princeton, NJ: Princeton University Press, 2010). On wealth inequality, see Rakesh Kochhar and Anthony Cilluffo, "How Wealth Inequality Has Changed in the U.S. Since the Great Recession, by Race, Ethnicity and Income," Pew Research Center Report, November 1, 2017, https://www .pewresearch.org/fact-tank/2017/11/01/how-wealth-inequality-has-changed-in-the-u-s-since-the -great-recession-by-race-ethnicity-and-income/. For income inequality, also see Pew Research Center Reports for 2018 and 2019, https://www.pewresearch.org/topics/income-inequality/.

improvisation the ways that gender, work, households, and families are formed, organized, and related.

Here feminists and Catholics diverge over how to address a shared concern: to identify, nurture, and support what is most fundamental to our existence and thriving as persons, families, and communities. Catholic thought has traditionally affirmed a God-created human nature in which male and female sexuality and corresponding gender identities are clearly distinguished, stable, and normative, and families are naturally grounded in monogamous, heterosexual, procreative, lifelong marriage. Honoring and conserving this God-given framework for sexual and family life are seen as essential to the bodily and spiritual health and well-being—including the economic well-being—of adults, children, society, and future generations.

Feminists, meanwhile, approach traditionally fixed and normative understandings of sexual nature and family formation with suspicion, deconstructing what they deem falsely universal and ideologically biased certainties, and opposing the constricting and harmful consequences of enforcing them, particularly for nonconforming persons and families. Catholic tradition has held that personal and social well-being requires both secure livelihoods and specific, stable sexual and family arrangements. Feminists affirm the former but promote openness to the diversity and fluidity of genderings, sexualities, partnerings, and family forms that increasingly define today's cultural landscape.

As we navigate these new diversities, however, the influence and pull of more traditional genderings remain strong. Both institutional patterns and people's affective sensibilities about the status obligations of womanhood and manhood—be they moms in high-powered political posts or dads coping with the loss of family-supporting factory jobs—continue to be drawn into traditionally gendered currents.[19] Here weighty policy questions cry out for reflective, data-informed public deliberation. How socially beneficial is it to continue to arrange labor markets and work-family policies assuming some version of a male-breadwinner, female-homemaker template? Catholic social teaching urges work-family policies that especially protect women's abilities to perform their family caregiving roles. Many feminists contend that a nongendered, "universal caregiver" family-work policy will yield more just, egalitarian, and flexible support for families' participation in the waged and household economies.[20]

---

19. Anne-Marie Slaughter, "Why Women Still Can't Have It All," *Atlantic*, July/August 2012, http://www.theatlantic.com/magazine/archive/2012/07/why-women-still-cant-have-it-all/309020/; "With His Job Gone, an Autoworker Wonders, 'What Am I as a Man . . . ?'" *New York Times*, May 27, 2019, https://www.nytimes.com/2019/05/27/us/auto-worker-jobs-lost.html.

20. See Nancy Fraser, "After the Family Wage: A Post-Industrial Thought Experiment," in *Gender and Citizenship in Transition*, ed. Barbara Hodgson (New York: Routledge, 2000), chap. 1.

Today, questions about fixed-versus-fluid sex, gender, marriage, and family forms spark visceral responses and heated arguments across the US social spectrum. And no wonder: at stake are the sustenance and welfare of our most intimate and tender personal and familial relationships. For family-work conservatives, precipitously abandoning tried-and-true gender, family, and work values is a risky, dangerously destabilizing social experiment. For change advocates like feminists, including many Catholic feminists, the key issue is not whether people enjoy performing conventional gender roles or the extent to which families' work and home lives hew to traditional shapes or scripts. Rather, it is how we in contemporary market economies can organize and support socially necessary labor in the waged and household sectors so that a dignified livelihood is accessible to every person, household, and family.

Practical Directions for Work-Family-Economy Relations Today

We conclude by posing several questions for further reflection, and perhaps action, about what work, family, and economic justice mean and require; how we might pursue these in our own lives and communities; and the cultural and institutional changes we need and ought to be promoting to ensure dignified work and well-being to all workers and families.

First, research suggests that in the United States, relatively privileged, college-educated middle and professional classes of people—the people most likely to read a book like this—are enculturated from a young age into an ethos that values individual self-expression, busyness and ambitious striving, competitive achievement, and securing fulfilling work that expresses one's identity and passions. Add to this the hyper-consumerism that infuses US culture today, and we have a recipe for a lifestyle of long work hours, chronic time squeeze, and default habits of compensatory, often ethically and ecologically questionable, consumption.[21] By contrast, both feminist and Catholic visions of good livelihood call for just wage work and ample time and support for the work of the home, but also time for rest, mindfulness, tending relationships, leisure and celebration, worship, ecological stewardship, and justice-promoting civic engagement.

- What is your reaction to this description of typical US middle-class cultural formation? What values or practices do you and your peers cherish that are not included in this list?

---

21. See, for example, the *Journal of Business Ethics* 84, Supplement 2 (2009); Schor, *Overworked American*; David Cloutier, *The Vice of Luxury: Economic Excess in a Consumer Age* (Washington, DC: Georgetown University Press, 2015).

- If feminists and Catholics are right that work, money, and consumption aren't everything, and that economic activities are meant to serve and support the noneconomic spheres of lives, and not vice versa, what challenges does this pose to our own attitudes and practices concerning work, time, and success? To our current economic and workplace cultures?

- What factors incentivize or discourage reorienting our personal and social compasses toward a vision of economic success that's measured by access to and enjoyment of a sustainable, amply sufficient livelihood not only for ourselves but for all families?

Second, it's well known that feminism and Catholic teaching take different stands on many issues surrounding sexuality, gender, marriage, and the makeup of families.

- With respect to family, work, and gender issues, what do you see as sources of these disagreements?

- Are there any aspects of these issues on which feminists who are not Catholics and Catholics who are not feminists might collaborate with one another? Legitimately critique one another? Learn from one another?

Finally, both feminism and social Catholicism posit relational and solidary understandings of reality and of humanity: we are all interconnected, with corresponding responsibilities. Both take active stands on the sides of poor, vulnerable, and marginalized persons and communities, including the vulnerable earth. Both advocate for reforms and structural changes aimed at sustainably redressing economic and social injustices and empowering historically excluded or oppressed peoples' participation and flourishing.

- What would it mean, practically, for faith communities and citizens to take seriously Catholic and feminist claims about solidarity, taking sides with the marginalized and oppressed, and working for universally inclusive, sustainable economic justice? What specific actions or practices might demonstrate their seriousness, or lack thereof?

- Is it even possible to meaningfully commit to such radically inclusive values while living within our mainstream US culture and economy? Or must one give up on one or the other? What steps can ordinary people take in their personal, family, work, and civic lives to respond to these radical claims with integrity?

Chapter 22

Wanting "the Best" for "Our" Kids

Parenting and Privilege

David Cloutier

In early 2019, news headlines were filled with a college admissions scandal. Rich parents, through an elaborate network of consultants and connections, sought places at elite universities for their sons and daughters. The consultants were paid large amounts of money to construct fake credentials for the students, fabricate records that they played a (usually obscure) sport, and even bribe coaches to accept those records and lobby their admissions office for the student's admission.[1]

In the wake of the scandal however, there followed a discussion of the many other ways—legal ways—that wealthy parents spend money to "game" the college admission system for the benefit of their children. It's no secret that parents pay hefty home prices to move into the best school districts in order to get an edge for their children, and others seek private schools that are very costly. In Washington, DC, even kindergartens at private schools are highly competitive, and later, these parents shell out money for extra classes or private tutors that prep students for admissions tests. On the athletic side, more and more parents support their children's participation in expensive "travel leagues" that give students a leg up on others for whom the only option is public school sports. Even many of these public schools now have "pay-to-play" policies that marginalize families who are just barely getting by. In all of these cases, parents are essentially paying in order

---

1. For an overview, see "College Admissions Scandal: Your Questions Answered," *New York Times*, March 14, 2019, https://www.nytimes.com/2019/03/14/us/college-admissions-scandal -questions.html?rref=collection%2Fnewseventcollection%2Fcollege-admissions-scandal&action= click&contentCollection=us&region=rank&module=package&version=highlights&content Placement=2&pgtype=collection.

to get their children in a better position to make it into the best colleges—and, from there, to get the opportunities that come from these colleges.

Is this all fair? On the one hand, in a society where educational credentials are so important, it seems that children who come from wealthy families have a pretty big advantage. On the other hand, these parents are just doing what we think anyone would do: trying their best to help their children have a good life. This is no different from my own parents, who saw that I performed really well in my neighborhood Catholic school growing up and who made sacrifices of time and money to send me to the excellent Jesuit high school located out in the rich suburbs. My parents were lucky that, at the time, these opportunities weren't that expensive. Neither of them went to college, but they had enough extra that (sacrificing other things; I don't remember any family vacations in my high school years) they could invest in my sister and me. So, if other parents happen to be really wealthy, why wouldn't they do exactly the same things, albeit at a higher level? Maybe they shouldn't outright lie or bribe, but shouldn't they do everything they can to benefit their children? Shouldn't they want "the best" for them? It turns out that, in contemporary American society, wanting "the best" for "our kids" is a tricky moral matter. In this essay, I explore these dynamics in light of Catholic teaching.

What Happens When Everyone Wants "the Best"?

One of the most important recent books on the American family is Robert Putnam's *Our Kids*. Putnam, a Harvard sociologist, has written for decades on the most important trends affecting American society. His book *Bowling Alone* (2000) documented the collapse in American community life. In *Our Kids*, Putnam documents the long-term phenomenon of the rise of family inequality, such that it has become absurd to claim that our society provides all kids with an "equality of opportunity." He has a personal stake in this. The book is framed by his 1950s childhood in a small, industrial Ohio town, where there was a shared sense that all the kids in town were "our kids." Putnam documents how the offspring of the rich and the poor shared the same playgrounds, the same sports teams, and the same classrooms. While this meant that poorer kids like himself could go to Harvard (as he did), it wasn't just about college admissions. In a whole host of ways, families took care of one another. Putnam tells the story of Don, who talks about coming from the "poor side of town" and having parents who "didn't have a clue about college" but who felt everyone "met as an equal in sports" and had a pastor who "kept an eye on him" and guided him toward a college path.[2] Even the few African

---

2. Putnam, *Our Kids: The American Dream in Crisis* (New York: Simon & Schuster, 2015), 4.

American kids in the town, though affected by a racism that meant they always felt like outsiders, had people looking out for them. Jesse (who beat Putnam out for class president) had a football coach who "was a figurehead" and connected him to a college coach, while Cheryl worked with her mom as a housekeeper for one of Port Clinton's CEOs whose wife, admiring Cheryl's work and "shocked to discover that no one had talked to her about college," intervened directly with the school principal to get Cheryl on the radar and eventually on a scholarship to a university.[3] When he returns to his town now, however, he finds it divided. Developers have built large, gated golf course communities all along the shore of Lake Erie, while a ten-minute walk away there are dilapidated trailer parks. The wealthy and the poor families no longer interact, no longer attend the same schools. Thus, their outcomes are much different.

Since one story cannot epitomize a whole society, Putnam's book has dozens of "scissors graphs"—that is, over time, one line for the kids of wealthier, educated parents rises while the other line for the poorer families stays flat or falls. He doesn't just chart relative family incomes over the last fifty years. He charts things like what he calls "Goodnight Moon time"—the amount of time parents spend on developmental activities, like reading to their kids (beyond activities like feeding them). In every case, Putnam finds that the gap between rich and poor families has grown, sometimes enormously. For Goodnight Moon time, he writes, "In the 1970's, there were virtually no class differences in how much [developmental] time a child got with mom or dad. By 2013, however, the average toddler of college-educated parents was . . . getting nearly three quarters of an hour more serve-and-return interaction every day."[4] And this is actually one of the more optimistic findings, since at least both upper- and lower-class kids are getting *more* time today than they did four decades ago. By comparison, routinely eating together as a family declined significantly more among lower-class families.[5]

Putnam concludes that we have gone from a society where "our kids" meant all the kids in a town to now where "our kids" just means our *own* kids. It is a collapse of social solidarity. What happened? Two factors stand out. One is the rise of single-parent households. In 1960, less than 5 percent of children were born outside of marriage but today over 40 percent are. In Putnam's Port Clinton, unwed births skyrocketed from 9 percent to 40 percent in the course of the 1980s.[6] Few factors so decisively correlate with economic poverty as does single parenting; in 2017, the Census Bureau reported 8.4 percent of children under

3. Ibid., 14–17.
4. Ibid., 127.
5. Ibid., 124.
6. Ibid., 21.

eighteen living in married-couple households were below the poverty line, but 35.8 percent of children not in married-couple households were in poverty.[7] Part of this is because families often have to rely on two incomes just to make ends meet. The issue, however, is more than economic. Some single parents may make enough money, but what they certainly lack is time. Indeed, one of the starkest "scissors graphs" in Putnam's study is how *dramatic* the class gap is on this issue. Children from birth to age seven whose parent or parents are college-educated are only slightly more likely *than in the 1950s* to be a single-parent household—still over 90 percent are in two-parent families. But for those whose parents have only a high school education, well over 60 percent are in single-parent families.[8] This is a cycle where those who start off disadvantaged in one way only suffer further disadvantages as they grow up.

But the single-parenting factor isn't the only one at play. Because single parents are now competing in an economy where many households *need* two incomes, they (or, rather, their kids) are fighting a losing battle against kids who have two parents. So, the second, and I think bigger, factor here is a situation of unequal competition. That's a bit trickier to explain, since clearly, even in 1959, some kids had parents with more privileges or more virtues than others. How do we explain the seeming greater equality in the earlier period?

The answer is to focus on the special nature of "positional goods." Some goods and services produced by an economy are not positional. That is, their consumption by one person doesn't affect the consumption of others. Food is an easy example. The fact that some kids have enough to eat doesn't mean others do not have enough. Indeed, one of the successes of industrial economies was to overcome these basic situations of scarcity. So, while some families in the United States might still today not have enough food, the problem of getting them food isn't a matter of worrying about what others are eating. We do not need to take food away from some to give to others. Other things we consume, however, are positional—that is, the quality of *my* good is related to the quality of *your* good. An obvious example, given our earlier discussion, is a good school. In theory, a society can provide "good schools" for every child, but what it cannot do is provide "better schools" for every child because "better" depends on one's position compared to others. So one person standing at an event gets a better view, a positional good, but if everyone stands, no one is actually better off. Thus, if everyone seeks a better school for their children, no one will actually get ahead.

---

7. See United States Census Bureau, "Income and Poverty in the United States: 2017," https://www.census.gov/data/tables/2018/demo/income-poverty/p60-263.html.

8. Putnam, *Our Kids*, 70.

In wealthy economies, this problem of positionality gets larger and larger over time, as people gain more and more resources that they don't have to spend on the basics. Thus, societies get richer—but also more competitive. Sometimes, especially among the very wealthy, this competition is kind of harmless or even silly—for example, over "genuine" works of art or brands of private jets. But let's be clear: in our society, plenty of people we call "upper-middle-class" spend plenty of time and money on seeking positional goods. After all, not everyone can have the "latest" phone.

Sometimes all this is derided simply in terms of "status" driven by "envy." But economist Robert Frank, who has done much work on this, notes that this isn't necessarily the psychology of positionality. Rather, it is a matter of the relative nature of quality judgments themselves. He notes a "special" anniversary dinner is necessarily positional, dependent on being distinguished from everyday dining. The judgment of a car or house as "small" is generally framed by what you experience others having—not because of envy but because "small" is an inherently relative term.[9]

Recognizing this is especially important because inequality is not typically a matter of well-intentioned parents wanting to use their kids as status symbols. It's a matter of getting their kids a "better" view. Richard Reeves documents the extensive "opportunity hoarding" that educated parents often do for their children—they look for scholarships, connections for internships at work, etc.[10] They aren't intentionally competing with other kids, but, in effect, they are trying to get as much as they can for their own kid. Some of this is also a matter of what Putnam describes as "air bags" that kids from wealthier families have—that is, a "crash" that happens in adolescence can be worked through, whereas these "crashes" for poor kids often cause them to fall off the rails and descend into cycles of problematic behavior.[11] Again, the fact that parents want to have "air bags" for their kids is not a matter of status envy. But it is relative. That some kids "bounce back" from challenges while others don't may be a nice line for a college essay—except a child "bouncing back" may have much more to do with positional advantages that cushioned the setback, advantages that others, fighting the same challenge, lack.

Once we recognize all of this, it's easy to become discouraged. Or even angry. Are people supposed to leave their kids in bad schools? (Even though one way a bad school improves is by parents who are committed to and have the time for

---

9. For a further overview, see Frank's *Falling Behind* (Berkeley: University of California Press, 2005).

10. Richard Reeves, *Dream Hoarders* (Washington, DC: Brookings, 2017).

11. Putnam, *Our Kids*, 198, 210.

educating their children stay put!) Before diving into particular issues, let's look more carefully at why all of this is problematic from a Catholic point of view.

Competition versus Solidarity

St. John Paul II insisted that "far from being closed in on itself, the family is by nature and vocation open to other families and to society" (*Familiaris Consortio* 42). He notes that the family's service to society is one of the family's "four missions"; besides being united within the family and raising children, the pope says that families "cannot stop short at procreation and education" (FC 44). Instead, they have to do more, contributing to a "worldwide solidarity" through "an inner energy that generates, spreads, and develops justice, reconciliation, fraternity, and peace" (FC 48). The internal relationships of the family are the "school for social virtue" because the "heartfelt acceptance, encounter and dialogue, disinterested availability, generous service, and deep solidarity" (FC 43) that happens within the family are meant to be shared with all those outside. As Pope Francis has reiterated, "Families should not see themselves as a refuge from society, but instead go forth from their homes in a spirit of solidarity with others" (*Amoris Laetitia* 181).

John Paul and Francis could well be describing Putnam's Ohio. To be thinking in terms of family solidarity is a matter of thinking not only of one's own kids but about others as well. But what is solidarity? In one place, John Paul describes it as the idea that "we are all really responsible for all" (*Sollicitudo Rei Socialis* 38). That can seem pretty overwhelming, but sometimes the easiest way of defining a term is to look for its opposite. The *opposite* of solidarity is *competition*. It is not "friendly competition" but rather a sense that I have to get some good before someone else does. It is a view of the world in terms of a zero-sum contest, where my victory is really a matter of someone else's defeat or, at least, falling behind.

Thus, to really address the issue of family inequality, we have to figure out why we fall into relations of positional competition so easily. Theologically, the answer is because we don't follow the basic Catholic teaching on "the universal destination of goods." The Catholic *Catechism* explains that, in the beginning, God destined "the goods of creation . . . for the entire human race." The ownership of property by individuals and families is meant as a means to achieve this end. People often take better care of things if they own them securely. But the use of this property should be governed by a very clear criterion: they are meant to help "each of them to meet his basic needs and the needs of those in his charge." Beyond this, their use "should allow for a natural solidarity to develop" between them (*Catechism of the Catholic Church* 2402). Thus, there is a two-part challenge: first, being clear on what "basic needs" are and then, second, using the rest not for enhancing competition between people but for building solidarity.

The phenomenon of positionality is a perilous temptation to disregard both of these. As we noted, positionality comes into play when goods and services are sought beyond a satisfaction of basic needs. Then, it inherently involves seeking advantages over others. If you stand up in front of someone at a baseball game, it certainly won't build "natural solidarity" with the people behind you. Families committed to the formation in solidarity that John Paul describes will figure out ways to either not stand up or help others also see better.

Practicing Solidarity

There are two aspects to acting on this challenge. One is what John Paul calls "political intervention," which is part of Vatican II's "appeal to go beyond an individualistic ethic" (FC 44). There are ways in which positional problems necessarily involve collective action to work for the good of the whole. Similar to the need to change the entire seating arrangement of a venue to make sure everyone has a decent view, there is a need to address the relationship between school funding and property taxes. In the Maryland suburbs of Washington, DC, for example, the schools in Montgomery County are considerably better than those in neighboring Prince George's County, and (unsurprisingly) the same 1960s ranch houses often go for hundreds of thousands of dollars more in Montgomery, even when they are located only a couple of miles apart. People are prevented from moving into these areas because of the high cost, but also, as Reeves notes, "exclusionary zoning" keeps the supply of houses limited.[12] Most places are now governed by zoning laws that direct a great deal of housing development. Of course, such laws are exactly a part of "arranging the seating." If we just let everyone build whatever they wanted, all sorts of problems could happen. Reeves, however, focuses especially on the extent to which many zoning laws limit the density of development and the size of units. They mandate fewer houses, spaced farther apart, and often specify minimum sizes. In effect, such laws make it much harder for smaller, more affordable housing options to be built in communities that might otherwise be very desirable for poorer families seeking good schools. While people do not want development that puts a neighbor's wall right up against their side window, many agree that these laws are also an effect of people simply wanting to keep their property values rising. Supply and demand in a positional situation means that even older, smaller houses in desirable communities start becoming more valuable, and, if one could suddenly develop similar houses anew, it would increase supply and moderate pricing. Even more important, Reeves points out

---

12. Reeves, *Dream Hoarders*, 102–6.

that one of the largest tax breaks in the American tax system is the one allowing deduction of mortgage interest. In effect, families who have the incomes and job stability to afford a large mortgage get an enormous subsidy, pushing prices up even further. Thus, they further secure their access to better schools and prevent others from doing so. Because changing the connections between school and housing requires political actions, Catholic families cannot do it alone. The call to solidarity means, however, that these families can certainly support such efforts and can at least avoid opposing efforts that they might perceive as "hurting" them.

Moreover, this divide in housing is compounded by racism. It's not a coincidence that in my example, Montgomery is majority white, while Prince George's is majority African American. While Putnam emphasizes that social class—measured by income and education—has become more and more determinative of social equality of opportunity, racism not only contributed to the privileging of whites in the housing market but also continues to preserve this privilege today.[13] For example, the well-documented phenomenon of "redlining"—a practice from the 1930s through the 1970s restricting mortgage loans in certain neighborhoods deemed "riskier"—was driven by race, systemically denying African Americans access to homeownership, the primary means of wealth accumulation for middle-class whites. Thus, in addition to "arranging the seating" as a way to maintain class separation, the laws and zoning restrictions also perpetuate racial divides. A solidarity that does not account for these intersecting effects of race and class will struggle to overcome inequality.[14]

While larger structural changes are needed and even called for in Catholic social teaching,[15] my focus here is on actions Catholic families can take to overcome positionality through solidarity. John Paul notes two key choices they can make. One, he emphasizes that families should engage in "social service," especially for "all people and situations that cannot be reached by the public authorities' welfare organization" (FC 44). A lot of what Putnam describes in his 1950s childhood involved *informal* sharing of opportunities. It can mean a lot to a poorer family if someone with better connections can help find an internship for their child. It can mean a lot if, in an "air bag" situation, someone can quietly step up and help out. A professor friend of mine who comes from a relatively poor town in the rural Midwest has noted how much it would help some families if they just

13. Kate Ward and Kenneth Himes, " 'Growing Apart': The Rise of Inequality," *Theological Studies* 75, no. 1 (2014): 128.

14. Baodong Liu, Yehua Dinnis Wei, Christopher Simon, "Social Capital, Race, and Income Inequality in the United States," *Sustainability* 9, no. 2 (2017); doi: 10.3390/su9020248.

15. For example, see John Paul II, *Familiaris Consortio*, part 3.

had someone to turn to who "knows the ropes" of the college admission process—for example, someone who could find genuinely good college opportunities that wouldn't force a student to take on excessive debt. Often, their high school counselors are overworked or just not that knowledgeable. What is needed is neighbors in solidarity with neighbors.

And importantly, the neighbors need to be there: another important way to address these problems is to be intentional about living somewhere where these connections might happen. Socioeconomic geographic division has become much worse in the United States over the past few decades, as people seek (or are forced) to live in local places where the neighbors are all basically "just like them." This harms the possibilities not only of the informal opportunity sharing described above but also of the other important task of the family John Paul names "hospitality in all its forms" (FC 44). The fact is doing a favor for a friend's child is more likely to happen if your families get together and socialize in each other's backyards on a regular basis. Sociologists like Putnam call these "weak ties"—"casual acquaintances in disparate social niches"[16]—with whom one has enough of a personal connection to give and receive help when needed. For example, one happens to know a lawyer down the block when something sketchy happens at work endangering your job or a college friend who is a psychologist offering a referral for your kid's needs.

Pope Francis has expressed this concern for this sense of hospitality and help in terms of "the larger family"—by which he means the extended family but also friends, groups of families, and close-knit communities. I'm sure I'm not the only one who grew up calling some folks "uncle" and "aunt" who were in fact not blood relatives. Francis states:

> This larger family should provide love and support to teenage mothers, children without parents, single mothers left to raise children, persons with disabilities needing particular affection and closeness, young people struggling with addiction, the unmarried, separated, or widowed who are alone, and the elderly and infirm who lack the support of their children. (*Amoris Laetitia* 197)

In sum, he calls the family to reach out and include not only those "who have made shipwreck of their lives" but also any who are abandoned or disadvantaged by society. Right now, those in the most challenging circumstances are precisely the ones who lack not only the strong core family relations but anyone who might

---

16. Putnam, *Our Kids*, 198.

be present and fill this role of "the larger family." That means those falling behind just fall further behind.

There's a third element that needs to be added here, one that draws on the "basic needs" part of the principle above. A big part of how children learn positionality is that their parents mistake "wanting the best" for their kids with "wanting the stuff that other kids have." In the college admissions scandal, one celebrity's daughter was clear that what she wanted from her elite college admission had nothing to do with high-quality education. She wanted the social scene and the posh amenities. Put in old-school terms, she was "spoiled." Spoiled children both intentionally and unintentionally make the world more competitive for everyone—unless we name them clearly as "spoiled." While Francis does not use the language of spoiled, he does insist on the importance of helping children develop good habits through "the strengthening of the will and the repetition of specific actions," such as being "trained . . . to say 'Please,' 'Thank you,' and 'Sorry'" (AL 266). Children also need "correction" (though without "discouragement") so as to recognize that "misbehavior has consequences" (AL 268).

Conclusion

While this essay has focused especially on the question of how inequality is related to raising children, many of its lessons also applied to the life of married couples more generally. All couples have an ongoing responsibility of solidarity, and a key element of that is managing positional considerations. Retired couples, for example, can consider how "aging in place" allows them to remain connected to networks of families who might have crucial needs. It's also the case that the social capital built up over time can be lost if one moves. But, in another scenario, moving might be a good choice: if it allows for providing child care to grandchildren, taking positional pressures off their own children. In these cases, what's crucial to notice is that a lifestyle choice—where to live—isn't made with an eye toward personal comfort or private amenities but rather with the perspective of using one's resources to enhance solidarity.

Younger couples also have considerations. One good that has become extraordinarily positional in our society is the wedding. Many couples either delay marriage or force themselves or family members into considerable expense by thinking that they need the "perfect" wedding—with unfortunately all too many voices in the society telling them what is "necessary" for it to be "perfect." The average wedding today costs more than $25,000. Certainly, it's appropriate to want a great celebration for one's marriage. If the spending is driven by positional considerations, however, the ceremony can not only actually take away from one's own delight but distract from the real meaning of what is going on. The celebration, and so the cost, should be driven by solidarity, by the gathering of one's community and the celebration of the marriage liturgy before God.

One of the key lessons of this essay should be that thinking about the problem of "our kids"—of the rising inequality between families in our societies—takes foresight and long-term thinking. Many of the choices discussed here aren't a matter of immediate consumer purchases or spur-of-the-moment toy donations. They involve longer-term life choices that, if made in the right way, orient one's family life toward solidarity and away from positional competition. That is, they involve the virtue of prudence. While the difference between the Catholic vision of families in solidarity and a vision of families in competition with one another is stark, people rarely face simply either/or choices on these matters. This can be a comfort. Raising kids in solidarity need not mean resettling in the most dangerous neighborhood, nor does it mean depriving them of basic needs or even wonderful experiences, like some travel or an excellent college. But it does mean that, when we make these choices for ourselves and our children, our considerations of what is "best" are not going to mirror the choices of the society around us. The factors we weigh in determining "better" will be different. If we all made somewhat different choices about what is best for our kids, we'd come to see the truth that both Putnam and the church emphasize: all kids are "our kids."

Chapter 23

Reading the Screens of Our Times

Attention and Resistance

Marcus Mescher

The intimate bonds of marriage and family life are increasingly being shaped by digital technology and personal devices. The average American spends at least eleven hours a day with a screen of some kind (computer, tablet, phone, or television), used to help with work, school, and family responsibilities as well as endless possibilities for information, entertainment, and connecting with others. These digital tools—encapsulated by the word "screen" in this essay—are not inherently good or bad, as their moral value is measured by their intended use, circumstances, and outcome. Neither are screens neutral, however, since they are situated in a specific social context that can influence the agency of users. This essay explores how screens are shaping marriage and family life and how a more virtuous use of screens can promote respect, responsibility, and the common good.

Screens and Belonging

Screens are often a double-edged sword. Screens help educate and empower us. They provide access to an immense array of content and connections, offer countless conveniences, help us to work more efficiently, communicate across great distances and differences, and join networks for support and collaboration. Screens also bring temptations for distraction, procrastination, and wasting time by spending an inordinate time shopping, playing video games, or scrolling through social media. Screens can reinforce social divisions, since social media algorithms are designed to confirm users' worldviews by presenting them with content and connections they are inclined to "like" and "share," reducing the likelihood that they will be exposed to views and voices that differ from their own. Although screens make it easier to work remotely, this can mean that job responsibilities seep into time at home. Screens keep us in contact with loved ones who are far away, whether they are traveling for work or school or deployed overseas. Screens can be a portal to other relationships and communities that provide greater attention, understanding, and encouragement. This is especially true for those with disabilities, who identify as LGBTQ, or who experience social isolation at home, school, or work and can often find a haven of support in online networks.

This last aspect is key. In our current social context, belonging includes connecting through a screen. Those who have the ability to participate in life with a screen enjoy access to more diverse content and greater freedom to engage others and express oneself to others than previous generations could have imagined. This also means that those who do not have reliable internet access—more often people of color, those with disabilities, the elderly, and sizable percentages of those living in the Global South—feel unseen and unheard. This digital divide often compounds other unjust inequalities arising from the unequal privilege and power produced by the interrelation of sex, gender, and sexual orientation, race and ethnicity, age and ability, class and creed, and nationality.[1] Individuals and families are disadvantaged if they are not able to contribute to and benefit from the same opportunities to connect with each other; learn, create, or complete tasks for work or school; or share in other social, cultural, or political activities. Those without screens are less likely to believe that they belong and matter to a world increasingly mediated by digital technology and social media.

Screens and Identity

Given the rising rates of digital interactions, people's identity is increasingly shaped by screens. Primarily through social media, people cultivate a "digital presence." They can change—to whatever degree desired—their identity. Some choose to distort their identity slightly, in the hope of seeming more attractive, accomplished, entertaining, intelligent, or popular. This can be liberating for those who would otherwise be judged by or discriminated against because of their physical appearance. Some use a digital avatar to benignly escape, experience fantasy, or pretend to be someone else. Others use screens as a cloak of anonymity, becoming more disinhibited for aggressive or deceptive behavior, feeling immune from the consequences of their digital interactions.

1. See Kimberlé Crenshaw, "The Urgency of Intersectionality," *TED Talk*, October 2016, https://www.ted.com/talks/kimberle_crenshaw_the_urgency_of_intersectionality?language=en.

In the mainstream, sharing pictures, experiences, and news articles all contribute to the work of curating a particular self-image. Psychologist Sherry Turkle describes the current trend through the credo, "I share, therefore I am," resulting in a more delicate sense of identity that demands constant validation from others.[2] Turkle warns of growing narcissism among social media users, who become less patient with the complex dimensions and needs of other people. If a user finds someone too dull or demanding, they can simply swipe or click on until they find someone more interesting or pleasing. Turkle laments that the endless options for content or connections threatens to turn users into "modern Goldilockses," who expect everything tailored to their preferences on-demand.[3]

Relatedly, anything that a person shares online can be judged, taken out of context, and sent to others without their knowledge or consent. This "public-by-default framework" can operate "as a mechanism of control," exacerbating insecurity among users or forcing them to filter out any unflattering digital interactions.[4] As a result, it is common for users to spend countless hours managing their profiles to "clean up" their digital presence.[5] The tension between what is public and what is private is a dynamic test of vulnerability and trust and sometimes the occasion for hard lessons about what to share and what not to share. It would be inaccurate to presume that files are consistently shared with consent when in fact many people are coerced, duped, or hacked. For example, when images from "sexting" (sending nude or seminude images) or "revenge porn" are spread, this can result in stigma, shame, severe emotional distress, and sometimes even suicide.[6]

Just as text messages, e-mails, and photos can be saved via screen-shot and shared with others, so also can social media posts and interactions. Personal views and information can be disseminated quickly and broadly, and something that might have been temporary, tentative, and private can be recorded and distributed as permanent and public. For some, this means becoming much more selective and guarded about what they share, fearing being exposed or exploited. Alternatively, others share everything indiscriminately, and digital interactions get flooded by banality. One illustration of this trend is Snapchat—a photo- and video-sharing

2. Sherry Turkle, *Alone Together: Why We Expect More from Technology and Less from Each Other* (New York: Basic Books, 2011), 302.

3. Ibid., 15.

4. danah boyd, *It's Complicated: The Social Lives of Networked Teens* (New Haven, CT: Yale University Press, 2014), 62, 74.

5. See Donna Freitas, *The Happiness Effect: How Social Media Is Driving a Generation to Appear Perfect at Any Cost* (Oxford: Oxford University Press, 2017), 48.

6. See Cyber Civil Rights Initiative at http://www.cybercivilrights.org/.

app popular among those thirty-five and younger—which boasts 300 million users (188 million per day), who create 3 billion images and view 10 billion videos each day. Insofar as the average Snapchat user has exchanged anywhere between 10,000 and 400,000 photos with friends, it can easily devolve into a tool of nearly endless distraction.

While some observers might point to apps like Snapchat as harmless and meaningless levity, such a perspective misses the "impact imprint" of these digital habits.[7] Brains can become used to—and actually crave—connection and interruption, making it difficult to concentrate on subjects and other people. More time spent with screens interferes with sleep, memory, attention spans, creativity, productivity, problem solving, and decision-making skills; the human brain is changing as a result of life spent increasingly with a screen.[8] In recent years, screen time has doubled for children under age two, and, while screens may help parents entertain or educate their children, they may not consider how so much time spent on YouTube or playing video games can make it more difficult for developing brains to cultivate deep and sustained thought, critical analysis, and creative problem solving. Even while screens offer convenience and efficiency, they can be the source of a love-hate relationship, since being tethered to a device produces pressure to be "constantly on," striving to enhance one's social acceptance and status. A growing number of users endure the effects of "technostress"[9] and feel trapped in a "cycle of responsiveness."[10] Although there are apps that can help us limit our time with a screen, the fact that we rely on technology to limit our use of technology might serve as yet another example of becoming ever more dependent on screens.

Given all the time and effort dedicated to cultivating an ideal digital profile, it becomes nearly impossible not to compare oneself to others' success, happiness, and popularity. The age-old "compare and despair" mind-set is hard to avoid on social media for both parents and children. Parents may feel pressured to appear successful at work and in raising their children while tempted to compare themselves to what other parents share. Young people—whose identity is more fluid—

7. For "Impact imprint," see Nancy K. Baym, *Personal Connections in the Digital Age* (Malden, MA: Polity Press, 2010), 26.

8. Nicholas Carr, *The Shallows: What the Internet Is Doing to Our Brains* (New York: W. W. Norton, 2011).

9. For "Technostress," see John Palfrey and Urs Gasser, *Born Digital: Understanding the First Generation of Digital Natives* (New York: Basic Books, 2008), 190.

10. Leslie A. Perlow, *Sleeping with Your Smartphone* (Cambridge, MA: Harvard Business Review Press, 2012), 7.

are also shaped by their peers' idealized social media posts that may contribute to making them feel like they cannot measure up, do not belong, or cannot admit they are struggling at school, at home, or in their mental or emotional state.[11] Researchers have found that the more time spent on social media, the higher the rates of feeling insecure, isolated, and lonely, a causal link to decreased mental and emotional well-being.[12] Mental health experts warn of a "sudden, cataclysmic shift downward in life satisfaction" as "only the tip of the iceberg" when it comes to the emerging mental health crisis that is linked to screens.[13] Overall, more teens report feeling left out, fragile, and afraid to fail, with girls experiencing these and other marginalizing effects (including cyberbullying) even more than boys. Teens' "depressive symptoms have skyrocketed" since 2011, a tidal wave of feeling inadequate, anxious, and alone.[14] Still, parents and children struggle to put their screens away. Screens have a drug-like effect on the brain, which is concerning for those under age twenty-five, whose brains are not yet finished developing.[15] Even as screens can pose a threat to healthy self-image and self-esteem, it is becoming more and more daunting to imagine life without being constantly connected.

Screens and Relationships

Screens impact not only our identity and sense of belonging but also our relationships. Nearly 30 percent of Americans report feeling lonely, an upward trend in recent years. Among older adults, this rate reaches over 40 percent, almost three times higher than was the case in the 1970s. This is even widespread among young people, who seem like "virtual hermits," glued to their screens, still experiencing isolation. Screens have created a "culture of elsewhere," directing our attention to other people and places, giving rise to loneliness, the "painful feelings of not belonging and disconnectedness from and abandonment by others."[16] Feeling

---

11. For example, see Kate Fagan, *What Made Maddy Run: The Secret Struggles and Tragic Death of an All-American Teen* (New York: Hachette Book, 2017).

12. Michelle W. Berger, "Social Media Use Increases Depression and Loneliness," *Penn Today*, November 9, 2018, https://penntoday.upenn.edu/news/social-media-use-increases-depression -and-loneliness.

13. Jean M. Twenge, *iGen: Why Today's Super-Connected Kids Are Growing Up Less Rebellious, More Tolerant, Less Happy—and Completely Unprepared for Adulthood* (New York: Atria, 2017), 96.

14. Ibid., 99–101.

15. Nicholas Kardaras, *Glow Kids: How Screen Addiction Is Hijacking Our Kids—And How to Break the Trance* (New York: St. Martin's Press, 2016).

16. Gerald Arbuckle, *Loneliness: Insights for Healing in a Fragmented World* (Maryknoll, NY: Orbis Books, 2018), xi–xiv.

lonely is desolation; it's related to feeling unworthy, unimportant, and unloved. It contributes to illness and early death. Loneliness can creep into marriages and despoil relationships between parents and children and between siblings.

While couples can use screens to share files and articles, use apps to coordinate schedules and plans, or stay in contact across distance, screens can also be a portal of content and connections that can make it harder to be physically, mentally, and emotionally present to their partner or spouse. Therapists warn that screens make it easier to connect with old flames, explore new relationships with others who share similar interests, or spend time doing other things—reading, shopping, gaming, watching sports and other entertainment programs, among other possibilities—instead of connecting with their spouse. In fact, some researchers point to screens in the bedroom as the culprit for the current "sex recession" that includes single as well as married adults.[17] In addition to screens serving as a gateway to more opportunities for distraction (social media and even Fortnite are increasingly blamed in divorce proceedings), they also can facilitate emotional infidelity and even financial infidelity (as spouses hide expenses or losses that result from addictions to shopping, gaming, and gambling, all exacerbated by screens). Perhaps the most distressing impact of screens on couples is pornography, as viewers become desensitized to the objectification of bodies and the physical and verbal abuse that fill the vast majority of pornographic film scenes.[18] Pornography is cited as a leading reason for divorce, both as an addiction and also because it can set unrealistic expectations, diminish sexual drive, and can lead to one or both partners feeling like their love life is inadequate. Pornography is now viewed more on tablets and phones than any other device, saved to a quarter of all smartphones. Pornographic websites like Pornhub attract about 30 billion visits per year (100 million visits per day, roughly a thousand visits per second, with more than 40 percent of traffic coming from the United States). Given its prevalence among adults and even many children (the average age of first exposure is eleven years old), porn is not just a public health crisis but one directly linked to the intimate ties of marriage and family life.

While screens can help with parenting, they can also become an obstacle to healthy relationships between parents and their children. Parents and kids are equally susceptible to being distracted by their screens, making it more difficult to be intentional about carving out opportunities for meaningful interactions off-

17. Belinda Luscombe, "Why Are We All Having So Little Sex?," *Time*, October 26, 2018, http://time.com/5297145/is-sex-dead/.

18. In *Pornland: How Porn Has Hijacked Our Sexuality* (Boston: Beacon Press, 2010), xviii–xxii, Gail Dines reports that popular internet porn has an average of twelve aggressive acts per scene.

line. Screens can also be a battleground for difficult decisions and power struggles between parents and children: while young people see screens as vital for information and entertainment, connecting with friends, and marking their digital presence, parents have to navigate how much or how little access is appropriate for their child's well-being. Screens can be useful to keep track of children as they experiment with increasing independence; apps like "Find My Phone" and parental control programs like "Net Nanny" provide the ability for constant surveillance while raising questions about whether this encourages or undermines trust between parents and children. Screens—especially when spent with social media—can turn children's focus more to the views and actions of their peers, eclipsing the strong attachments between parents and children where unconditional love and acceptance are first experienced and sustained over time. Physician and psychologist Leonard Sax points to screens and social media as dominated by the conditional and contingent nature of peer relationships, which can exacerbate a young person's sense that their value or belongingness is also conditional or contingent. Sax points to this trend as a root cause of the growing rates of loneliness, anxiety, and fragility among young people today. He asserts that it is the job of parents to supplant screens, peer relationships, academics, and other activities to reclaim as central to the parent-child relationship.[19]

Screens can also take a toll on relationships between siblings. The same issues with distraction can make it harder for siblings to connect, converse, and play together. Screens can be a way for younger siblings to be exposed to content more appropriate for older siblings. The way to solve this problem is to give each child their own screen, which can ensure that everyone is able to engage the content or connections of their own choosing. When each child is glued to their own screen, however—while in transit, in a restaurant, store, or at home—this is a lost opportunity to engage the same material together, and it becomes something less than a shared experience. It might be nice to avoid a fight over what to listen to in the car or watch on the weekend, but, when everything is catered to individual preference, there is less communication across differences, fewer opportunities to compromise, negotiate, and practice conflict resolution. Siblings—just like spouses and parents—can get lost in their own digital worlds and miss out on the conversations and experiences that form family members in identity and belonging. This tendency to cater everything to personal taste, or fill every lull with a screen, not only confirms Turkle's warning about "modern Goldilockses" but becomes a threat to prosocial dispositions and commitments.

19. Leonard Sax, *The Collapse of Parenting: How We Hurt Our Kids When We Treat Them Like Grown-Ups* (New York: Basic Books, 2016), 105–13.

Screens and Social Bonds

Finally, screens impact our social bonds. For every way they connect us, screens also have the potential to divide us. Screens make it possible to connect with more information, perspectives, experiences, and possibilities than ever before. This can reduce isolation in those who feel like they do not quite fit in their physical surroundings. It can lead to promising developments for those looking to find a romantic partner: today, nearly 1 in 5 brides report finding their spouse online or through a dating app. Associations mediated through a screen can also strengthen the social fabric and produce democratic goods like social trust and courage, as well as civic participation and efficacy. We can connect with others wherever we are and wherever they are, bringing new meaning to William Wordsworth's phrase from 1807: "The world is too much with us."

Screens can also foster division, however. In the face of rising social segregation based on race and class, families already experience greater social separation from people who look, think, and live differently from them.[20] These social divisions are reinforced by social media algorithms designed to expose users to content they will be inclined to engage, creating echo chambers of the same ideas and perspectives that bolster our beliefs and worldview. Even though countless connections are constantly being mediated by screens, they do not always take place across real differences where everyone is included and empowered to participate together. In the case of fake news and social media accounts that intend to deceive people, screens can also become instruments to distort truth, erode trust, generate cynicism, and foment despair.

Screens can make it possible to demonstrate Christian neighbor love to people across great physical distances. Insofar as screens can help us become more attentive and responsive to others unencumbered by physical or geographic barriers, screens provide new possibilities for solidarity across differences. While they may not be corporeal connections, screens are still a means of social connection. The danger arises when screens replace—rather than complement—meaningful connections. The lack of facial cues and tone in text and e-mail can impoverish interactions, making it hard to understand the full picture of what the other person is trying to share. Without more practice reading body language and imagining what the other person intends to communicate, people lose important opportunities to develop their emotional and social intelligence. In a time when empathy rates are down 40 percent among young people, screens can actually be part of

---

20. See Robert Putnam, *Our Kids: The American Dream in Crisis* (New York: Simon & Schuster, 2015), 39, 41.

the problem in making it harder to authentically understand and meaningfully relate to others.[21]

Screens can play a vital role in civic society, with immense potential to advance love, justice, and solidarity for a more inclusive common good. Screens have proven to be powerful tools to enhance democracy, capable of changing the landscape of social and political imaginations. Facebook, Twitter, and YouTube can and often do raise the social and ecological consciousness of their users. Hashtags collect posts from all over the world, uniting people by shared cause. #BlackLivesMatter and #MeToo help document the ongoing prevalence of racial and gender-based violence. Even more than raise awareness, these trends have resulted in actual policy and legal changes.[22] The #IceBucketChallenge raised more than $115 million for ALS research, resulting in a medical breakthrough. Hashtags can galvanize support for a range of causes, from mental health to human rights, from environmental protection to interfaith solidarity.

Still, activism on social media is often reduced to what is currently trending and rarely lasts past the daily news cycle. Laudable as it is to become more informed, awareness does not automatically generate commitment to creating change. For these reasons, this "hashtag activism," or "clicktivism," is more aptly described as "slacktivism," a simplistic and superficial level of engagement compared to what is required by social or environmental "activism."[23] Because it caters to a person's interests and does not really require them to change their behavior or social location, this temptation to click "like" or "favorite" or "share" falls well short of the individual's and family's responsibility to the common good. In some cases, "slacktivism" hurts more than it helps, since it convinces people they have fulfilled their social duty by adding a filter to their profile picture or sharing an article or petition, without taking more time to listen to and learn from the poor and marginalized and working with them for systemic change.

While screens can be portals to connect, they can also become buffers to passively observe, unnoticed by others, without any demands being placed on the

21. Jamil Zaki, "What, Me Care? Young Are Less Empathetic," *Scientific American*, January 1, 2011, https://www.scientificamerican.com/article/what-me-care/.

22. Brittany Packnett, "Black Lives Matter Isn't Just a Hashtag Anymore," *Politico*, September/October 2016, https://www.politico.com/magazine/story/2016/09/black-lives-matter-movement-deray-hacknett-politics-protest-214226; Rebecca Beitsch, "#MeToo Has Changed Our Culture: Now It's Changing Our Laws," *Pew*, July 31, 2018, https://www.pewtrusts.org/en/research-and-analysis/blogs/stateline/2018/07/31/metoo-has-changed-our-culture-now-its-changing-our-laws.

23. Shaunacy Ferro, "Just Liking a Cause Doesn't Help: Internet Slacktivism Harms Charities," *Popular Science*, November 8, 2013, http://www.popsci.com/article/science/just-liking-cause-doesnt-help-internet-slacktivism-harms-charities.

viewers. Screens can tempt users to fall into a "spectator culture" that produces more bystanders than active participants. "Spectator culture" relies on endless entertainment, streaming videos, and social media algorithms that will keep users scrolling for hours. In this way, screens can appease and disempower; users can choose to engage only what entertains and/or confirms their worldview without confronting other content or connections that might challenge them. This allows people to ignore other parts of reality or even hide from it.

For all these reasons, we should carefully evaluate to what extent our digital tools make us complicit in digital "structures of vice."[24] The potential of these digital tools and structures to deform our moral identity and agency points to the need for a more virtuous approach to screens in everyday life. This is especially true for marriages and families that might be tempted to turn inward, given the unpredictable and sometimes daunting state of the world. The Catholic vision of marriage and family, however, always involves a public commitment involving social and ecological duties. This corrects against the trend that Edward Banfield described sixty years ago: "amoral familism" that maximizes the self-interest of one's own family and assumes that other families are doing the same.[25] Families need to be on guard for the way that screens might numb us to distant suffering and our duty to serve the common good. As Americans become less aware of the needs of others, their obligations to others, and their abilities to help others, screens can play a key role in restoring right relationships between the individual, family, and society.

A Virtuous Approach to Screens

Screens are not sinful, but an immoderate attachment to using them endangers the ability to be attentive and responsive to one's spouse, children, and other family members. Three virtues—temperance, prudence, and fidelity—are crucial for preventing screens from deforming moral identity, agency, and relationships within and beyond family life. The virtue of temperance aids in defining a limit. It moderates the drive for more and seeks fulfillment in what is sufficient. Temperance and fidelity remind us of our proper relation to God and others, which can be useful for keeping screens from becoming an inordinate attachment. The virtue of prudence serves to integrate practical wisdom so that knowing the good becomes striving to do good. Prudence helps individuals to reflect on human experience, distinguish good from evil, and form their conscience to discern the most fitting

---

24. Daniel J. Daly, "Structures of Virtue and Vice," *New Blackfriars* 92, no. 1039 (2011): 341–57.

25. Edward C. Banfield, *The Moral Basis of a Backward Society* (Glencoe: The Free Press, 1958), 85.

way to love God, self, and others. The virtue of fidelity aims to help people to be properly attached to people and things in the right way, for the right reasons, and to the right ends or goals. Taken together, these virtues serve as dispositions and habits to become more mindful of how, when, and why we use screens.

This more intentional approach to screens can be helpful for creating a healthy distance between one's identity and one's digital profile, especially so that a failure to garner "likes" or "shares" for a particular post should not lead a person to question their value. Strong, secure attachments offline can provide more stability and support than the fickle nature of what catches fire or is ignored online. Digital fasts—scheduled time free from screens—can be helpful to connect with a spouse or child or as a family offline. Family dinners, date nights, and bedrooms can and should be screen-free. Schools and churches as well as other local communities and organizations can make these digital fasts potent shared practices. Since people are formed by what they repeatedly do, these commitments are easier when they enjoy the agreement and accountability of others.

A virtuous use of screens can and should place love of God, self, and others at the forefront. Screens should be used to enhance intimacy, rapport, and love, which is more likely when their use leads to or flows from mutually respectful and responsible interactions offline. For screens to be virtuous tools to affirm human dignity, right relationships, and inclusive, vibrant, and equitable communities, their usage should be marked by appropriate vulnerability, integrity, and trust. Donna Freitas recommends several virtues for practicing a more life-giving approach to screens. They include the willingness to engage others honestly; authenticity to dispel myths of perfection; toleration to make room for difference and dissent; forgetting, in order to let memories fade; being present instead of dwelling on past highlights or hurts; play and silliness; digital fasts, time spent in solitude, untethered from technology; and even quitting some social media to be liberated and empowered to interact with others in more meaningful ways.[26]

When screens function as a bridge to connect people in mutual respect and responsibility, it makes it possible to create new spaces for shared knowledge and expands the boundaries of community. When used virtuously, screens can positively influence identity, family relationships, and social bonds. This means disrupting the temptation for mindless entertainment, endless distraction, and comfortable convenience that caters to personal tastes, contributing to a "spectator culture" that promotes passivity and indifference to injustice. Every person who uses a screen should consider their choices of what content and connections fill

26. Freitas, *The Happiness Effect*, 256–64.

their time, who benefits from these choices, and who suffers as a result of them.[27] They should reflect and discern whether and how their time with a screen helps or hinders a healthy sense of identity, the quality of their most intimate bonds, and their social and ecological duties.

Conclusion

How do we love well in a digital age? By being present to those who rely on us the most and applying temperance, prudence, and fidelity to our screen time. Each person can and should use screens as part of their commitment to love and justice. We will have to answer for how, when, and why we used screens as well as the impact this had on ourselves and others. Sometimes this means embracing the incredible possibilities afforded by digital technology and online networks. And other times this will mean heeding the advice of Pope Francis, who suggests that we put our screens away, since they cannot actually fulfill our deepest desires.[28] Only love—often in marriage and family life—can do that.

27. These questions come from a model of social analysis developed by Joe Holland and Peter Henriot in *Social Analysis: Linking Faith and Justice* (Maryknoll, NY: Orbis Books, 1980), 28.

28. Liz Dodd, "Don't Waste Time on 'Futile' Internet and Smartphones, Pope Tells Youth," *The Tablet*, August 6, 2014, https://www.thetablet.co.uk/news/1038/don-t-waste-time-on-futile -internet-and-smartphones-pope-tells-youth.

Chapter 24

A Spirituality for Parenting in a Hurried Age

Tim and Sue Muldoon

Love needs time and space; everything else is secondary. Time is needed to talk things over, to embrace leisurely, to share plans, to listen to one other and gaze in each other's eyes, to appreciate one another and to build a stronger relationship. Sometimes the frenetic pace of our society and the pressures of the workplace create problems. At other times, the problem is the lack of quality time together, sharing the same room without one even noticing the other.

—Pope Francis, *Amoris Laetitia* 224

The Christian vocation to family life regularly invites us to attend to imminent beauty. Whether it is the emotional excess of birth or adoption, the celebrations of birthdays, graduations, or weddings, the memories of shared family vacations or the simple reminiscences of ordinary school days, the experiences that constitute a parent's spiritual journey offer regular glimpses of the divine goodness for those who have eyes to see. Every person who has taken the emotional risk of parenting understands, on some level, that at its root parenthood is a willingness to allow one's own happiness to be inextricably linked with the life story of a young person. Our challenge and opportunity is to practice a spirituality of attentiveness to these experiences so that they might not be lost amid the torrents of practical matters. This essay invites readers to consider a focal point for a parenting spirituality: the practice of *kairos*, the biblical Greek word for "acceptable time," time set apart from the usual tick-tock of daily life.

Every Christian vocation calls forth a spirituality, understood as the constellation of practices that nurture and promote a faithful pilgrimage in imitation of Christ. A parenting spirituality is a shared pilgrimage, and as such it involves practices that nourish both the individual and the family. In this essay, we explore some contours of such a spirituality, mindful that over the past half century there has developed a theological and indeed ecclesial vocabulary with which to speak about it as a vocation. Our aim is to offer a parenting spirituality rooted in the church's sacramental tradition and to consider parenting as a spiritual lens through which we might discern "indistinctly, as in a mirror" (1 Cor 13:12) the hand of God in the reality of everyday life. Both of these aims seek to promote an understanding of the vocation to family life in the context of our hurried age and to suggest that, at its core, parenting spirituality is about a fundamental reorientation of time, a responding to the insistent invitations to practice *kairos*.

Time in the Family

In our experience, raising children is an invitation to an often profoundly meditative way of being-in-time. Whereas the workday proceeds with predictable regularity, punctuated by meetings, tasks, and to-do lists, family life exists in a different kind of time. Especially when our children were younger, it felt like we had to take off the workaday world's approach to time as if it were an overcoat and enter a new world with them. Children's sense of time differs from adults. Frederick Buechner puts it beautifully:

> For a child, time in the sense of something to measure and keep track of, time as the great circus parade of past, present, and future, cause and effect, has scarcely started yet and means little because for a child all time is by and large *now* time and apparently endless. What child, while summer is happening, bothers to think much that summer will end? What child, when snow is on the ground, stops to remember that not long ago the ground was snowless? It is by its content rather than its duration that a child knows time, by its quality rather than its quantity— happy times and sad times.[1]

On top of this difference in the perception of time are the trials that every parent we know has had to face, whether the illness of a child, or issues at school, or social problems, or any number of others. Parents lose sleep, make and change plans, negotiate and argue, spend hours on homework, take days off from work to be with their child, plan vacations around school schedules, and so much more. Family work can often be demanding, and sometimes it even pushes us to despair.

---

1. Frederick Buechner, *The Sacred Journey* (San Francisco: HarperOne, reprint 1991), 9–10.

In the midst of these challenges can be profound joy: celebrating our children's successes, enjoying holidays or other celebrations as fruits of much preparation and planning, taking time together to play games or engage in leisure activities, reflecting on warm memories and shared experiences. The texture of family life over the years varies, including times of sun and rain, consolation and desolation. It is, in a word, life itself, life that the Lord invites us to live to the full.

Those who enter fully into the vocation to family life will understand how the various relationships within the family constitute the focal points of their ministry. According to the church, the Christian family is "a sign and image of the communion of the Father and the Son in the Holy Spirit" and is called "the domestic church" (*Catechism of the Catholic Church* 2205 and 2204). The family vocation is also one that redounds to the benefit of society. As the *"original cell of social life"* and "an initiation into life in society" (*Catechism of the Catholic Church* 2207), it represents the way that humans practice what it means to live in community. Practicing *kairos*, we suggest, is a life-giving way to live mindfully within the context of the family vocation and can bear fruit for the broader communities of which families are constitutive parts.

What Is *Kairos*?

The word *kairos* is one of the biblical Greek words for "time" and is sometimes translated as "acceptable time." In Paul's second letter to the Corinthians, he describes what it is like to receive the salvation offered by Christ:

> "In an acceptable time [*kairos*] I heard you,
>   and on the day of salvation I helped you."
> Behold, now is a very acceptable time [*kairos*]; behold, now is the day of salvation. (2 Cor 6:2)

There is a certain urgency in what Paul is describing here: *now* is the day of salvation; *now* is when the Lord is helping you. Lest we fall into the trap of thinking that what God is doing is somewhere in the future, Paul suggests that we need do no more than pay attention to this acceptable time.

Paul's use of the word *kairos* here is different from our usual approach to time and, indeed, the approach to time that was common in the ancient world. For the ancients, time was an objective reality, and human beings were utterly subject to it. To use one example, the name given to the Greek titan Cronus—father to the Olympian gods Zeus, Hera, and others—may have come from *chronos*, the root of our word *chronology*, meaning measured time. According to the Roman orator

Cicero, Cronus was so named because he governed the "course and revolution of periods and times."[2] Time was, for Cicero and many others, the realm of the gods, and human beings were but players in a vast cosmic drama over which they had little control.

The ancient Israelite theology of time shared some similarity with that of the Greeks and Romans in that time was a constant in the order of creation and governed by the hand of God. But the distinctly Israelite practice of Sabbath called for a community response to a larger reality—that everything in the cosmos, including time itself, came from God and was ordered to God's purposes.

Today, we may retain some of that sensibility, especially during times of feast. Consider the Christian celebration of the Eucharist and its roots in the Jewish celebration of Passover. Every year, Jews celebrate the Passover at the Seder meal, during which participants recall and make present the story of Moses leading the Israelites out of Egypt. Similarly, Christians recall and make present the Last Supper between Jesus and his disciples, who themselves may have been celebrating a Seder meal. Such celebrations are interruptions in our normal experience of time; we make ourselves present to the past, as it were.

Celebrations such as these remind us that time is not only about getting things accomplished and marking days off a calendar; it is also about seeking the Lord's hand active in creation, if we but pause long enough to recall that he died in order to redeem it.

A New Approach to Time

The biblical writers describe time in ways that can inform the way we approach family life. Lest we get too caught up in daily chores, the texts remind us that the Lord has established time itself (Gen 1:14); he has ordered the nations and their time on the earth (Dan 2:21; Acts 17:26). The Lord's designs prevail (Prov 16:4; Isa 46:10) because he is not limited by time (Ps 90:4), nor does he grow tired (Isa 40:28). He will bring about the consummation of history when Jesus returns (Eph 1:9-10; 1 Tim 6:15). He is the Alpha and the Omega, the beginning and the end of all time (Rev 22:13).

Even though we experience time as passing (Ps 144:4; Jas 4:14), still our well-being is in the hands of the Lord (Ps 31:15). Now, according to Paul's traveling companion Luke, is a time "acceptable to the Lord" (4:19) because of Jesus coming to announce good news to the poor. The Lord has sanctified all time; nothing

---

2. Cicero, *De natura deorum* 2.25.

else is necessary—not the end of the school year, not the next vacation period, not the next free weekend. Now!

What emerges as an essential dimension in Jesus' preaching is a sense of expectant hope, that the time to change our lives and our approach to time is right in front of us. Time is not only about a steady march toward adulthood and old age. It is also about taking advantage of the limited opportunities we have to experience a foretaste of the heavenly banquet. It is about inviting the Lord to act in our daily lives, transforming them into opportunities to see the good, true, and beautiful amid the mundane.

Kairos is about opportunity, while often *chronos* is about measuring time. It is about stepping out of the usual chronology of our days—that is, whatever appears in our schedule books or calendar apps—and making room for spontaneity, discovery, and wonder with our families.

Anyone with small children or grandchildren certainly can remember experiences of "wasting time" with children and how wonderful such experiences can be. The imaginative worlds that young people inhabit can be hilarious, insightful, creative, surprising—the list goes on. You cannot rush a child's experience of the world any more than you can make a flower bloom by yanking it up from the ground. Family life ought to have a natural rhythm of *kairos*: an attentiveness to God's presence amid the noise and clutter.

God's time is, to use an allegory, what existed in the garden of Eden: a place of serene receptivity to the good things that God has made. Seeking *kairos* is about being willing to suspend ourselves from whatever the immediate objective of the moment is—getting ready for school, finishing a project, doing chores—and simply attending to the revelation of the moment.

Recently we had an experience of such a *kairos*. It was Memorial Day weekend, the gateway to summer. Our oldest was home from her first year of college, so we were mindful of how precious time is as her summers home are numbered. She had a last-minute change in her work schedule that allowed us to plan a day trip with the whole family, so we packed up the car and drove to a favorite destination. We enjoyed walking along a scenic route and then had dinner together—one of the increasingly rare opportunities that our busy teenagers' lives afford us.

We have found that such times away from the day-to-day plant themselves in our memories in important ways and help us to appreciate the richness of our family life. Days and weeks can go by with little to distinguish them from any other stretch, but *kairos* moments are memorable. As we grow older, we become mindful that we cannot take these opportunities for granted. To be sure, there are graces that come with every life stage. But with each passing year, we sometimes find ourselves saddened at the loss of the graces of earlier life stages. Living mindful of the acceptable time that is now is a call to practice gratitude for the gifts that are present always: the relationships that we nurture with our dynamic, growing children in whom God is always present.

Contemplation

Openness to *kairos*, and the practice of seeing God present in those we love, grows out of the practice of contemplation. The Carmelite William McNamara describes contemplation as "a long, loving look at the real."[3] That is an apt description of what parenthood summons from us: eyes to see not only what is most evident but also the deep meanings unfolding before us as our children navigate the mysteries that are their very selves. What is necessary for *kairos* time is not necessarily time off of work or vacations away from home. Rather, what is necessary is contemplation, which opens us to the possibility of finding *kairos* moments throughout the day. Now is an opportune time.

In several places throughout the Bible, the writers point to the ways that people often go through life without really understanding the meaning of what they experience. The prophet Isaiah describes God's lament for his people: "They do not know, do not understand; their eyes are too clouded to see, their minds, to perceive" (44:18). Matthew describes Jesus trying mightily to make people understand the kingdom of God in their midst, devoting several parables to the ways that people tend to miss what God is doing among them. Jesus says, "This is why I speak to them in parables, because 'they look but do not see and hear but do not listen or understand'" (13:13). Again and again, we see similar comments. People are blind to the reality of God right underneath their noses.

Consider the past twenty-four hours. No doubt you, like us, can point to things that got done, from mundane things like eating a meal or going shopping to more meaningful things like having a phone conversation with a family member. We have mental to-do lists—and sometimes written or digital ones—that tend to guide our daily choices. If you're like us, what you see on a daily basis are the "necessary" activities, the things you perceive as important for the daily functioning of your life. You see the world primarily through a lens we might call "utility"—that is, a lens that allows us first to see what is useful.

Now, consider the past twenty-four hours through a different lens, one we'll call "relationship." Through this lens, you can pay attention to the ways that you interacted with people to build relationship with them. Pay attention to the key relationships in your life, especially those in your immediate family, and ask what

---

3. See Walter Burghardt, "Contemplation: A Long, Loving Look at the Real," in *An Ignatian Spirituality Reader*, ed. George W. Traub (Chicago: Loyola Press, 2008), 89–98.

the interactions with those people were like. What did you communicate? What did you seek to understand? In what ways did you demonstrate your love and care for that person?

Let's apply a third lens, which we'll call "grace." As you consider the past twenty-four hours, when did you discern signs of God's grace? When, for example, did you experience yourself practicing generosity toward someone? When did you feel loved? When did you recognize something beautiful, whether in nature or in something made by human beings—a song, a work of art, a book, or something else? When did you notice yourself responding to an injustice, or feel sympathy for someone going through a hard time? When were you moved to pray or to express a hope to God?

There are many lenses we can use to look at the world, but the important practice is switching out the one we use most often—utility. Contemplation, we'll suggest, arises when we move away from seeing the world through the lens of utility and start seeing it in ways suggested by Jesus' parables and actions. Prayer is the daily practice of switching lenses: it is the regular practice of adapting our vision more and more to that of Jesus. Contemplation is a posture of receptivity to the world that God has made and has invited us to help shape toward his plans. Practices of prayer, mindfulness, reflection, and journaling cultivate in us the habit of contemplation.

Happiness, writes St. Thomas Aquinas, consists in contemplation, for it is a participation in the divine life (ST I–II, q. 3, a. 5). Thomas, though, writing in the thirteenth century, believed that contemplative life was reserved for those who enter a religious order, distinguishing that life from the more active life of families. To be sure, there is a vocation to contemplative life, a call that God issues to some who will choose lives of prayer in a cloister or monastery. Yet, we are convinced that it is possible and, in some sense, necessary for active people—like those called to the vocation of family life—to develop habits of contemplation that center their busy lives on the Lord's invitation to relationship.

Thomas exhorts those engaged in a contemplative life to "give to others the fruits of contemplation" (ST III, q. 40, a. 1, ad. 2). This exhortation—a motto of the Dominican Order, of which he was an influential early member—suggests for us an approach to the balance between prayer and the busyness of family life. Through contemplation, we become attuned to the daily workings of grace—God "laboring" (as St. Ignatius of Loyola suggested) in his creation, moving it toward the good.[4] Developing the habit of seeing God laboring in the daily lives of our families is about developing the visions to "see and understand" in a manner suggested by Jesus.

---

4. St. Ignatius writes, "God works and labors for me in all things created on the face of the earth—that is, behaves like one who labors—as in the heavens, elements, plants, fruits, cattle, etc., giving them being, preserving them, giving them vegetation and sensation, etc." *Spiritual Exercises*, "Contemplation to attain divine love," third point.

Giving to others the fruits of contemplation is nothing less than sharing our most authentic selves with others—including our children—and also sharing with them a life compass well calibrated toward the divine life. It is about daily attempts to switch out the lens of utility for lenses more apt for seeing the way God sees. It is about what St. Paul described as the "fruits of the spirit": love, joy, peace, forbearance, kindness, goodness, faithfulness, gentleness, and self-control (Gal 5:22-23). It is resisting the temptation to hurry through tasks, taking time to listen to a child, even in the midst of a tantrum. It is bringing children along to serve at a migrant shelter or at the home of a neighbor and reflecting on the experience before bedtime. It is engaging kids' questions about politics or social issues, gently nudging them to critique what they hear around school. It is about planning a day with one of your children who needs some Mom or Dad time. It is about recognizing in kids' complaints the seeds of some insecurity or fear and returning to it when there is time for conversation. It is about interrupting your day when a child wants time outside and the sun happens to be shining. It is about riding bikes together in freezing winter weather, just because that's what will give your newly adopted son a sense of excitement about the new home he lives in.

Festivity

One of the most delightful contemplative practices is festivity. From the ordinary family dinner, to birthday parties, adoption days, and holidays, festive celebrations are *kairos* times. Festivity can be thought of as a kind of spiritual practice, inasmuch as it gives us the opportunity to suspend the usual demands of our lives and simply enjoy the goodness of one another. It calls for a certain renunciation, a certain ascesis, defined as the willingness to give up something in order to achieve a spiritual benefit. The paradox, of course, is that unlike other forms of ascesis like fasting or abstaining from meat—practices proper to other seasons of the year—festivity calls for the renunciation of utility in favor of extravagance.

Jesus himself gave the example *par excellence* at the wedding at Cana (John 2:1-12). It was Mary who exhorted Jesus to perform his first miracle in order to enhance festivity. Mary, ever the mother, possessed a wisdom that Jesus himself had yet to discern: that a family celebration may well be the closest we get to the heavenly banquet. She understood what the bridegroom was feeling: a sense that the party was likely to wind down as the wine ran out. Perhaps she knew that the young man did not come from means and struggled even to provide food for his guests so that they might share his joy.

Jesus was still a young man, and he certainly desired his Father's will in all things. Yet he did not then rank festivity as his highest concern. Mary, though, saw an opportunity, a *kairos*: changing the water into wine so that the gladness of the guests might not be cut short. Perhaps she knew the sentiment expressed by another man named Jesus, son of Eleazar, son of Sira: "Gladness of heart is the very life of a person, and cheerfulness prolongs his days" (Sir 30:22). She urged Jesus to take another look at the way that this festivity might be a sacrament of divine gladness.

Our hearts are very often like that of Jesus before the urging of his mother: good, holy, well intentioned, yet removed from the immediate moment. The summons to festivity is indeed sacramental, in the sense that it calls us to invite the Lord to sanctify the ordinary people and places where we set aside time simply to be in one another's presence. The kitchen, the site of so much of our daily labor—cutting and chopping, cooking and washing—becomes the locus of holy gladness. The living area, where we do laundry and where we are constantly picking up discarded shoes and socks, becomes a kind of sanctuary where, in an acceptable time, festivity unfolds.

What we have noticed in times of festivity—summer vacations with extended family or Christmas gatherings with people dear to us—is that they are times when our kids return to themselves. To put it crassly, we like being around them more. Gone, for a time, are the usual preoccupations with appearance and the social dramas that push and pull on a daily basis. With adequate sleep, no stress from homework, and time to do what they enjoy, times of festivity summon from them a greater willingness to be in the moment, perhaps playing a game with cousins or friends or talking with a relative who can't believe how big they are getting.

Perhaps it is because festivity often coincides with holidays that mark the passage of years; we connect in our minds the memories from past years' celebrations and recognize the ways our children have grown and changed over the years. Perhaps it is because festivity offers the chance to draw families closer together, saying, effectively, "These are the people you will celebrate with many years from now, long after most of your current friends have moved on with their lives." To be sure, that is a message we sometimes voice, particularly now as our children are in their teen years and likely to be drawn away from family toward friends. But festivity issues a reminder of the transitoriness of life, even as it draws us to celebrate the life we have now.

Our family has had to wrestle with sickness, job insecurity, strained relationships, and death, to name a few issues. Festivity is not about ignoring the reality of life. Rather, it's about choosing to find *kairos* even in the midst of difficulty, to offer to the Lord our hopes and our desires even in the midst of it. Festivity is, in this sense, a kind of hopeful expectation, a microcosm of the hope expressed by the entire pilgrim people of God anticipating Christ's return. "You changed my mourning into dancing; you took off my sackcloth and clothed me with gladness," writes the Psalmist (30:12), expressing the hope of all God's people.

Ignatian Spiritual Practice

Like all forms of spirituality, a parenting spirituality is a practice more than a vague objective. In *Six Sacred Rules for Families* and *The Discerning Parent*, we have written about the Ignatian tradition and how it can inform a parenting spirituality. At root, the spirituality proposed by St. Ignatius is a secular spirituality, in contrast to earlier forms of fundamentally monastic spirituality. It is oriented toward life in the world and to the transformation of vision that is constitutive of the practice of discernment.

Central to Ignatian spirituality are practices of the Examen, the prayer of review of one's day.[5] The Examen is a prayer of contemplative attention to experience, inviting God to inform the understanding of our daily lives and to attend to *kairos*. The fruits of Examen are many: gratitude, insight, and love arising from reflection on positive experiences, but also compunction, sadness, or remorse arising from negative ones. All of these fruits, when offered to God in prayer, are opportunities for a deepening of relationship with God, by which we sharpen our eyes in discernment.

It is possible, we have argued, to teach the Examen to even very young children, inviting them at the end of a day to reflect on their experiences. We also suggest that parents can cultivate discernment in many ways, by inviting children at different ages to reflect on and pray about their experiences. Similarly, the Ignatian practice of imaginative prayer using scriptural stories—a practice that any good religious educator will recognize—can be woven into seasons of Advent or Lent in age-appropriate ways. In the Ignatian tradition we have discovered tools that help us to share the gift of faith and attentiveness to *kairos* in everyday life with our children.

Conclusion

What we are proposing in this essay is something that is easy to say yes to: celebrate the time you have with your family! Celebration is a spiritual practice, for it arises out of a life lived in God's *kairos*. For our family, commitment to this spirituality means taking advantage of opportunities to enjoy each other's company and creating opportunities whenever we can. A spirituality of *kairos*, rooted in practices of contemplation, is a way of first seeking God in all things. Do we always get it right? No. But we are convinced that the vocation to family life is indeed a call from God to live abundantly.

5. See David Fleming, *What Is Ignatian Spirituality?* (Chicago: Loyola Press, 2008), 20.

Chapter 25

Cultivating Resistance

Youth Protest and the Common Good

Mary M. Doyle Roche

On March 25, 2019, the Solemnity of the Annunciation, following a Synod on Youth, the Faith, and Vocational Discernment held the previous fall, Pope Francis issued *Christ Lives*, an exhortation to young people and the entire people of God. It is a celebration of young people and a call for them to embrace their faith, restlessness, and roles in the church and world. It is also a call to resist injustice and the dehumanizing effects of forms of technology and consumerism. Francis exclaims, "Make a ruckus!" Finally, it is a summons to intergenerational solidarity marked by patience, humility, and a willingness to listen to and hear the good news of the Gospel as it is preached by young and old alike. The document closes with these lines, "Dear young people, my joyful hope is to see you keep running the race before you, outstripping all those who are slow or fearful. . . . May the Holy Spirit urge you on as you run this race. The Church needs your momentum, your intuitions, your faith. We need them! And when you arrive where we have not yet reached, have the patience to wait for us" (CV 143, 299).

The occasion of *Christ Lives* provides an invitation to consider more deeply the rights, relationships, and roles of young people in the mission of the church and the building of the common good of society. In particular, it offers a theological vision to guide reflection on the participation and leadership of young people in movements of resistance and protest. This chapter lifts up several key passages of *Christ Lives* as a way to frame several examples of youth protest and critique responses to these protests on the part of some adults. Recognizing the tension and friction that youth protest, resistance, and rebelliousness can create in families and communities, the chapter proposes practices of intergenerational solidarity for the common good that can be taken up in families, schools, and churches.

Christ Is Alive! Make a Ruckus!

The opening line of Pope Francis's exhortation proclaims, "Christ is alive!" He begins the document with a number of brief reflections on youth and young people (including Jesus as a child and adolescent) found in the Scriptures. These reflections highlight the dignity of young people, God's presence with them, and their place of honor within the Christian community. Francis writes, "Let us also keep in mind that Jesus had no use for adults who looked down on the young or lorded it over them. On the contrary, he insisted that 'the greatest among you must become like the youngest' (Lk 22:26). For him age did not establish privileges, and being young did not imply lesser worth or dignity" (CV 14).

Francis finds in epistles to the earliest Christian communities, signs of intergenerational tensions and cautions against the discouragement that these can bring:

> The word of God says that young people should be treated "as brothers" (1 Tim 5:1), and warns parents not to "provoke your children, lest they become discouraged" (Col 3:21). Young people are not meant to become discouraged; they are meant to dream great things, to seek vast horizons, to aim higher, to take on the world, to accept challenges and to offer the best of themselves to the building of something better. That is why I constantly urge young people not to let themselves be robbed of hope; to each of them I repeat: "Let no one despise your youth" (1 Tim 4:12). (CV 15)

For Francis, the Holy Family stands as a witness to parenting that honors young people, "Thanks to the trust of his parents, Jesus can move freely and learn to journey with others." That Mary and Joseph lost track of Jesus on a visit to the temple is a sign, not of neglect, but of trust and confidence in Jesus and in their wider family and community—a bit of "free range" parenting, if you will (CV 29).

Francis is jubilant about the possibilities for young people, saying, "For whenever you are united, you have marvelous strength. Whenever you are enthused about life in common, you are capable of great sacrifices for others and for the community" (CV 110). This optimism is not a saccharine view of the cultural icon of youth. Francis recognizes and honors the power, strength, and real sacrifice made by young people as signs of authentic moral agency. He also recognizes the gift of *restlessness* that accompanies youth as well as the tendency toward impatience that is characteristic not only of youth but of the wider culture: "Restless discontent, combined with exhilaration before the opening up of new horizons, generates a boldness that leads you to stand up and take responsibility for a mission." He cautions against "anxiety" that causes people to give up on dreams for the world when change is not immediate. Patience is required but must be differentiated from hesitance and endless waiting. Francis calls on young people to risk and "take chances" even if it means making mistakes (CV 138, 142). The same could be said of adults who might be more risk averse in a variety of ways.

Though *Christ Lives* praises the ability of young people to "take on the world," Francis rejects a view of the social order that pits young people against adults and elders. In a similar vein to the church's resistance to other models of change that place races, classes, and genders in conflict, he writes, "The world has never benefited, nor will it ever benefit, from a rupture between generations. That is the siren song of a future without roots and origins. It is the lie that would have you believe that only what is new is good and beautiful" (CV 191). Yet the relationship does not fall into a stifling pattern of obedience and deference. Rather, old and young are called to listen and learn from each other. Both must be open to being changed by the experiences of the other and transformed by the Spirit breathing life into what is old and new.

Youth Resistance and Protest

Though Catholic teaching calls for generations to work together peacefully, this value does not require the absence of tension. Tension between generations may in fact be necessary if old and young, parents and children, are to grow in the moral life. Parents face protest, resistance, and rebellion at many stages of their children's development. Infants may reject pureed peas, and toddlers any food that is green, by spitting it right back at that hand that feeds them. Young children may wail and stomp their feet at schooltime, bath time, or bedtime. In adolescence and young adulthood, protest, resistance, and rebellion may take other forms: an avant-garde style of dress, unconventional hair color or cut, tattoos, and body piercings. Teens test the boundaries set by curfews, tune in (or out) to music only they can hear through earbuds, and challenge expectations regarding education and career choice. Of course, naming these as forms of protest and resistance assumes that parents have "conventional" styles of dress and presentation, schooling and employment, and socially sanctioned patterns of relationships. So, it is probably wise to think as broadly as possible about the kinds of tensions that emerge as young people encounter, question, and challenge the status quo, however that status quo presents itself. Though I have argued elsewhere that families are schools of solidarity, friction is par for the course in any family's journey, even in the best of circumstances.[1] *Parents and children both are growing and developing; both are*

1. Mary M. Doyle Roche, *Schools of Solidarity: Families and Catholic Social Teaching* (Collegeville, MN: Liturgical Press, 2015). This essay accepts the premise that there are moral and developmental

in an ongoing process of resisting some roles and taking on others. Acts of resistance and rebellion can be responses to the movement of the Spirit shaking up a status quo of complacency that stifles moral and spiritual growth.

Alongside rebelliousness at home, young people have long been active in public movements for justice and social change. Recall the young people involved in the sit-ins and marches during the Civil Rights movement and figures including the Little Rock Nine and Ruby Bridges whose courage both inspired a generation and shamed the ugliness of racist hatred. Their participation was not without tension in the movement and within their families. Parents were committed to racial justice but also to the safety and well-being of their children who took great risks that included the possibilities of being jailed, beaten, and killed. These young people, no mere actors in a play directed by others, were actively engaged in the struggle for justice for themselves and their communities. They made real moral decisions in the context of oppressive circumstances and limited options.[2]

Sometimes the values for which young people stand up and speak out put them at odds with their parents and other adults. We might think about the kinds of organized protests and marches that accompanied the "sexual" revolution and antiwar movements but also the many smaller, but no less important, forms of resistance undertaken by teens to challenge the kinds of conformity that adulthood seems to represent. Children and young people engaged in the struggle for a more just and inclusive society often challenge our unacknowledged assumptions about childhood and adolescence: that childhood should be marked by innocence and freedom from responsibility and that children participate in public life only insofar as they do not upset the status quo maintained by adults. Rebelliousness is considered an adolescent phase that young people should grow out of as they take on increasing responsibility for themselves and others. In reading *Christ Lives*, we see that restlessness and the desire to resist the status quo, as characteristic of youth, could also be considered a moral virtue to be cultivated. Rather than a stage to grow beyond, rebelliousness could become a kind of deep practice, a posture, and a set of skills to be called on in crises and situations of injustice and oppression. Adolescence, which can certainly be a time of strife in families, for

---

reasons for the protection of children and young people from harmful risks but that these can and should be differentiated from the kinds of risk, resistance, and rebellion that might lead to personal growth and social transformation. This task of differentiation is difficult, requires considerable prudence, and ought not be underestimated.

2. See David Halberstam, *The Children* (New York: Random House, 1998); Wilma King, *African American Childhoods: Historical Perspectives from Slavery to Civil Rights* (New York: Palgrave/Macmillan, 2005); and Robert Coles, *Children of Crisis: A Study of Courage and Fear* (Boston and Toronto: Little, Brown, 1967).

both parents and children, can also inspire in adults and elders a new or renewed commitment to justice and the common good.

In January 2017, my spouse and I traveled with our oldest child, then eighteen years old, to the Women's March in Boston, Massachusetts. It was the first protest march for them and the first in many, many years for me. I thought those days may have been behind me and would have probably been content to support the movement from home were it not for the determination of our daughter. We had a sign raised in support of feminism and LGBTQ+ rights. We were overwhelmed by the turnout and the streets flowing like a river of pink hats. While the Women's March movement, like the feminist movement generally, has struggled with issues around diversity and pluralism, its intergenerational appeal seemed evident that day and in the coverage of other marches taking place in Washington, DC, and cities all over the globe. There were infants, young children, teens, college students, young parents, middle-aged people, and older folks. I imagine many were first-time protesters, though many others had in a sense been marching for decades: *for* civil rights, women's rights, LGBTQ+ rights, and *against* wars, corruption, and abuse in its many forms. Motivated by anger and fear that decades of progress on a number of social issues could erode rapidly before our eyes, marchers engaged in peaceful protest as a counter-witness to the inaugural festivities of the incoming presidential administration. Once there, the homemade signs, crocheted hats, and the presence of tens of thousands of other marchers left many participants feeling not only angry but also hopeful and empowered.

Cut to a subsequent scene, the March for Our Lives on March 24, 2018, at the US capital. Again, hundreds of thousands of demonstrators came to protest gun violence and advocate for stricter gun control legislation in the wake of the mass school shooting at Marjory Stoneman Douglas High School in Parkland, Florida, on February 14, 2018. They came also with stories from Sandy Hook Elementary, Columbine, and other sites of school violence. They came with stories about gun violence in American cities and the havoc it wreaks on families and communities.

March for Our Lives was also intergenerational in terms of turnout for the event, but it is primarily a student-led movement. Though young people rely on parents, teachers, and other adult allies for assistance and support, the high school students themselves are the key players and the movement is shaped by their experiences. Emma Gonzalez has become one of the many faces of March for Our Lives and its efforts to pass gun control legislation and increase voter participation. In an op-ed for *The New York Times*, she wrote,

> On the 16th, I was asked to speak at a gun control rally by a woman on the school board. For what seemed like the first time, adults were treating me and my peers as though they cared about what we had to say. I started writing my speech and didn't

stop until I got up to the lectern. I gave it my all. All of my words, my thoughts, my energy, every political fact I knew. . . The speech followed a pattern: I had a thought, I wrote a new paragraph, I filled in the gaps, I ranted, and then deleted the rants. I had waves where all I wrote was a kind of *scream* of consciousness: "How could this have happened? So many people died, so many people died. I can't do this. How do I do this? How do we do this?"[3]

Supporters of gun rights were unsurprisingly critical of March for Our Lives and its student leaders. The NRA has martialed its considerable resources to fight any legislation that would restrict gun ownership and access and has raised the claim that the solution to gun violence is more guns in the hands of students and teachers. More surprising than criticisms rooted in gun rights ideology, however, was a criticism about the mobilization of young people itself.

Some dismissed the moral and political agency of youth, suggesting that young people limit their participation to the personal, private, familial, and, at best, local spheres. Some cast protesters as people doing nothing but waiting for someone else (the "someone else" in this case are their elected officials) to solve their problems. Protest on the part of young people in this instance is characterized as a form of laziness or an abdication of proper social roles and moral responsibility, rather than as a prophetic witness to the sanctity of life.[4] A devastating implication is that elected officials do not represent children and young people as constituents. Adult responsibility is determined solely by privileged adult experience and does not involve structural change to get at the roots of the multifaceted problem of violence that involves and impacts young people.

The Black Lives Matter movement, which predates March for Our Lives, is also a response to violence that impacts young people, especially police violence that targets boys and young men of color. It is a movement spurred by young people on behalf of justice for young people and has drawn attention to the complex dynamics of racism and the root causes of both physical and institutionalized violence. Though #BlackLivesMatter began in earnest in the wake of the 2013 acquittal of George Zimmerman for the murder of Trayvon Martin, youth participation in protest for racial justice has a long tradition. It is also important to note that long before the organized public protests, one had only to "pay careful attention to the lyrics of their songs, the verses of their poems, the scripts of their

---

3. Emma Gonzales, "A Young Activist's Advice," *New York Times*, October 5, 2018, https://www.nytimes.com/2018/10/05/opinion/sunday/emma-gonzalez-parkland.html. Emphasis added.

4. For an example, see CNN, "Marching for Change," March 25, 2018, http://transcripts.cnn.com/TRANSCRIPTS/1803/25/sotu.01.html.

plays, and to their discourses and images on Facebook, Instagram, Snapchat" to see the fervent and creative critique of the status by young people of color.[5]

Black Lives Matter pledges to be intergenerational, noting in their platform, "We cultivate an intergenerational and communal network free from ageism. We believe that all people, regardless of age, show up with the capacity to lead and learn."[6] Another organization, The Movement for Black Lives, also centers the experiences of young people in its call to end "the criminalization and dehumanization of black youth across all areas of society including, but not limited to, our nation's justice and education systems, social service agencies, media and pop culture."[7] Black Lives Matter and the many organizations that contribute to the movement not only address issues impacting young people of color but also bear witness to the ways in which young people can challenge prevailing images of youth as people either apathetic or to be feared.[8]

Another current example of youth-inspired and youth-led protest is the Youth Climate Strike, in which students organize to leave school and engage in peaceful protest, issuing demands for political and corporate responsibility in the face of the existential threat to the future of the planet and its occupants. One of the faces of the movement, Greta Thunberg, a teenager from Sweden, entered the international media spotlight to press elected officials to make greater strides to halt global climate change. Thunberg has been the target of atrocious personal attacks in the media from pundits who rely on funding from the fossil-fuel industry. Nevertheless, she has persisted in her mission and has motivated young people across the globe to act for climate justice. Youth Climate Strike brought millions of people to the streets all over the world on September 21, 2019, to rally for change and to urge world leaders to act.

Thunberg is not the only prominent youth climate activist, and neither is she the first. Young people have been organizing for environmental justice for years

5. Alcinda Manuel Honwana, "Youth Struggles: From the Arab Spring to Black Lives Matter and Beyond," *African Studies Review* 62, no. 1 (March 2019): 8–21, 14.

6. See Black Lives Matter, "What We Believe," https://blacklivesmatter.com/about/what -we-believe/.

7. See The Movement for Black Lives, "End the War on Black People," https://policy.m4bl .org/end-war-on-black-people/.

8. See also Elan C. Hope, Micere Keels, and Myles I. Durkee, "Participation in Black Lives Matter and Deferred Action for Childhood Arrivals: Modern Activism Among Black and Latino College Students," *Journal of Diversity in Higher Education* 9, no. 3 (2016): 203–15; William Julius Wilson, "Black Youths, Joblessness, and the Other Side of 'Black Lives Matter,'" *Ethnic and Racial Studies* 39, no. 8 (2016): 1450–57; and Ileana Jiménez, "#SayHerName Loudly: How Black Girls Are Leading #BlackLivesMatter," *The Radical Teacher* 106 (2016): 87–96.

and a number of them spoke before the United Nations Youth Climate Summit. A number of young activists represent indigenous peoples or are from regions in the Global South that are already facing acute climate crises: Autumn Peltier is a Canadian advocate for indigenous people's water rights; Bruno Rodriguez from Argentina calls on corporations to end the use of fossil fuels; Helena Gualinga of Ecuador speaks out for the indigenous peoples of the Amazon rainforest. US-based activists also represent the diversity within the movement: Mari Copeny, "Little Miss Flint" began the fight for clean water when she was eight years old; Isra Hirsi, a black Muslim young woman, helped found the US branch of Youth Climate Strike; Varshini Prakash organizes sit-ins outside of Congress; Xiuntexcatl Martinez is a plaintiff with twenty other young people who are suing the federal government in the 9th Circuit for protection of the environment as a civil right. These young people make passionate and persuasive cases for change and they highlight the need for an intersectional approach that attends to environmental racism and sexism.[9] They are leveraging the power they have to disrupt the school day, provocatively claiming that their education is for a future that must be secured in the present in order to have meaning for themselves and their communities.[10]

Again, there has been criticism from adults. Like the involvement of powerful lobbies including the NRA to squash March for Our Lives, the fossil-fuel and energy company lobbyists have been making the rounds to critique the Youth Climate Strike. Some criticize the goals of the movement and policy proposals they deem ill-informed, unrealistic, or inadequate. Others criticize the strategy of striking at school and walking out of classes. Students have been accused of "wasting lesson time." One commentator, a partner in a law firm that represents energy companies, said, "I do not like the symbolism of sacrificing education to make political points." Others suggest that students protest "after school or on weekends."[11] "After school and on weekends" suggests that youth protest ought not to be disruptive of business as usual. Activism is considered an extracurricular

---

9. For information on Youth Climate Strike, the Youth Climate Summit, and the stories of young activists see United Nations, "Climate Action," https://www.un.org/en/climatechange/youth-summit.shtml; BBC, "Climate Change: 7 Young Climate Activists from Around the World," https://www.bbc.co.uk/newsround/49676291; Hope Howard, "5 Youth Climate Activists You Need to Know," ABC News, https://abcnews.go.com/US/youth-climate-activists/story?id=65721725.

10. Youth Climate Strike, "May 3rd We Strike Again," https://www.youthclimatestrikeus.org.

11. Jeff Brady and Jennifer Ludden, "Skipping School Around the World to Push for Action on Climate Change," *National Public Radio*, March 14, 2019, https://www.npr.org/2019/03/14/703461293/skipping-school-to-protest-climate-change.

activity, not something constitutive of the academic endeavor itself. Youth protest then becomes a kind of window dressing and a practice that is regulated by adults.[12]

March for Our Lives, Youth Climate Strike, and Black Lives Matter are but three examples of youth protest addressing urgent moral questions of our time. To these, we could add young people participating in the #MeToo movement, #TimesUp, Take Back the Night, Dreamers standing up for DACA and immigration reform, demonstrations for LGBTQ+ rights, and student involvement in political, economic, and educational reforms across the globe. The list goes on. Shaped by their experiences of fear, grief, and outrage at being abandoned by adult leadership, young people raise their voices and their bodies in protest. Their demands for change and the risks they take give prophetic witness to justice and the common good for all people.[13]

Obedience and conformity to expectations are not the only virtues proper to children and young people any more than they are to adults. Sometimes resistance is required for growth. Resistance and protest can be important indicators of dignity, autonomy, interdependence, and the exercise of conscience. So resistance too is a moral virtue and an acquired skill. Yet parents and other adults often think about resistance by youth as an unruly, even if natural, urge that hopefully comes under control after spiking during periods of childhood and adolescence. It is thought of as a habit to be broken rather than cultivated over time. The lesson of many of the films of youth rebellion during my "coming of age," however, was that breaking the habit of resistance in favor of conformity to expectations can be soul sucking for young and old alike. This is the lesson of youth protest today.

A primary implication is that rebelliousness and resistance among children and young people are not morally problematic in themselves, nor are they necessarily a sign of an unruly will or sinfulness. In fact, young people may be taking the lead on important moral issues of our day, including entrenched racism, the specter of environmental devastation, the epidemic of gun violence, sexual assault and rape culture, the future of education, and civil rights for all people. Young people are moral agents, fully engaged participants in building the common good and transforming unjust social structures. They claim not only resources but also

12. Some young activists in rural communities have adopted this strategy in an effort to build political bridges, particularly in communities that rely on mining, timber, and agriculture for their livelihoods. See Kirk Siegler, "Rural Students to Join in Classroom Walkout Over Climate Change," *National Public Radio*, May 3, 2019, https://www.npr.org/2019/03/14/703461293/skipping-school-to-protest-climate-change.

13. See Honwana, "Youth Struggles."

relationships that are just and merciful. They demand roles in family and community that are honored and nurtured. They embody intrinsic human dignity in all of its vulnerability and strength. Their peaceful protest challenges the logic and cynicism of the adult world.

Protest and Intergenerational Solidarity

Young people have witnessed and experienced much: terrible violence rooted in racial hatred, religious intolerance, gender injustice, and a disregard for the gift of creation. Many have responded with public protest. In these protests, adults and young people alike have witnessed tremendous courage. Critics see a fly in the ointment. The Body of Christ, alive in the world, could see a graced moment and hear an invitation to solidarity. If resistance to injustice often involves protest, how, then, can the habits of protest and the courage they require be cultivated in community? What are the responsibilities of young people and elders? Of children and parents? Students and teachers? Members and ministers of the church?

Adults, parents, teachers, and ministers must respect the dignity and agency of young people. Even as adults recognize the vulnerabilities of the young and respond by protecting them from harm, adults can also honor the many ways in which children and young people carve out a unique space for full participation in our common life. Adults must discern carefully the kinds of rebelliousness that might cause real and maybe irrevocable harm to young people and even in these contexts call young people to relationship and responsibility rather than capitalizing on fear and isolation.

Adults must approach positions of authority with humility, recognizing that trust is earned. They can use the privileges and freedoms of maturity to enhance the freedom and empowerment of young people. They can provide space at home, school, and houses of worship for young people to take risks, to challenge, to resist. They can model many forms of resistance and protest, including choices regarding patterns of consumption, the businesses they patronize, campaigning for important issues, voting, and worship. They can model authentic argument and informed critique of structures of power. Parents, teachers, and ministers can be open and honest about their own desires and struggles to resist expectations (including the expectations of children and students) that inhibit their growth as disciples. Intergenerational solidarity does not require the absence of tension. It does require that absence of violence and authoritarian control.

According to Pope Francis, "Youth ministry has to be synodal; it should involve a 'journeying together'" (CV 206). Journeying together implies that young and old are sometimes side by side on the way. It also suggests shared responsibility for setting the goal, planning the route, and knowing when to lead and when to follow. This is a "march for our lives" moment in the church. It is a moment for resistance and protest in a spirit of solidarity. Young people can join adults in this and stand up when the spirits of their elders are flagging. They can demand accountability from ministerial leadership. They can be strengthened in this task by listening to the stories of those who have been challenging the church for decades, those who have taken the long view and possess a different perspective on time. *Christ Lives* calls young and old to be patient, but patience is the virtue that helps us to know when, how, and how long to wait. The patient know how to use time, and they know when the wait has been too long. Children and young people's agitation often spark the recognition that time is short. Their refusal to wait for justice and inclusion is not necessarily impatience but may be a sign of true patience when inaction and deference are masquerading as virtue. Like Jesus in the gospels, young people can make trouble, make a mess, make noise, and "make a ruckus" that shakes the status quo in the church and society.

Contributors

Elizabeth L. Antus is an assistant professor of the practice at Boston College. Her essay "'Was it Good for You?' Recasting Catholic Sexual Ethics in Light of Women's Sexual Pain Disorders" received the Catholic Theological Society of America LaCugna Award in 2018. She is currently working on a book titled *Steady My Soul: An Augustinian Feminist Account of Self-Love*.

Tom Beaudoin is professor of religion at Fordham University. Among his numerous books and articles on theology and culture are "Teaching Theology in an Atmosphere of Deconversion" in *Horizons* and "Secular Catholicism and Practical Theology" in the *International Journal of Practice Theology*.

Jana Marguerite Bennett is professor of moral theology at the University of Dayton. She is the author of *Singleness and the Church: A New Theology of the Single Life* (Oxford University Press) and coeditor of *Naming Our Sins: How Recognizing the Seven Deadly Vices Can Renew the Sacrament of Reconciliation* (Catholic University of America Press).

Jennifer Beste is College of Saint Benedict Koch Chair in Catholic Thought and Culture and professor of theology at the College of Saint Benedict and Saint John's University in Collegeville, Minnesota. She is the author of *College Hookup Culture and Christian Ethics: The Lives and Longings of Emerging Adults* and *God and the Victim: Traumatic Intrusions on Grace and Freedom*, both from Oxford University Press.

Victor Carmona is assistant professor of theology and religious studies at the University of San Diego. He is the author of "Love and Conflict in U.S. Immigration Policy" in the *Journal of Hispanic/Latino Theology* and "Theologizing Immigration" in the *Wiley Blackwell Companion to Latino/a Theology*.

Hoon Choi is a transgeneration Korean American Catholic theologian from Bellarmine University who teaches and writes on race, gender, and ethics. His publications include "Brothers in Arms and Brothers in Christ? The Military and the Catholic Church as Sources for Modern Korean Masculinity" in the *Journal of the Society of Christian Ethics.*

David Cloutier is associate professor of moral theology at The Catholic University of America. He is the author of *The Vice of Luxury: Economic Excess in a Consumer Age* (Georgetown University Press) and the coeditor of *Naming Our Sins: How Recognizing the Seven Deadly Vices Can Renew the Sacrament of Reconciliation* (Catholic University of America Press).

Kathryn Lilla Cox is a research associate at the University of San Diego. Her publications include "Toward a Theology of Infertility and the Role of *Donum Vitae*" in *Horizons: The Journal of the College Theology Society* and *Water Shaping Stone: Faith, Relationships, and Conscience Formation* (Liturgical Press).

Gemma Tulud Cruz is senior lecturer in theology at Australian Catholic University. She is the author of *Toward a Theology of Migration: Social Justice and Religious Experience* (Palgrave Macmillan) and *An Intercultural Theology of Migration: Pilgrims in the Wilderness* (Brill).

Craig A. Ford Jr. is assistant professor of theology and religious studies at St. Norbert College. He received his PhD from Boston College. He has published "Transgender Bodies, Catholic Schools, and a Queer Natural Law Theology of Exploration" in the *Journal of Moral Theology* and "LGBT Catholics are a Reality" in *Commonweal.*

Richard Gaillardetz is the Joseph Professor of Catholic Systematic Theology at Boston College. In addition to numerous articles and books on ecclesiology, authority, and Vatican II, he has published *A Daring Promise: A Spirituality of Christian Marriage* (Liguori/Triumph) and *Transforming Our Days: Finding God Amid the Noise of Modern Life* (Liguori).

Christine Firer Hinze is professor of Christian ethics and director of the Curran Center for American Catholic Studies at Fordham University. Her many publications include *Glass Ceilings and Dirt Floors: Women, Work, and the Global Economy* (Paulist Press) and *Radical Sufficiency: Legacy and Future of the U.S. Catholic Livelihood Agenda* (Georgetown University Press).

Jason King is professor of theology at Saint Vincent College in Latrobe, Pennsylvania. He received his PhD from The Catholic University of America in Washington, DC. He is the author of *Faith with Benefits: Hookup Culture on Catholic Campuses* (Oxford University Press). Currently, he edits the *Journal of Moral Theology*.

Kent Lasnoski is an associate professor at Wyoming Catholic College. He received his PhD from Marquette University. He is the author of *Vocation to Virtue: Christian Marriage as a Consecrated Life* (Catholic University of America Press). He lives in Wyoming with his wife and eight children.

Julie Donovan Massey has worked at St. Norbert College for over two decades, initially in campus ministry roles and more recently serving as the associate and then interim vice president for Mission & Student Affairs. She coauthored *Project Holiness: Marriage as a Workshop for Everyday Saints* (Liturgical Press) with Bridget Burke Ravizza.

Megan K. McCabe is an assistant professor of religious studies at Gonzaga University. She is the author of "A Catholic Feminist Response to the Sin of Campus Rape Culture" in the *Journal of Religious Ethics*, "Signs of the Times: Theological Anthropology in Light of #MeToo" in *New Theology Review*, and "Create in Me a Just Heart: Treating Pornography as a Structure of Sin" in *America* magazine.

Marcus Mescher is assistant professor of Christian ethics at Xavier University in Cincinnati, Ohio. He is the author of "Beyond Slacktivism" in the *Journal of Catholic Social Thought* and the book *The Ethics of Encounter: Christian Neighbor Love as a Practice of Solidarity* (Orbis Books).

Tim and Sue Muldoon are the authors of *Reclaiming Family Time: A Guide to Slowing Down and Savoring the Gift of One Another* (Word Among Us Press) and *Six Sacred Rules for Families: A Spirituality for the Home* (Ave Maria Press). Tim is the director of mission education for Catholic Extension and an adjunct professor at Boston College. Sue is a therapist and director of family ministries at Good Shepherd Parish in Wayland, Massachusetts. Together, they and their teen/young adult children live outside of Boston.

Daniel Olsen is the director of the Office for Ecumenical and Interreligious Affairs of the Archdiocese of Chicago. He represents the archdiocese in ecumenical and interreligious settings and furthers the Catholic Church's commitment to religious dialogue and collaboration in Chicago. His research focuses on the gifts and pastoral challenges of interchurch families.

Timothy P. O'Malley is director of education at the McGrath Institute for Church Life and teaches in the Department of Theology at the University of Notre Dame. He is the author of *Off the Hook: God, Love, Dating, and Marriage in a Hookup World* (Ave Maria Press) and *Bored Again Catholic: How the Mass Could Save Your Life* (Our Sunday Visitor).

Bridget Burke Ravizza is a professor of theology and religious studies at St. Norbert College in De Pere, Wisconsin, where she contributes to the Women's and Gender Studies program and the Master of Theological Studies program. She coauthored *Project Holiness: Marriage as a Workshop for Everyday Saints* (Liturgical Press) with Julie Donovan Massey.

Emily Reimer-Barry is an associate professor and chair of the Department of Theology and Religious Studies at the University of San Diego. She is the author of *Catholic Theology of Marriage in the Era of HIV and AIDS* (Lexington Books). She draws on ethnographic research to engage questions of sexual ethics and social justice.

Mary M. Doyle Roche is associate professor of religious studies at the College of the Holy Cross. She is the author of *Children, Consumerism, and the Common Good* (Lexington Books) and *Schools of Solidarity: Families and Catholic Social Teaching* (Liturgical Press). Mary and her spouse Dennis are the parents of two children, Emma Rose and Declan.

Julie Hanlon Rubio is professor of social ethics at the Jesuit School of Theology of Santa Clara University in Berkeley, California. She is the author of *Family Ethics: Practices for Christians* and *Hope for Common Ground: Mediating the Personal and the Political in a Divided Church*, both published by Georgetown University Press.

Kathryn Getek Soltis is director of the Center for Peace and Justice Education and assistant professor of Christian Ethics at Villanova University. Her publications include "The Christian Virtue of Justice and the U.S. Prison" and "*Gaudium et Spes* and the Family," both in the *Journal of Catholic Social Thought*.

Sandra Sullivan-Dunbar is associate professor of Christian ethics at Loyola University Chicago, where she teaches and writes on sexual and family ethics, political and social ethics, and their intersections. She is the author of *Human Dependency and Christian Ethics* (Cambridge University Press).

Cristina L. H. Traina is professor and chair of religious studies at Northwestern University. She is the author of *Erotic Attunement: Parenthood and the Ethics of Sensuality* from the University of Chicago Press and *Feminist Ethics and Natural Law: The End of Anathema* from Georgetown University Press.

Kari-Shane Davis Zimmerman is an associate professor of theology at the College of Saint Benedict and Saint John's University in Collegeville, Minnesota. Her publications include "Hooking Up: Sex, Theology, and Today's 'Unhooked' Dating Practices" in *Horizons*.

Index